LAW, MORALITY, AND SOCIETY

Best wishes

Lee & Cally

Dick

May 1980

H. L. A. HART

LAW, MORALITY, AND SOCIETY

Essays in Honour of H. L. A. Hart

EDITED BY
P. M. S. HACKER
AND
J. RAZ

CLARENDON PRESS · OXFORD

Oxford University Press, Walton Street, Oxford OX2 6DP

OXFORD LONDON GLASGOW NEW YORK
TORONTO MELBOURNE WELLINGTON CAPE TOWN
IBADAN NAIROBI DAR ES SALAAM
KUALA LUMPUR SINGAPORE JAKARTA HONG KONG TOKYO
DELHI BOMBAY CALCUTTA MADRAS KARACHI

© *Oxford University Press* 1977

First published 1977
Reprinted in Paperback form 1979

British Library Cataloguing in Publication Data
Law, morality, and society: essays in honour of
H.L.A. Hart.
Bibl. – Index.
ISBN 0 19 824610 2
1. Hart, Herbert Lionel Adolphus   2. Hacker,
Peter Michael Stephan   3. Raz, Joseph
340.1   [Law]
Jurisprudence – Addresses, essays, lectures

*Printed in Great Britain by
The Pitman Press, Bath*

Preface

AT mid-century political philosophy was said to be dead and legal philosophy appeared to be dying. The only fruits that could be obtained from that field of intellectual activity were the gleanings from ancestral sowings. A quarter of a century later a transformed landscape is revealed—legal philosophy flourishes as never before. The responsibility for this renaissance is H. L. A. Hart's. His work provides the foundations of contemporary legal philosophy in the English-speaking world and beyond. His teaching, in Oxford and elsewhere, has inspired many a young philosopher to turn to jurisprudence in the reasonable expectation of a good harvest.

Herbert Hart has done for twentieth-century legal philosophy what Bentham did for eighteenth-century jurisprudence. He has integrated it into the mainstream of general philosophical thought. He has brought his knowledge of contemporary philosophical method to bear upon the questions of philosophy of law, and, as he has said of Bentham, 'We are too often forced to the conclusion that . . . [he] . . . has provided us with a new question, rather than merely a new answer, for his innovation to be considered matters of method alone.' He has clarified and strengthened the links between legal philosophy and moral and political philosophy, philosophy of mind and of language, and philosophical logic. To each of these subjects he has made a serious contribution. Finally, again following in Bentham's footsteps, he has been a forceful spokesman for the liberal tradition in morals and politics. The endeavour to strike a judicious balance between the liberty of the individual and the social good lies at the core of his political morality.

This year, 1977, sees Herbert Hart's seventieth birthday. We, the contributors to this volume, wish to honour him and his great achievement in philosophy. The range of essays collected here reflects the wide variety of his interests and contributions to philosophy. Being composed by sixteen authors, the essays lack the unity of thought and style which informs his work. Being written by colleagues, former pupils, and devotees, they reflect his profound influence. Like all reflections they can do no more than indicate the lustre of their original.

Oxford, 1977   P.M.S.H.
                                                      J.R.

Contents

1

Hart's Philosophy of Law

P. M. S. HACKER*

* Fellow of St. John's College, Oxford.

INTRODUCTION

In 1961 Professor H. L. A. Hart's *The Concept of Law* was published.[1]
It was immediately recognized as a major contribution to philosophy
of law, and a distinguished contribution to moral and political
philosophy, and social theory in general. Since then it has achieved
the status of a classic in its field. No serious writing upon the subjects
with which Professor Hart dealt can afford to neglect his work, and
the key concepts with which he was concerned will, for a long time,
be discussed within the parameters he laid down.

Since the publication of Hart's great work a substantial number of
articles and books have been written which are concerned with
central topics of *The Concept of Law*. While there have been shining
exceptions, most of these writings were of poor quality. Yet some
pertinent points emerged from these discussions. *The Concept of Law*
is more of a pioneering work of synthesis in legal philosophy than a
conclusive study. Many of the novel distinctions drawn by Hart are
not wholly sharp nor unambiguous. Many of the central theses of the
book are not merely (as might be expected) controversial, but also not
wholly clear. Moreover a number of quite clear distinctions and
theses have been subjected to widespread misinterpretation.

In view of these more recent writings I shall attempt to survey
some of the central themes of the book. My remarks will necessarily
be synoptic, for the issues are manifold and the requisite arguments
often too complex and lengthy for detailed elaboration. Thus
clarification of misinterpretation will be brief, and often relegated to
footnotes. The discussion falls into two parts: in the first I shall
discuss methodological aspects of Hart's philosophy; in the second

[1] Page reference to *The Concept of Law* will be preceded by the abbreviation *CL*.

I shall examine the jurisprudential core of *The Concept of Law*, but space will not permit investigation of the host of other topics with which Hart deals with the characteristic insight and elegance which informs all his work.

PART 1: METHODOLOGICAL REMARKS

I remarked that *The Concept of Law* is a work of synthesis. This requires elucidation. Written at a time when English analytic philosophy was at full fruition, part of the originality of *The Concept of Law* lay in its author's insights into the relevance of new analytic techniques and advances in general philosophy for classical questions in legal theory. By his ingenious application and adaptation of such developments Hart sharpened methods of jurisprudential analysis, illuminated numerous outstanding issues, and made it possible to raise a wide range of new problems. This can be seen by a survey of the salient methodological features of the book.

The family of philosophical styles commonly referred to as 'linguistic' or 'analytic' (or occasionally even 'Oxford') philosophy has often been condemned as arid, superficial, and philosophically unilluminating—at best high-grade lexicography. *The Concept of Law* provides a brilliant refutation of such nonsense. Methods of linguistic analysis are employed to clarify important distinctions implicit in our language which will themselves yield a rich harvest of jurisprudential insights. The distinctions between being obligated and being obliged, between mere regularities of social behaviour and rule-governed social behaviour, between following rules and accepting rules are illuminated by analysis of linguistic use, and are brought to bear upon questions of legal philosophy. It is noteworthy that adopting methods of 'linguistic analysis' in no way precludes stipulative introduction of technical terminology where necessary (e.g. 'primary and secondary rules'), nor explication which intentionally strays from ordinary or even technical-legal use, where such explication is justified by its illuminative power (e.g. 'legal power', 'power conferring rules'[2]). The linguistic analysis undertaken in the book is designed, Hart claims (quoting J. L. Austin) to give us 'a sharpened awareness of words to sharpen our awareness of the phenomena'. It

---

[2] L. J. Cohen castigated Hart for his extension of the term 'power' beyond its normal limits in legal discourse (*Mind*, 71 (1962), 395 ff.). Hart's employment of the term, like Bentham's, clearly involves an explication (in Carnap's sense). See J. Raz, 'Voluntary Obligations and Normative Powers', *Proceedings of the Aristotelian Society*, Suppl. Vol. 46 (1972), 79 ff.

will not only reveal linguistic facts, but also 'the similarities and differences, recognized in language, between various social situations and relationships,' (*CL*, p. 235).

The nature and limits of lexical definition was widely discussed in mid-century, and much influenced Hart's methods of analysis, both for good and ill. Here, to be sure, there were august precedents within and without jurisprudence. Bentham's brilliant discussion of paraphrastic definition, and his insistence upon the limits of usefulness of Aristotelian definition by genus and differentia were brought to light after a century of oblivion by Wisdom's *Interpretation and Analysis*[3]. The similarities between Bentham's techniques of eliminating 'fictions' by paraphrasis and Russellian methods of eliminating singular referring expressions were striking. In addition to these precedents Austin's sharp awareness of the pointlessness of pursuit of definition by 'characteristic marks',[4] Wittgenstein's discussions of family resemblance, and Waismann's influential notion of open-textured concepts[5] made it inevitable that the application of these semantic advances to jurisprudence should be attempted sooner or later.

This trend made a deep impact upon Hart's work. Already in his Inaugural Lecture[6] Hart assailed the issue of definition of key legal concepts vigorously, and in *The Concept of Law* he returned to the same theme in the opening chapter. Generic definition, he argued (following Bentham) is powerless when the genus term is philosophically no less perplexing than the *definiendum*. It is inappropriate when the unifying features, which justify application of a term, do not consist of characteristic marks, but of analogy (e.g. 'foot' of a mountain) or of different connections to a central case (e.g. 'healthy' complexion or exercise) or by way of being constituents in a complex institutionalized activity (railway stations, tickets, shares, companies). It can be misleading when the concept in question has a penumbra of vagueness and is open to extension. This led to a salutary refusal to force key jurisprudential concepts into a uniform straitjacket, and to a heightened awareness that the central concepts employed in discourse about social phenomena are, by the nature of their diverse subject matter and the very different needs they are designed to meet

[3] J. Wisdom, *Interpretation and Analysis* (Kegan Paul, London, 1931).

[4] J. L. Austin, 'The Meaning of a Word' in *Philosophical Papers*, pp. 23 ff., ed. J. O. Urmson and G. J. Warnock (Clarendon Press, Oxford, 1961).

[5] F. Waismann, 'Verifiability', *Proceedings of the Aristotelian Society*, Suppl. Vol. 19 (1945).

[6] H. L. A. Hart, *Definition and Theory in Jurisprudence* (Clarendon Press, Oxford, 1953).

in the different domains of social activity (i.e. law, social morality, personal or professional ethos), unlikely to possess the intellectually and aesthetically attractive features of sharply determined concepts definable by the traditional means after which we characteristically hanker. In his analysis of social obligation Hart clarifies the analytic proto-phenomenon of obligation, but it is no part of his claim that all the features that characterize social obligation, which provide the analytical roots of the concept of obligation, will also apply to the more complex phenomenon of legal obligation. Similarly, his brilliant analysis of rights in his recent 'Bentham on Legal Rights'[7] stresses that the needs met by the use of the term 'a right' by the constitutional lawyer or the individualistic critic of the law, let alone the moral philosopher, preclude the simple extension of the elegant choice-theory of rights.

Though beneficial in these respects, Hart's preoccupation with the sins of classical definition also led him astray. He begins *The Concept of Law* by pointing out the perplexing oddity of the answers given by jurists to the central problem of analytical jurisprudence—'What is law?', citing some of the more notorious utterances of Llewellyn, Holmes, Gray, and Kelsen. Their slogans conflict with our ordinary conception of law, and are prima facie readily refutable by reference to features of legal systems which even a layman can identify. So whence the persistent puzzlement?

Not, Hart rightly claims, because of the existence of borderline cases of laws or legal systems (primitive or international law) which are, after all, clearly understood. Nor because these eminent jurists had forgotten the truisms about law familiar to the layman. Hart identifies three recurrent issues which come together in the quest for a definition of law. These are (1) the binding nature of law which renders conduct obligatory; (2) the differences between law and morality which overlap in content, concepts, and values; (3) the philosophically perplexing nature of rules and their role in social and legal activities. Resolution of these three general issues, Hart contends, has been the chief aim of most speculation about the nature of law. Yet, he stresses, no *definition* of law could resolve the complex issues at stake. Traditional genus and differentia definitions of law as a species of rule would be useless since the term 'rule' is no less perplexing than 'law'. The variety and complexity of the various

---

[7] H. L. A. Hart, 'Bentham on Legal Rights' in A. W. B. Simpson, ed. *Oxford Essays in Jurisprudence*, 2nd series (Clarendon Press, Oxford, 1973), pp. 171–201.

problems is too great to be resolved by a quest for definitions. Nevertheless bringing these issues together is, Hart suggests, correct —and 'it is possible to isolate and characterize a central set of elements which form a common part of the answer to all three' (*CL*, p. 16).

I think there is something misleading about this way of posing the central matter. The kind of perplexity Hart cites, and the oddity of the traditional answers is, after all, characteristic of every branch of philosophy. Reflect a moment upon the oddity of the answers philosophers have given to the question 'What is a material object?' —a substance qualified only by geometrical properties (and hence strictly colourless, odourless, tasteless, etc.), a congeries of qualities which qualify nothing, a bundle of sense impressions, a logical construction out of sense data, and so forth. Yet the Cartesians, Subjective Idealists, and Logical Positivists were not oblivious to the fact that apples are red and sweet, tables hard and solid, and that one listens to Beethoven's Ninth in a concert hall and not in one's mind. The point is that philosophical perplexity arises with regard to any categorial concepts in any domain of thought. These are not concepts we learn by verbal definition or ostension, and so quests for a definition are bound to be problematic. Moreover the pervasiveness of the categorial concepts, person and object in the metaphysics of experience, moral obligation and goodness in ethics, and law and legal obligation in jurisprudence, together with the fact that we are not normally called upon to define them, implies that these concepts themselves display a high degree of complexity, involve multiple ramifications in their logical connections with adjacent concepts and that no ordinary criteria of adequacy by reference to common definitional practices will be available. Rather we must ourselves determine criteria of adequacy by reference to very general considerations pertaining to the domain of the categorial term in question.

The concept of law fulfils as central a role in jurisprudence as Kant claimed for the concept of moral obligation in ethics. No simple definition will satisfy us in the absence of a clear grasp of the ramifications of the concept throughout its domain and an acceptable criterion of adequacy. So a definition, though it may be produceable at the end of our investigations into the structure of a categorial concept, is at best a decoration upon the keystone of the arch we build. Hart's specification of the purpose of his book goes to the core of the issue: 'it is to advance legal theory by providing an improved analysis of the distinctive structure of a municipal legal system and a better understanding of the resemblances and differences between law, coercion and morality as types of social phenomena' (*CL*, p. 17). The central jurisprudential task therefore is the analysis of the structure of a legal system. If desiderated definitions emerge from this, as I believe they do, they may serve a decorative purpose. If the concept of a rule can first be adequately clarified, then maybe that of a law can be defined in terms of it; if the concept of a legal system can be satisfactorily analysed, then maybe that of a law can be characterized in terms of its internal relation to the system of which it is a member. But the philosophical illumination will stem not from the concise definition but from the expository analytic matter which precedes it. The defects of Hart's predecessors stem less from a misguided quest for sharp definition than from inadequate analysis of the distinctive structure of a municipal legal system.

A further aspect of *The Concept of Law* which reveals the impact of work in analytic philosophy in the fifties is its preoccupation—for legal theoretical purposes—with doctrines of presupposition on the one hand, and intimately related issues of pragmatics on the other. The Fregean notion of presupposition was revived in this period by Strawson's famous paper 'On Referring'[8] where it was introduced as a non-logical relation obtaining between putative statements such that the truth of a presupposition was alleged to be a condition of a presupposing statement having any truth-value at all (i.e. having the status of a statement). The term quickly burst these narrow confines and was widely used to designate a set of conditions which must obtain if the use of a certain form of words is to have a point, or if it is to conversationally imply what it normally, conventionally, can rightly be taken to so imply. Positively, this looser, pragmatic, conception of presupposition plays a central role in Hart's distinction between internal and external statements of law. For certain types of normative statements are only appropriately used if the speaker has a distinctive attitude towards the norm thus expressed, and the utterance, although it is no part of its meaning that that attitude obtains, presupposes the existence of the attitude on behalf of the speaker, and hence can be taken to imply (non-logically) that it obtains.

In the more strict use of the term, statements concerning the validity of a law are held to presuppose the existence and general efficacy of the legal system of which the law is allegedly a member.

    [8] P. F. Strawson, 'On Referring', *Mind* 59 (1950).

For if the system does not, and never did, exist, then ascription of validity is neither true nor false.[9] This doctrine is duly brought to bear, by way of criticism, upon Kelsen's claims regarding the presuppositional status of the basic norm.

It is interesting to note, *en passant*, that elements in the analysis of key jurisprudential concepts which Hart had earlier included in the truth-conditions of statements containing them are, in *The Concept of Law*, relegated to presuppositions of assertion (e.g. the existence of a legal system was held, in Hart's Inaugural Lecture, to be part of the truth-conditions of '*A* has a legal right to . . .'). A similarly significant shift was Hart's abandonment of speech-act analyses as a panacea for all manner of ills in jurisprudence. In 'Ascription of Responsibility and Rights'[10] a speech-act analysis of action dominated the account, and a crucial component of the analysis of claim-rights in the Inaugural Lecture is the contention that statements of rights are used to draw a conclusion of law, where the latter phrase is interpreted in speech-act terms. This emphasis upon speech-act analyses has almost completely disappeared in *The Concept of Law*, being replaced by the notion of 'statements made from an internal point of view' (below).

A final, large, area of Hartian jurisprudential doctrine, which displays the profound impact of contemporary work in the philosophy of language, concerns the interpretation and application of law. A salient theme of Wittgenstein's philosophy, which was given widespread circulation by Waismann's paper 'Verifiability',[11] concerns a complex range of issues pertaining to the gap between rules and their application, the vagueness and the open texture of concepts. Open texture, in Hart's view, is an ineliminable feature of language. But this necessity is to be welcomed rather than deplored. For in a world characterized by a relatively unpredictable future, inhabited by creatures confronting diverse and constantly changing circumstances with relatively indeterminate and often competing goals, 'mechanical jurisprudence', were it possible, would secure greater predictability only at the price of reasonableness and flexibility. Rules can never dictate their own application: any appearance of inexorability stems

[9] This claim is not explicitly made in *CL*, where the constant emphasis is upon the *pointlessness* of assertions of legal validity when the requisite presupposition is false (cf. *CL*, pp. 100 ff.). It may well be, therefore, that the only notion of presupposition at work is the contextual one.

[10] H. L. A. Hart, 'The Ascription of Responsibility and Rights', *Proceedings of the Aristotelian Society* 49 (1948–9).

[11] F. Waismann, loc. cit.

from the inexorability of our methods of application of rules in standard cases. But non-standard cases will perforce arise, requiring the exercise of judicial discretion. To be sure, such discretion is guided, according to Hart, by antecedently specified *legal standards* which impose legal obligations to exercise that discretion according to those standards (*CL*, pp. 128 f, 132).

Thus far I have emphasized the impact of contemporary analytic philosophy upon Hart's jurisprudence. Another large area of methodological adaptation and innovation in his work lies in the sociological dimension. 'Notwithstanding its concern with analysis,' Hart writes in the Preface, 'the book may also be regarded as an essay in descriptive sociology', and, it will be remembered, one of the aims of the book is to produce 'a better understanding of the resemblances and differences between law, coercion and morality as *types of social phenomena*'.

That laws and legal systems are abstractions from highly complex social facts is a common tenet of English analytical positivism in jurisprudence. Part of Bentham's laudable demystification of law consisted of his constant insistence that law is not a divine phenomenon nor a product of nature, but a human artefact. It is, in Bentham's view, the expression of the will of the legislator, a person (or persons) who stands in a complex but specifiable relation to members of the political society in question. A consequence of this insistence upon law as social fact is Bentham's famous distinction between expository and censorial jurisprudence. What the law is, is one matter—to be discovered by examining social facts. What the law ought to be is another matter—to be discovered by applying moral principles. Hart's jurisprudence agrees with classical positivism on these two very general principles (as well as others). There are however important differences, although only those pertaining to the first general principle need concern us here.[12] Classical English social theory was dominated by methodological monism,[13] the *locus classicus* for which is to be found in the sixth book of Mill's *System of Logic*. The converse methodological doctrine that human, social, phenomena are essentially intentional and teleological, and that the

[12] With respect to censorial jurisprudence Hart, unlike Bentham, is an ethical pluralist, and hence accepts no simple uniform principle by reference to which to evaluate laws.

[13] For a synoptic account of positivist methodological monism as well as the competing pluralism which insists upon the propriety of hermeneutics for explanation and understanding in the human sciences, see G. H. von Wright, *Explanation and Understanding*, ch. 1 (Routledge & Kegan Paul, London, 1971).

logical structure of their description and explanation is not assimil-able to the patterns of explanation in the physical sciences was only belatedly assimilated into the mainstream of English philosophy. Collingwood's work was largely neglected, and it was mainly through Wittgenstein's later philosophy that hermeneutics began to influence English philosophical psychology, and hence philosophy of history and social theory in general. The impact upon jurisprudence is revealed in *The Concept of Law*.

In the Preface Hart declares that 'one of the central themes of the book is that neither law nor any other form of social structure can be understood without an appreciation of certain crucial distinctions between two kinds of statement, which I have called "internal" and "external" and which can both be made whenever social rules are observed'. Later in the book Hart again insists that 'until its import-ance is grasped, we cannot properly understand the whole distinctive style of human thought, speech and action which is involved in the existence of rules and which constitutes the normative structure of society' (*CL*, p. 86). One of the salient themes of hermeneutics is that description of distinctively human phenomena must involve under-standing the situation described as it is apprehended by the agent whose behaviour is to be explained and understood. So it must make reference to the conceptual framework of the agent. The social phenomena whose structure is the concern of jurisprudence is paradigmatically normative. A central feature of Hartian analysis is that normative phenomena in general, and legal phenomena in particular can only be understood if reference is made to the attitudes of human beings towards their behaviour. If social behaviour is to be understood as normative then it must be grasped as being seen by at least some of its participants as conforming to, or deviating from, general standards of conduct. This 'internal point of view' is manifest in characteristic normative responses, in critical attitudes expressed in demands for conformity, criticism of deviation, acceptance of the legitimacy of criticism, and distinctive kinds of justification of action expressed in normative language. This aspect of Hartian analysis constitutes a marked deviation from classical positivism, and informs his analysis of all the fundamental legal concepts discussed in the book. For where the classical positivists had attempted to explain internal legal relations largely in terms of a probabilistic nexus, or a psychological (but not normative) connection, Hart's explanations are characteristically normative.

A different aspect of the sociological dimension of Hart's juris-prudence is his repudiation of Kelsen's pure theory of law. The key methodological doctrine of Kelsen's pure 'normative science' of law is that in the explanation of legal concepts the sole admissible elements must be found in the 'legal material', and no reference to extra-legal phenomena is permitted. By contrast, Hart insists that a wide range of legal concepts and phenomena can only be adequately explained when reference is made to underlying social facts. This is, in a sense, a corollary of Hart's hermeneutics. For if normative phenomena and concepts are only intelligible by reference to the internal point of view which informs all distinctively social pheno-mena, then jurisprudential analysis which omits all reference to social facts must be misguided. Hart's rejection of 'pure theory' is manifest at many levels. Conceptual distinctions (e.g. between a fine and a tax levied at source) cannot be understood without reference to social purposes of the law. The concept of legal validity is essentially relative, and at the apex of the 'pyramid' of validity lies a norm (the rule of recognition) whose validity is not 'postulated by the juristic consciousness' (as is the Kelsenian basic norm) but which is neither valid nor invalid. Its existence is a social fact, manifest in the norma-tive behaviour of legal officials. Consequently the key to the unity of a legal system does not lie in a Kantian postulate of pure normative science, but in a legal norm which exists in the practice of a human community. A proper typology of legal norms must make reference to the social functions of laws, e.g. to facilitate and give legal status to citizens' private arrangements (disposal of property after death, contractual arrangements, marriage, etc.), to discourage socially undesirable behaviour, and so forth.[14] Any attempt to grapple with the problem of the necessary content of a legal system must allude to salient social, as well as psychological and economic, facts of the human condition.

Hart's hermeneutics and his repudiation of pure theory merge in his illuminating analysis of social (and subsequently legal) norms. Like Kelsen,[15] and unlike classical legal positivism, Hart rejects the imperatival analysis of law. Laws are rules or norms, not imperatives

---

[14] For a careful distinction between normative and social functions of law, and a general typology, as well as criticism of *The Concept of Law* on this matter, see J. Raz, 'On the Functions of Law', in A. W. B. Simpson, ed. *Oxford Essays in Jurisprudence*, 2nd series, pp. 278–304.

[15] In the *General Theory of Law and State* (Russell & Russell, N.Y., 1961), but variously qualified and obfuscated in *The Pure Theory of Law*, 2nd edn. (University of California Press, Berkeley and Los Angeles, 1967).

or expressions of will backed by threats. But whereas Kelsen's explanation of what a norm is, is extremely obscure, and his doctrine of purity precludes giving a general account of the existence conditions of norms, Hart's analysis of rules suffers from no such limitations. To be sure, he does not say, in so many words, what a rule is. But he gives a detailed and elaborate account of what it is for a rule to exist. And in conformity with the classical 'social realist' approach of English analytical positivism in jurisprudence, the specification of existence conditions of rules is in terms of complex social facts, of patterns of behaviour and response, critical attitudes and dispositions, characteristic reasons and justifications. Consequently Hart's analysis of fundamental normative and legal concepts (e.g. obligation, power, rights, validity, etc.) constitute a major advance over those of his predecessors. And the key notions employed throughout are those of rules, reasons, and justifications.

The final methodological feature to which I wish to draw attention here is Hart's espousal of the genetic-analytic method of exposition. This, while it has time-honoured antecedents (e.g. the social contractualists of the seventeenth century) and great expository advantages, is always liable to misinterpretation. Hart's analysis of social obligation commences by delineating the salient social facts which give rise to the need for the concept of obligation, and give point to its use. The concept continues to be of use in far more complex social situations, and its use in these complex situations can be much clarified by reflection upon similarities to and differences from the proto-phenomenon of obligation in the simpler context. But it is not claimed that other types of obligation, in particular legal obligation, are related to the concept of social obligation as species to genus, nor that all the features of social obligation also characterize legal obligation.[16]

Another, even more striking, employment of the genetic-analytic method occurs in Hart's elaboration of the illuminative virtues of the conception of a combination of primary and secondary rules as characterizing the complex social structure of which a legal system consists. This is done by means of describing the defects of a notional

[16] This has indeed occasioned much misunderstanding, see e.g. R. J. Bernstein, 'Professor Hart on Rules of Obligation', *Mind* 73 (1964), 563–6, or R. E. Hill, 'Legal Validity and Legal Obligation', 80 *Yale Law Journal* 47 ff. (1970). Bernstein's criticisms stem from failure to distinguish social or positive morality from personal and critical morality, a distinction which is crucial for Hart's purposes. Hill's criticisms stem from failure to realize that the analysis of social obligation does not, and is not intended, to apply, in any simple way (e.g. by addition of specific differentia), to legal obligation.

social group which has only primary rules. Each of the three salient defects would be remedied by supplementing the primary rules with different types of secondary rule. Each remedy is *a* step from the pre-legal world into the legal world, and all three remedies convert a 'regime' of primary rules into a legal system. It is important to understand that this revealing analysis is not a piece of armchair anthropology, but is conceptual analysis.[17] We are asked to envisage a purely notional situation in order to perceive what crucial features characterize our own complex situation, and to understand the structure of the concepts with which we describe it.

PART 2: ASPECTS OF HART'S LEGAL PHILOSOPHY

Having thus far examined Hart's methodological contribution to jurisprudence, it is time to turn to the substance of his philosophy of law. In this part of the discussion the following central themes from *The Concept of Law* will be surveyed: (a) Hart's discussion of the internal aspects of rules, and the application of his hermeneutical analysis to the concept of social obligation; (b) his distinction between primary and secondary rules and his conception of law as a union of rules of these two types; (c) the concept of a rule of recognition and Hart's solution to the problem of the unity of a legal system.

A. *Hermeneutics and the Concept of Social Obligation*

Rules, according to Hart have an 'internal aspect' which habits do not. Where rules, with their internal aspect, exist, then there is room for two distinct points of view with respect to them, an external and an internal point of view. Corresponding to the different points of view there are different types of statement whose use can only be understood if they are seen as standardly used by a speaker who has one or the other point of view. These types of statement are distinguished by the terms 'internal (external) statement' or 'statement made from the internal (external) point of view'. Hart's exposition of these distinctions is not wholly clear, and he employs the distinctions for different purposes. The following discussion does not

---

[17] L. J. Cohen (op. cit., p. 410) makes much of the existence of secondary rules relating to property, marriage, contract, etc. in primitive pre-legal societies. To be sure a human society could hardly exist in a regime of purely primary rules. But not every addition of secondary rules constitutes *the* step into the 'legal world', only *a* step. Of course the institutions of marriage, promising and primitive rules of ownership are the most law-like components of primitive societies. But it is the conjunction of the three types of secondary rules which convert a pre-legal into a legal system; less than that and we merely hover on the borderline between 'primitive law' and full-blooded legal systems.

mirror Hart's distinctions between internal and external points of view, aspects and statements, point for point. But I hope they may be used to shed some light upon his remarks.

Hart is concerned with the description of social behaviour that is rule governed.[18] One can distinguish different kinds of descriptions of such behaviour along a spectrum of increasing complexity. At one extreme one can describe such an action simply in terms of physical behaviour in a given circumstance, and give a similar description of the actions which commonly accompany its non-performance in the circumstance. Here neither teleological nor intentionalistic elements are invoked, and normative expressions are not used. Such a description would, in most instances of distinctively human action, display complete lack of understanding of the action. Further along the spectrum of possible descriptions lie increasingly complex intentionalistic descriptions of behaviour which variously describe the action as intentional, specify the intention with which the action was done, give the agent's reason for doing it, and specify the social context of the action. The minimal level of intentionalistic description will only further our understanding of it minimally. Such descriptions might be invoked by anthropologists encountering an alien society whose social behaviour (viewed 'externally') is clearly teleological, but as yet unintelligible. They are also commonly invoked by social satirists. But more complex intentionalistic descriptions of action will invoke a welter of factors pertaining to the agent's conception of his action and goals. At the complex level which is of interest for present purposes a description which displays an understanding of the action will refer to features such as the agent's beliefs, values, and desires with respect to the social institutions which play a role in his practical reasoning. A person can be described as making scratches on paper, or as making a will, as emitting sounds or as pronouncing a judicial verdict. The normative descriptions are the normal ones of a person who understands the significance of what he describes. Moreover such understanding (from an 'internal point of view') is a prerequisite to explaining the agent's behaviour (in motivational terms). Here the complex descriptions of action will employ a host of normative words which characterize the social practices which normally inform the agent's understanding of the social context of his actions.

The rules of a social group need not apply, individually, to all

---

[18] Both conformity to and violation of the rules.

members of the group. The norm-subjects of a rule may be limited to women, or to men over the age of forty-five, or to children. But whether a rule applies to a person or not, he may have a range of distinctive attitudes towards the rule, and the conduct governed by it. Cognitively, he may or may not be aware of the existence of the rule. If aware of its existence, he may or may not be aware of the fact that it applies to a given situation. Given that the general form of a rule includes specification of the occasion for performance of the norm-act, which we may call 'the operative facts', then cognizance of the rule implies cognizance of the fact that such-and-such conditions are the operative facts for performance of the norm-act. When an agent knowingly complies with a rule, he must be aware that the operative facts obtain. If he so acts with the intention of complying with the rule, those facts must be *part* of his reason for compliance, but they are not a complete reason.[19] The crucial feature for Hartian purposes is the question of what the agent's other (partial) reasons are, which, together with the operative facts, constitute a complete reason for him to perform the norm-act. For it is by reference to such considerations that Hart's distinction between two *attitudes* towards rules, namely *acceptance* and *rejection* can be clarified.

The circumstances which justify asserting that an agent accepts a rule divide into two main types: instances in which the rule applies to the agent on a particular occasion, and instances where the rule does not apply to the agent on a given occasion. The latter group involves different cases. (1) The agent's behaviour in circumstances in which the rule does not apply at all, but e.g. its rationale is under discussion, hypothetical cases are examined, and the agent's verbal behaviour manifests his attitude. (2) The agent's behaviour in respect of the behaviour of norm-subjects of a rule of which the agent is not a norm-subject. His responses to their conformity or violation of the rule are grounds for asserting his acceptance (or rejection) of that rule. (3) The agent's behaviour in respect of norm-subjects of a rule under which he too falls *upon other occasions*, but in this type of circumstance the rule does not apply to him. His responses to their behaviour will be a criterion of his acceptance, but so will his own behaviour on those occasions where the rule applies to him. The two criteria may converge or conflict.

[19] For a detailed discussion of the notion of a complete reason for action, see J. Raz, *Practical Reason and Norms* (Hutchinson, London, 1975); note especially the conception of an exclusionary reason tacitly invoked here in the sequel.

Where the agent's own rule-conformity or violation is not in view his acceptance of the rule is manifest in his attitude towards the actual or possible behaviour of others. He must take violation of the rule as a backward-looking reason for criticism. His rationale for so doing must manifest *respect for the rule*, be it moral, social or legal. This can be seen in a variety of factors: reference to the conventionality of the conduct in the circumstances, it is 'the done thing', or 'that's the law'; it may take the form of insistent reference to the operative facts e.g. 'But the lights are red', or to antecedent facts which institutionally provide the operative facts with their normative status e.g. 'But you promised' or 'He lent you the money'; it may be accompanied by justifying reasons for the rule itself, which may in turn conform with the generally accepted rationale for the rule, or may be of a private nature, and may but need not be moral considerations. It does not appear inconsistent, on the Hartian conception of rule acceptance, that the justifying reasons for the rule should be wholly prudential. For that is compatible with the contention that the accepting agent's reasons for complying with the rule preclude purely prudential considerations. To be sure, acceptance is also manifest in an agent's demands for conformity, and the types of factors the agent countenances as excuses and justifications for non-conformity.

Where the agent's own behaviour is in view, his acceptance of the rule is to be seen from the additional reasons which, together with the operative facts, constitute his complete reason for conformity, and from the normative status he accords to the operative facts. If the obtaining of the operative facts is (defeasibly) taken to preclude consideration of other possible reasons, so that the question of non-compliance does not arise for him on the occasion in question, then there is a prima-facie case for judging him to accept the rule. If his rationale for so apprehending his situation manifests respect for the rule in the way sketched out above, then there is a stronger case for taking him to accept the rule. Acceptance of a rule does not require uniform conformity, but the accepting agent's nonconformity must be accompanied by certain types of excuse and justification the necessity of which is felt by the agent, and in the absence of which responses of guilt, shame, and remorse are, for him, natural. Moreover, where criticism is directed at the agent for his rule-violation, he must, in the standard case, view it as legitimate.

An agent's rejection of a rule is characterized negatively, as excluding the complex phenomenon of acceptance, and positively, in terms of the prominence, among the additional reasons, which, together with the operative facts, constitute the agent's complete reason for conformity, of 'external' reasons. For the agent who rejects a rule, conformity upon any occasion is always an open question, to be settled by reference to forward looking considerations provided by the incentives (e.g. winning approbation) or disincentives (e.g. sanctions) which are provided by the consequences of compliance or non-compliance. The only kinds of criticism of actual or potential rule violation by others likely to be evinced by one who rejects a rule will concern the imprudence of failing to obtain the advantages of conformity or of incurring the disadvantages of nonconformity. Again it is noteworthy that rejection of a rule by no means requires uniform violation of it.

Hart further characterizes acceptance of rules by reference to the fact that those who accept a rule *use* it as a guide to social life. Since rules are not 'real entities', the notion of *using a rule* is opaque. It can be given an obvious use, e.g. where rule-statements are constantly consulted in rule-books we might say that rules are used. But this is hardly characteristic of common normative behaviour, and the income tax evader is likely to use rules more than the law-abiding citizen. We might claim that rules are used when circumstances are recognized as operative facts for performance of a norm-act. But this too will not, in itself, distinguish acceptance from rejection. Hart also stresses that for those who accept rules, violation of a rule is a reason for criticism. But for one who rejects a rule, the fact of violation, in conjunction with the fact that undesirable consequences will probably ensue, is also a reason for (prudential) criticism. So what differentiates the attitudes is not mere recognition of the operative facts, but the normative status accorded them in practical reasoning, not the justificative nexus with criticism, but the types of criticism.

It is clear that acceptance or rejection is not an all-or-nothing affair, for we are concerned with general dispositions to act in like circumstances, and to justify, criticize, or excuse in certain ways, as well as to advise and prescribe. Humans, being what they are, may combine attitudes of rejection in their own case, and critical attitudes characteristic of acceptance towards the behaviour of others. Finally, the notions of acceptance and rejection, here, as in *The Concept of Law*, are applied only to mandatory norms. This is a lacuna which needs filling in, but that will not be attempted here.

We have distinguished types of description of, and types of attitude towards, normative behaviour. These schematic distinctions, it is hoped, illuminate Hart's notions of internal and external aspects of rules and points of view. Hart also places considerable emphasis upon the idea that certain types of statements are 'naturally' used only if the speaker has a certain point of view relative to a norm. A very wide range of types of deontic sentences, types of normative statements and kinds of speech acts performed by using such sentences or expressing such statements is doubtless discernible. The issue will not be pursued here, for it has little bearing upon the sequel.

Hart's jurisprudence can best be approached via the question of what it is for a customary (non-legal) duty-imposing rule to exist. Here the internal/external distinctions are invoked constructively to clarify the existence conditions of such rules, and critically to refute predictive analyses of obligation. For a social duty-imposing rule to exist eight conditions must be met: (1) a duty-imposing rule must require its norm-subjects to do or abstain from a given act upon specified occasions; (2) the rule must be thought, by most members of the social group, to be important because it is believed necessary to the maintenance of social life or some valued feature of it; (3) the required conduct may conflict with the wishes of the norm-subjects; (4) compliance must be general. In the event of deviation from the rule (5) serious critical reactions of the type characteristic of rule-acceptance usually ensue, making nonconformity less eligible; (6) deviation is generally accepted as a good reason for the ensuing critical reaction; (7) such critical reactions are commonly regarded as legitimate, i.e. are not met with counter-criticism; (8) normative language is extensively used in the expression of critical responses.

These existence conditions require that most members of the social group must accept the duty-imposing rule. Hart's conditions stress the expression of acceptance of the rule in minatory, critical, reactions to deviation. No doubt the acceptance of the rule must be manifest also in hortatory responses to actual and possible occasions for conformity. Consequently norm-applying statements are likely to be commonly used by members of the group in manifestation of their acceptance of the rule, or, as Hart puts it, of their 'internal point of view'. Finally, a description of the behaviour governed by the rule which will render the behaviour intelligible must involve reference to the normative situation as apprehended by the agents and members of the group.[20]

Hart's account of the existence conditions of duty-imposing customary rules contains the core of his refutation of imperative and predictive analyses of duty, as well as the grounds for his distinction between being obligated and being obliged. Though his account is related to classical sanction theories of duty, it differs from its positivist ancestors largely as a consequence of the hermeneutical methodology adopted throughout and the resultant appreciation of the significance of normative connections. Hart summarizes his objections to the predictive theory of obligation by saying that it defines 'the internal aspect of obligatory rules' out of existence (*CL*, p. 88).

B. *Law as Union of Primary and Secondary Rules*

The foregoing analysis provides the foundation for the subsequent jurisprudence. We can imagine, Hart suggests, a social group which lives solely by a code of such duty-imposing rules, which he calls 'primary rules'. Such a code would not be a normative *system*, for although it might be informed by a common ideology, it would lack that unity which transforms a group of rules into a system, namely internal relations between rules such that behaviour according to one rule will normatively, rather then causally, affect the existence, incidence and scope of other rules. Moreover the membership of a rule in the code is exclusively determined by its customary existence conditions, and not by its having internal relations to the other rules. The defects from which such a wholly notional social group would suffer are (1) uncertainty, for the group would lack means of conclusive identification of its own rules and their scope; (2) staticness, for there would be no means of creating or abrogating rules at will, nor for altering the scope of existing rules; moreover (although this could hardly be envisaged in a human society) there would be no means of voluntarily altering the incidence of duties, of releasing people from onerous duties which, on particular occasions, may serve no purpose, or of intentionally changing the beneficiendiary of a duty; (3) inefficiency, for there would be no means of authoritative ascertainment of violation in disputed cases, and the informal

[20] For a more detailed discussion of Hart's analysis of duty see P. M. S. Hacker, 'Sanction Theories of Duty', in A. W. B. Simpson, ed. *Oxford Essays in Jurisprudence*, 2nd series, pp. 160 ff.

social pressures providing quasi-sanctions are inefficient in application and execution in all but the smallest and closest knit social group.

The remedy for each of these defects lies in supplementing the primary rules of obligation by distinctive kinds of secondary rules, which are rules of a quite different type. Conjunctively the *three* remedies convert a regime of primary rules into a legal system where the constituent primary rules are no longer necessarily customary rules of obligation (indeed most will probably be enacted obligatory rules). Uncertainty is resolved by introducing a rule of recognition for conclusive identification of the rules of the group. Staticness is eliminated by introducing rules of change which confer *public or private* powers upon officials or persons at large to enact, abrogate, and alter the incidence of, rules. Inefficiency is reduced by rules of adjudication empowering authorities to determine whether a rule has been violated, defining the procedure to be followed in adjudication, and empowering adjudicators to direct the application of penalties by other officials, thus centralizing the sanctions of the system. It is in this union of primary rules of legal obligation[21] and secondary (legal) rules of recognition, change, and adjudication that we have, according to *The Concept of Law*, the heart of a legal system, and a most powerful tool of jurisprudential analysis.

Hart's distinction between primary and secondary rules of law has occasioned much confusion.[22] It must be admitted that the fault lies in the fact that different dichotomous principles of classification are

---

[21] M. Singer ('Hart's *Concept of Law*', *Journal of Philosophy* 60 (1963), 197 ff.) criticized Hart for restricting legal primary rules to obligation-imposing ones, and excluding permissive rules assigning rights. Singer cites three ways of acquiring such rights: (1) by express legal permission; (2) by legal prohibition upon interference; (3) by absence of prohibition. This is confused; all these rights are liberties to do or abstain from ordinary (non-power-exercising) acts. The third way of acquiring such rights shows that they are not assigned by laws. So does the second, for the penumbra of duties of non-interference does not confer a correlative right, only protection of an antecedent liberty. Whether a statute expressly permitting something otherwise forbidden by another law which it thus restricts is itself a law conferring a liberty-right is a more controversial question. Hart would deny that it is an independent law.

[22] Thus L. Fuller in *The Morality of Law* (Yale U.P., New Haven, 1964), p. 134, thought the distinction coincided with the Hohfeldian right–duty relations and power–liability relations. But primary rules do not confer rights, and Hohfeldian rights are, as Hart has shown, a species of powers. R. Sartorius in 'Hart's *Concept of Law*' (*More Essays in Legal Philosophy*, ed. R. S. Summers (Blackwell, Oxford, 1971), pp. 131–61) argues that the distinction to which Hart assigns greatest weight is between constitutional rules of recognition, change, and adjudication, and rules which impose duties and confer powers upon private individuals. But private power-conferring rules are not primary rules, and secondary rules encompass both more and less than constitutional rules.

misguidedly assimilated, and wrongly thought to coincide exten-
sionally. Hart's remarks are neither clear nor obviously consistent.
Sometimes he equates the distinction with that between duty-
imposing and power-conferring rules (*CL*, pp. 27, 32, 78–9). But the
rule of recognition is a secondary rule, although it is apparently a
duty-imposing rule (see below). Elsewhere he suggests that secondary
rules are second-order rules. They are all on a 'different level' from
primary rules (*CL*, p. 92), being *about* such rules, specifying ways in
which they may be conclusively ascertained, introduced, eliminated,
etc. But secondary rules can be *about* secondary rules as well as
primary ones, and they are no more *about* rules than about behaviour,
for they guide behaviour no less than do primary rules. Moreover
primary rules too may be *about*, i.e. include reference to, other rules,
e.g. if the operative facts for the performance of the acts they guide
involve reference to the existence and scope of other rules, or to the
fact of violation of or compliance with other rules. Consequently
invoking the distinction between rules which presuppose the existence
of other rules, as opposed to those which do not, will not serve the
purpose either. Finally, it is clear that the desired contrast cannot turn
simply upon the deontic character of the rule, primary rules being
mandatory (and so duty-imposing) and secondary rules being
permissive. Since officials may be obligated to exercise powers, this
cannot be right either.

One can classify rules according to their deontic character, e.g.
whether they are duty-imposing or not. One can classify rules
according to the nature of the norm-act they guide, i.e. whether it is a
power-exercising act or not. One can classify rules according to their
normative function, i.e. whether they aim at regulating the scope,
incidence, application, and existence of other rules or not. Each of
these principles of classification is jurisprudentially significant, and
bears upon the concerns of *The Concept of Law*. But application of
the different principles to legal rules will not yield equivalent classes
of rules; nor will any of the principles yield the class of rules picked
out as secondary rules, namely rules of recognition, change and
adjudication.

This, if correct, suggests that Hart's distinction between primary
and secondary rules is a distinction by enumeration. Secondary rules
are rules of recognition, change, and adjudication, primary rules are
not. That this is so, however, does not prejudice the importance of
the distinction, nor the general thesis that the distinction provides the

'key to the science of jurisprudence'. It is also clear that the notion of a normative power is the most important concept involved in the conception of a legal system as a union of primary and secondary rules. For all secondary rules either confer powers or guide acts which are exercises of legal powers. To be sure, some may permit them, and others require (or even forbid) them; and Hart lacks principles of individuation of norms which will determine whether a duty to exercise a power can or cannot be imposed by the same norm which confers the power.[23] The notion of a power-conferring rule is one of Hart's main instruments in demolishing the obsessive picture of legal norms as hugely complex, imposing duties only (Bentham) or directed exclusively at officials (Kelsen) and containing in their antecedent conditional clauses as much legal material as would fill some several volumes. Constructively the notion not only provides a basis for a proper analysis of legal relations which will supersede the inadequate Hohfeldian analysis, but is a first step towards a proper typology of laws.[24]

The contention that law is best understood as a union of primary and secondary rules draws attention to, and explains, the institutionalized, systematic nature of law.[25] A legal system regulates its own creation and application (by rules of change and adjudication), provides criteria of identity for its parts (by a rule of recognition) and ensures its efficacy (by sanction stipulating laws which render violations of law less eligible courses of conduct). It is only within an institutionalized normative order, produced by the union of primary and secondary rules, that an obligation can exist, as some legal obligations do, without being efficacious. For social obligations exist through their practice, while legal obligations may exist only by means of the legal validity of the norm which imposes them, and the

---

[23] At *CL*, p. 29, Hart claims that a duty not to exercise a power is imposed by a different rule from the rule conferring the power. Is it then a primary or a secondary rule, or neither?

[24] This latter endeavour has been much furthered by J. Raz, *The Concept of a Legal System* (Clarendon Press, Oxford, 1970).

[25] M. Singer (op. cit., pp. 201–2) points out that morality contains power-conferring rules and argues that mere fusion of two types of rule cannot distinguish law from other kinds and types of rule. But positive morality is not institutionalized. It has no general rules of change empowering a moral legislature, no rules of adjudication setting up a moral judiciary, nor a rule of recognition for identification of the positive morality of a society. So not only does the claim that law is best understood as a fusion of primary and secondary rules not conflate law and morality, it sharply distinguishes them. The four cardinal features of social morality specified in *CL* are in part reflections of its non-institutionalization. It does not, however, follow that law can be fully characterized by form and structure alone.

notion of legal validity is explained by reference to the systematic unity, conferred by the rule of recognition, of that fusion of primary and secondary rules of which a legal system consists.[26]

C. *Rules of Recognition and the Problem of Unity*

One of the central problems of jurisprudence is that of the unity of a legal system. What is it that confers unity upon a legal system in virtue of which a law can be said to belong to a given legal system? Traditional resolutions to the problem divide into two types, those that locate the principle of unity in some aspect of law-creation, and those that locate it in some aspect of law-application. A different principle of classification can also be employed, for we can distinguish theories that search for the principle of unity in a legal organ from those which search for it in a legal norm. Bentham and Austin find the principle of unity in a law-creating organ (the legal sovereign), Kelsen in a law-creating norm (the 'basic norm'). Hart's analysis in *The Concept of Law* rejects attempts to resolve the problem by reference to law-creation.

The principle of unity, in his view, is to be found in a law-applying norm, the rule of recognition, not in an organ. Yet he does justice to the insights of positivist social realism by his insistence that the unifying norm exists only in the *customary practice of legal organs*, i.e. the courts which have to apply the law.

Hart's conception of a rule of recognition has occasioned much puzzlement,[27] for his analysis is incomplete and often obscure. The following theses are clear: (1) every legal system necessarily contains one and only one rule of recognition; (2) the rule is ultimate, i.e. it

---

[26] Sartorius (op. cit., pp. 145 f.) argues that fusion of primary and secondary rules is not employed in the analysis of obligation, one of the three central concerns of jurisprudence. But this confuses the analysis of social obligation with the analysis of legal obligation, for while the concept of social obligation is explained without reference to secondary rules, that of legal obligation presupposes the notion of validity, which is in turn explained by reference to the fusion of primary and secondary rules.

[27] L. J. Cohen (op. cit.) argued that the rule of recognition does not confer on anyone a power to make law, but sets up criteria of validity, and hence is not a secondary rule. It is true that a rule of recognition does not confer law-creating powers, but false that it is not a secondary rule. Sartorius (op. cit.) argues that the rule of recognition is neither necessary nor sufficient for the existence of valid law. But his arguments rest on four confusions: (a) of 'bindingness' of pre-legal rules with validity of rules of law; (b) validity of constitutional law with the ultimacy of the rule of recognition; (c) the validity of a law with the fact of its application; (d) applying existing laws recognized as valid with making and applying a new law by way of legally guided judicial discretion. Much light is cast upon the problem by J. Raz's illuminating paper, 'The Identity of Legal Systems', 59 *California Law Review* 795 ff. (1971), to which the above discussion is indebted.

is neither valid nor invalid, for its membership in the system is not determined by reference to any further rule; (3) consequently its existence is solely as a customary legal rule, to be seen in social practice; (4) it contains criteria for identifying rules of the system,[28] and where it contains a multiplicity of criteria (statutory enactment, custom, precedent, etc.) it ranks the various criteria to establish a supreme criterion and the relations of subordination between the other criteria in order that conflicts may be resolved; (5) it may be open-textured, and may be changed by judicial legislation; (6) as a customary rule, its existence requires that it be accepted and viewed from an 'internal point of view'.

It is not clear what the norm-act of the rule is, nor who the norm-subjects are. Nor is it obvious what the deontic character of the rule is, whether it is duty-imposing or not. Consequently the relationship between the act guided by the rule and the criteria of validity it contains is unclear. These unclarities can be resolved in a way which will preserve the spirit of Hart's approach even though it will controvert some of his claims.

To whom is the rule of recognition addressed? Hart speaks of private citizens using the rule of recognition to identify the law, but their use of the rule, like a spectator's use of the scoring rule of a game, does not imply that it is addressed to them. It is rather addressed to judicial officials (*CL*, p. 113), and its existence as a customary norm is to be seen in their normative behaviour. Courts have law-applying powers conferred upon them by rules of adjudication. When exercising their adjudicative powers they have a duty to apply only those laws satisfying certain criteria of validity. But the duty-imposing norm is distinct from the power-conferring norm, for the duty is not coextensive with the power (since courts may, given an appropriate rationale, refuse to adjudicate in certain kinds of cases despite being empowered to do so), and the norm imposing it is ultimate, whereas the power-conferring norm is not. Moreover, failure to comply with the rule of recognition does not nullify the adjudicative act. So a rule of recognition is a rule imposing a duty upon judicial officials to exercise their adjudicative powers by applying laws satisfying certain criteria.

If this is an acceptable explanation of Hart's view, it has further consequences which conflict with some of his remarks although they

---

[28] Hart occasionally slips on this, suggesting (*CL*, pp. 92, 97) that it merely identifies the primary rules of the system, but compare *CL*, p. 102.

do not destroy the general thrust of his argument. Firstly, given the multiplicity of judicial and quasi-judicial organs and the diversity of legal matter with which they may be severally concerned, there is no reason why there should not be numerous distinct rules of recognition, addressed to different judicial organs, having distinct content although similar form.[29] They will all require their norm-subjects to apply only valid laws in exercise of their adjudicative powers, but the criteria of validity specified in one rule of recognition addressed to one adjudicative body need not be identical with those specified in another addressed to a different body. Hence there may be derived (non-ultimate) rules of recognition. Secondly, and consequently, there need be no rule of recognition in a system which specifies all the criteria of validity of the system. So the principle of unity does not lie in a single norm but in *aspects* of a number of norms. A systematized, single, and highly complex criterion of validity specifying a supreme criterion and ranking subordinate criteria may be *extractable* from the various rules of recognition that exist in the system, but it need not be part of any rule of recognition. So we must sharply distinguish rules of recognition, which are norms imposing duties to exercise adjudicative powers, from the ultimate, complete, criterion of identity of the system. To properly specify the latter might be a difficult, unrewarding, and pointless task of particular expository jurisprudence. The concept of such a criterion is an illuminating and fruitful tool in general analytic jurisprudence. Thirdly, although some rules of recognition are ultimate, and although they severally serve to identify all the valid rules of the system, they are not the only ultimate rules. For there may exist other ultimate rules of judicial organs, e.g. duty-imposing laws of discretion.[30] So the principle of unity of a legal system lacks the tidiness of the favoured pyramidal picture.

Finally, a remark upon Hart's claim that the rule of recognition *must* be accepted by the judicial officials and must be viewed, by them, from the internal point of view. This, Hart claims, is a necessary condition for the existence of a legal system. There is no disputing that this is the normal condition of the life of a legal system. But it is not obvious that, if the previous discussion of acceptance is on the right lines, there cannot be pathological circumstances in which even judicial officials do not accept the rules of recognition under which

---

[29] Interestingly, in *CL*, p. 113, Hart talks of a legal system's *rules* of recognition.
[30] Cf. J. Raz, 'The Identity of Legal Systems', loc. cit. 810 f.

they fall. There is no conceptual necessity that the reasons for the judicial organs' compliance with the rules of recognition should satisfy the conditions of acceptance. It is undoubtedly the case that from a socio-psychological point of view the likelihood that officials, whose task it is to apply law, should not accept the rules guiding the application of rules is extremely remote. But whatever necessity obtains is, it seems, empirical. The only conceptual requirement is that the rules of recognition have the 'internal aspect' which is necessitated by the very claim that there exist such rules. And, to be sure, the norm-subjects must view their adjudicative acts as falling under such rules. But it is not logically necessary that their reasons for compliance should not be wholly prudential. It is striking that this contention, if correct, nevertheless does very little damage to the over-all picture of the structure of a legal system which Hart delineates. For the central features of Hart's resolution of the problem of the unity of a legal system stand intact. And here, in his doctrine of the rule of recognition, as elsewhere, Hart has fundamentally reoriented the debate about the central problems of legal philosophy.

2

Defeasibility and Meaning

G. P. BAKER*

HART conceives the purpose of jurisprudence to be the increase of understanding, not of knowledge; the generation of new insight, not the discovery of new facts. Well-trained lawyers know how to answer such questions as whether A is the owner of this property, whether B murdered C, whether D was negligent in ϕ-ing. Though they can employ such legal concepts, they may not be able to explain them. A Socratic question may produce perplexity. Lawyers are not ready with satisfactory and illuminating answers to the questions 'What is a contract?', 'What is a legal right?', 'What is negligence?'. Hence there is room for jurisprudence to come to the aid of beleaguered lawyers. It silences such questions, if not by answering them directly, at least by clarifying those concepts to such an extent that these questions are no longer thrown up in the search for understanding.

Hart's quest for understanding is guided by two fundamental principles. First, that it is possible to give genuine explanations of legal concepts and legal statements. Second, that legal concepts and legal statements are *sui generis*; i.e. that they cannot be shown to be logically equivalent to non-legal concepts and non-legal statements. The first principle is the practical justification of Hart's jurisprudence. It also underlies his rejection of 'realist' theories in the law—theories that tell us that legal words like 'corporation', 'contract', and 'right' stand for something extraordinary, different from other things that we see, feel, hear, touch, i.e. theories that take the *end* of wisdom to be the recognition that a right (duty, corporation, etc.) is what it is and is no other thing.[1] It is closely allied with other central motifs in Hart's work, and it bears the weight of his rejection of reductionist

---

* Fellow of St. John's College, Oxford.
[1] *Definition and Theory in Jurisprudence* (hereafter abbreviated *D*), p. 6 and n. 1.

theories in the law (especially 'Scandinavian fiction' theories and 'American Realism').[2]

In the eyes of many philosophers these twin principles are irreconcilable. The ground of this perceived incompatibility lies in very general considerations about what it is to explain the meaning of an expression and what it is to understand what an expression means. A sentence is explained by determining the conditions under which it is true (and those under which it is false), i.e. by stating its truth-conditions. Relativized to concept-words, this conception yields the claim that a concept is explained by stating its *Merkmale*, the conditions individually necessary and jointly sufficient for its correct application to an object. It is but a short step from this conception of meaning to the conclusion that there is a non-trivial explanation for every legal concept and every legal statement only if legal discourse can be reduced to non-legal discourse. Any complex legal concept can be analysed by means of a definition *per genus et differentiam*, but the *summa genera* (e.g. rights) can be analysed only if they can be reduced to concepts of some other type. Such basic concepts are either indefinables whose meaning cannot be explained or else logical constructions out of different sorts of concepts. Consequently, if there is a genuine explanation of *every* legal concept, then some reductionist theory must be correct. Conversely, if legal concepts are *sui generis*, then some of them are not susceptible of non-trivial explanation. The fact that theories in jurisprudence both grow on the back of definitions and polarize into two types (realism and reductionism)[3] does not result from intellectual perversity, but from the invisible but universal force of gravitation exerted almost everywhere in philosophy by a truth-conditions conception of meaning.

Hart himself feels the tension between his two basic principles. Much of his work can be regarded as an attempt to find an equilibrium position in the field of forces that they generate. He seeks a middle way between realism and reductionism, a way that acknowledges both the possibility of non-trivial explanation of all legal concepts and the distinctive irreducible character of these concepts. This search is one of the main concerns of his early article 'The Ascription of

---

[2] *D*, pp. 6–7.

[3] Hart distinguishes three, not just two, main types of legal theory. The rationale for this is historical, since, as he himself concedes, both Fiction theories and 'American Realism' are forms of reductionism (*D*, p. 6, n. 1).

Responsibility and Rights' (hereafter 'Ascription').[4] It is the centre-piece of his inaugural lecture *Definition and Theory in Jurisprudence* (hereafter *Definition*). It is one of the most important enterprises in *The Concept of Law*.[5] Each of these works marks an important advance and contains major insights, even if none of them alone constitutes the discovery of a *via media*. Moreover, by connecting it with other concerns, they show the central position of this problem in Hart's jurisprudence. Defence of the anti-reductionist principle is directly linked with criticism of definition *per genus et differentiam* as the only proper method for explanation of meaning and also with the ineliminable vagueness or open texture of all legal norms. Less directly it is linked with the use of the distinction between primary and secondary rules as a main tool in the analysis of a legal system; also with a simultaneous rejection of rule formalism and rule scepticism as adequate accounts of the application of laws. The defence of his two basic principles directly motivates some of Hart's most influential work and further ramifies into other issues central to much of his writing.

In this essay I discuss these two principles and the apparent conflict between them. Like Hart, I assume that the first is unproblematic, viz. that every legal concept or every legal statement can be explained or elucidated. If challenged, this would be defended on the ground that meaning is not ineffable: there must be criteria for correct understanding linked with any significant expression, and the specification of these criteria gives scope for non-trivial explanations of meaning. As a consequence, I focus on the second anti-reductionist principle and its apparent conflict with the first. In the first section I discuss Hart's attempts to justify its application to legal discourse by claiming that legal concepts are irreducibly defeasible. His arguments are so problematic that his conclusion is generally dismissed as unintelligible. In the second section, after clarification of the concept of defeasibility, I sketch a conception of meaning that makes sense of his analysis of legal concepts and dissolves the apparent conflict between his two principles. My hope is to arrive at the beginning of wisdom by getting to the Hart of this matter.

I

In 'Ascription' Hart offers a rationale for his anti-reductionist stand in jurisprudence. His principal claims are that legal judgments are

---

[4] 'The Ascription of Responsibility and Rights', *Proceedings of the Aristotelian Society*, 49 (1948–9). Reprinted in A. Flew, ed. *Logic and Language*, 1st series (Oxford, 1960), pp. 145–66. References will be to this reprint, indicated by the Abbreviation 'A'.
[5] *The Concept of Law* will be abbreviated *CL* in giving references.

primarily ascriptive, not descriptive, and that legal concepts are typically defeasible. (He mentions, but does not develop, a different line of argument based on a degree of freedom in identifying the *ratio decidendi* of cases cited as precedents in support of legal judgments.[6]) The main business of his article is to extend the anti-reductionist analysis of legal discourse to prove that the concept of human action is ascriptive and defeasible; i.e. that sentences of the form 'He did it' are primarily used to ascribe responsibility for actions, not to describe a person's actions. Though flawed in several respects, this article is a landmark. It is also essential for proper understanding of the development of Hart's own defence of his anti-reductionist principle. He moves gradually away from its emphasis on speech-acts (the contrast between ascription and description, between verdicts and statements) while the notion of defeasibility quietly disappears. In view of the double affinity of 'Ascription' to the work of J. L. Austin,[7] these developments might be summarized as the decreasing influence of Austin on his jurisprudence.

On the basis of speech-acts, Hart elaborates a strong criticism of reductionism in jurisprudence. The primary use of legal concepts is in the formulation of judicial decisions.[8] In the judge's mouth, sentences applying legal concepts are 'operative words' or 'performatory utterances'.[9] The judge does not, e.g., describe the facts in saying that a contract exists between *A* and *B*, he issues a decision.[10] What he decides may be affirmed or reversed, but it cannot be said to be true or false.[11] To issue a decision is a speech-act that cannot be assimilated to making a descriptive statement. Therefore decisions cannot bear truth-values. There can be no question of their being entailed by the facts cited in their support. Only a statement, not a performance, can be entailed by a set of facts. A correct explanation of a legal concept-word must take its distinctive primary use into account, and this will of course make impossible its explanation in terms of clarifying the contribution that it makes to the truth-conditions of those sentences in which it occurs.

This aspect of Hart's article has been subject to much criticism. In later work he himself makes telling points against it. The thesis that

---

[6] 'A', p. 147.

[7] Especially to his discussion of speech-acts in *How To Do Things with Words* (Oxford, 1962), and in 'Other Minds' and 'Performative Utterances' (*Philosophical Papers*, Oxford, 1961), and to his discussion of 'trouser-words' such as 'real' and 'voluntary' in *Sense and Sensibilia*, (Oxford, 1962), pp. 62–83, and 'A Plea for Excuses' (*Philosophical Papers*).

[8] 'A', p. 156. [9] 'A', p. 157. [10] 'A', p. 155. [11] 'A', p. 155.

the primary use of legal concepts is in judges' decision is radically mistaken. Especially so if associated with the claim that rules of law are primarily addressed to judges, not to citizens; that they are not so much rules guiding the actions of private individuals, as rules guiding judges in reaching decisions.[12] This mistaken outlook is perhaps fostered by a confusion between finality and infallibility in the case of judicial decisions.[13] The finality of a decision seems to carry the implication that it cannot be challenged as false. Either the decision that there is a contract between *A* and *B* makes it true that there is such a contract or, being a decision, not a statement, it cannot be assessed as either true or false. In either case, the decision, being final, is infallible, i.e. it cannot turn out to be false. Judges' verdicts carry a weight altogether different from applications of legal concepts by private individuals. Yet this difference is not correctly characterized by saying the judges' use of legal concepts is the primary one, others merely derivative; nor by claiming infallibility for judges' judgments. It must be understood in terms of legal powers that give an authoritative status to judges' decisions. Laws are typically directed to the citizen and are intended to guide his actions. But the smooth functioning of a legal system is promoted by establishing authorities whose decisions are to be taken to be final in cases of disputes among citizens about the application of laws. Such institutions are set up by secondary rules. Hart's distinction between primary and secondary rules is not only the principal tool in his analysis of a legal system, but also the means for proper elucidation of the distinction between finality and infallibility and some of the differences in speech-acts performed by different subjects of a legal system.

These criticisms, though sufficient to account for Hart's later repudiation of 'Ascription',[14] do not exhaust the problems even with this aspect of it. First, there is the general problem of relating meaning to the performance of speech-acts. The thesis that the primary use of legal concepts is found in judges' verdicts is difficult to reconcile with the use of these concepts in negative statements, in questions, in the antecedents of hypotheticals, in disjunctive statements, and in the formulation of norms. Secondly, if the speech-act analysis were dropped, Hart's argumentative strategy would be undercut. For it is

---

[12] 'A', p. 156.

[13] Both of these mistakes are later fully exposed by Hart himself. See especially *D*, pp. 10–11, and *CL*, pp. 35–41 and 138–41.

[14] In his preface to the collection of his papers *Punishment and Responsibility*, p. v.

fallacious to conclude from the thesis that no judicial decision is entailed by the evidence cited in its support that legal concepts or legal statements cannot be reduced to non-legal concepts or statements.[15] Reductionist theories are generally taken to be compatible with absence of entailment even in singular statements of the problematic kind, provided that each such statement is taken to be logically equivalent to an infinitely complex statement in the reduction class.[16] Some extra premiss is needed to prove that a reductionist account of legal discourse is impossible.

A second support for Hart's anti-reductionist principle is found in the concept of defeasibility. This concept is explained by reference to the notion of contract in English law.[17] There is a list of positive conditions required for the existence of a valid contract (e.g. at least two parties, an offer by one, an acceptance by the other). Knowledge of these conditions does not give a full understanding of the concept of contract. What is necessary in addition is knowledge of the distinctive ways in which the claim that there is a valid contract may be challenged and thereby reduced or defeated. Such defences include fraudulent misrepresentation, duress, lunacy, and intoxication. The concept of contract may best be explained by setting out a list of conditions necessary and normally sufficient for the existence of a valid contract together with 'unless' clauses that spell out the conditions under which this existence claim is defeated. It is this distinctive feature of the explanation of 'contract' that is singled out by the term 'defeasible'. Hart's thesis is that contract is an irreducibly defeasible concept.[18] Though developed with reference to the concept of contract, the notion of defeasibility is intended to have a much wider application. Indeed, this is the 'characteristic of legal concepts . . . which makes the word "unless" as indispensable as the word "etcetera" in any explanation or definition of them.'[19] Defeasibility is argued to be a fundamental characteristic of the concept of human action.[20]

There are three main consequences that follow from the fact that a

[15] Reductionism would be excluded only if legal judgments had semantic features either independent of or incompatible with the features of non-legal statements. The speech-act analysis seeks to establish the first case. Hart has an argument based on the timelessness of conclusions of law that purports to establish the second ('A', p. 156).

[16] e.g. A. J. Ayer in *Language, Truth and Logic* (London, 1936) held that statements about material objects were logically equivalent to infinite conjunctions of statements about sense experiences; hence that no singular statement about material objects was entailed by the descriptions of any actual sense experiences.

[17] 'A', pp. 148 ff.   [18] 'A', pp. 148, 150.   [19] 'A', p. 147.   [20] 'A', p. 160.

concept is defeasible. The first concerns onus of proof. If a concept ϕ
is explained in terms of necessary and usually sufficient conditions
for its application together with a list of heads of exception, then the
onus is on a person who challenges a particular application of ϕ on
the basis of satisfaction of these normally sufficient conditions to
show that ϕ cannot correctly be applied in this instance because the
case can be brought under a recognized head of exception. No defence
of the application of ϕ is necessary unless a prima-facie case is made
against its applicability. It is not required to show that no such prima-
facie case *can* be argued in order to justify the application of ϕ. This
point about onus of proof for defeasible legal concepts consists in (or
is typically reflected in) the allocation of the burden of proof in the
procedural principles of English law. The second consequence of
defeasibility is that applications of defeasible concepts are justified
in particular instances only on the assumption of total evidence, i.e.
the assumption that the relevant evidence actually stated is in fact
the only available evidence. Adding to the body of evidence may
verify an 'unless' clause that is otherwise not known to be true, and
hence it may defeat an application of the concept that would be
justified by its definition in absence of this additional evidence. The
citation of satisfaction of conditions normally sufficient for applying
ϕ does not justify its application in a case where it is known that other
conditions are satisfied that would defeat its application. The third
consequence of defeasibility is that a defeasible concept cannot be
defined *per genus et differentiam*. It cannot be explained on this
model. There are no circumstances severally necessary and jointly
sufficient for its correct application; merely conditions necessary and
normally sufficient. A defeasible concept might be explained on the
classical model by coupling with the necessary and normally sufficient conditions of application the negation of the disjunction of
the various defeating conditions. Hart condemns such a move as
'obstinate loyalty to the persuasive but misleading logical ideal that
all concepts must be capable of definition through a set of necessary
and sufficient conditions'.[21] One objection is that such a definition is
vacuous or trivial.[22] A more telling objection is that it would misrepresent the onus of proof, suggesting that the justification for
applying a defeasible concept is incomplete until it is shown that there
is no prima-facie case defeating its application.[23] The illegitimacy of
transforming the explanation of contract into a set of necessary and

[21] 'A', p. 152.   [22] 'A', p. 152. n.   [23] 'A', p. 151.

sufficient conditions is summarized in the claim that the concept of contract is 'irreducibly defeasible'.[24] This feature of defeasible concepts is often obscured in their explanations. The 'unless' clauses in the explanation of 'contract' may, e.g., be replaced by the positive-looking condition that 'consent must be true, full, and free'.[25] It is essential to recognize that such formulae are merely a 'comprehensive and misleadingly positive-sounding reference to the absence of one or more of the defences, and are thus only understandable when interpreted in the light of the defences, and not vice versa'.[26] Hart thus links the thesis that legal concepts are defeasible with the principle that they are not reducible to concepts of another kind.

Is the thesis that legal concepts are defeasible less trouble-ridden than its companion that they are fundamentally ascriptive? There is room for doubt here. Apart from the point about onus of proof, the irreducibility of defeasibility rests on a distinction between positive and negative conditions. Absence of a defence should not be seen as a positive condition whose satisfaction is sufficient for the application of a defeasible concept, whereas, presumably, definition *per genus et differentiam* proceeds by stipulating a positive condition for something to fall within a genus itself determined by a positive condition. It is far from clear that there is any intelligible way to segregate conditions into negative and positive ones. On the other hand, difference in onus of proof might well be thought not to support any *logical* distinction between defeasible concepts and those admitting of a reductionist analysis. Given the procedural rules for English law, we can determine that the burden of proof is put on a person who argues that satisfaction of the normally sufficient conditions for the existence of a contract does not license the conclusion that there is in this case a contract between *A* and *B*. This is an objective question to be settled by appeal to procedural principles. Outside courtrooms there are no similar rules to settle questions of onus of proof. This obstructs the extension of the concept of defeasibility to any non-legal concepts; in particular to the concept of human action.[27] Even for legal concepts there is a problem. The defeasibility of the concept of contract puts the onus of proof on someone who challenges a prima-facie case for the existence of a contract, and yet it is admitted that in certain exceptional cases the onus of proof in the courtroom

[24] 'A', p. 150.   [25] 'A', p. 151.   [26] 'A', p. 163.
[27] 'The notion of defeasibility then is inextricably tied up with an adversary system of litigation and its complex and diverse (procedural) rules . . .' (J. Feinberg, 'Action and Responsibility', in M. Black, (ed. *Philosophy in America* (London, 1964), p. 136.).

may be cast on a person to show that a certain defence cannot be pleaded.[28] This concession requires either the elaboration of a non-legal notion of onus of proof or the abandonment of the claim that there is a uniform connection between defeasibility and legal onus of proof. In either case we must return the verdict 'not proven' on Hart's thesis that legal concepts are irreducibly defeasible.

Apart from these sins of omission, the concept of defeasibility might be charged with sins of commission. Hart argues that the concept of contract is explained by a combination of conditions necessary and normally sufficient for the existence of a valid contract with a list of conditions that can defeat the claim that there is a valid contract. Also that this form of explanation is taken to be typical of the analysis of legal concepts.[29] But, if there are any *necessary* conditions for the existence of a contract, there are *sufficient* conditions for there not being a contract. The statement that there is no contract between *A* and *B* is an application of the term 'contract', albeit a negative one. Therefore it is incoherent to explain defeasibility by stating that there are only necessary and normally sufficient conditions, but never sufficient conditions, for the *application* of a defeasible concept.[30] If there are no sufficient conditions for its application, there cannot be any necessary conditions either. Certainly a truth-functional explanation of negation leaves no room for an essential asymmetry in the sense of positive and negative legal statements, whereas Hart's account of defeasibility requires such asymmetry. To avoid this incoherence, it seems best to amend his thesis so that a defeasible concept is explained by conditions normally necessary and normally sufficient for its application together with a list of conditions that can defeat a claim applying it (positively or negatively). (This modification will henceforth be made by transforming Hart's phrase 'necessary and normally sufficient' into the phrase 'normally necessary and sufficient'.)

Hart's defence of his anti-reductionist principle in 'Ascription' is also marred by the fact that his two main arguments war against each other. The explanation of a defeasible concept like contract consists in a list of conditions normally necessary and sufficient for its application together with a series of 'unless' clauses stating defeating conditions. These are conditions of its being *true* that there is a

---

[28] Hart cites the case where one party to a contract stands in a fiduciary position to the person against whom he wants to enforce it ('A', p. 151).
[29] 'A', p. 154.   [30] 'A', p. 154.

contract between A and B. Moreover, satisfaction of an 'unless' clause presumably makes it *false* that such a contract exists. The explanation of defeasible concepts presupposes that their central applications are in making statements with determinate truth-values. But Hart's speech-act defence of anti-reductionism for legal concepts rests on the contention that their primary use is not to make statements, but to formulate verdicts that cannot be assessed as being true or false. An explanation of a legal concept must primarily explain its primary use. This cannot take the form of setting out conditions normally necessary and sufficient for the *truth* of statements applying it. It is inconsistent to claim that any concepts at all are both defeasible and ascriptive. On Hart's early view of performative utterances, each of these claims, if true, would render the other unintelligible.[31]

The defence of his anti-reductionist principle is taken up again in *Definition*, but the thrust of Hart's argument there is unclear. He claims that a fundamental legal concept cannot be defined *per genus et differentiam*; that words like 'corporation', 'right', and 'duty' do not have 'the straightforward connexion with counterparts in the world of fact which most ordinary words have and to which we appeal in our definitions of ordinary words'.[32] The proper method for explaining them is contextual definition. We should take a sentence where such a word plays its characteristic role and explain it first by specifying the conditions under which the whole sentence is true, and secondly by showing how it is used in drawing a conclusion from legal rules in a particular case.[33] Instead of vainly trying to answer the question 'What is a right?', we should focus our efforts on explaining how to use the sentence-form 'X has a right'.[34]

So far everything is perfectly clear. What remains obscure is whether this amounts to a denial of the possibility of a reductionist analysis of fundamental legal concepts. Hart does criticize prevailing reductionist theories, 'American realism' and 'Scandinavian fiction theories'. But this criticism might be interpreted as a quarrel about details, not about fundamentals. On this view, such theories err in giving too simple a statement of the connection between legal concepts and the world of facts: they assume that there is something of a complex and unexpected sort that corresponds to these legal words,

---

[31] There are alternative accounts of performative utterances according to which they may be assigned truth-values. (Even the possibility of treating them as self-verifying statements.) In later writing Hart implicitly subscribes to some such view of performatives (cf. esp. *D*, p. 14).

[32] *D*, p. 5.   [33] *D*, p. 14.   [34] *D*, pp. 16–17.

and they use these counterparts to define legal concepts. They assume that such words 'stand for and describe something'.[35] An alternative reductionist analysis of legal words would be built on contextual definitions. The model for such a procedure is Russell's theory of descriptions:[36] although, where a definite description is used as the grammatical subject of a sentence, the sentence as a whole is equivalent in meaning to a complex sentence beginning with an existential quantifier, there is nothing for which the description stands. But this minimal interpretation seems too weak in view of the lingering speech-act analysis. Such a word as 'duty' not only 'does not stand for or describe anything', but also 'has an altogether different function which makes the stock form of definition, " a duty is a . . .", seem altogether inappropriate'.[37] Such a word 'has meaning only as part of a sentence the function of which as a whole is to draw a conclusion of law from a specific kind of legal rule'.[38] It appears that *Definition* is intended to defend Hart's anti-reductionist principle. But there is no new argument here to warrant this conclusion. Definition *per genus et differentiam* is not essential to reductionist analyses, and hence even if it were necessary to give contextual definitions of fundamental legal concepts, this would not prove that they were *sui generis*. This conclusion might be derived from the premisses that explanations of legal concepts must make reference to the existence of legal rules and that the statement that a particular legal rule exists cannot itself be reduced to 'brute' facts.[39] Hart does not develop such a line of reasoning.

One might try to extract from *The Concept of Law* one fresh argument for the anti-reductionist principles.[40] This starts from the thesis that there is room for discretion or decision in the application of rules to concrete cases. Hart argues that it is logically impossible to eliminate the need for such discretion because it is always possible to generate a borderline case for the applicability of any rule. Like all utopias, the jurists' heaven of absolutely determinate and mechanically applicable concepts is unattainable. This excludes the possibility of reducing legal discourse to any form of discourse in which all

---

[35] *D*, p. 23.

[36] Or Bentham's method of paraphrase (*D*, pp. 8, 13, 15).

[37] *D*, p. 5.

[38] *D*, p. 10. (This thesis is absurdly strong. Instead of 'has meaning *only* . . .' it might better read 'has meaning *primarily* . . .'.)

[39] Cf. the explanation of '*X* has a right' at *D*, p. 16.

[40] This argument is perhaps adumbrated at 'A', p. 147, but certainly not fully developed there.

concepts are absolutely determinate and mechanically applicable; hence it might be thought to exclude the possibility of reduction to factual or 'scientific' language for describing the material world and human behaviour.[41] As previously argued, even the assumption that a description of the facts in a case never entails a legal conclusion (that a law applies) is not sufficient to establish the impossibility of a reductionist analysis of laws or legal concepts. The major premiss of this argument is also open to question. What shows that it is logically impossible to frame laws in such a way that there is no need for judicial discretion? Hart has a two-pronged attack on this problem.[42] A law must be determined either by explicit statute or by authoritative example (precedent). In the first case, the ineliminability of scope for discretion is traced to the open texture of all empirical concepts. In the second, it is traced to indeterminacy in the sense of any expression explained by ostensive definition or paradigms.

Unfortunately, the argument from open texture seems circular. This concept is borrowed from Waismann,[43] who deduces the thesis that all empirical discourse is open textured from the claim that no rule can be formulated in such a way that no cases can arise in which its application is open to doubt.[44] From this generalization about rules, he concludes that the sense of any empirical sentence must be ineliminably indeterminate since sense is explained by reference to rules governing the application of its constituent expressions.[45] Hart's thesis about legal statutes is simply a restriction of this completely general statement about rules that Waismann takes as a datum in introducing the concept of open texture. Consequently, appeal to open texture provides no independent support for Hart's contention that a statute cannot be framed so that it removes the need for the exercise of discretion in its application.[46]

[41] On Hart's view, no plausible form of reductionism would be excluded, since *all* empirical concepts whatever are taken to be open-textured, hence neither absolutely determinate nor mechanically applicable.

[42] *CL*, pp. 121 ff.

[43] *CL*, p. 249, for the reference to F. Waismann's 'Verifiability' in A. Flew, ed. *Logic and Language*, 1st series, pp. 117–44.

[44] Waismann does not explicitly make this completely general claim, but it follows immediately from his demonstration that the open texture of empirical concepts follows from the essential incompleteness of empirical descriptions (Waismann, op. cit., pp. 122–3). If this thesis could not properly be attributed to Waismann, then Hart's argument would not strictly be circular.

[45] Waismann, op. cit., pp. 120–1, 122–3.

[46] Although this is not generally recognized, the notion of open texture makes sense only within a particular form of semantic theory. (See below, p. 51, n. 76). As a result it might well be impossible for Hart to incorporate it into his philosophy of law.

The argument from ostensive definition is also dubious, though doubt may be dulled by familiarity. It is almost a commonplace that ostensive definitions determine the meaning or sense of an expression only vaguely or approximately. A definition of a colour-word, e.g., consists in pointing at some objects and saying 'This, this, and this are blue'; this process leaves the learner with the task of intuiting in what respect objects must resemble these samples to count as being blue and also how close this resemblance to the samples must be. This conception of ostensive definition is radically mistaken. In pointing at an object and using it as a sample for defining 'blue', I produce a complex and partly concrete symbol consisting of the word 'this', the gesture of pointing, and the object pointed at. This whole complex symbol can be substituted (when it can be produced) for the word 'blue'. There is absolutely no reason why an expression so defined should be any less determinate in sense than one given an explicit wholly verbal definition. If this conception of ostensive definitions can be defended, then the stipulation of legal norms by reference to paradigms or authoritative examples does not exclude the possibility of a system of laws whose applications would every-where take care of themselves without any need for the exercise of discretion.

The whole argument for the impossibility of eliminating the need for judicial discretion is inconclusive.[47] If *The Concept of Law* had advanced on this basis an argument for the anti-reductionist princi-ple, it would have added to the support of this principle only the weight of a fallacious deduction from a dubious premise.

Apart from this putative argument from discretion, the reasoning by which Hart supports his anti-reductionist principle in *The Concept of Law* is identical with the argument in *Definition*, although it is differently expressed. It rests on the distinction between the internal and external aspects of legal rules. A social rule of a group of people has an 'external aspect . . . which consists in the regular uniform behaviour [of members of the group] which an observer could record', i.e. in 'a fact about the observable behaviour of most members of the group'.[48] In addition, it has an internal aspect that is manifested by

---

[47] Hart has important non-logical arguments for the desirability of a degree of indeterminacy in the framing of laws. The right degree is determined by balancing the demands of equity (fairness and flexibility) in the application of laws with the demands of predictability in their operation (to allow citizens to plan their lives free from unforeseeable interference by legal authorities). Cf. *CL*, p. 125.

[48] *CL*, p. 55.

its use 'in the criticism of others and demands for conformity made on others when deviation is actual or threatened, and in the acknowledgement of the legitimacy of such criticism and demands when received from others'.[49] The 'characteristic expression' of the internal aspect of rules is 'in the normative terminology of "ought", "must", and "should", "right" and "wrong" '.[50] Hart uses this distinction to produce an argument against the possibility of a reductionist analysis of legal language. He distinguishes statements incorporating normative terms into two types: internal and external. An internal statement is a form of expression manifesting the internal point of view of a person who expresses it, i.e. his acceptance of the relevant rule and his willingness to use it for the appraisal of his own and others' behaviour.[51] An external statement, by contrast, is non-committal, the natural form of expression for an outsider to use in describing rule-governed behaviour within a group. Using this distinction, one can state one of the major premises of Hart's argument: the primary use of legal language is in making internal statements. The second premiss is that no internal statement is the logical consequence of any set of 'scientific', external descriptions of the facts of the behaviour of any person or group of people. Together these premisses yield the conclusion that legal discourse cannot be reduced to non-legal, factual discourse. The proof of the anti-reductionist principle emerges from the logical abyss that divides the internal aspect of rules from their external aspect.

This reasoning is more of a logical reconstruction of a line of Hart's thought than an argument explicitly advanced in *The Concept of Law*. None the less it seems to be required to do justice to many of his remarks there. In particular, he claims that 'most of the obscurities and distortions surrounding legal and political concepts arise from the fact that these essentially involve reference to the internal point of view'.[52] It is this that 'requires more detailed attention in the analysis of legal and political concepts than it has usually received'.[53] We must learn to resist the 'constant pull' towards analysing them 'in terms of ordinary or "scientific", fact-stating or predictive discourse', since 'this can only reproduce their external aspect'.[54] Does this not amount to the thesis that the internal aspects of legal language cannot be accounted for by any reductionist analysis of legal concepts? Moreover, only the ascription of this thesis to Hart makes sense of

[49] *CL*, p. 56.   [50] *CL*, p. 56.   [51] *CL*, p. 99. (cf. p. 96).   [52] *CL*, p. 96.
[53] *CL*, p. 96.   [54] *CL*, p. 96.

his contrast between 'statements of law' (e.g. that the successor of Rex I has the right to legislate) and 'statements of fact' (e.g. that he is likely to be obeyed if he does legislate).[55] Otherwise statements of law would be a proper subclass of statements of fact.

If this is Hart's reasoning in support of his anti-reductionist stand in *The Concept of Law*, then it is essentially identical with his argument in *Definition* and even harks back to distinctive elements in 'Ascription'. (One might turn this argument inside out, using it to support this interpretation of *The Concept of Law* as a persistence of reasoning familiar in his earlier writing.) Hart relates the internal point of view to a distinctive *use* of rules, viz. their use as standards for the appraisal of one's own and others' behaviour.[56] His notion of use is not altogether clear. But the salient point is that rules viewed from the internal point of view play an essential role in the speech acts of *criticizing* others' behaviour, of *demanding* conformity with norms, and of *acknowledging* the legitimacy of such criticism and demands addressed by others to oneself.[57] Further, it is characteristic of these speech-acts that one uses normative terminology in their performance.[58] Granted that 'normative language' will figure in any adequate analysis of legal concepts, Hart's remarks add up to the thesis that what is crucial for the correct analysis of legal concepts is the elucidation of their role in the performance of a certain distinctive range of speech-acts. This is a restatement of the kernel of 'Ascriptivism', divested of the restrictive claims that utterances used in performing these speech-acts cannot be assigned truth-values and that the use of legal language in the decisions of judges is its primary use.[59] This, as we have seen is the position laid down in *Definition*.

What is crucial for this account of *The Concept of Law* is the connection between the internal point of view and certain speech-acts. That Hart does make such a connection seems clear not only from his explanation of what the internal aspect of rules consists in, but also from his distinction between internal and external statements. The difference between these kinds of sentences is explained in terms of the different speech-acts that they are typically used to perform. An internal statement like 'Out!' or 'It is the law that . . .', is 'the language of one *assessing* a situation by reference to rules which he . . . acknowledges as appropriate for this purpose'.[60] It is the language

---

[55] *CL*, pp. 57–8.   [56] *CL*, p. 96.   [57] *CL*, p. 56.   [58] *CL*, p. 56.

[59] But for an echo of Hart's earlier view about the primacy of judicial decisions, see *CL*, pp. 102 and 112–14.

[60] *CL*, p. 99 (italics added).

appropriate for *applying* a rule to a situation in order to draw a conclusion of law,[61] presumably for such purposes as criticizing others' performances, demanding conformity to a norm, etc. An external statement, by contrast, is a mere statement of fact. It is 'the natural language of an external observer' of a system of rules and is used for stating of a rule 'the fact that others accept it'.[62] The reference to speech-acts is essential to Hart's development of this distinction. Since the distinction between internal and external statements is the linguistic reflection of the difference between the internal and external points of view, its dependence on speech-acts indirectly establishes the connection between the internal point of view and certain speech-acts.

The multiple ambiguity in Hart's contrast between the external and internal points of view makes difficult a thorough assessment of his reasoning in support of his anti-reductionist principle. If, however, this distinction is used in this context simply to give a new formulation to the argument familiar from *Definition*, then the difficulties with that argument are common to this one as well. The crucial problem is to vindicate the connection between meaning and speech-acts in the face of powerful and well-known objections. A secondary problem will be to prove that the use of legal words in certain speech-acts is primary or essential. Only thus can it be demonstrated that a correct analysis of legal concepts must make reference to their use in utterances performing that range of speech-acts that are distinctive of the internal point of view.

The existence of this unsolved problem makes Hart's anti-reductionist stance in *The Concept of Law* at best unproved. In fact the situation is even worse. For, it seems inconsistent to combine the thesis that meaning is connected to speech-acts with the view that the internal point of view is a matter of person's attitude towards rules. Hart insists that the analysis of legal concepts must make reference to the internal point of view.[63] On the other hand, the distinction between expressions of the internal and external points of view, i.e. the distinction between internal and external statements, is pragmatic, not semantic. To make an internal statement does not entail, but at best contextually implies, that the speaker shares the internal point of view towards the relevant rule. To make such a statement without this attitude of commitment is misleading, perhaps reprehensible, but it is perfectly intelligible and semantically in order. Its

[61] Cf. *CL*, p. 100. [62] *CL*, p. 99. [63] *CL*, p. 96.

truth-value does not depend on the speaker's attitude. There is no form of words that cannot correctly be used by someone who is merely pretending to share the internal point of view, and there is no speech-act that he cannot perform. Whether or not they include reference to speech-acts, the conditions under which meanings are assigned to utterances cannot ensure that the meaningfulness of any utterances is a guarantee of its speaker's sincerity in making it. Therefore, it is incoherent to maintain both that the internal point of view is an ingredient in the analysis of some concepts and that the internal point of view is essentially a matter of a person's attitude to rules. Hart has an inconsistent division between semantics and pragmatics. In view of this problem, it might be best to drop the claim that consideration of speech-acts performed by sentences incorporating legal words plays an essential role in the analysis of legal concepts. This need not prejudice one important truth encapsulated in Hart's thesis that the analysis of legal concepts must make reference to the internal point of view. This truth is that it must make sense to speak of certain activities (whether linguistic or non-linguistic) as criticisms of conduct, demands for obedience to norms, acknowledgements of obligations or guilt, etc., if it is to make sense to speak of the members of a group as having legal rules and making use of them as guides for their conduct. Unless the truth-conditions of some statements of the form 'A criticized B for ϕ-ing', 'A required B to ϕ', etc. are satisfied for some members of the group, it cannot be true to say of the group that its activities are rule-governed. Through the use of the phrase, 'the internal point of view', Hart conflates this conceptual truth with various theses about speech-acts and observers' attitudes towards rules and thereby commits himself to a range of statements that seem indefensible.

The upshot of this examination is that there is no cogent argument in Hart's writings for the irreducibility of legal concepts. The most striking candidate is the original speech-act argument in 'Ascription'. Like Hare's parallel argument for the autonomy of ethics, this one would be decisive if only its premises could be established. But Hart has explicitly and advisedly retreated from this position. This leaves no support for the irreducibility of legal concepts and no demonstration that it is possible to combine non-trivial explanations of every such concept with opposition to reductionism. If to say that a concept is irreducibly defeasible presupposes that its correct analysis satisfies both his fundamental principles, then it is not clear that there *can* be *any* defeasible concepts. It is therefore problematic whether legal concepts are rightly characterized as being irreducibly defeasible. Hart has certainly not driven us out of the jurists' heaven of concepts nor out of a reductionist conception of the language of the law even if he has made us eager to leave it of our own accord.

II

From this examination one comes away much wiser but also somewhat sadder. There is a sense of disappointment, reflecting that one's hopes were so very high. Hart's work holds out the prospect of major clarification of legal concepts because his view of the law seems informed and free from the distorting influence of philosophical commitments. His achievements in most respects measure up to these heady prospects. The disappointment comes at the highest level of abstraction. What we hoped for was a cogent diagnosis of the ills of legal philosophy, not just an identification of the most prevalent diseases; a general rationale for his own analyses in addition to a number of conspicuously successful examples of elucidating legal concepts; the delineation of a method to be followed or of a correct logical point of view. What seems lacking is a developed synoptic view of jurisprudence, something that would give us a feeling of knowing our way so that we could dispense with the need for philosophical vision or genius in constructing a systematic philosophy of law. Though we learn a great deal from his work, too little of what we learn seems transferable to treating other problems.

Disappointment is doubly acute. Hart's notion of defeasibility seems enormously suggestive and potentially fruitful. It fills our heads with ideas and apparent insights. It seems to have applications in many areas, particularly in the analysis of certain words that are productive of philosophical controversy, e.g. 'real', 'certain', 'voluntary'. The recognition that these expressions are 'trouser-words' or 'excluders',[64] i.e. that these concepts are defeasible, seems a great advance in clarification. None the less, in spite of its promise, the concept of defeasibility seems too frail to support any important conclusions. Its application to non-legal concepts is as fraught with difficulties as its application to legal ones. It is impossible to marry the concept of defeasibility with our conception of meaning based on truth-conditions, and this prevents our consolidating the impression

---

[64] J. L. Austin, *Sense and Sensibilia*, pp. 70–1, and R. Hall, 'Excluders', *Analysis* 20 (1959), 1–7.

of insight that it generates and our exploiting its apparent potentialities.

Unless we are to abandon hope, we must make a fresh start on the basis of a new strategy. Previously we have taken for granted that a truth-conditions conception of meaning is correct, that understanding the sense of a sentence is knowing the conditions under which it is true (and hence by complementation, those in which it is false), and that explaining the sense or meaning of a word is clarifying the contribution it makes to the sense of sentences in which it occurs. We then studied the possibility of accommodating Hart's concept of defeasibility within this framework. The result was an accumulation of difficulties that led inexorably to a negative verdict. The obvious alternative strategy is the polar opposite of the previous one. Instead of taking the theory of meaning as fixed and testing Hart's analyses of legal concepts against it, we take his analysis of legal concepts as fixed and search for a theory of meaning that makes sense of as much of it as possible. We take for granted his thesis that legal concepts are irreducibly defeasible and study the possibility of constructing semantics in accord with this datum. Such a strategy offers several possible advantages, even apart from charity, and certainly seems worth trying.

The first step is to establish the constraints that must be met by a theory of meaning for it to accommodate Hart's analyses of legal concepts. These constraints fall into two categories. The strong ones are imposed by his analyses. The weak ones in other ways, especially by his *obiter dicta* in giving these analyses (Austin's 'cackle'). In so far as possible, all these constraints should be met, but the strong must prevail over the weak.

The strong constraints are summarized in the slogan that legal concepts are irreducibly defeasible. The implications of this remark are spelt out in Hart's analysis of contract and highlighted by his own comments on this analysis. We have already noted them. (1) A defeasible concept is explained by giving a list of conditions normally necessary and sufficient for its application together with a list of conditions under which the claim that it applies may be defeated. (2) The defeating conditions associated with a defeasible concept are naturally expressed as a series of 'unless' clauses. (3) The onus of proof is typically on a person who challenges the application of a defeasible concept on the evidence of satisfaction of the conditions normally sufficient for its application; he must show that the disputed instance can be brought under a recognized head of exception, i.e. that one of the defeating 'unless' clauses is verified. (4) The principle of total evidence is necessary in justifying typical applications of defeasible concepts. (5) There are no necessary and no sufficient conditions for applying a defeasible concept, merely normally necessary and sufficient conditions.

Although these theses seem quite unproblematic, they do stand in need of some clarification. The concept of defeasibility is somewhat indeterminate. Its ambiguity is best explored by asking what are the implications of the defeasibility of legal concepts for the logical structure of legal arguments. It seems reasonable to suppose that there are such implications. For knowing how evidence bears on the application of a concept seems at least in part a consequence of grasping a concept.[65] (This presumably is the rationale for some aspects of legal training, in particular of the institution of moot court trials.) Grasping the concept of contract, e.g., requires knowing what sort of evidence is *a priori* relevant to the claim that A has a contract with B to ϕ and being able to assess the extent to which any such actual evidence supports this claim, i.e. knowing whether it constitutes a prima-facie case, or conclusive evidence, or even incontrovertible evidence for this claim, or whether it directly licenses no decision at all. There is room for some disagreement in these matters, and the conclusion to be drawn from some sets of facts may not always be determinate. None the less, there must be at least a broad measure of agreement in drawing legal conclusions from evidence unless the functioning of a legal system is to be capricious (both unfair and unpredictable). Hence, if the application of legal concepts is rational and regular, we might expect to find the defeasibility of legal concepts to have implications for the structure of legal arguments.

In an adversary system of trial, these implications should be clearly visible in the structure of arguments in courts of law. Here the judge or jury is supposed to start from a *tabula rasa* in respect of evidence relevant to the dispute to be decided. A decision should be reached solely on the basis of evidence actually submitted by at least one of the parties or implicitly conceded by both. The logical description of a trial must specify the legal question to be settled and the evidence presented, e.g. as a list of statements $p_1, p_2 \ldots p_n$ (perhaps pruned of

[65] In part, too, a matter of inductive inference. But it will be assumed here that inductive inference, being grounded in observed correlations, presupposes identification of what constitutes *a priori* evidence for the instantiation of the related concepts.

any irrelevancies). This could be presented in the form of a tree-diagram. The nodes of the tree represent states of information. The 'root' (at the top) is the initial state of no relevant information. The assignment of a letter 'p_i' to a node represents the supposition that it is established that the proposition p_i is true, and information is assumed to be transmitted downwards along the branches, (i.e. p_i is tacitly assigned to any node below a node marked 'p_i').[66] Someone's grasping the sense of the disputed legal statement q (e.g. that A has a contract with B to ϕ) has the consequence that he can determine whether or not any particular body of relevant evidence establishes *a priori* that q is true.[67] This will be represented on the tree by the assignment of other symbols to the nodes: viz. '+' indicates that the evidence so far presented supports q, '−' that this evidence supports the negation of q, and '0' that no decision is possible on the established evidence (i.e. either no evidence at all is established or the bits of established evidence cancel each other out). The logical description of a trial (or any legal proceeding) might then have the form exemplified in the following tree-diagram:[68]

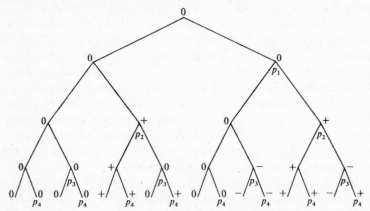

A person with a complete grasp of the sense of q should be able to fill in the symbols '+', '−', '0' correctly on any such tree constructed

[66] This condition might be applied only to certain kinds of non-legal statements, e.g. to descriptions of behaviour, but not e.g., to attributions of mental states (intentions, desires, motives, etc.). This complication will be ignored here.

[67] This is a very strong requirement, perhaps too strong. It excludes vagueness, or at least any vagueness that might be reflected in uncertainty about what counts as evidence for a statement. It could be relaxed. The account of tree-diagrams would need appropriate modifications.

[68] If each p_i is independent of every p_j ($i \neq j$, $i, j, = 1, 2 \ldots n$), then the tree will be the full binary tree of length n. Any logical dependence among $p_1, p_2 \ldots p_n$ will be

on any set of relevant evidential propositions $p_1, p_2 \ldots p_m$ (for any m). The job of the judge or jury, on this model, is to determine which of the evidential statements actually presented ($p_1, p_2 \ldots p_n$) are established as true and thus to reach a verdict as to whether q is established or not.[69]

If there were (finite) necessary and sufficient conditions for the application of any legal concept, then there would be the possibility of embedding any tree-diagram of this kind in a larger tree Γ in any extension of which each branch would be stable; i.e. for every nontrivial branch of Γ terminating in node α all nodes below α in any extension of Γ would have the same value ($+$, $-$, 0) as α itself. This simply reflects the fact that entailments are immune to revision on the strength of increasing evidence. (If $p \vdash r$, then p, $q \vdash r$.) Hart associates the defeasibility of legal concepts with the thesis that there are no sufficient conditions for their application. What property of tree-diagrams does this thesis encapsulate?

One property might be that for any legal concept ϕ there is some statement q incorporating ϕ for which there is a tree at least one of whose branches is not stable: i.e. there is an infinite sequence of independent relevant evidential statements such that any positive (resp. negative) verdict on q that is justified by the first n of them is reversed for some n' by the first $(n+n')$ of them. On this interpretation, there being no sufficient conditions for the truth of ϕ consists in there being the possibility that the truth of some statements incorporating ϕ be indefinitely unresolvable in an incontrovertible way, even though nearly all statements employing ϕ have a truth-value that can be incontrovertibly established. Defeasibility of ϕ here amounts to the possibility of indefinitely hard cases of applying ϕ. This interpretation of the defeasibility of legal concepts seems to accord with Hart's own expansion of the claim that there is an ineliminable need for judicial discretion in applying laws. There are clear cases where a concept can be applied, and others where it cannot. But there is always a penumbra of uncertainty surrounding any legal concept, and this gives the possibility of there being judgments incorporating this concept whose truth or falsity is not dictated by any set of relevant facts, however extensive. What cannot be got rid of is the possibility of unsettlable borderline cases.

reflected in the truncation of some branches of the corresponding tree. This complication will be ignored here.

[69] The verdict will also typically depend on empirical confirmation (inductive support).

Another much stronger property would be that, for any legal concept ϕ, every finite tree Γ associated with any statement q incorporating ϕ non-vacuously can be embedded in a larger tree Γ' such that, for every terminal node α in Γ, Γ' contains a node below α to which an assignment of the values $+$, $-$, 0 is made that is different from the value assigned to α. On this interpretation of there being no sufficient conditions for ϕ, no statement q incorporating ϕ non-trivially has a truth-value that can be established incontrovertibly. However extensive the evidence supporting it or disconfirming it, this evidence can always be extended in such a way that the previous verdict on the truth-value of q is reversed. The defeasibility of ϕ here amounts to impossibility of any incontrovertible applications of ϕ, whether positive or negative. This interpretation of defeasibility seems to accord with Hart's invocation of open texture in establishing the necessity for judicial discretion. No application of an open-textured concept is incontrovertible; there is always a possibility that further evidence will undermine its application to an object, and this possibility can never be eliminated from language. Waismann makes this point by imagining bizarre contingencies.[70] What for many years has romped around my house and garden, barked, gobbled down dog-biscuits, and otherwise behaved in a paradigmatically canine manner may none the less now suddenly explode or float off upwards into the clouds, or start reciting the *Iliad* in Greek, or fall apart revealing an internal constitution of clockwork and springs. Since such possibilities can never be excluded, and since each of them alone (or at least some combination of them and others of the same sort) would defeat the application of the term 'dog' to this problematic object, no application of an open-textured term, however fully supported, is proof against revision in the light of further evidence. The explanation of such a term proceeds, as it were, by laying out the conditions normally sufficient for its application. These conditions must be understood to be accompanied by a *ceteris paribus* rider, and there is no possibility of spelling out explicitly the content of this clause. If it is plausible to attribute to Hart the thesis that legal concepts are themselves open-textured, this is the lineal descendant of his early claim that they are irreducibly defeasible.

In terms of the logical machinery here introduced, there are at least six other interpretations of defeasibility which are intermediate in strength between these two. These will not be explored further.

[70] Waismann, op. cit., pp. 119–20.

Instead, we will simply split the claim (5), that there are no sufficient conditions for applying defeasible concepts, into three theses: (5a) Some applications of defeasible concepts can never be determined incontrovertibly. (5b) No application of such a concept can be determined incontrovertibly. (5c) The full explanation[71] of a defeasible concept cannot have the form of stating necessary and sufficient conditions for its application; it cannot be a definition *per genus et differentiam*. This completes the catalogue of the strong constraints on the semantics for defeasible concepts.

The weak constraints can be dealt with more summarily.

(1) Compatibility with Hart's two fundamental principles, viz. that it be possible to give a non-trivial explanation of the meaning of every legal expression and that this explanation not be a reductionist one.

(2) There must be the possibility of certainty in the application of legal concepts. Hart is as much opposed to rule scepticism as to rule formalism. It must be possible to settle at least most legal disputes in ways that are recognized to be rational, i.e. by appeal to evidence that justifies assigning a particular truth-value to a legal judgment. It is thus natural to think that a legal statement can, at least in a favourable case, be known to be true, that it can be established with certainty (when the evidence is conclusive). This possibility is precisely what rule scepticism denies.

(3) The explanation of a concept by stating necessary and sufficient conditions for its application is not the only legitimate form of definition. Concepts may be fully and adequately defined in other ways. The demand that every definition take the form of a definition *per genus et differentiam* is procrustean and eliminates the possibility of clarifying most concepts that raise philosophical problems.

(4) It must be possible to distinguish positive and negative properties. Hart requires this distinction in order to defend his thesis that non-satisfaction of the 'unless' clauses linked with a defeasible concept cannot be represented as a positive condition for its application. In order, e.g. to defend his contention that the condition on contracts that 'consent be true, full, and free' is not a positive condition for the existence of a contract.[72] (The distinction is also required by the

---

[71] The qualification 'full' is necessary since a complex legal concept (e.g. ownership) might be defined *per genus et differentiam* (e.g. as a species of right).

[72] To Hart might be attributed a weaker thesis, the objection to treating the phrase 'True, full, and free consent' as a positive description of a *psychological* or *mental* element necessary to the existence of a valid contract (cf. 'A', pp. 151 and 153). This interpretation seems weaker than what he intended (cf. 'A', pp. 161–2).

related doctrine that words such as 'voluntary' and 'real' are 'trouser-words' or 'excluders'.)[73]

(5) It must follow from the fact that no legal judgment is entailed by the non-legal evidence presented in support of it that there is no possibility of reducing legal statements to non-legal ones. Hart presupposes that this second thesis is entailed by the first one, that the open texture of laws directly established his anti-reductionist principle. This argument is invalid provided that it makes sense to speak of infinitely complex logical constructions (as many philosophers do). Hart's reasoning can be secured, however, by arguing that there is no such thing as logical equivalence with an infinite conjunction of statements. Therefore, this thesis is a (weak) desideratum of a semantics to fit his analysis of legal concepts.

(6) The clarification of legal concepts must make reference to the distinctive speech-acts performed by means of the different sentences that incorporate these concepts non-vacuously. It is a desideratum of the required semantics that it establish some connection between meaning and illocutionary force.

This is a formidable catalogue of constraints on a semantic theory. Can any theory meet them? Or even a significant proportion of them? *Mirabile dictu*, the answer is 'Yes'. There is a theory of meaning that satisfies *all* of the strong constraints and most of the weak ones. This theory may even be familiar, though neither recognized nor understood, from Wittgenstein's *Philosophical Investigations*. It is a little-known form of a little-recognized kind of semantics, a form of constructivism. This needs some elucidation.[74]

Constructivism is a genus of semantic theories marked off from the more familiar truth-conditions theory by taking sense to be related to evidence, i.e. to the conditions under which a statement can be recognized to be true or false. A truth-conditions theory explains the sense of a sentence by specifying the conditions under which it is true, whether or not we have any effective method for determining whether these conditions actually hold. Constructivism, by contrast, explains the sense of a sentence by specifying the conditions under which we correctly judge it to be true (and those under which we

---

[73] '. . . [the] attempt to find a characteristic common to all things that are or could be called "real" is doomed to failure; the function of "real" is not to contribute positively to the characterization of anything, but to exclude possible ways of being not real . . .' (J. L. Austin, *Sense and Sensibilia*, p. 70; cf. *Philosophical Papers*, p. 140). Also Hall, op. cit., p. 5.

[74] A fuller account is given in G. P. Baker, 'Criteria: A New Foundation for Semantics', *Ratio* 5 (1974).

correctly judge it to be false), where these conditions must be ones such that we do have an effective method for determining whether they hold. Alternative formulations of constructivism are that the sense of a sentence is determined by its assertion-conditions (the conditions that fully justify its unqualified assertion) or that its sense is determined by its verification-conditions (the conditions that fully justify its being assigned the truth-value true). (The difference is most obvious in considering sentences involving universal quantification over domains that cannot be exhausted by a finite list.) The most widely known form of pure constructivism is the Intuitionistic account of the meaning of statements in mathematics. A more comprehensive but adulterated form is familiar from logical positivism (built on the 'strong' principle of verification). The only explicit attempt to outline a general constructivist semantics bears the label 'anti-realism'.[75] Constructivism may take various forms even as regards the sense of non-basic sentences. The *a priori* relation of evidential support used in the explanation of sense may be taken to be entailment (as in anti-realism) or (*a priori*) probabilification.[76] Yet another species may be built on a notion to be called the C-relation. This evidential relation, like the relation of *a priori* probabilification, can be undermined by addition of further evidence; it is 'defeasible' both positively and negatively, and therefore subject to the principle of total evidence. But, unlike probabilification, it may yield conclusions that are certain: indeed, if a sentence is C-supported by statements known to be true, it *is* certain. To grasp the sense of a non-basic sentence is to know what statements C-support it, i.e. to know the conditions under which it is correctly taken to be certain. (Wittgenstein's concept of a criterion is built on the C-relation.)[77] It is this species of constructivism that gives maximal satisfaction of the constraints set up by Hart's analysis of legal concepts.[78]

---

[75] M. A. E. Dummett, 'The Reality of the Past', *Proceedings of the Aristotelian Society* 69 (1969), 239–58, and *Frege: Philosophy of Language* (London, 1973), s.v. 'verificationism versus realism, as theories of meaning'.

[76] This form of constructivism was explored by Wittgenstein in the early '30s, when the notions of hypothesis, symptom, and probability dominated his account of meaning. (See especially *Philosophical Remarks*, Part XXII.) Waismann's concepts of open texture and language strata belong to this conception of meaning. (See F. Waismann, *Logik, Sprache, Philosophie* (Stuttgart, 1976), ed. G. P. Baker and B. F. McGuinness, Nachwort and Anhang 'Ueber Hypothesen'.)

[77] Baker, op. cit., pp. 170–5.

[78] If Wittgenstein's account of the sense of third-person psychological sentences in terms of behavioural criteria fits this semantics, then Hart's analysis of legal concepts can be thought of as a formal parallel to Wittgenstein's analysis of psychological concepts.

All the strong constraints are met.

(1) A defeasible concept is determined by the conditions that C-support its attribution to an object and by those that C-support the negation of its attribution to this object. The first set of conditions is normally sufficient for its application, i.e. they make its application certain *ceteris paribus*. The second set of conditions are those that may, unless counterbalanced, defeat its application. The defeating conditions cannot be given by a closed list, but membership in the open list can be determined by reference to a closed list of types of conditions instances of which figure on this open list.[79] The 'unless' clauses associated with a defeasible concept thus determine its sense by fixing the types of conditions instances of which may defeat claims that the concept may be applied in a particular case.

(2) Unproblematic.

(3) The C-relation gives rise to a *logical* conception of onus of proof. This removes the principal obstacle to treating defeasibility as a *semantic* feature of legal concepts. Since C-support makes a conclusion certain at least *ceteris paribus*, the person who challenges the certainty of a statement C-supported by established evidence must show that some further condition is satisfied that defeats the claim that there is C-support for the conclusion. To refuse to acknowledge that the onus of proof is thus placed on the challenger (in particular on the sceptic) constitutes misunderstanding or redefinition of the sense of the disputed sentence.[80]

(4) The 'defeasibility' of the C-relation, i.e. the fact that C-support may always be undermined by addition of evidence, requires that assessment of C-support is always made on the assumption that the stated evidence is the total evidence known to be available.

(5) The 'defeasibility' of C-support is equivalent to the strong thesis that no application of a defeasible concept, whether positive or negative, is incontrovertible, i.e. to (5b). Moreover, if a full explanation of a legal concept must show how its applications are C-supported and C-defeated by non-legal evidence, then such an explanation does not state conditions necessary and sufficient for its application. This establishes (5c).

This form of semantics also satisfies most of the weak constraints.

---

[79] Compare the recognition that criterial-support for someone's being in pain may be defeated by establishing that he is pretending, play-acting, anaesthetized, hypnotized, etc.

[80] This doctrine about semantic onus of proof is prominent in Wittgenstein's refutation of scepticism about other minds.

(1) It reconciles Hart's two fundamental principles. Explanation of legal concepts is non-trivial: it proceeds through clarification of what evidence C-supports a legal statement. It is not a form of reductionism: there is no non-legal sentence, however complex, that is logically equivalent to any sentence containing a non-vacuous occurrence of a legal concept-word.

(2) It establishes the possibility of certainty in the application of legal concepts and thereby refutes rule-scepticism. The essential feature of the C-relation is that C-support establishes a conclusion as certain in spite of the fact that any C-support can be overturned by further evidence. Evidence C-supporting a conclusion is conclusive evidence for this conclusion even though it is not incontrovertible. It cannot be strengthened though it can be increased. To many the features in each of these pairs appear to be irreconcilable. The dissolution of this difficulty is a crucial part of elucidating the C-relation. It raises deep issues about possibility, certainty, and the dependence of probability on the possibility of certainty.[81] These cannot be discussed here.

(3) The *Merkmal* definition of concepts is just the truth-conditions theory of meaning relativized to concept-words. It is not necessary for constructivism to give any special role to this form of explanation, and the full explanation of concepts essentially connected with sentences whose sense is a matter of C-support cannot be cast into this mould.

(4) A limited defence of the distinction between positive and negative properties can be erected on constructivist foundations. It is natural to suppose that the logic generated by any form of constructivism will differ from Classical Logic in lacking the principle of bivalence; hence that it will be (or be similar to) Intuitionistic Logic and lack of the Law of the Excluded Middle. If so, absence of verification for a statement need not verify any other statement; therefore, lack of evidence verifying an 'unless' clause need not verify anything else, in particular not its negation. Hence if the sentences describing the defeating conditions of a legal judgment are not all decidable, then the positive-sounding reformulations of the 'unless' clauses in its explanation are indeed logically objectionable. Since there need be nothing in common among the conditions in which, e.g. it would be correctly judged that a contract exists, the condition that consent be true, full, and free cannot be a statement of such a common condition.

[81] These issues are explored in Baker, op. cit., pp. 176–82.

(5) According to any coherent form of constructivism, there is no such thing as a logical equivalence between one statement and an infinite conjunction of other statements.[82] The phrase 'infinite conjunction' has no sense. Hence there is no *non sequitur* in the argument attributed to Hart, viz. that it follows from the fact that no legal judgment is entailed by the non-legal evidence presented in support of it that legal statements cannot be reduced to non-legal ones. Since we 'mere mortals' could not come to grasp the sense of a legal sentence if it were given as an infinite conjunction of non-legal sentences, this cannot be a correct way of accounting for its sense.

(6) Constructivism makes no explicit provision for a connection between speech-acts and the clarification of concepts, between sense and illocutionary force.[83] Hence it gives no rationale for this aspect of Hart's analysis. Yet, since the importance of speech-acts in his analysis of legal concepts diminishes, indeed almost vanishes, this may not be reckoned a serious obstacle to the claim that a particular form of constructivism satisfies the constraints laid down by Hart's work. There are serious objections to the claim that semantics need or can include reference to speech-acts in the analysis of meaning. Perhaps Hart's later explanation of the different functions of legal statements by reference to secondary legal rules points to a general way towards a better account of speech-acts.

Apart from its satisfying the constraints of Hart's analysis of legal concepts, this particular form of constructivism has considerable intrinsic plausibility in application to legal discourse. First, explanation of legal concepts by reference to what constitutes evidence for and against their applicability gives a very direct account of the rationality of certain legal institutions. In particular, it gives a justification for the practice of choosing juries from legal 'laymen'. A jury's decision turns on non-legal questions of fact, and if the judge in instructing a jury is giving a constructivist explanation of a legal statement with special reference to the arguments presented in court,

[82] This is one respect in which orthodox logical positivism deviates from a pure form of constructivism. It uses the notion of verifiability in principle to legitimate such infinite analyses.

[83] It is sometimes thought that a liberalization of constructivism might connect speech-acts with meaning. By explaining sense by reference to *assertion*-conditions, constructivism restricts the semantic relevance of speech-acts to the single case of assertions. Why should sense not be explained in terms of *utterance*-conditions? Why should the sense of a word not be taken as the contribution to the conditions under which it is appropriate to utter any sentence (of whatever semantic mood) in which it occurs? Some have detected intimations of this line of thought in Wittgenstein, esp. *Philosophical Investigations*, §§ 22–4.

then the whole procedure of trial by jury has a transparent rationale and objectivity. Secondly, the notion of onus of proof is a crucial component of this form of semantics. Consequently, the allocation of onus of proof in the courtroom is shown typically to have its justification in the very analysis of legal concepts. Of course, procedural rules may impose the burden of proof in an exceptional manner,[84] and here presumably the justification would be a matter of moral values or of policy considerations. No alternative semantics gives any role to the notion of onus of proof in explanations of meaning. Finally, this form of semantics gives the most direct possible account of the relation between grasping a legal concept and knowing how to make particular applications of it in the light of specific bodies of evidence. The relation is simply one of identity.[85] The tree diagrams of legal arguments presented above are simply a representation of what it is to grasp the sense of a legal sentence and hence the sense of legal concept-words.[86] It is the heir to Frege's conception of sense:[87] that the sense of a concept-word is determined by determining how it is applied to any object in any possible situation. A possible state of affairs can be specified constructively only by giving a sequence of propositions supposed to be true. Hence, the ability to determine on *any* tree whether or not a legal statement incorporating the concept ϕ is verified or refuted just as the ability to determine for any object whether the concept ϕ can be applied to it in any possible situation.[88] Moot court trials are far from being indirect means for establishing whether law students have a grasp of the relevant legal concepts. What they test directly is the understanding of these concepts.[89]

In spite of its merits, especially its satisfaction of the constraints laid down by Hart's analysis of legal concepts, a constructivist semantics based on the C-relation is not fully worked out for any

[84] 'A', p. 151.

[85] At least if attention is restricted to *a priori* evidential support.

[86] If this form of constructivism were a completely general semantic theory, it would be natural to restrict the extent to which evidence was cumulative, i.e. inherited by lower nodes from higher ones.

[87] See G. Frege, *Grundgesetze der Arithmetik*, v. ii (Jena, 1903), 56 (translated in Geach and Black, eds. *Philosophical Writings of Gottlob Frege* (Oxford, 1952), p. 159).

[88] This formulation incorporates a Fregean demand for determinacy of sense. This could be relaxed.

[89] It is sometimes argued that support of a legal judgment by factual statements is a distinctive form of inference, different from both induction and deduction (e.g. J. R. Lucas, *The Principles of Politics* (Oxford, 1966), pp. 22–3 and 139–41). This might constitute another independent argument for the particular constructivist analysis proposed here.

region of language, least of all for legal discourse. It might better be called a 'programme' than a 'theory'. At best what I have accomplished is a 'relative admissibility proof'. Relative to the nearly universal truth-conditions account of meaning, this form of semantics is a viable one. In other words, the central problems to be solved about legal language are common to *both* of them. Neither account deals immediately with rules or norms, only with statements or assertions. This is a particularly urgent problem in this area of language since it is at least plausible to think that the primary application of legal concepts is in the formulation of rules, not judgments. Similarly, nothing definitive is said about the possibility of relating illocutionary force to meaning, and nothing about the degree of determinacy of sense of legal language.[90] If Hart's conception of meaning is at root the truth-conditions account, then conversion to a constructivist conception would leave him no worse off as regards unsolved problems, yet better off in another respect since the thesis that legal concepts are irreducibly defeasible could be reconciled with his underlying conception of meaning instead of warring against it.

Finally, out of abundant caution, I should point out that the suggested constructivist framework for analyzing the language of the law has been presented *very* schematically. An enormous amount has been left out of consideration. There has been no discussion of the complexity of legal judgments (e.g. second-level charges such as the violation of *A*'s civil rights), the policy constraints on legal decisions (arising from the role of decisions as precedents in common law), the complexity of rules, the different standards of proof in civil and criminal cases, or the explanation of expressions referring to legal entities (e.g. 'Smith & Co. Ltd.', 'Nusquamia'). Such matters will have to be examined carefully in any thorough constructivist analysis of legal language.

III

Even Hart in his jurisprudence can know without understanding. The twin principles of the possibility of non-trivial explanation and of the possibility of a non-reductionist explanation guide and inform his analysis of legal concepts. At an early stage he summarized this pair of principles in the thesis that legal concepts were irreducibly

---

[90] In particular, use of the C-relation in explaining legal concepts does *not* prove that it is logically impossible to remove the need for judicial discretion in the application of laws to particular cases.

defeasible. Although this slogan then disappeared, the underlying principles soldiered on unchanged. Hart's own defence of the anti-reductionist thesis took different forms at different times. The original defence borrowed some gaudy plumes from Austin's work, while the later ones were more soberly dressed in the garb of contextual definition, open texture, and the internal point of view. These changes seem rather external: the negative thesis (no reductionism) is what wears the trousers. Hart did not succeed in articulating a cogent defence of this insight. Certainly he did not pass on an understanding of it that is proof against the variety of objections marshalled against his claim that legal concepts are irreducibly defeasible. This is hardly surprising. There is no way to graft the notion of defeasibility onto the tree of the truth-conditions conception of meaning. Hence, there is no way to develop Hart's insights except in the framework of a kind of semantics radically different from any that he explicitly contemplated. Like criteria, defeasibility can be harvested only as the fruit of a new species of semantics. I have tried to plant the seed of this Tree of Knowledge. If it should flourish, then eating of its fruit might give full understanding of the pair of principles on the foundation of which Hart has built the most substantial contribution to jurisprudence in modern times.[91]

[91] I am very grateful to the editors for their criticism and advice in the preparation of this essay.

3

No Right Answer?[1]

RONALD DWORKIN*

I. WHAT IS THE QUESTION?

Is there always a right answer to a question of law? Suppose the
legislature has passed a statute stipulating that 'sacrilegious contracts
shall henceforth be invalid'. The community is divided as to whether
a contract signed on Sunday is, for that reason alone, sacrilegious. It
is known that very few of the legislators had that question in mind
when they voted, and that they are now equally divided on the
question of whether it should be so interpreted. Tom and Tim have
signed a contract on Sunday, and Tom now sues Tim to enforce the
terms of the contract, whose validity Tim contests. Shall we say that
there is a right answer to the question of whether Tom's contract is
valid, even though the community is deeply divided about what the
right answer is? Or is it more realistic to say that there simply is no
right answer to that question?

That issue is central to a large number of controversies about
what law is. It has been debated under many titles, including the
question of whether judges always have discretion in hard cases, and
whether there are what some legal philosophers call 'gaps' in the law.
For some time the weight of opinion has been on one side of the
issue. I myself am often accused of thinking that there is almost
always a right answer to a legal question; the accusation suggests
that if I were to confess to that opinion anything else I said about
legal reasoning could safely be ignored. In fact the issue is much more
complex than is often supposed. I now wish to defend the unpopular
view, that in the circumstances just described the question of Tom's
contract has a right answer, against certain arguments on which its

* Professor of Jurisprudence, University College, Oxford.
[1] I wish to thank Gareth Evans, and also members of the seminar he and I jointly
offered at Oxford in 1975.

opponents knowingly or unknowingly rely. I shall also try to show what sense there is in the no-right-answer thesis, and why the occasions in which a legal question has no right answer in our own legal system must be much rarer than is generally supposed. I shall begin, however, by insisting upon a clarification of the issue that removes a troublesome ambiguity.

Certain legal concepts, like the concept of a valid contract, of civil liability, and of a crime, have the following characteristic. If the concept holds in a particular situation, then judges have a duty, at least prima facie, to decide some legal claim one way; but if the concept does not hold then judges have a duty, at least prima facie, to decide the same claim in the opposite way. I shall call such concepts 'dispositive' concepts. Lawyers seem to assume, in the way they talk and argue, that in every case a dispositive concept either holds or does not hold, even when it is controversial whether it does or does not. They assume that an exchange of promises either does or does not constitute a valid contract. If it does, then judges have a duty to enforce these promises if so requested within their jurisdiction; but if it does not, then they have a duty not to do so. They seem to assume that a particular person is either liable in law for the damage his act has caused or he is not; if he is, then judges have a duty to hold him in damages, but if he is not, then they have a duty not to. They seem to assume that a particular piece of conduct, taking into account intention and circumstances, either constitutes a crime or it does not; if it does, and the actor has no other defence, then the judge has a duty to hold him guilty; but if it does not, then the judge has a duty to find him innocent.

I can now state the ambiguity latent in the thesis that in some cases a question of law has no right answer. We may distinguish two versions of that thesis. The first version argues that the surface linguistic behaviour of lawyers just described is misleading because it suggests that there is no logical space between the proposition that a contract is valid and the proposition that it is not valid; that is, because it does not contemplate that both propositions may be false. In fact, however, if we look deeper into the matter, we find that it might be false both that a contract is valid and that it is not valid, false both that a person is liable and that he is not liable for some act, and false both that a particular act constitutes a crime and that it does not. In each case both propositions may be false because in each case they do not exhaust the logical space they occupy; in each case there is a third independent possibility that occupies the space between the other two. On this first version of the thesis the question 'Is Tom's contract valid or invalid?' makes a mistake like the question 'Is Tom a young man or an old man?' The latter question may have no right answer because it ignores a third possibility, which is that Tom is a middle-aged man. According to the first version, the legal question also ignores a third possibility, which is that an exchange of promises may constitute neither a valid contract, such that judges have a duty to enforce the exchange, nor a contract that is not valid, with the consequence that judges have a duty not to enforce it, but something else that might be called, for example, an 'inchoate' contract.

The second version of the no-right-answer thesis, on the other hand, does not suppose that there is any logical space, in that sense, between the propositions that a contract is valid and that it is not valid, or that a person is liable or that he is not, or that an act is a crime or that it is not. It does not suppose that there is any third possibility, and yet it denies that there is always a right answer to the question of which of the two possibilities it does recognize holds, because it may not be true that either does. On this second version of the thesis, the question 'Is Tom's contract valid or not valid?' is like the question 'Is Tom middle-aged or not?' There may be no right answer to the latter question if Tom is of an age that lies on the border between youth and middle age, not because we recognize categories of age distinct from both middle age and non-middle age, but because, at the border, it is a mistake to say of someone either that he is or that he is not middle-aged.

I do not mean to suggest, by offering this comparison, that the second version of the thesis must suppose that the concepts of a valid contract, of legal liability, and of crime are vague like the concept of middle age. Though, as we shall see, some arguments for the second version are based on claims about vagueness, others are of the different character suggested by the following comparison. Some philosophers believe that there is no right answer to the question of whether Charles was brave if Charles is dead and never faced any occasion of danger during his lifetime, not because 'brave' is vague but because the concept of truth does not allow us to say either that a man was brave or that he was not brave if we could have no evidence bearing on the question of which he was.[2] The second version of the

[2] See M. A. E. Dummett, 'Truth' (*Philosophical Logic*, ed. P. F. Strawson (Oxford University Press, Oxford, 1967)).

thesis may be defended, as we shall also see, in a manner that seems closer to this argument than to the argument from vagueness.

We may state the difference between the first and second version of the no-right-answer thesis more formally. Let $(\sim p)$ be defined as the logical negation of (p), so that if (p) is false $(\sim p)$ is true, and if $(\sim p)$ is false (p) is true. Let the proposition that Tom's contract is valid be represented by 'p' and the proposition that his contract is not valid as 'non-p'. The unpopular theory both versions of the thesis oppose holds that the question about Tom's contract must have a right answer, even if we are not sure what it is, because (non-p) is identical with $(\sim p)$ and either (p) is true or $(\sim p)$ is true because $((p)$ or $(\sim p))$ is necessarily true. The first version argues that the supposition that (non-p) is identical to $(\sim p)$ is a mistake; (non-p) should be represented as a proposition (r) that is not the logical negation of (p). (I do not mean, by the choice of 'r' in that representation, to suggest that the first version must hold that (non-p) is unstructured, but only that it is not the negation of (p)). Plainly, $((p)$ or $(r))$ is not necessarily true; it does not allow for the possibility of (q) which is neither (p) nor (r) but something in between. The second version, on the other hand, does not deny that (non-p) is identical to $(\sim p)$; instead it holds that in some cases neither (p) nor $(\sim p)$ is true, that is, that in some cases bivalence does not hold.

If either version of the thesis is right, then there will be lawsuits in which we cannot say that either party is entitled to a decision, and therefore must concede that the judge has a discretion to decide either way. But there is this important difference. If the first version holds, then this discretion is affirmatively provided by law, because the law distinguishes circumstances in which exchanges of promises, for example, fall into a distinct category which has discretion as a consequence. If the second version holds, on the other hand, discretion follows, not by affirmative provision, but by default: since the law stipulates nothing, even discretion, the judge must do what he can on his own.

II. THE FIRST VERSION

We can easily imagine a legal system such that if any one claimed that there is always a right answer to the question of whether judges have a duty to enforce an exchange of promises or a duty to refuse to enforce the exchange, he would be making a mistake of the sort the first version supposes. Even under our own law, after all, there are

many decisions that a judge has no duty to make either way. That is
so, for example, when the plaintiff requests an early adjournment on
some particular day and the defendant asks that the request be denied.
It is also so when the defendant has been convicted of a crime for
which the statute provides a sentence of from three to five years, and
the prosecution asks for the maximum, while the defence asks for the
minimum, sentence. The concept of duty provides a space between
the proposition that the judge has a duty to decide one way and the
proposition that he has a duty to decide in another; this space is
occupied by the proposition that he has no duty to decide either way,
but rather a permission, or as lawyers say a 'discretion', to decide
either way.

That space might easily be exploited to introduce a form of
contract that is neither valid nor invalid, as we now use those terms,
but inchoate. The law might provide, for example, that if a contract
otherwise unobjectionable is agreed between two people each over
twenty-one years of age the contract is 'valid', and judges have a duty
to enforce it; if either party is less than sixteen years of age, the
contract is 'invalid', and judges have a duty not to enforce it; but if
the younger party is between sixteen and twenty years of age the
contract is 'inchoate', and the judge has a discretion to enforce it or
not depending upon whether, all things considered, he thinks that
the right thing to do. The law might stipulate, in a similar way,
circumstances in which someone who has caused damage is neither
liable nor not liable for that damage, but rather, as we might say,
'vulnerable to liability', or circumstances in which a particular act is
neither a crime nor not a crime but, perhaps, 'criminous'. In a legal
system like that it would, of course, be wrong to translate 'Tom's
contract is valid' as '(p)' and 'Tom's contract is not valid' as '$(\sim p)$',
and therefore wrong to appeal to the law of bivalence to argue that
one of these propositions must be true.

The first version of the no-right-answer thesis argues that, contrary
to how lawyers seem to talk, our own legal system is really like that;
that is, that there is space between a dispositive concept and its
apparent negation that is occupied by a distinct concept, like the
concept of an inchoate contract, though, as it happens, we do not
have a separate name for that distinct concept. But what argument is
available to support that claim? It is a semantic claim, about the
meaning of legal concepts, and it would therefore be natural to
support the claim by some appeal to a linguistic practice that is

decisive. But since lawyers do seem to treat 'not valid' as the negation of 'valid', 'not liable' as the negation of 'liable' and 'is not a crime' as the negation of 'is a crime', the argument cannot take that natural course. It cannot be like the argument that 'old man' is not the true negation of 'young man'. That argument may proceed simply by calling attention to a widespread linguistic practice, or, more likely, simply by reminding the speaker who has made the mistake of how he, as a speaker of the language, ordinarily speaks. Since the legal argument cannot proceed in that direct way, it is unclear how it can proceed at all.

It would plainly be fallacious, for example, to argue for the first version in the following way. There is logical space between the proposition that a judge has a duty to enforce the contract and the proposition that he has a duty not to. That space is occupied by the proposition that he has discretion to enforce it or not. Since it is a consequence of the proposition that the contract is valid that a judge has a duty to enforce it, and a consequence of the proposition that the contract is not valid that he has a duty not to enforce it, there must therefore be a parallel space between these two propositions about the contract, which is left available for the proposition that the contract is inchoate.

That would be a fallacious argument because it does not follow from the fact that the concept of duty has, in this sense, three values, that the concepts used to define occasions of duty must also have three values. In tennis, for example, judges have a duty to call a fault if a serve falls wholly outside the service court, and a duty not to call a fault if it does not. There is space between the propositions that a judge has a duty to call a fault and that he has a duty not to, but it does not follow that there is space between the propositions that the serve fell wholly without the service court and that it did not. Dispositive concepts are used to describe the occasions of official duty, but it does not follow that these concepts must themselves have the same structure as the concept of duty.

Someone who wishes to defend the first version of the thesis will properly object, however, to that analogy. He will rightly say that the concept of a valid contract does not simply describe the factual circumstances under which, as it happens, judges have a certain duty. We can easily imagine the rules of tennis being changed so that, for example, the judge will have a duty to call a fault if the ball lands on the service-court line. But we cannot imagine a change in the rules of law such that judges would no longer have even a prima-facie duty to refuse to enforce a contract that is not valid; in any case, if such a change were made, we should certainly say that the concept of validity had itself radically changed. For we use that concept (and the concepts of tort liability and crime) not simply to report in a neutral way that certain events, comparable to the ball landing in a certain area, have occurred, but as an argument in itself that certain legal consequences, and in particular official duties, follow from these facts.

But though this is certainly right, it is unclear what useful conclusions a defender of the first version is able to draw. Suppose he were to take the point further, and say, not simply that statements about contracts always provide grounds for claims about official duty, but that such statements are indistinguishable from statements about duty. He might say, for example, that it means the same thing to say that a contract is valid as to say that a judge has a duty to enforce the promises that compose it, and the same thing to say that it is invalid as to say that he has a duty not to enforce these promises. If these equivalences in meaning hold, then the first version of the thesis follows in a straightforward way. Since there is space between the two propositions about judicial duty, and since the two propositions about contracts mean the same thing as the propositions about judicial duty, there must be space between the two latter propositions as well.

This argument would be impeccable if the semantic theory on which it is based, that propositions of law are equivalent in meaning to propositions about official duties, were sound. But that theory is not sound. There must be some differences in meaning between the proposition that a contract is valid and the proposition that judges have a duty to enforce the promises that compose the contract, because the former statement is ordinarily taken as providing an argument for the latter, not simply as a question-begging restatement of it. If there is a conceptual, and not simply a contingent, connection between dispositive concepts and legal rights and duties, there is also a conceptual, and not merely a contingent, connection between such concepts and the types of events they report. If a lawyer says that his client has a right to win a judgment because the contract on which he sues is valid, or because the contract on which he is being sued is invalid, he indicates his readiness to make certain sorts of arguments rather than others, to point to facts having to do with offer, acceptance, capacity, illegality, or mistake rather than to other sorts of facts, to support his client's claim.

The semantic theory which simply translates statements about contracts into statements about official duties therefore obscures the interesting and distinctive role of dispositive concepts in legal argument. These concepts provide a special kind of bridge between certain sorts of events and the conclusory claims about rights and duties that hold if these events can be demonstrated to have occurred. They both designate tests for conclusory claims and insist that if the tests they designate are not met, then the opposite conclusory claim, not simply the denial of the first, holds instead. The need for concepts having that function in legal argument arises because the concepts of right and duty in which conclusory claims are framed are structured, that is, because there is space between the opposite conclusory claims. The function is the function of denying that the space thus provided may be exploited by rejecting both the opposing claims. Dispositive concepts are able to fill this function just because the first version of the no-right-answer thesis is false; if there were space between the propositions that a contact is and is not valid, that concept could not close the space the concepts of right and duty provide.

The correct analogy, on this account of the matter, is not between dispositive legal concepts and factual events in a game, like a ball landing within or without a physical area. The correct analogy is between these concepts and dispositive concepts that fulfil the same function within a game. The concept of a tennis serve being 'in' or 'out' *tout court*, rather than within or without a physical area, is a dispositive tennis concept. The events that make a serve 'in' may change, within limits, as when the rules change so that a serve on the line is 'out', but the dispositive concept nevertheless has the function of connecting whatever events do constitute a serve's being 'in' to official duties in such a way as to close the space left open by the structure of claims of duty.

Someone who defends the first version of the no-right-answer thesis will, of course, challenge my description of the function of dispositive concepts. He will say that the function of these concepts is to enforce, rather than to suppress, the structure of claims of rights and duties. But he cannot win that dispute with me in advance; if he believes that the way lawyers use the concept justifies his description of its function rather than mine, he must provide affirmative evidence drawn from their practice. I am able to point to the fact that lawyers treat the claim that a contract is not valid as the negation of the claim that it is valid, the claim that someone is not liable as the negation of the claim that he is, and so forth; and I am also able to show that lawyers do not use words of the sort his description suggests they would, like 'inchoate' contracts or 'vulnerability to liability' or 'criminous' acts. These are powerful arguments in my favour against his account, and though they are not conclusive, I do not see any arguments that he might make on his own side.

I shall mention one apparent argument that he might urge, which we might call the argument from realism. He might say that my description of the function of dispositive concepts must be wrong, because if it were right legal practice would be grossly unrealistic in the following way. If we look to the actual tests the law provides for claims about the validity of contracts, we see that in fact there is sometimes no right answer to the question of whether these tests are met in a particular case. Since there may be no right answer to the question whether an agreement is sacrilegious or not, for example, there can be no right answer to the question whether Tom's contract is valid or invalid, whether lawyers think there is a right answer or not. This kind of indeterminacy occurs with such frequency that it would be unrealistic and indeed perverse for lawyers to insist that there is nevertheless no logical space between the concept of a valid and an invalid contract. The frequency of such cases, that is, provides a strong motive for adjusting legal semantics to accommodate the case, and we should therefore expect that lawyers have already made that adjustment. They may not have actually developed separate names for the third categories they have been forced to acknowledge —perhaps they regret such third categories and wish to keep them secret from the public at large—but they nevertheless must recognize such cases as distinct. If we attend very carefully to the nuances of their arguments, therefore, we may expect to see traces of an un-named concept actually in use.

I set out this argument from realism because I think it has been influential. We must now notice, however, that it is not an independent argument for the first version; on the contrary, it assumes that, the second thesis has already been made out. The common-sense lawyers are supposed to have is the common sense necessary to accept the second version of the thesis, and therefore to adapt their semantics to its truth. We may therefore safely ignore the argument from realism, and turn instead to the second version of the no-right-answer thesis itself. If the second version fails, the argument from realism collapses; if the second version holds, the argument from realism is of no independent philosophical interest.

III. THE SECOND VERSION

I shall consider three arguments that might be thought to support the second version of the no-right-answer thesis. The first supposes that the inevitable vagueness or open texture of legal language sometimes makes it impossible to say that a particular proposition of law is either true or false. The second supposes that propositions of law, like the proposition that Tom's contract is valid, have a hidden structure, explicated by legal positivism, that explains how it may be true neither that Tom's contract is valid nor that his contract is not valid. The third fixes on the fact that sometimes, as in our example, a proposition of law is contested in such a way that neither side has any hope of proving that the other is wrong; this argument supposes that propositions of law that are inherently controversial cannot be either true or false.

1. *The Argument from Vagueness*

It is a very popular idea among lawyers that the vagueness of the language they use guarantees that inevitably there will be no right answer to certain legal questions. But the popularity of this idea is based on a failure to discriminate between the fact and the consequences of vagueness in canonical legal language.

Consider the argument that since the word 'sacrilegious' is vague there can be no right answer to the question whether Tom's contract is valid. I should want to insist that the argument makes one mistake not presently important. It confuses the case in which a legislature uses a vague term, in the sense that it could have said what it meant to say more precisely, with the different case in which it lays down a concept that admits of different conceptions. I shall not press that distinction here, however, because someone who accepts the distinction might simply add that in either case what the legislature has said does not dictate a particular answer to the question of Tom's contract, either because it used a vague term or, if I am right, for the different reason that it used a concept that admits of different conceptions. I shall therefore assume, in this essay, that 'sacrilegious' is vague, and that the statute in question is therefore vague in the way that a statute providing that contracts signed by people of middle age are invalid would be vague.

In any case the argument from vagueness makes a further mistake. It assumes that if a legislature enacts a statute, the effect of that statute on the law is fixed by nothing but the abstract meaning of words it has used, so that if these words are vague, it must follow that the impact of the statute on the law must be in some way indeterminate. But that assumption is plainly wrong, because a lawyer's tests for fixing the impact of a statute on the law may include canons of statutory interpretation or construction which determine what force a vague word must be taken to have on a particular occasion, or at least make its force depend upon further questions that in principle have a right answer. These tests may refer to matters of intention or other psychological fact. It is open for a lawyer to argue, for example, that the extension of 'sacrilegious', on this occasion of its use, must be confined to cases which at least a majority of those who voted for the statute had in mind, or would have wished to embrace if the case had been put to them. But the tests may not rely on psychological facts. It is open for a lawyer to argue, as I have myself,[3] that the impact of the statute on the law is determined by asking which interpretation, of the different interpretations admitted by the abstract meaning of the term, best advances the set of principles and policies that provides the best political justification for the statute at the time it was passed. Or it is open for him to argue the much more conservative position that if a statute uses vague language it must be taken to have changed the legal *status quo ante* only to the extent justified by the indisputable core of the language employed.

The charge that there is no right answer because 'sacrilegious' is vague therefore assumes that no general theory of legislation can be defended that will always provide an answer to the question of what happens to the law when some institution has used vague language. But why should he accept that jurisprudential position? It might be said that there is no such theory of legislation in general use. If we look, for example, at the decisions of courts called upon to interpret statutes containing vague terms, we find that the courts either disagree about techniques of statutory construction or agree only on canons that critically use terms like 'intention' and 'purpose' that are in their own way as vague as 'sacrilegious'. But what of that? Even if we treat these pronouncements by courts as canonical statements of law, like statutes, we still leave open the question of what the impact

---

[3] Dworkin, 'Hard Cases', 88 *Harvard Law Review* 1057 (1975).

on the law is of the fact that courts, in these canonical statements, have used vague terms.

Suppose we put our question about Tom's contract, to which there is supposed to be no right answer, this way. Given that the legislature has enacted a statute which provides that 'sacrilegious' contracts are void, given whatever we may suppose about the state of mind of the legislators who did this, given whatever we might suppose about the attitudes of the general public towards the Sabbath, and given whatever else may be relevant, is Tom's contract valid in law, so that he is entitled to have the exchange of promises enforced, or is the contract invalid, so that Tim is entitled not to have the exchange enforced? The vagueness of the term 'sacrilegious', and the vagueness inherent in any description the legislators might have given of their own state of mind, or members of the public of their own attitudes, are simply facts which our expanded question invites us to take into account. They do not mean that our question has no right answer. If someone now points out that the statements judges make about the construction of statutes themselves contain vague terms, he simply supplies a further fact. If we agree that that further fact is relevant to our question, as it plainly is, then we might add, to our list of considerations, that judges have made such statements. Nothing has yet been said, relying on the vagueness, to make us doubt that our question has an answer.

I emphasize that qualification because I think that the popular idea, that some legal questions have no right answer because legal language is sometimes vague, does not depend on any argument from vagueness after all, but rather on the different argument, which I describe later, that there can be no right answer to a legal question when reasonable lawyers disagree about what the right answer is. The concept of a valid contract is not itself vague like the concept of middle age, and it does not follow from the fact that some statutory language pertinent to the validity of a contract is vague that the question is also vague whether, given that statute, the contract is valid. That fact does make it more likely, however, that lawyers will disagree about whether the contract is valid than if the statute contained no vague terms; not because the meaning of terms is decisive of questions of validity, but because lawyers do disagree about the techniques of interpretation and construction properly used to answer such questions.

2. *The Argument from Positivism*

Legal positivism has many different forms, but they all have in common the idea that law exists only in virtue of some human act or decision. In some forms of positivism this act is the command of a person or group with actual political power; in other forms it may be an act as passive as the general and casual acceptance of a customary rule; but in every form some set of acts is defined as necessary and sufficient. We may therefore state the structure of positivism, as a type of legal theory, this way. If 'p' represents a proposition of law, and '$L(p)$' expresses the fact that someone or some group has acted in a way that makes (p) true, then positivism holds that (p) cannot be true unless $L(p)$ is true.

It might therefore seem that positivism, in any of its different forms, provides an argument for the second version of the no-right-answer thesis. Suppose (p) cannot be true unless $L(p)$ is true, and that ($\sim p$) cannot be true unless $L(\sim p)$ is true. For any plausible value of 'L', in some cases both $L(p)$ and $L(\sim p)$ are false. If 'L' expresses the fact that a sovereign has issued a particular command, for example, it might be false that he has commanded that act, and also false that he has commanded that the act not be done, that is, that he has prohibited that act. But if $L(p)$ and $L(\sim p)$ are both false, then neither (p) nor ($\sim p$) can be true, which is what the second version of the no-right-answer thesis holds.

Of course, the fact that legal positivism supports the second version of the no-right-answer thesis would not count as a complete proof of the second version without an independent proof that positivism is right. Nevertheless, since positivism in one form or another is a very popular legal theory, the apparent connection between that theory and the second version, if it can be sustained, would provide important support for the second version and also explain the great popularity of the no-right-answer thesis. It can quickly be shown, however, that none of the familiar forms of positivism does support the second version, and that the only form that might do so would support it to only a very limited degree.

We can distinguish types of positivism not only by distinguishing the different values given to 'L' in the general structure I described, but also by distinguishing different relations supposed to hold between (p) and $L(p)$. Semantic positivism holds that (p) is identical in meaning to $L(p)$ so that, for example, 'Tom's contract is valid' means the same thing as 'A sovereign has commanded that contracts like Tom's be enforced' or something of the sort. Plainly, semantic positivism cannot offer an argument for the second version of the no-right-answer thesis. The second version concedes that 'Tom's contract is not valid' is the logical negation of 'Tom's contract is valid'; it concedes that if the latter proposition is represented as 'p' the former must be represented as '$\sim p$'. If a particular form of semantic positivism supplies a value of 'L' such that $L(p)$ and $L(\sim p)$ cannot both be false, then the argument for the second version of the thesis just described does not, for this form of positivism, go through. But if it supplies some value for 'L' such that $L(p)$ and $L(\sim p)$ may both be false (as the command form of semantic positivism does) then it contradicts itself, because, since (p) and ($\sim p$) cannot both be false, it cannot be that (p) means the same as $L(p)$ and ($\sim p$) means the same as $L(p)$. Semantic positivism must therefore deny that 'Tom's contract is not valid' is the negation of 'Tom's contract is valid'; it is entitled to deny that, of course, only if it has already been shown that the surface linguistic behaviour of lawyers is misleading in the way that the first version of the thesis claims.

There are, however, forms of positivism that do not claim that the relation between (p) and $L(p)$ is identity of meaning. Some forms of positivism claim only the relation of mutual logical entailment, so that it is logically necessary, for example, that Tom's contract is valid if a sovereign has commanded that contracts like his be enforced, and vice versa. Others claim only the still weaker relation of truth-functional equivalence, so that whenever Tom's contract is valid it will always also be true that some sovereign has commanded judges to enforce contracts like his, and vice versa.

It is easy to show, however, that neither mutual-entailment positivism nor truth-functional-equivalence positivism can support the second version of the no-right-answer thesis. I will make the argument for the latter, weaker form of positivism; the same argument obviously holds for the stronger form. If (p) is truth functionally equivalent to $L(p)$, then (p) is false, and not simply not true, when $L(p)$ is false. Therefore when $L(p)$ is false, ($\sim p$), which is the logical negation of (p), must be true. Since $L(p)$ must be either true or false, then either (p) or ($\sim p$) must be true, which is what the second version denies.

The argument from positivism I described earlier in this section is misleading, because it capitalizes on the supposed distinction between the internal negation of $L(p)$, which is $L(\sim p)$, and the external negation of $L(p)$, which is $\sim L(p)$. If (p) is truth functionally equivalent to $L(p)$, then it seems naturally to follow that $(\sim p)$ is truth functionally equivalent to $L(\sim p)$. That seems to leave $\sim L(p)$ equivalent to nothing, so that it seems plausible that neither (p) nor $(\sim p)$ is true when $\sim L(p)$ is true. But all that overlooks the fact that if $L(p)$ is indeed equivalent to (p) and $L(\sim p)$ is equivalent to $(\sim p)$, then it follows from the former equivalence that $\sim L(p)$ is equivalent to $(\sim p)$ and therefore that $L(\sim p)$ and $\sim L(p)$, being equivalent to the same thing, are equivalent to each other. Truth functional positivism, if it concedes that the first version of the no-right-answer is false, provides an argument against, not for, the second version.

That has the following interesting consequence. It has always been assumed that the values traditional forms of positivism assign to 'L' use the ordinary meanings of the terms they employ; that the command theory uses, for example, the ordinary meaning of 'command'. But unless positivism maintains the first version of the no-right-answer thesis, that cannot be so. In the ordinary meaning of 'command', the proposition that someone has commanded that a contract not be enforced is not equivalent to the proposition that he has not commanded that the contract be enforced. But if it is maintained that 'Tom's contract is valid' is truth functionally equivalent to 'Lawmakers have commanded that such contracts be enforced' and that 'Tom's contract is not valid' is the logical negation of 'Tom's contract is valid', then it follows that 'Lawmakers have commanded that the contract not be enforced' is equivalent to 'Lawmakers have not commanded that the contract be enforced.'

In any case, no form of positivism that stipulates truth functional equivalence or mutual entailment between a proposition of law and some proposition about lawmaking acts can support the second version of the no-right-answer thesis. If the argument from positivism is to be effective, some form of positivism must be found that makes the connection between these propositions a special one such that a proposition of law is true if and only if a proposition about lawmaking acts is true, but is not false when that proposition about lawmaking acts is false. None of the orthodox forms of positivism seems to make that special and limited connection plausible. If a proposition of law is true when and only when a sovereign has issued a particular sort of command, then why should it not be false when he has not issued that command? If a proposition of law is true only when some rule from which the proposition follows has been enacted or adopted or accepted pursuant to some rule of recognition, why should it not be false when no such rule has been enacted or adopted or accepted?

I shall try to suggest, through an analogy, how a positivist might succeed in answering these difficult questions and thereby making that special one-way connection more plausible than it might seem. Suppose a group of Dickens scholars proposes to discuss David Copperfield as if David were a real person. They propose to say, for example, that David attended Salem House, that he was industrious, and so forth. They might well develop the following ground rules governing these various assertions.

(1) Any proposition about David may be asserted as 'true' if Dickens said it, or said something else such that it would have been inconsistent had Dickens denied it.

(2) Any proposition may be denied as 'false' if Dickens denied it, or said something else such that it would have been inconsistent had Dickens said it.

The first version of the no-right-answer thesis would not hold in this enterprise. Consider any concept we use to describe real people such that if it is true that a person has the property in question it is false that he does not, and if it is false that he has the property it is true that he does not. That concept will have the same logical behaviour in the literary discussion. If it is true that David attended Salem House, then it must be false, under the rules, that he did not, and vice versa. If it is true that David had an affair with Steerforth there, then it must be false, under the rules, that he did not, and vice versa. If it is true that David had type-A blood then it is false that he did not, and vice versa. We can even say, of David as of real people, that for any property it is true that either David had that property or not, because the law of the excluded middle is a necessary truth that it would have been inconsistent for Dickens to deny once he had said anything at all about David.

But the second version of the no-right-answer thesis would hold in the literary enterprise, for there would be many propositions about David that the participants would know were neither assertable as true nor deniable as false. Dickens never said that David had a homosexual affair with Steerforth, and it would not have been inconsistent with anything he did say if he had denied it. But he did not deny it, and it would not have been inconsistent with anything he said if he had asserted it. So the participants can neither assert nor deny the proposition, not because they lack sufficient information, but because they have sufficient information to be certain that, under their rules, the proposition is neither true nor false.

This story suggests a form of positivism that provides for the special connection I described between propositions of law and propositions about lawmaking acts. Law is an enterprise such that propositions of law do not describe the real world in the way ordinary propositions do, but are propositions whose assertion is warranted by ground rules like those in the literary exercise. A proposition of law will be assertable as true, under these ground rules, if a sovereign has issued a command of a certain sort, or if officials have adopted rules of a certain form in a certain way, or something of that sort. The same proposition will be deniable as false only if a sovereign has commanded to the contrary, or if officials have adopted a contrary rule, or something of that sort. This form of positivism does not presuppose the first version of the no-right-answer thesis, because it does not suggest that there is any conceptual space, within the institution of law, between any proposition and its apparent negation. It does not suppose that the proposition that a contract is valid and the proposition that it is not valid may both be false. But it does support the second version of the thesis, because it shows how a particular proposition may be neither true nor false, not because of some vagueness or open texture in canonical language, but because the ground rules of the legal enterprise, like the ground rules of the literary enterprise I described have that consequence.

But we must now notice that this form of positivism differs from more familiar forms in one important respect. Orthodox positivism, in each of its forms, claims some sort of conceptual connection between law and the particular act or act designated by the theory as the distinctive law-creating act. For an Austinian positivist, for example, the fact that law is the command of the sovereign is not simply the consequence of the particular legal practices in some countries, but constitutive of the very ideal of law. But the new version of positivism I constructed, based on the analogy of the literary game, cannot make so global a claim. Everything turns on the question of which ground rules of assertion the participants in the legal practice in fact follow, and we can easily imagine ground rules very different from those that positivism supposes.

The participants in the literary game (to return to that analogy) might easily have chosen less ascetic ground rules for themselves. We might, in fact, distinguish a great many varieties of the literary exercise by progressively relaxing these ground rules. The second form of the exercise might provide, for example, that further propositions about David are assertable as true (or deniable as false) if it would be very likely indeed (or very unlikely indeed) that a real person having the properties true of David under the standard game would also have the properties asserted in the further propositions. The second version of the no-right-answer thesis would still hold for the second form of the literary exercise, but there would be many fewer cases of questions that have no right answer in the second form than in the first, not because the raw data of what Dickens said has changed, but because the ground rules now warrant the assertion or denial of much more. We can imagine a third form of the exercise in which the number of such questions would be reduced to very boring questions no one would wish to ask. The rules of this third form provide that as further proposition about David is assertable as true (or deniable as false) if that further proposition provides a better (or worse) fit than its negation with propositions already established, because it explains in a more satisfactory way why David was what he was, or said what he said, or did what he did, according to those already established propositions. In fact, literary criticism often takes the form of an exercise much closer to this third form of the exercise than to either of the other two.

We can correspondingly imagine different forms of the legal enterprise by supposing progressively less strict ground rules of assertion and denial for propositions of law. We can imagine an enterprise like the first form of the literary exercise, in which participants assert or deny propositions of law only if some stipulated lawmaker asserted or denied those very propositions, or propositions that entail these propositions. But we can also imagine an enterprise much more like the third form in which participants assert (or deny) propositions provide a better (or worse) fit with the political theory that provides the best justification for propositions of law already established.

The issue of whether there is a right answer to any particular question of law will crucially depend upon which form of the legal enterprise is in play. If it is like the first form of the literary exercise, then the question of whether Tom's contract is valid will not have a right answer on the simple facts I stipulated at the start of the essay. But if it is like the third form, on the other hand, that question will almost certainly have a right answer, because, for reasons I consider more fully in the next section, it is very unlikely that one answer will not provide a better fit in the sense just described. If a positivist wishes to argue that in cases like Tom's case there is no right answer, so that judicial discretion must be exercised willy-nilly, then he must show that our own legal practice is like the first form of the literary exercise and not like the third. (I leave aside the question of whether the latter would count as a positivistic account of law at all.) But whether our system is more like the first than the third form is a question of fact. So even if we accept the general account of law I described, which holds that legal propositions are not directly true or false of some external world but are rather propositions whose assertion or denial is licensed by ground rules that vary with practice, nothing follows, from that general theory of law, about the extent, if any, to which the second version of the no-right-answer thesis is true of any particular legal jurisdiction.

3. *The Argument from Controversy*

I shall now consider what I think has been the most influential argument in favour of the second version of the no-right-answer thesis, even though this argument has not always been recognized or clearly set out in the thoughts of those whom it has influenced. The argument may be put in the form of a doctrine which I shall call the demonstrability thesis. This thesis states that if a proposition cannot be demonstrated to be true, after all the hard facts that might be relevant to its truth are either known or stipulated, then it cannot be true. By 'hard facts' I mean physical facts and facts about behaviour (including the thoughts and attitudes) of people. By 'demonstrated' I mean backed by arguments such that anyone who understood the language in which the proposition is formed must assent to its truth or stand convicted of irrationality.

If the demonstrability thesis holds, then there must be legal questions to which no right answer can be given because neither the proposition that some dispositive concept holds nor the proposition that it does not hold can be true. If reasonable lawyers can disagree whether Sunday contracts are sacrilegious within the meaning of the statute, because they hold different views about how statutes containing vague terms should be interpreted or construed, then the proposition that Tom's contract is valid cannot be demonstrated to be true, even when all facts about what the legislators had in mind are known or stipulated. Therefore, on the determinacy thesis, it cannot be true. But the same holds for the proposition that Tom's contract is not valid. Since neither of these propositions can be true, and since they are assumed to exhaust the range of possible answers, then there is no right answer to the question.

The demonstrability thesis therefore provides a conclusive argument for the second version of the no-right-answer thesis. But why should he accept the demonstrability thesis? Anyone will accept it, of course, who holds a strict form of empiricism in metaphysics. If we believe that no proposition can be true except in virtue of some fact that makes it true, and that there are no facts in the world but hard facts, then the demonstrability thesis follows from that metaphysics. The proposition could rationally be believed to be true, even though its truth is not demonstrated when all the hard facts are known or stipulated, only if there were something else in the world in virtue of which it could possibly be true. But if there is nothing else, then the proposition cannot rationally be believed to be true; the failure of hard facts to make it true would have exhausted all hope of making it true.

But if, on the other hand, we suppose that there is something else in the world beside hard facts, in virtue of which propositions of law might be true, then the demonstrability thesis, in the form I set it out, must be false. Suppose, for example, there are moral facts, which are not simply physical facts or facts about the thoughts or attitudes of people. In that case a proposition of law might be true in virtue of a moral fact. The proposition that Tom's contract is valid might be true in virtue of the fact that, given the statute and the data I mentioned about the beliefs etc. of officials and people, judges have a moral duty to enforce the promises that compose the contract. If there are such moral facts, then it might be rational to debate whether a particular moral fact exists even after all hard facts are known and stipulated. It would not follow, from the fact that a proposition cannot be demonstrated to be true when all hard facts are known or stipulated, that the proposition cannot nevertheless be true.

The demonstrability thesis, therefore, seems to depend upon an answer to the question of what there is. I shall not, in this essay, try to make plausible the idea that moral facts exist, but I shall try to support the idea that some facts beside hard facts do. I wish, for this purpose, to consider again the third form of the literary exercise I described in the last section. Participants assert a proposition about

David as true (or deny it as false) if that proposition provides a better (or worse) fit than its negation with propositions already established, because it explains in a more satisfactory way why David did what he did, or said what he said, or thought what he thought, according to the established propositions.

I do not mean to raise the question, through this story, of whether fictitious persons are in some sense real so that all these propositions may be said to be true of someone or something. I do not meant to suggest, that is, that in addition to hard facts there are facts like the fact that David Copperfield first read Hamlet at Salem House. The literary exercise I imagine does not require that assumption to make it a sensible exercise. But it does require the assumption, I think, that there are facts of narrative consistency, like the fact that the hypothesis that David had a sexual relationship with Steerforth provides a more satisfactory explanation of what he subsequently did and thought than the hypothesis that he did not.

That is not, I take it, a hard fact. It is not the sort of fact that is even in principle demonstrable by ordinary scientific methods. Since no one ever did have just the history and character Dickens said David did, we cannot provide ordinary arguments of probability, even when all the histories of real people are known, that would necessarily convince any rational man either to accept or reject the hypothesis. In some cases the argument will be so strong for a particular proposition, no doubt, that we should say that any participant who did not agree with that proposition was simply incompetent at the exercise. In other cases we should not say this at all; we should say that there is so much to be said on both sides that competent participants might reasonably disagree.

Suppose that the exercise proceeds with fair success. The participants often agree, and even when they disagree they understand the arguments on both sides well enough to rank each set, for example, in rough order of plausibility. Suppose now that an empiricist philosopher visits the proceedings of the group, and tells them that there are no such things as facts of narrative consistency or that, in any case, there are no such facts when reasonable men can disagree about what they are. He adds that therefore no one can have any reason to think, in response to the terms of the exercise, that the argument that David had an affair with Steerforth is stronger than the argument that he did not. Why should they be persuaded by what he says? This case is not like Dummett's example of Charles's bravery I mentioned earlier. The participants do have reasons for preferring one proposition to another, or at least they think they do, and even when they disagree each of them thinks he can distinguish cases when his opponents have genuine reasons on their side from cases when they do not. If they have all made a mistake, and no reasons exist, it is difficult to see why they think they do, and how their exercise can have had the success it has.

The philosopher's argument would be compromised, moreover, by the following consideration. It is very likely that if he is asked to take part in the exercise he will find, at least after listening to the group for a while, that he himself will have beliefs of narrative consistency, and that he will be able to provide arguments that others recognize as arguments, and so forth. But how can he say that he believes it is more likely that David had an affair with Steerforth, and offer reasons for that belief, and nevertheless maintain that no one can have reasons for such a belief, or that all such beliefs are illusions?

Suppose he says that while it is true that he and the other participants have such beliefs, they have these only as participants, so that it would be quite impossible for an independent observer or critic to say that one participant's beliefs are superior to another's. Would the independent observer or critic himself have beliefs, if he became a participant, even in controversial cases? If not, then the participants will properly doubt whether he has the capacity to judge their debates. But if so, then he does think, after reflection, that some of the participants have the better of the argument, namely those with whom he would agree. Why should he lose that belief, and whatever reasons he has to support it, when he steps back from the debate and reassumes the role of critic? Of course, he cannot demonstrate his beliefs, either as participant or critic, any more than the other participants can demonstrate their beliefs. But the fact that a critic is in that position offers no more argument for the demonstrability thesis than the fact that a participant is in the same position.

We might now assume the offensive against the philosopher and argue that the fact that the enterprise succeeds in the way it does is a reason for supposing that there are facts of narrative consistency about which the participants debate. He might oppose that argument in this way. He might try to show that the fact that a particular participant holds a particular belief of narrative consistency can be satisfactorily explained by considering only the participant's own personality and tastes and history, so that it is not necessary, to explain his beliefs, to suppose any objective fact to which he is responding, in the way in which we ordinarily suppose objective facts in explaining why people hold beliefs about hard facts. It is unclear how he might conceivably show this. Perhaps he might invent a machine which would be able to predict, with great accuracy, what a participant's belief would be with respect to any question about David that might be asked, once highly specific information about the participant's blood chemistry was programmed into the machine. It is, of course, very speculative that if such a machine were built it would yield such predictions in the case of this literary exercise, but not also in the case of, for example, astronomers who debate about the number of Jupiter's moons. If the demonstrability thesis depends on the speculation that the machine would yield positive results in the one case, but not in the other, then it rests on very shaky ground.

Let us assume, nevertheless, that such a machine could be built, and that it would yield that discriminatory information about the literary exercise. What follows? The philosopher might be justified in concluding that the literary exercise was special in the following sense. In many exercises, including the experimental sciences, participants are trained to respond to their observations of the external world in a way which, we suppose, increases our collective knowledge of the world. In the literary exercise, participants are trained to respond to certain questions of a highly specific form which, as the machine is supposed to have proved, cannot be said to be questions about the external world. They are trained to subject their responses to the disciplines of reflection and consistency, and then to make certain assertions that their training authorises them to make on the authority of these responses so disciplined. The exercise, conducted by participants so trained, serves some purpose other than to increase our collective knowledge of the external world, which might be a recreational or cultural or some other purpose.

Suppose this distinction, or some more sophisticated version, can in fact be made out between enterprises like astronomy and enterprises like literary games. That would be an important discovery, and we should certainly wish to mark the distinction in some way. Suppose a philosopher argues that, in consequence of the distinction, we should not say that propositions asserted by participants in the literary exercise can be either true or false. If he explained that he wished to mark the important distinction in this way, we might or might not agree that the constraint he suggests is an appropriate way to do this. But we should be careful to stipulate what must not follow from the decision to restrict the use of 'true' and 'false' in that way.

It must not follow, for example, that the participants have no reason to think one judgment of narrative consistency superior to another when they disagree about which is superior. They still have just the reason the enterprise teaches them to recognize, which is the fact of their disciplined and reflective response to the distinct questions the enterprise requires them to ask. The philosopher might concede this, but then say that they must recognize that the enterprise that encourages them to make judgments of this sort is based on an illusion. But if the exercise serves its purpose, whatever that might be, what reform would be justified in consequence of what he says? If no reform would be justified, what is the illusion?

Our philosopher might say that the illusion is the supposition that facts about narrative consistency are part of the external world in the same sense in which facts about the weight of iron are part of the world. But the participants certainly do not think that narrative consistency is the same sort of thing as the weight of iron, or that it is part of the external world in anything like the way that the weight of iron is. The philosopher may say that they think that their judgments of narrative consistency are objective, whereas it has now been shown that they are merely subjective. But his own theory makes us lose our grip on that ancient distinction. Whatever sense statements about narrative consistency may have, they are given that sense by the enterprise that trains participants to make and respond to such statements. The philosopher's claim that the reasons of one are no better—provide no superior warrant for his assertion—than the reasons of another is a claim that can only be made from *within* the enterprise. From within the enterprise (except in certain circumstances I shall discuss in a moment) that claim is simply false, or, if we choose to avoid that word, simply not warranted. Our philosopher may, of course, say that an institution so constructed is a silly one and˙ that may or may not be so. Whether it is so will depend upon whether the enterprise, taken as a whole, serves some worth while purpose, and serves it better than a revised form of the enterprise would.

The third form of the literary exercise is therefore an enterprise that makes trouble for the determinacy thesis. I suggested, in the last section, that our own legal system might resemble that form of the

literary exercise. In a recent article,[4] in fact, I offered a theory of
adjudication which supports the following description of our legal
enterprise. A proposition of law, like the proposition that Tom's
contract is valid, is true if the best justification that can be provided
for the body of propositions of law already shown to be true provides
a better case for that proposition than for the contrary proposition
that Tom's contract is not valid, but is false if that justification
provides a better case for that contrary proposition than for it. There
are important differences between the idea of consistency used in this
account of legal reasoning and the idea of narrative consistency used
in the literary exercise. Legal reasoning makes use of the idea of
normative consistency which is plainly more complex than, and may
be thought to introduce grounds for claims of subjectivism not
present in, narrative consistency. Nevertheless the comparison may
help to explain why it is sensible to suppose that there might be a
right answer to the question of whether Tom's contract is valid even
when that answer cannot be demonstrated.

The comparison is useful in another way as well. It helps us to
understand why, even though we reject the demonstrability thesis and
therefore reject the idea that there is no right answer whenever the
right answer is not demonstrable, it might nevertheless be sensible to
say that there is no right answer to a question of law in certain very
special cases. In certain circumstances, even in the third form of the
literary exercise, it might be right for the participants to refuse to
assert either that David had some property or that he did not.
Suppose the question is raised whether David had type-A blood or
not, and there is no reason to think that a boy with that blood type
would be more likely to have had the history and character Dickens
stipulates than a boy with any other blood type. The proposition that
David had type-A blood is not vague; we can say that any historical
boy would either have had type-A blood or not, and that there is a
right answer to the question whether he did, even though we shall
never know. But the assertion conditions of the literary exercise
forbid saying that of David; it seems more sensible, given these
conditions, to say that though the proposition that he had that
blood type is not true, the proposition that he did not is not true
either. In such a case the grounds for saying that there is no right
answer to the question are not based on any external criticism of the
enterprise, or on any external philosophical position like the deter-

[4] 'Hard Cases', ibid.

minacy thesis. The grounds are simply that that is the right response *within* the terms of the enterprise itself. We may imagine a genuine controversy within the enterprise as to whether, in any particular case, that *is* the right response. One party may say that there is a reason for thinking that boys like David would for that reason have been more likely to have type-A blood and another that there is a reason for thinking that they would more likely not, and a third thinking either that there were no reasons either way, or that whatever reasons there were were so equally balanced that no sensible discrimination could be made.

The occasions on which the participants would be tempted to say that there was no right answer to some question about David would be a function of two considerations. The first is the length of the novel, or, rather, the density of the information that Dickens does in fact supply. The second is the character of the question. If it is a question about a feature that is randomly distributed throughout a population, so that the fact that a boy had the specific characteristics Dickens described, no matter how dense the description, can have little bearing on the question of whether he had the feature in question, then it is more likely that the question will have no right answer.

We can imagine questions that might be raised within a legal system that would have no right answer for the same sort of reason. We must concede the theoretical possibility that the political theory that provides the best justification for the settled law is for some reason entirely neutral on the question whether, in some particular case, an exchange of promises must be taken to constitute a contract or not. We must also concede the theoretical possibility that two different political theories, which suggest different answers to that question, for some reason each provide exactly as good a justification of the settled law as the other. We can also imagine a case in which the issue of whether one or another of these grounds of neutrality holds is itself in dispute, with one party contending for one answer, another for the other, and a third for no answer at all.

Once again, however, the claim that there is no right answer, made on these grounds, would be a claim within the institution, not one forced upon the institution by external philosophical considerations. Once again, the occasions on which this claim might properly be made would be a function of two considerations: the density of the information supplied by the settled law, and the degree to which the question put by the case could be thought independent of whatever information is so supplied. This fact suggests that though these occasions might be frequent in immature legal systems, or in legal systems treating of only a limited range of the conduct of its constituents, they will be so rare as to be exotic in modern, developed, and complex legal systems. In these jurisdictions the intersections and interdependencies of different legal doctrine will be so intense that it will not be possible to maintain the third position against the other two. The argument from controversy therefore suggests what sense there might be in the second version of the no-right-answer thesis, and why that version will have little application in our own legal experience. For all practical purposes, there will always be a right answer in the seamless web of our law.

4

The Phenomenon of Law[1]

J. R. LUCAS*

IT IS ungenerous to pick holes in *The Concept of Law*. It is a great work. Its clarity is luminous, and its argument sustained and convincing. Hart is eminently successful in rescuing the concept of law from the Legal Realists, the Positivists, and the Formalists, who attempt to straitjacket it within schemata which are too narrow or too vague to give an adequate elucidation of it. But sometimes Hart is not carried along by his arguments as far as he should. He makes too many concessions to his opponents, and his own account of the law is, in consequence, too formalist, in spite of having himself adduced cogent considerations elsewhere for rejecting the purely formalist line of argument.The rule of recognition, although important, is not fundamental. We should, rather, see law as a social phenomenon, to be distinguished from other social phenomena, but intelligible only in a social context, and not—as lawyers are too ready to suppose—an autonomous discipline which can be explained and understood entirely in its own terms.

Hart elucidates law in terms of rules. He argues, quite convincingly, against the positivist programme of taking an entirely external attitude to the law. It cannot be explained either in terms of mere *habits* of obedience or as a purely predictive enterprise. It is, rather, a rule-governed activity. Almost all officials, and indeed most other citizens, are primarily concerned with the internal aspect of rules, regarding them as guides for action, and using them as the basis for their own justifications and criticisms. Hart is quite right to stress the internal aspect of the law, but the word 'rule' suffers from an unfortunate ambiguity. It may mean a rule explicitly formulated in words, or it

* Fellow of Merton College, Oxford.
[1] I have benefited greatly in writing this from discussions with Professor R. S. Summers of Cornell University, and from a class given in Lincoln College many years ago by A. W. B. Simpson and the late H. H. Cox.

may mean a rule implicitly revealed in action. In Chapter VII Hart
shows how much of contemporary jurisprudence has arisen from the
desire of legal philosophers to operate with one consistent concept of
rule, and argues that the two concepts of rule are complementary, and
therefore both necessary. But elsewhere he tends to assume that rules
are explicitly formulated rules, whereas what his argument against
the positivists has established is that people in behaving lawfully have
a *reason* for so acting, whether or not they can cite a formulated rule
—they are acting μετὰ λόγου, as Aristotle would have said, and not
necessarily κατὰ τὸν ὀρθὸν λόγον.[2] This has an important bearing
on the need for legislation and the separation of law and morals.
If law is rule-governed behaviour in the sense of being in accordance
with explicitly formulated rules, then the role of that body which
formulates the rules becomes central to our concept of law, and there
is no incoherence in supposing rules being promulgated that run
counter to every tenet of morality. If, however, law is a sort—a sort
yet to be characterized—of rational response by a man to his social
situation, then the simple legal systems which Hart stigmatizes in
Chaper VI as being pre-legal will seem much more fully legal in spite
of their lack of sophisticated adjuncts, and the interplay between law
and morals will become much easier to understand.

Hart lays great emphasis on another distinction among rules. In
Chapter V he distinguishes primary from secondary rules, and
believes that this distinction furnishes him with 'the key to the science
of jurisprudence'. But the distinction is uncharacteristically unclear.
It seems to be a conflation of at least three different distinctions.
There is a distinction between rules imposing duties and rules conferring powers; there is a distinction between simple legal rules and
somewhat more sophisticated meta-rules; and there is the ghost of a
positivist distinction between rules concerning actions involving
physical movement or changes, and those which lead to the creation
of duties or obligations.[3] It is easy to see why Hart has run these
three distinctions together. Primary rules thus characterized are the
closest analogue he can offer to the gunman situation of Austinian
analysis, and, by going along with Austin thus far, he is enabled to
point out the more convincingly its defects, and accommodate within
his own theory its insights. Nevertheless, it is misleading. Not only
are secondary rules awkwardly heterogeneous, but it accommodates

---

[2] *Nicomachean Ethics*, VI. 13. 5, 1144b 26–7.
[3] *The Concept of Law*, p. 79.

one characteristic feature of law, that it is enforced by sanctions, at the cost of distorting other features, equally characteristic, which bring out the resemblances between law and other aspects of social life.

The distinction between operations that lead merely to physical movement or change, and those that lead to the creation of duties or obligations, is a difficult one, and not really very relevant to Hart's purposes. It is important to the positivist, because he believes in the former, while he suspects the latter of being metaphysical; and therefore if primary rules of law concern *pukka* positivist behaviour, they provide a way into legal concepts which the positivist can follow. But Hart is not in this sense a positivist, and should start not from the merely physical but from the social. Laws seldom characterize actions by reference to mere physical movement, but construe them in a social context and often with reference to the agent's intention. Stumbling into you differs from banging into you only in that I didn't mean to: if I swat the horse-fly that is about to feast on your sun-bathing thigh, I have not assaulted you, although I may have hurt you as much as if I had been administering corporal punishment: and physical actions which would be quite illegal if performed by me on you, would be entirely lawful if done by a policeman on a suspected criminal resisting arrest. Or, to take a very different case, my obligation to pay taxes derives from a rule Hart would reckon as primary, since it requires men to do certain actions whether they wish to or not, and yet is characteristically discharged by my signing a cheque, which varies the duties and obligations of my banker. It is a mistake to try to peel off the social or legal characterization of actions from a basic description in behaviouristic terms. Most of our actions are social actions, undertaken for social reasons in a social context, with social consequences and often endued with a social significance. One very fundamental human action is that of giving. To give is not just to hand over, but to authorize the recipient to retain and use, and if he so chooses to dispose of, what is given, and to extinguish one's own rights to do likewise. Giving cannot be understood except with regard to these rights and powers—else how should we distinguish giving from lending?—and these rights and powers only make sense in a social setting and cannot be explicated in purely physical terms. It may, of course, still be useful in jurisprudence to distinguish actions, such as promising, signing a cheque, or going through a marriage ceremony, whose primary significance is that they are meant to

alter the legal situation, from those, such as eating, hitting, or travelling, which are normally performed for other than social reasons and
whose social consequences, if any, are only contingently caused by
them and are not part of the significance of the act. But it is not a
very fundamental distinction, and will not unlock for us a way into
the central features of a legal system.

The distinction between rules which impose duties and rules which
confer powers likewise softens under scrutiny. Not that it is a useless
distinction—it remains a valuable tool for analytical jurisprudence—
but it is neither as fundamental nor as directed as Hart supposes. In
spite of the inadequacies he perceives in Austin's analysis, and the
ways in which having a legal obligation cannot be reduced to being
obliged by the threat of sanctions to act in a particular fashion, Hart
tends to assume that having an obligation is more fundamental than
having a power, so that rules imposing the former are primary, and
those imposing the latter only secondary. But really the rules are
correlative. The rules proscribing my driving a self-propelled vehicle
on the public highway, unless I and it are licensed, and the rules
prescribing the procedure for obtaining a driving and a vehicle licence
interlock. I cannot explain the one except with reference to the other.
So, too, although less obviously, with Hart's favourite examples of
solemnizing a marriage or making a will. The laws prohibiting rape,
adultery,[4] seduction, and fornication, are clearly primary rules in
Hart's view, but equally clearly presuppose an already intelligible
concept of marriage—no man, however attractive, can ever hope to
seduce his own wife. Equally, the laws against theft presuppose laws
of property, including therefore laws defining the conditions under
which property may be disposed of. If after Aunt Agatha's funeral I
walk out of her house with her Sèvres dinner service, I am stealing it
unless she left it me; and whether I had stolen it or not might turn on
whether her will leaving it me was valid or not—on whether she had
signed it at the top, instead of the bottom (cf. *The Concept of Law*, p. 12)
or whether the witnesses have seen her sign it only in a mirror, not
being visibly present to her (as in Dorothy Sayers's *Unnatural Death*).
These examples are, I shall argue, typical. Every primary rule is
correlative with some secondary rules, and vice versa. For rules imposing duties apply only in certain circumstances and subject to some
exceptions, and since I have some control of circumstances, I can
take steps to put myself beyond the scope of the rule or within the

[4] See H. L. A. Hart, *Law, Liberty, and Morality* (Oxford, 1963), pp. 26–7.

ambit of some exception, and thus possess the power of making it lawful for me to do what I want to do. To take the most favourable case to Hart's thesis, even the rule prohibiting homicide does not apply to soldiers in time of war, persons defending themselves against violent attack, or executioners carrying out judicial sentence of death. Jesebel was able to compass Naboth's death under due form of law. Laws can be manipulated. Even straightforward prohibitions can be read as giving guide-lines on how the desired action may be performed without breaking the law, and thus as conferring powers to restyle the legal position so as to accomplish one's purposes. Of course, in some cases such purposes can be achieved only by devious or dishonest manoeuvres, and the rule is correctly seen as imposing a duty rather than conferring a power, but in other cases the emphasis is reversed. So the distinction is valuable. But just as rules conferring powers would have no point unless somewhere down the line a person could by their aid bring about some alteration in the bearing on someone of some rule imposing a duty, so rules imposing duties create also a web of interlinked rights and powers, which they implicitly confer on various people. Any system, whether of law or of morality or of social custom, which imposes duties will also confer rights and powers, and he cannot reasonably regard the rules imposing the former as more primary than those conferring the latter.

Nevertheless, Hart has a point. Although rules imposing duties are not more basic than those conferring powers, it is, among other things, in the enforcement of duties that a legal system is to be distinguished from a system of morality or a set of social customs. Hart's account is illuminating and persuasive. Legal and moral rules differ from rules of grammar and etiquette in being insistently demanded of us, and differ among themselves in that legal rules are enforced, if need be, by sanctions, even physical sanctions. Although men are invited to regard a legal rule from an internal point of view—and indeed many do so—if a man refused to acknowledge the claims of the law, he will be made to comply none the less, because there are annexed to non-compliance consequences sufficiently disagreeable to make compliance the preferable course. With morals there is an ultimate emphasis on authenticity— no moral merit attaches to the right thing being done for the wrong reasons. But with the law the ultimate emphasis is on conformity—the lawyer would far prefer that a man should discharge his legal duties for the wrong reasons than that he should not discharge them at all, even though he might regard it as still more preferable that his reasons as well as his actual actions should be the right ones. This distinctive feature of law shows itself directly only with regard to duties. With regard to powers, I can tell only indirectly whether they are legal or moral or social powers, by following out the consequences until some question of duty is in issue. If we fail to have a properly ordained priest to marry us, we run the risk of being punished for adultery if we honeymoon in America, and being made to pay Capital Transfer Tax in Britain when one of us dies. It is therefore a legal rule we have failed to follow. If a man tells me he is leaving me his house in his will, and I undertake to live in it and not to sell it, then he has exercised a legal power in leaving me his house, because in due course the bailiffs will uphold my being in the house rather than anybody else, whereas I have exercised only a moral power in making a promise, because if I subsequently sell the house, the courts will not intervene, although my conduct will be regarded as reprehensible by my friends and at the bar of my own conscience. We need to be careful, as Hart is, not to make the connection between a rule's having the status of law and its being enforced by sanctions too rigid. Sometimes, especially in developed legal systems, there may be duties which cannot be enforced, perhaps for procedural reasons, e.g. a statute of limitations. Where the body of rules is sufficiently organized to constitute a system, it is of the system as a whole, rather than of isolated parts of it, that we ask the question whether it is a legal system or a system of morality or social custom. And a system is a legal system if, should arguments and appeals to self-respect and enlightened self-interest fail, recourse is had to more external and tangible pressures to ensure that its rules imposing duties are generally observed.

Enforceability is a feature that characterizes not only a fully developed legal system but what Hart calls a 'pre-legal' regime. The difference between a pre-legal regime and a fully developed legal system is that the latter possesses a number of meta-rules which the former lacks. These meta-rules do not necessarily impose duties but provide for the authoritative adjudication of disputes, the effective enforcement of sanctions and the deliberate alteration of laws. Hart therefore regards these meta-rules as secondary rules, along with rules conferring powers. But it is evident that pre-legal regimes, even though they lack meta-rules, have rules regulating the solemnization of marriage, which Hart takes as paradigms of secondary rules. The distinction between rules and meta-rules, although not the same as that between rules imposing duties and rules conferring powers, is nevertheless of great importance to the philosophy of law, and Hart's discussion of the demerits of pre-legal regimes is illuminating and profound. We see why pre-legal regimes need to develop into full-blown legal systems. Hart may be right in regarding a certain degree of sophistication as essential to a regime's being a proper legal system, but a strong case could be put forward the other way for regarding primitive legal systems as genuinely legal, and not merely pre-legal. In either case it is important not to allow the specific differences between the pre-legal regime and the fully developed legal system to obscure their generic similarities. Legal and pre-legal regimes differ in sophistication, but both have the hallmark of enforceability which distinguishes them from systems of morality and social custom, and both share with morality, but not etiquette, a high degree of seriousness. Hart's emphasis is different. He stresses the difference between a fully developed legal system and a pre-legal regime. The important thing, according to him, about a legal system is that it has certain meta-rules, notably a rule of recognition, and that the system as a whole is enforced. The effect of this emphasis is to play down the connection between a fully developed legal system and its roots in a pre-legal regime and other systems of social control, and to make law appear a much more abstract and autonomous discipline than it really is. Marriage is not, as one might suppose from *The Concept of Law*, an institution created by law, nor do wills exist because Henry VIII passed an Act enabling us to make them. Rather, marriage is a social institution, and laws about marriage do not so much *constitute* the state of matrimony as *specify* the procedure for getting married and the rights and duties of husband and wife. If the law did not facilitate the making of wills, it would be necessary to invent ways of bequeathing property, as the Romans did in ancient days[5] and Britons have been doing since the imposition of death duties. The social institution or business arrangement comes first, and only later, when there are disputes, does the law have to spell out the respective rights and duties of the various parties. (Indeed, once the law has reached a certain stage of sophistication, and enables people to enter into contracts and create trusts, further legislation is unnecessary. I tell my solicitor what I want, and he devises means to give legal effect to my wishes.) The function of the law is not to initiate forms of life

[5] Sir Henry Maine, *Ancient Law* (Oxford, 1931), Ch. VI, pp. 169–78.

but to obviate and resolve disputes. It does not create institutions, but gives them definition, tidying up the exact conditions under which they obtain and determining various rights and duties arising from them, so that if we fall out, and cannot resolve disagreements amicably, a solution can none the less be obtained. The law provides a skeleton, which needs to be fleshed out by the social arrangements of our everyday life. It is reasonable for professional purposes to abstract this skeleton, and study the law without overmuch concern with its social setting: but for a philosophical understanding of law, we shall misconstrue it if we abstract too much, just as if we were to study anatomy on its own, without reference to the physiology of the bodies in which the bones are built.

Hart is at his unhappiest in his controversy with Professor Fuller over the legal status of wicked edicts enacted by an iniquitous regime.[6] If the defining property of a law is that it should satisfy the rule of recognition of a regime whose laws are generally enforced, then the decrees of the Nazis were valid law, and the only question left is whether it should none the less be disobeyed. But this is to abstract too much and put on the rule of recognition more weight than it can properly bear. It is, after all, only a meta-rule, and, as Hart himself points out,[7] not always fully formulated, and sometimes itself an object of controversy. The rule of recognition need be neither explicit nor clear. It was only very gradually that it changed in England, and shifted sovereignty from the monarch to parliament.[8] It was not clear for centuries what the fundamental law of the land was, but laws were made, applied, and enforced none the less, because for the most part king and parliament were working together rather than in opposition. Legal disputes were much more about the scope or application of laws rather than their validity. The rule of recognition is implicit rather than explicit, and rests upon a number of tacit understandings about the way in which various functionaries will co-operate and will be guided by public interests rather than private purposes. It may be a matter of considerable difficulty to say exactly what the rule of recognition is. It therefore may be not a very usable criterion of validity. Moreover, meta-rules, however useful they may be in remedying the inadequacies of a pre-legal regime, are 'in some

---

[6] 71 *Harvard Law Review* 593–672 (1958); reprinted in F. A. Olafson, *Society, Law and Morality* (Englewood Cliffs, N.J., 1961), pp. 439–505; see also *The Concept of Law*, pp. 204–7, 254–5.

[7] *The Concept of Law*, pp. 149–50.

[8] J. W. Gough, *Fundamental Law in English Constitutional History* (Oxford, 1955).

sense parasitic upon'[9] primary rules and cannot stand on their own. Hart makes the point very clear by his analogy with a scorer in a game. We may, for good reasons, have a scorer and may have the meta-rule that his decision is final, but this meta-rule operates, and can operate, only against the background that scoring is something which players by and large can do themselves, and that the scorer is trying to do the same thing as the players are, and on the whole succeeding. Else the game is different, and becomes what Hart illuminatingly describes as the game of 'scorer's discretion'.[10] Exactly similar arguments apply to the rule of recognition. It makes sense only as a development of a pre-legal regime in which most people know most of the time what their legal rights and duties are, and look to the civil authorities only to enforce them if need be and to adjudicate the relatively rare cases of dispute. Provided, but only provided, that the developed legal system satisfies these requirements, its various meta-rules will serve a social function and be generally accepted. But if we divorce the meta-rules from the substantive rules of social intercourse, they no longer fulfil their role and so cease being the rules they were. So long as rulers are trying to do the same thing, in regulating social behaviour, as the ordinary members of society are, and on the whole succeeding, we can make sense of their activity, and see a developed legal system as an improved version of a pre-legal regime. But once the tacit understandings which direct the rulers' activities on lines congruous to the aims of ordinary citizens are dissolved, and the sole requirement for legal validity is that it should conform to the rule of recognition, the game has been changed, and we are no longer faced with a legal system, but a potentially disastrous analogue of scorer's discretion.

'Scorer's discretion' is as much a pathological case of a legal system as breakdown due to unenforceability—indeed more so, for since most laws are mostly obeyed without their having actually to be enforced, they may continue to be obeyed even though no longer backed up by the coercive powers of the state; whereas 'scorer's discretion' has an essentially different view of rules, which no longer can be viewed from an internal aspect at all, but only an external one. But law, although it has its external aspect, in which it differs from morality and social custom, has much more importantly an internal aspect, in which it resembles them. They all give guidance. Most of

[9] *The Concept of Law*, p. 79.
[10] Ibid., p. 139.

us most of the time, once we know what the law is, do not, in the
absence of special reasons for doubting its obligatoriness, ask a further question of why we should obey it, but obey it in the same un-
thinking way as cricketers abide by the rules of cricket. Just as the
rules of cricket are shared rules which cricketers all acknowledge and
internalize, so the laws of a society are ones which each member
shares and can, by and large, act on by himself. This is why medieval
men contrasted being governed by law with being governed by will
and 'sought liberty by enlarging the number of rules under which they
lived'.[11] The long-held belief that law not only is not opposed to
freedom, but positively constitutes it, makes sense only if law is
regarded primarily from the internal point of view. The law makes
me free because it enables me to know of myself what to do, without
having to be told by a superior on each particular occasion. It makes
me a full member of the community, able to embody communal
standards in my own actions and my own approbation of the actions
of others. The maxim 'Ignorance of the law is no excuse' makes sense
if law is part of the common stock of the community which we all
share in and make part of our daily lives, whereas it is manifestly
absurd if the law is viewed entirely externally as what the scorer is
going to decide. Hence the position of the unofficial scorer is stronger
than Hart allows.[12] It is not merely that he is doing in an unofficial
and non-authoritative way the same as what the official scorer does,
but that it is an essential condition of the intelligibility of the official
scorer's activity that he is doing, only in an official and authoritative
way, the same as the unofficials are doing, and what they are doing is
something which, although for convenience sake made the responsibility of an official scorer, can essentially be done by unofficials at large.

   One lesson which Hart draws from his discussion of 'scorer's
discretion' is that the scoring rule 'has a core of settled meaning . . .
which the scorer is not free to depart from, and which, so far as it
goes, constitutes the standard of correct and incorrect scoring . . .
The same is true in law.'[13] In particular it is true of pathologically
wicked regimes. We can criticize the iniquitous edicts of the Nazis in
just the same way as Hart allows that we could criticize a scorer
whose aberrations became frequent or who repudiated the scoring
rule. Although within a certain game the scorer's rulings are final,

---

[11] R. W. Southern, *The Making of the Middle Ages* (London, 1953), p. 108.
[12] *The Concept of Law*, p. 140.
[13] Ibid., p. 140.

they are—and are *necessarily*, I would add—not infallible, and if they are often wrong, 'there must come a point when either the players no longer accept [them] or, if they do, the game has changed'.[14] It is a conceptual necessity. It applies to systems of law just as much as to games. And it applies to systems of law whose aberrations are evil just as much as to those which are merely randomly wrong. The rule of recognition cannot override great substantive wrong. It is only a meta-rule, subsidiary to the system of substantive rules, often unformulated and depending on the substantive rules for its real significance. A German under the Nazi regime was in the same position as a cricketer when the umpire starts giving all black men out and awarding sixes to all Australians over six feet tall. It is not any longer cricket. He can either continue to play cricket and take no notice of what the umpire says, or if that is inexpedient—if the umpire is armed—humour the umpire but recognize that what he is doing is not playing cricket, and gives rise to no cricketing obligations, rights, or privileges. So too the German who was not in a position to resist the Nazis might obey them to save his skin, but could not claim that rulings of the Hitler regime had any legal validity, even though Hitler's original appointment to office, like the umpire's, had been legally valid.

Hart does not apply his arguments of Chapter VII to the problems of Chapters VIII and IX. He is very cautious in allowing moral considerations any entry into legal argument, perhaps for fear of a too easy identification of the two. Clarity is served if we maintain the distinction, and allow the conceptual possibility of a law's being morally wrong, and in need of reform or resistance. But although the connection between law and morality is not an analytic one, it is not merely a contingent one either. Hart more or less concedes this in the case of a pre-legal regime, but claims that in a developed legal system it is much easier for the law to be out of line with morality.[15] And so indeed it is. But once we see a developed legal system as a pre-legal system, only in a developed form, we shall be ready to recognize the connection between law and morals, although attenuated with growing sophistication, as stemming from a fundamental common concern. We are concerned about what to do in the various situations of our everyday life. To a large extent we acquire by a form of social osmosis a knowledge of how to behave. From this general know-how some principles can be distilled, and we could justify

14 Ibid., p. 141.   15 Ibid., pp. 165, 197–8.

either those principles or particular decisions in part by giving the reasons for them and in part by referring to the customs of our society. Thus far law and morals overlap. Both are rule-governed activities, in the wide sense of 'rule' (noted above, pp. 85 f.), in which it can be more or less equivalent to 'reason'. Hart instances four features of morality which particular laws need not manifest,[16] but it is worth looking at the distinction from the opposite side, not how morality differs from law, but how law differs from morality. In addition to the funda-mental criterion of enforceability, I shall note two others: conven-tionality and impersonality.

There is great social utility in conventions. Often they are obviously matters indifferent in themselves, but with great importance attaching to everyone's abiding by the same convention, as with the rule of the road. In other cases the convention may not be a *mere* convention, and there may be dispute whether some other convention than that actually observed would not be better; nevertheless, unless and until a new convention is adopted, it is better that we should all be guided by the existing one than that some people should be out of step with everybody else. Even questions of justice are often not fully deter-minate, and have to be decided in the context of the reasonable expectations of each party, which themselves depend on previous decisions arrived at in comparable cases. Hence the rule of preced-ence, and hence also the considerable element of artificiality in case law. The law rapidly becomes very complicated, in which the layman is lost, and the expertise of the lawyers can diverge a long way from the deliverances of morality.

Although the law becomes very complicated in one way, it re-mains coarse-grained in another. Justice is, in an important sense, no respecter of persons. It treats like cases alike, not like persons. There are many morally relevant features, particularly those concerning purity of motive, which the law cannot take cognizance of. The bad man has his rights as well as the good, and often will be able to manipulate the law to serve his own fell purposes. As a legal system develops, therefore, it comes to contain many rules for which no convincing rational justification can be offered, and will often yield results repugnant to our moral sense. These are rationally opaque, but nevertheless enforced by the powers-that-be. And in some cases we may well want to say, with Hart,[17] 'This is law; but it is too iniquit-

---

[16] *The Concept of Law*, pp. 169–76.
[17] Ibid., p. 203.

ous to be obeyed.' But such cases, although too common, are relatively rare. For the most part the law, as it is popularly understood, either is a specification of morality or at least congruous with it, and the legal system as a whole can, therefore, 'carry' the cases which seem to be morally wrong. Where they occur, they are felt to be a blot, not merely a moral blot, but a legal blot, on the legal system. For many centuries the Court of Equity sought to remedy legal iniquity, and judges avoid reaching unconscionable decisions not simply because they are nice men or because, as in Switzerland,[18] they are directed to do so by statute, but because the law, they believe, ought to be congruous with morality, and would be legally less good law if it were not.

In writing *The Concept of Law*, Hart set out to rehabilitate the concept in the aftermath of positivism. He succeeded brilliantly. The tough-minded sceptic is forced to recognize problems he cannot dismiss, and cannot solve so long as he takes up an exclusively external point of view. He has to recognize the internal aspect of the law, if he is to understand how it functions, at least so far as officials are concerned. And the tough-minded sceptic is the readier to be led by Hart to this recognition in as much as Hart is evidently sympathetic to the aims of the Austinian analysis, and anxious to go along with it so far as possible. His criticisms are telling, because they are reluctant. In the end the sceptic is forced to concede that laws must be construed as rules of conduct, and that jurisprudence must be, as Vinogradoff terms it,[19] a moral science, to be understood and reasoned about from the inside. This point once adequately established, Hart goes on to elucidate many of the difficulties which have hitherto beset philosophers who have sought to expound the nature of law. But he draws back from giving full weight to the internal aspect of law, and is led, largely owing to the confused distinction between primary and secondary rules, to place too much emphasis on a rule of recognition too formally construed, and to deny the conceptual connections between law on the one hand and morality and social custom on the other. The distinction between rules imposing duties and rules conferring powers is not one between primary and secondary rules properly so called, but is one that throws enforceability into focus as the characteristic feature of a legal, as opposed to a moral or social, system. The distinction between rules and meta-rules *is* a distinction

---

[18] § 1 of Civil Code of 1907.
[19] P. Vinogradoff, *Common Sense in Law* (Oxford, 1946), p. 13.

between what is primary and what is secondary. It serves to characterize what Hart counts as a legal, in contrast to a pre-legal, system, but implies that the centre of gravity of a legal system is not in its meta-rules, but in the primary rules of the pre-legal system and the social *mores* it embodies. If we concentrate too much on formal meta-rules, we shall abstract too much. If we concern ourselves only with formal criteria of legal validity, we shall fail to see that these arise out of the law's fulfilling a social function, and presuppose that the substantive law is in line with social customs and moral principles. Moreover, even if we wanted to, we could not give an entirely formal definition of law, for whereas rules imposing duties and rules conferring powers may be explicitly formulated in words, and usually become more fully formulated with the passage of time and the growing sophistication of a legal system, meta-rules, and especially the rule of recognition, are not, and cannot be, fully formulated, but must always be at least in part implicit in a diffused recognition of what is rationally acceptable. They thus cannot provide completely adequate criteria of legal validity, since the crucial question—whether the meta-rules are operated in such a way as to produce results that are by and large rationally acceptable—is one that no formal decision-procedure can always settle. The concept of law, therefore, cannot be given too tidy a definition. It can be elucidated, but only as a social phenomenon that arises when men, who are rational but not very rational, and moral but not very moral, live their lives together.

Real Laws

A. M. HONORÉ*

To attack or defend in this article some item of Herbert Hart's corpus of contributions to legal theory would be both impertinent and inauspicious. It would be so because his work, more than that of most contemporaries, naturally attracts the metaphor of a seamless web, in which, over time, topic, and context, the same or related doctrines constantly recur in differing combinations. One who wishes to take Hart seriously must approach his work as the neo-classical expression of a liberal social and political philosophy which the radical utilitarians first expounded but which he has, with sober eloquence and ingenious shift, remodulated and redressed for the eyes and ears of our age. To the liberal mainstream other aspects and characterizations of his work (analytical, positivist) are, I believe, no more than subordinate rivulets or embankments. But if the Hartian themes are too subtly contrapuntal to be isolated in a brief essay we can neither escape nor wish to escape their pervasive echoes. The debt which I in particular owe to the agile sensitivity of our honorand cannot be liquidated and could not be paid. In Oxford, in the English-speaking world, among legal philosophers ever widening circles have converged, if not *chez* Hart, then *Du côté de chez Hart*. In the pedestrian remarks which follow, therefore, the discerning reader will track down a certain parentage.

What I shall try to do is to describe real laws, as opposed to the laws which the theorist remodels in the shape of his theories. The enterprise will constitute a minor piece of descriptive sociology. Traditional questions such as 'What is a single law?', 'What is the general form of a law?', 'What sorts of law are there?' can, I believe, be answered in a way which, possibly unexciting, presents within limits an accurate reproduction of the shape of the material with

* Regius Professor of Civil Law, All Souls College, Oxford.

which in teaching, practising, or judging lawyers operate. To attempt to answer these questions in any other way, is, I shall argue, to embark on a wild-goose chase. There is no theoretical way of settling the form, identity or individuality of laws other than to scrutinize them as they appear in professional discourse. To suppose otherwise is to become the victim of a strange form of analytical metaphysics.

A. METAPHYSICAL LAWS

Yet eminent men have thought otherwise. To Bentham, in the words of Raz

the discovery that a law is not identical with a statute or a section in a statute etc., that many statutes from all the branches of the law, including civil as well as penal law contribute to the content of every law, was the most important turning-point in his thinking on legal philosophy. This discovery and the problems it raised were crystallised in one central question 'Wherein consists the identity and completeness of a law?' And again 'What is a law? What are the parts of a law? The subject of the questions, it is to be observed, is the *logical*, the *ideal*, the *intellectual* whole, not the physical one: the law and not the statute'.[1]

It is something of a mystery why anyone should have thought that behind 'physical laws' there lie 'logical' or 'ideal' legal units, real entities[2] which are the ultimate furniture of the legal universe. It may be that the analogy of physical science counted for something. Chemistry made great advances when the atomic theory was revived, and there might seem to be a parallel between the physical and social sciences. But it cannot really be suggested that law consists of units waiting to be discovered by some 'empirical' procedure analogous to experiment: Dalton's atomic theory rested, after all, on quantified observations of interacting substances.

A second possible source of analogy is as follows. Lawyers talk freely about particular rules of law and sometimes name them: for example the 'rule against perpetuities' or the 'rule in *Rylands* v. *Fletcher*'.[3] This suggests that there is a professional use of the term 'rule' or 'law' in which laws or rules are individuated. But this use of 'rule' or 'law' does not identify a law with a section of a statute or the statement of a judge in deciding a case. The legal adviser, advocate, or writer who sets out the 'rule in *Rylands* v. *Fletcher*' does not copy

[1] J. Raz, *The Concept of a Legal System* (1970), p. 71, citing Bentham, *Principles of Morals and Legislation*, 122, 429.
[2] *Of Laws in General*, ed. H. L. A. Hart (1970), pp. 251 f.
[3] (1866) L.R. 1 Ex. 265; (1868) L.R. 3 H.L. 330.

it exactly from the case of *Rylands* v. *Fletcher*. He takes account of subsequent decisions, of the traditional formulation in textbooks and in general of professional tradition to add and subtract touches from the raw rule. Indeed, he may go further and extract from the raw material a law which is implicit in it but has not been enunciated, for example, that an interest in property of a certain type exists.

If, then, the ordinary lawyer retouches raw rules or helps them to give birth when he is engaged in the activities of advising, arguing, teaching, or deciding, perhaps the legal theorist, who has greater insight into the nature of law, will be able to do even better. The rule in *Rylands* v. *Fletcher* says something like

> (i) An occupier who collects on his land something which is likely to do mischief if it escapes is liable to his neighbour if it does escape, and do damage, unless . . .

The rule does not appear to instruct the occupier to take steps to keep the dangerous thing (for example, water in a reservoir) in. On the contrary it is said to impose a strict liability, independent of fault. But perhaps it *really* amounts to a very strenuous instruction to the occupier to take precautions against the escape, or to pay damages in the event of escape. The ordinary lawyer would if called upon to meet these suggestions have to draw certain distinctions. He would say that one of the *purposes* of the rule is no doubt to encourage occupiers either not to collect dangerous things on their land or to take stringent precautions if they do. But it would be wrong to re-write the rule in order to change its *content* by making it one which imposes a duty to take precautions, since this is not the law. The law says that precautions are irrelevant. The ordinary lawyer would also agree that the consequence and *point* of saying that someone is liable is that the occupier must in certain conditions pay damages. One cannot however *identify* 'being liable' with having to pay damages, if only because there are many other legal consequences of liability, not all of which are statable in terms of duties. For example, if the occupier is liable time runs in his favour under the Limitation Act. The ordinary lawyer would, or should, not therefore accept either proposed reformulation of the rule in *Rylands* v. *Fletcher*. It is simply a rule (of the sort I later call a 'position-specifying rule') which draws conclusions as to the legal position of an occupier in certain events. The rule is of course also a part of the law of tort, of which the general function is to impose duties on subjects and compel them to pay compensation in certain events. In that sense it may be said to have an indirectly duty-imposing or normative function, but this is to speak elliptically, and to court danger. For it is to risk falling into Bentham's confusion, namely that of treating the content of a particular rule as if it were deducible from the function of a network of rules, a branch or a system of law to which the particular rule belongs.

Bentham's search for 'logical' or 'ideal' legal units seems to have been influenced by two preoccupations. One was his conviction that all laws are concerned with imposing duties and that these are imposed by legislative volitions which can be individuated. Hence a logical or ideal law should impose a duty. But existing laws, as formulated by legislators, judges, or writers, often do not on the face of them impose duties. Think not just of the rule in *Rylands* v. *Fletcher* but of such laws as

(ii) A young person is any person who has attained the age of 14 years and is under the age of 17 years;[4]

(iii) Part VII of the Rent (Scotland) Act 1971 does not apply to a contract which creates a regulated tenancy;[5]

(iv) A beneficial joint tenancy may be severed only by agreement or by a disposition by one co-owner of his interest in law or in equity;[6]

(v) An order against an accused person convicted on indictment to pay the whole or part of the prosecution costs is a 'sentence' for purposes of the Criminal Appeal Act 1968 s. 9;[7]

(vi) An agreement is not a binding contract unless it is made under seal or for some consideration.[8]

The theorist will have to torture not just the raw laws as they appear in statutes or cases but even the processed laws which inhabit the books if he is to carry through his programme.

Once we abandon the notion that all laws are concerned to impose duties (or have some other uniform purpose, such as prescribing sanctions or guiding behaviour) and free ourselves from the metaphysics of real entities and legislative volitions, the Benthamite programme falls away. There is no need to restate laws which do not

---

[4] Children and Young Persons Act 1933 s. 107(1), third schedule.
[5] Rent (Scotland) Act 1971 s.85(3) (c).
[6] *Nielsen-Jones* v. *Fedden* [1974] 3 All E.R. 38.
[7] *R.* v. *Hayden* [1975] 2 All E.R. 558.
[8] G. H. Treitel, *The Law of Contract*, 3rd edn. (1970), p. 57.

impose duties, prescribe sanctions, or seek to guide people's behaviour as if they did. Nor is there any case for accepting *a priori* his view that laws should be individuated on the basis that every act-situation governed by the law is the core of a separate law.[9] It may be that in Bentham's mind this view was connected with his desire that codes (and by a parity of reasoning statements of the existing law) should set out the obligations of each class of persons in the various situations in which they might find themselves. Now there is undoubtedly a place for works such as the average 'Executor's Manual', which do just this, listing the thirty-nine steps that an executor should take. But such works are written on the assumption that executors do not need to understand the law but only to apply certain rules by rote. Any general programme of restating the law in terms of act-situations would speedily reduce it to sterility, because such a programme must jettison the general rules, principles, and concepts which generate change, progress, and adaptation. The laws, normative and non-normative, which are not tied to any particular act-situation are in the nature of things likely to be the most important.

B. ACT-SITUATION LAWS

Nevertheless Raz wishes to individuate laws according to Bentham's principle that every act-situation that is guided by a legal system should be the core of a law. His reason is worth quoting in full.[10]

Law is universally regarded as a special social method of regulating human behaviour by guiding it in various ways and directions. This function of the law, which is also the main reason for learning and referring to the law, should be made clear in its theoretical analysis. The way in which this function is pursued is best shown and brought to the forefront of the study of law by adopting this requirement.

On a certain interpretation there is nothing to object to in this passage. Raz is entitled to credit for having shown that not all laws are normative or coercive. He does not share Bentham's view that all laws should be formulated in terms of act-situations but believes only that some should be set out in this way. Nevertheless his approach is misleading. It rests on the view that certain laws should be formulated in terms of act-situations not because this is the way in which they are expressed in statutes, cases, or textbooks but because the function, or one of the main functions of the law is to guide

---

[9] Bentham, *The Limits of Jurisprudence Defined*, pp. 234–5, cited by Raz, op. cit., p. 76.

[10] Raz, op. cit., p. 145.

behaviour. But even if, as I believe, the main function of a legal system is to strengthen the motives which citizens have to obey certain prescriptions in certain situations, it does not follow that this is done by enacting laws which purport to guide behaviour or secure obedience in those situations. For on the one hand, some of the main normative laws which guide behaviour may not be tied to any particular act-situation; and on the other, laws the social purpose of which is to guide behaviour may not be norms at all but may simply say, for example, that in a certain situation a person falls into a certain category, e.g. that he is guilty of an offence. How laws are in fact framed cannot be deduced from their social function. If laws are enacted or expounded in a way which does not seem to reflect their social function there is probably some good reason for this which we had better try to discover. The tail must not be allowed to wag the dog.

It seems, therefore, worth while to underline by illustrations the fact that not all laws are normative or built round act-situations. For example, laws protect people against exploitation, folly, fraud, and injustice, sometimes by means of norms but sometimes by invalidating certain transactions or posing requirements which cannot be satisfied in circumstances of injustice. Thus:

(vii) *Mens rea* (intention, knowledge, or negligence) is presumed to be a constituent of every criminal offence;[11]

(viii) A will must be signed by the testator at the foot or end thereof or by some other person in his presence and by his direction.[12]

Another example is (vi) above, dealing with the requirement of consideration in contract.

The rule of *mens rea* is certainly not intended to guide the conduct of prospective criminals. They are not being advised to avoid criminal responsibility by doing wrongful acts without the appropriate intention or knowledge. Rather the rule of *mens rea* gives effect to the principle that voluntary and intentional conduct is a prerequisite of guilt. On any reckoning it is one of the most important rules of criminal law, and any individuation of rules which devalues it on the ground that it is not concerned with an act-situation is to be

---

[11] 'It has frequently been affirmed and should unhesitatingly be recognized that it is a cardinal principle of our law that *mens rea*, an evil intent or a knowledge of the wrongfulness of the act is in all ordinary cases an essential ingredient of guilt of a criminal offence': *Sweet* v. *Parsley* [1970] A.C. 132, 152 per Lord Morris of Borth-y-Gest.

[12] Wills Act 1837 s. 9.

deplored. Of course one must make two concessions. The requirement of *mens rea* may be regarded as part of the definition of murder,
rape, theft, and arson. An act of killing is not murder unless committed intentionally or with similar mental attitude. There certainly
is a norm which requires us to abstain from committing offences and
so, given that murder so defined is an offence, from committing
murder. But the norm in question is hardly to be thought of as attaching to particular act-situations, and even if it were it would still not be
true that the rule of *mens rea* played a normative role in relation to
that situation. The second concession is that any rule of law (including the *mens rea* rule) necessarily operates as a norm to a person
whose duty it is to state, teach, apply, advise on, or decide the law.
The judge therefore *must* apply, the law professor *must* teach, and the
prosecutor *ought* to take account of the rule of *mens rea*. But these
are not, I think, the act-situations that the individuator has in mind.
The point of the *mens rea* rule is that it is *not* tied to any particular
situation. This is why it is a more significant rule of law than the
act-situational rule which makes it an offence to use premises as a
slaughter-house or knacker's yard without a licence.

Many of the most important rules of English law (and there is no
reason to suppose that other systems differ in this respect) are rules
which are not normative and not intended to guide behaviour, at
least in any straightforward sense. Thus, the rule of consideration in
contract expresses the idea that there must be a good reason for the
law to enforce a promise, and that promises are legally invalid in the
absence of such a good reason. This is not meant as advice to pro-
misors to make promises only when (or avoid making promises only
when) there is a good reason to enforce them, such as a compensating
advantage to the promisor. Nor is it meant as advice to the promisee
to offer a tomtit or a canary[13] in return for a proposal to release him
from a debt of £100,000, though he could try to exploit the rule in
this way if he knew it. What the consideration rule does (whether
successfully or not is debatable) is to give effect to a principle that,
roughly speaking, a promisor should get or expect something in
return for his promise before the law will intervene, and to protect the
rash or inexperienced promisor against his own folly. It is an item of
legal paternalism which works by the mechanism of refusal to enforce

[13] 'According to the English common law a creditor might accept anything in
satisfaction of his debt except a less amount of money. He might take a horse or a
canary or a tomtit if he chose . . . but he could not take 19s. 6d. [97½p] in the pound':
Jessel M. R. in *Couldrey* v. *Bartrum* (1881) 19 Ch.D. 394.

certain agreements. On the one hand it is a rule which possesses a general moral and commerical significance: it is tied to no particular act-situation. On the other hand its connection with legal norms is negative. There is no norm requiring the performance of a promise not supported by consideration.

Neither is rule (viii) which requires a will to be signed by the testator at the foot or end a normative rule. It simply states one of the conditions of the validity of a will; it is what will later be termed a categorizing law. A testator or legal adviser who knows it can of course take it as a guide to ensuring (if he wishes to do so) that a testamentary disposition is valid. But its main purpose is to ensure the authenticity of documents propounded as wills after the testator's death when he is no longer in a position to settle the matter. In this aspect the rule is a protective one, whose point it is to safeguard the interests of the intestate heirs, the beneficiaries under earlier wills, and the testator himself in his ultimate abode. It is also perhaps concerned with the dignity of the law, which would be undermined by the admission to probate of false testamentary dispositions.

Having examined a few examples of non-normative laws, how are we to take Raz's statement that these laws 'derive their legal relevance from their internal relations with legal norms'?[14] The answer depends on what is meant by 'legal relevance'. Certainly their importance is not dependent in the way he suggests on a connection with legal norms. Thus, the *mens rea* rule might exist and be considered a guarantee of liberty even in a society with no criminal law. For it would serve to reassure everyone that if any criminal offences were created they would at least not be offences of strict liability. Nor is it true, in my view, that the definitions of murder, rape, theft, and arson, into which *mens rea* enters as an element, are norms. At most one may concede that rules such as *mens rea*, consideration or the like cannot be applied in individual cases unless there are *also* some normative rules. But this does not make them dependent or derivative.

Any programme of individuating all laws according to act-situations, or treating the non-act-situation laws as qualifications, adjuncts, or derivatives of the act-situation laws, is therefore to be rejected, because:

(i) its execution would obscure the place of general rules, principles, and legal concepts in the operation of the system;

[14] Raz, op. cit., p. 183; cf. p. 145.

(ii) it would obscure the fact that there are laws which protect people by invalidating transactions and processes rather than by regulating human conduct;

(iii) it reintroduces by the backdoor a subtle form of reductivism which was expelled with a pitchfork *in limine*. This holds that while of course not all laws are norms, the non-normative are significant only by virtue of their relationship to the normative ones.

Indeed one can go further. Any programme of individuating laws, fixing their canonical form and settling their classification is mistaken except in so far as it reflects the exigencies of legal argument and the legal process. For it rests either on a Benthamite belief in metaphysical legal units or on a determination to reconstruct laws in such a form as to show that they function in the way in which the theorist has *ab initio* decided that they are meant to function. If the function of laws is to guide human conduct in act-situations, act-situation becomes the central individuating concept. It will not improve the matter to substitute something else for 'act-situation', for example 'classes of person'. The remodelling operation is possible but will prove nothing except that, given freedom to individuate as he chooses the theorist can restate laws in terms of a variety of central concepts. Abandoning reconstruction and reductivism let us therefore turn to laws and rules as they exist in professional discourse and argument. This will be the subject of the remainder of the article.

C. PROFESSIONAL LAWS AND RULES

Laws and rules of law can be said to exist in the sense either that they are actually observed by members of a group or that they conform to criteria of recognition accepted by that group. Is it possible and is there any point in going further? Do these legal entities possess identities? If so, are they alike? Do they have the same form or structure? How should they be classified?

There is no point in individuating laws in order to count them. The question how many laws are contained in the Code civil is no more sensible then the question how many facts there are in the *Oxford English Dictionary*. But laws do have to be learned one by one, and arguments about the formulation and limits of laws must take the form of arguments about units if legal discourse is to possess a minimum of clarity and discipline. The main consideration in settling their identity and form is dialectical. They are to be separated and expounded in such a way as to make clear the issues involved in fixing their scope rather than their functions.

A good starting-point is the generality of laws and rules. There can indeed be one-off laws, for example those (a variety of what are later called existence laws) setting up particular institutions or repealing previous laws. Since they cannot apply more than once they are not rules. They give rise to problems of interpretation but not to those of dialectical development, and their formulation will appropriately follow that of the relevant statute or authoritative source. For example 'the provisions of s.2–5 of the Animals Act replace the rules of the common law imposing a liability for cattle trespass'[15] is not a rule, and 'there shall be a Crown Court in England and Wales which shall be a court of record'[16] does not state a rule.

Most other laws however possess a certain generality and one can either say that such general laws are all rules or that rules are a species of general laws. There is a natural reluctance to term definitions and interpretations 'rules', because they tend to look as if they applied only to particular words in statutes or common law rules. But definitions and interpretations of general terms are themselves general.

'A child is a person under 14 years of age' means 'all persons under 14 are children and all children (for purposes of the Children and Young Persons Act) are under 14'. For this reason I include them under the term 'rule' while appreciating that some may find such a usage artificial.

A second feature of which account must be taken is that rules of law are subject to actual or potential exceptions. This has been neglected in the brief summaries of rules so far given and to be given. But many rules, for instance the rule of consideration, have acknowledged exceptions, and of those that have not it is always arguable that an exception should be carved out.

If we are looking for a canonical form in which to state rules we should presumably choose a form which brings out their generality, shows how they function in legal argument and conforms so far as possible to the way in which they are learned and formulated in statutes, cases, textbooks, and the like. These desirable features are satisfied if

(a) rules are stated in the form of prima-facie universal propositions applying to a defined range of cases

but

[15] Animals Act 1971 s.1(1).   [16] Courts Act 1971 s. 4(1).

(b) their range of application is understood to be inherently debatable and so is the existence of exceptions, qualifications, and reservations (here called 'exceptions') to them

(c) as their scope is widened or narrowed and as exceptions are grafted on to them their formulation changes

(d) while there is no uniquely correct formulation of a rule that expression should preferably be selected which stands closest to its authoritative formulation in a statute, etc. or which represents a professionally acceptable formulation.

From these desiderata it follows that rules are entities persisting in time. They have a history and a development. The life and identity of a rule in time is however dialectical. Its genealogy consists in the fact that its present state has been derived by a process of argument, amendment, and modification from its former state. It also follows that rules overlap, since exceptions to rules and propositions defining the scope of rules are themselves prima facie universal propositions of an inherently debatable character and so are themselves rules. Whether they are to be stated as substantive rules or as fragments of other rules depends on the context of discussion. Thus:

(ix) No revoked will can be revived except by re-execution or by express incorporation in a subsequent will[17]
will be the appropriate formulation if the question to be debated is whether there is a third way of reviving revoked wills, but

(x) All revoked wills can be revived by re-execution
will be appropriate if the debate is whether a person who was sane at the time of revocation but is now insane may revive it by re-execution.

The canonical form of a rule will on this analysis be:

Prima facie / / for the purpose of X / within limits Y / /
All / no / any / whenever / only etc. . . . / / unless . . .

The operative part of the rule is left blank for the moment since it involves a discussion of types of rules.

The form involves no more rewriting of 'raw rules' as they appear in statutes or digested rules as they appear in textbooks and cases than is necessary in order to display two features: their generality and the fact that it is always possible to argue in favour of an exception to a rule, even if none has at the time of argument been recognized.

Unlike generalizations or laws of the physical world which are

---

[17] American Model Probate Code s. 55.

designed so far as possible to be exceptionless or to be expressed in continuous variables a rule of law is no way invalidated because it is subject to one or more exceptions and, even if there are no recognized exceptions, it is always open to someone to argue in favour of a hitherto unrecognized exception. This is of course because law is a practical discipline which requires a margin of flexibility in order to cater for situations not so far envisaged or for changes in circumstance not taken into account when the rule was formulated in universal terms.

Here are some examples of raw rules and their translations into canonical form on the principles stated:

(iv) A beneficial joint tenancy can be severed only by mutual agreement or by the assignment by one owner of his share in law or equity.

(ivA) All beneficial joint tenancies can be severed . . . and no beneficial joint tenancies can be severed otherwise (e.g. by unilateral action).

(ii) A young person is a person over 14 and under 17 years of age.

(iiA) For purposes of the Children and Young Persons Act all persons between 14 and 17 years of age are children and all children are persons between 14 and 17 years of age.

(xi) It shall be an offence for the occupier of any premises to use them as a slaughterhouse or knacker's yard unless he holds a licence.[18]

(xiA) Any person who occupies premises and uses them as a slaughterhouse or knacker's yard without holding a licence is guilty of an offence.

(xii) All goods are movable or immovable.[19]

(xiiA) All goods which are not movable are immovable and all goods which are not immovable are movable.

(iii) Part VII of the Rent (Scotland) Act 1971 does not apply to a contract which creates a regulated tenancy.

(iiiA) No contract which creates a regulated tenancy is governed by Part VII of the Rent (Scotland) Act 1971.

For purposes of the canonical form performatives have to be turned into descriptive language and in order to bring out the prima-facie universal character of rules a single proposition has in a number of

[18] Slaughterhouses Act 1974 s. 1(1).
[19] French Code civil art. 516.

cases to be turned into two or more (three, for example, in the case of a threefold classification). The importance of the principles of the system in the formulation of rules emerges with special clarity when exceptions are introduced. Here is a statement about police powers:

> (xiii) The police have no general power to compel any person to disclose facts within his knowledge or to answer questions put to him. [Specific powers are conferred by individual Acts].[20]
> (xiiiA) No person may be compelled by the police to answer questions unless . . .

or should it be

> (xiiiB) A policeman may compel any person to answer questions provided that . . .

Most lawyers would say that (xiiiA) is professionally correct while (xiiiB) represents the cynic's view of police powers. But how do we know this? Only by virtue of the fact, which of course the Halsbury formulation reflects, that the primary concern of this area of the law is the protection of personal freedom not the facilitation of police investigation.

D. INDIVIDUAL RULES OF LAW

Rules exist, albeit not in a settled, determinate form. Is it sensible to ask what constitutes a single rule? It will be so only in a context of legal debate. From that point of view every prima-facie universal proposition of law which may be the subject of debate is a separate rule. Take for example

> (xiA) Any person who occupies premises and uses them as a slaughterhouse or knacker's yard without a licence is guilty of an offence.

This should be taken to state two rules, since a person might (I suppose) be charged either with using premises either as a slaughterhouse or with using them as a knacker's yard or both. A separate, individuated rule is simply the reflection of a separate arguable point of law or item in the legal process. It is only in the context of legal procedure and argument that there is any point in individuating laws.

The principle adopted for individuating laws governs their classification, since the classes of laws must, given the principles we have adopted, reflect the matters about which lawyers argue and the

[20] Halsbury's *Laws of England*, 3rd edn. (1959), vol. 30, p. 129 and note (g).

categories in which they teach or expound the law. Any attempt at classification of this sort risks descent into the narrowing circles of a taxonomic hell. It may however help to show something of the nature of legal characterization and reasoning if the attempt is made.

E. TYPES OF LAW

The law is concerned with the relations between human beings and between them and animate or inanimate objects viewed from a special point of vantage. To attain this point of vantage requires the transformation of the data of ordinary life into those of a special drama with its own personages, costumes, and conventions, not to mention the invention of new personages and relationships not found in the state of nature. To set the stage for this drama the law categorizes actions, events, personalities, and conditions in a special way and then, from their subsumption into the appropriate category, draws conclusions as to the legal position of the *dramatis personae* and *res*, their possibilities of acting and suffering, and their mutual relations. The various types of law are concerned with the parts of the dramatic dialectic.

There is no point in multiplying classes of law beyond the minimum necessary to delineate the course of legal argument. Even so, one must allow for six sorts of law:

1. *Existence* laws create, destroy, or provide for the existence or non-existence of entities.
2. *Rules of inference* provide how facts may or must or should preferably be proved and what inferences may or must or should preferably be drawn from evidence.
3. *Categorizing rules* explain how to translate actions, events, and other facts into the appropriate categories.
4. *Rules of scope* fix the scope of other rules.
5. *Position-specifying rules* set out the legal position of persons or things in terms of rights, liabilities, status, and the like.
6. *Directly normative rules* (which are few in number but important) guide the conduct of the citizen as such.
(Someone can surely think of more elegant names!)

Here are two examples taken from classes 1, 3, and 5. First: an existence law prescribes that there is a legal interest in land known as an estate in fee simple in possession. A categorizing rule specifies how

[21] Treitel, op. cit., p. 111.

such an interest may be acquired, transferred, or lost. A position-specifying rule prescribes what the legal position (rights, liabilities, etc.) of the holder of the fee simple in possession is. Again, an existence law sets up a Crown Court in England and Wales.[22] A categorizing rule prescribes its constitution. A position-specifying rule lays down its powers.

The first class (logically) is the existence law. This will either create an entity or specify the sorts of entity which do or may exist in the universe of law, or destroy them. These laws set up (as opposed to prescribing how to set up) courts, legislatures, boards, and other bodies, prescribe what interests in property may exist (as opposed to how they are created), and in general list the *dramatis personae* of the law. They are not called rules since their operation is a one-off affair, whether of creation or destruction. The enactment of statutory and other rules, or their repeal, is however brought about by an existence law of a performatory sort. Examples are:

(xiv) It is hereby enacted that . . .

(xv) There shall be a Crown Court in England and Wales.

(xvi) The statutes listed in this schedule are hereby repealed.

(xvii) The only estates in land which are capable of subsisting . . . are (a) an estate in fee simple in possession (b) a term of years absolute.[23]

The next three classes of rules are concerned with establishing and categorizing facts. First the facts must be determined, and for this a class of rules which I term rules of inference may be called into play. These provide that from evidence *A* conclusion *B* may or must or should preferably be drawn, or must be drawn in the absence of *C*, or that *B* must or may or should preferably be proved by establishing *A*. The law of evidence consists mainly of this sort of rule: rules of construction also feature here. Examples are:

(xviii) Where there is no acceptable evidence that a person was alive during a continuous period of seven years and there are persons who would be likely to have heard of him but have not despite due inquiry heard of him he is presumed to have died at some time within that period.[24]

[22] Courts Act 1971 s. 4(1).
[23] Law of Property Act 1925 s. 1(1).
[24] Paraphrase of Sachs J. in *Chard* v. *Chard* 1956 P. 259, 272.

(xix) In interpreting a will, effect must be given so far as possible to the intention of the testator.

The third class of rules is concerned with the translation or transformation of the raw facts of human existence into a form in which they can be subsumed under legal categories and are fit to perform on the legal stage. In the process of translation or categorization four main tools are available:

(a) definitions of legal categories, e.g. a young person is a person who has attained the age of 14 but is under the age of 17;
(b) specifications of the necessary conditions for subsumption under a legal category, e.g. a contract not under seal requires consideration:[25]
(c) the listing of one or more instances as falling within a given category e.g. an occupier who uses premises as a slaughterhouse without a licence is guilty of an offence;[26]
(d) the division of a category into classes e.g. all goods are either movable or immovable.[27]

These four subclasses illustrate four logical forms:

(a) All As are Bs and all Bs As (all young persons are between 14 and 17 and all persons between 14 and 17 are young persons).
(b) No non-As are Bs (no agreements other than those under seal or for consideration are valid contracts).
(c) All As are Bs but not all Bs are necessarily As (all occupiers of unlicensed slaughterhouses are guilty of an offence but not all persons guilty of an offence are occupiers of unlicensed slaughterhouses).
(d) All non-As are Bs and all non-Bs are As (all non-movable goods are immovable and all non-immovable goods are movable).

These four logical forms yield four subtypes of rule, (a) the semantic, (b) the constitutive, (c) the instantiating, and (d) the classifying. All four function as elements of the legal dialectic in the same way, by making it possible to categorize conduct, facts, or events. In practice the second and third are the most important. The second subclass specifies the constitutive elements of contracts, wills, marriages, property interests, legislatures, courts, associations, and of course of

[25] Above, n.7.
[26] Above, n.18.
[27] Above, n.19.

rules themselves. The third subclass includes most interpretations of legal terms, for these are normally enunciated in the instantiating rather than the defining form (e.g. an order against a person to pay the costs of the prosecution is a 'sentence' for purposes of the Criminal Appeal Act 1968 s.9).[28] For this type of rule it is a simple matter to fill out the canonical formula given earlier by inserting the appropriate logical form in the middle. For example: 'Prima facie / / so far as concerns contracts governed by English Law / / no agreements other than those under seal or for consideration are valid contracts / / except . . .'

Rules of scope determine the limits of rules and settle demarcation disputes between rules. The conflict of laws contains many rules of this sort. Thus, apart from the question whether a will is formally valid under the rules of English domestic law there may arise a question whether the rules of English domestic law are applicable to the facts in issue. The first issue is settled by categorizing and the second by scope-fixing rules. A reductivist might wish to represent the second as a version of the first. He might say that the sort of issue settled by scope-fixing rules is whether a given set of facts falls into the category 'fact-situation governed by English law' or whether a contract falls into the category 'contract governed by Part VII of the Rent (Scotland) Act'. The reason for rejecting this reduction is that the concept 'fact-situation governed by English law' is not thought of as representing a legal entity. There is however an uncertain borderline between the two classes. Scope-fixing rules, apart from being a class of rules in their own right, feature as elements in all other classes of rule. Examples are:

(xx) Part VII of the Rent (Scotland) Act 1971 does not apply to contracts creating a regulated tenancy.

(xxi) As a general rule the law of the matrimonial domicile is applicable to a contract in consideration of marriage.[29]

Account is taken of this feature in fixing the canonical form of rules (above, p. 109).

Categorizing rules and laws may be thought of as laying the ground for the application of a further class of rules which I shall call position-specifying rules, i.e. those which specify the legal position of a person, animal, or thing falling within one of the legal categories specified by

[28] Above, n.6.
[29] *Re Fitzgerald* [1904] 1 Ch. 573, 587 per Cozens-Hardy M.R.

the categorizing rule. These are the rules which tell one about the legal position of a contracting party, a possessor, a legislature, an executor, a parcel of land subject to a compulsory purchase order or a dangerous dog. They enable us to draw out the consequences of categorization in terms of the rights, duties, liabilities, status, capacity, remedies, exemptions—in short the *incidents of the legal condition* of the parties or things in issue. Some of these incidents will be normative. They will provide that a citizen or an official may perform, must perform, may abstain, must abstain, ought to take into account, should preferably decide,[30] is well advised to do *X*. Others regulate the passive condition of the person or thing by providing that he or it is not liable, subject, exempt, affected, comprised, eligible, or capable of taking.

The position-specifying rules are often also categorizing rules. Thus suppose the Secretary of State may in certain circumstances set up a joint planning board.[31] The rule providing for this from one point of view specifies the legal position of the Secretary of State (whose existence and qualifications are provided for by other rules) while from another point of view it specifies the manner of constituting a joint planning board. There is of course no reason why a rule should not fall into more than one class, the more so since the individuation of rules is, as we have seen, significant only in relation to legal process or argument. The fact that position-specifying rules are often also categorizing rules helps to explain how legal reasoning proceeds from stage to stage.

The rule that enables the Secretary of State to set up a joint planning board categorizes the institution 'joint planning board'. The position-specifying rule that empowers the board to fix the appointment, tenure, and vacation of office of its members categorize the entity 'member of a joint planning board'. So the matter continues until an ultimate conclusion is reached as to the legal position of the person or thing involved, for example that a member convicted of fraud vacates office. Such an ultimate conclusion may or may not be normative. This one is not. As we saw, an exclusive preoccupation with the normative aspects of law, important as they are, is distorting. Besides guiding people's conduct laws sometimes protect them and sometimes subject them to deprivation.

[30] The 'should' or 'ought' forms, not stating a rule since they are not prima facie of universal application are common in relation to discretionary areas of the law such as sentencing.
[31] Town and Country Planning Act 1962 s. 1(2).

By contrast with the classes of rule we have picked out—creating, categorizing, and position-specifying—the type of rule which the uninstructed in common with the old-fashioned legal theorist supposes to be typical is in fact rare. This is the class which may be called 'directly normative': laws addressed to the citizen telling him 'do this', 'no one may do that', 'X is forbidden', 'Y is permissible'.

Why are criminal statutes couched in terms such as 'A person who does X is guilty of an offence' rather than 'No one may do X'. So far from being a draftsman's quirk, which the theorist can helpfully correct by translating it into a proper form, this piece of legal technique has both a professional and a moral significance. To begin with the former, 'No one may do X' provides no information as to what form of unlawfulness is involved in doing X. Is doing X a crime? If so, what class of crime? Is it a civil wrong? Is it simply a matter of which the administration may take note, as by refusing a licence? Or is the prohibition of X *lex imperfecta*, without remedy or sanction? The form 'No one may do X' is inherently imperfect. On the other hand the form 'One who does X is guilty of an offence' implies the prohibition of X. It does so because it is self-evident that we should abstain from crime. To put the matter more formally there exists a rule or assumption of law to the effect that 'no one may behave in a manner which constitutes an offence, save in circumstances of self-defence, coercion . . .' Is this assumption too obvious to be called a rule? Perhaps, but it possesses in other respects the characteristics of a rule, since it is prima facie general but may be challenged or cut down in particular classes of case such as those constituting instances of self-defence.

In conjunction with this rule or assumption a law which provides that certain conduct instantiates the notion 'offence' has the consequence of prohibiting that conduct. But while the *effect* and *purpose* of a rule constituting X an offence is to prohibit X, that is not its *content*. It should not therefore be classed as a normative rule. Rules are what they are. This is a rule which characterizes conduct by providing that it falls into the category 'offence'.

In the balmy days of the 1950s Hart was a central and I a peripheral figure in the movement called 'linguistic philosophy' which has since passed from fashion but from which lawyers can still learn much. We learned to pay precise attention to the way people speak and write. We repeated to ourselves and to anyone who would listen the salutary maxim that everything is what it is and is not something else.

The fact that criminal legislation by and large defines what constitutes an offence and does not directly forbid the obnoxious conduct illustrates the value of resuscitating the lessons of those days. For what this form reveals, if taken seriously, is that the directly normative rules of a modern system are for the most part platitudinous generalities. 'Do not commit an offence.' 'Abstain from torts.' 'Perform contracts.' 'Pay debts.' 'Discharge liabilities.' 'Fulfil obligations.' If anything should qualify as the basic norms of a system it is these self-evident propositions rather than some tortuous hypothesis about 1066. These basic norms are not tied to specific act-situations, and this confirms, if it needed confirmation, how unsatisfactory would be any general programme of individuating laws on the basis of act-situations. But of course the norms presuppose for their application in legal discourse that the system contains rules which do specify the act-situations falling within the general categories 'offence', 'tort', 'contract', 'debt', 'liability', 'obligation'. So with the famous 'rule of recognition'. This can, I believe, be understood as a categorizing rule or set of rules which specify (of course never exhaustively) what counts as a rule of a system and which should be read in conjunction with a platitudinous norm 'judges and officials must give effect to the law'.

In the main the legal process and dialectic assumes that members of society are disposed to perform their obligations and abstain from wrong: that it is not necessary to bombard them with commands. Such a technique, which reduces to a minimum the incidence of orders directed to citizens is psychologically sound from the point of view of legislators and officials as it is from the standpoint of parents and managers. It pays the members of society the compliment of treating them as responsible beings, not manipulable puppets. In this as in other respects the world of real laws is both more rational and more reassuring than the Benthamite maze.

6

Naïve Instrumentalism and the Law[1]

R. S. SUMMERS*

I. INTRODUCTION

In the opening pages of *The Concept of Law*, Professor Hart lists those salient features of a legal system which he thinks 'the educated man' would be able to identify without consulting the *cognoscenti*, and in the rest of the book goes on to supplement and revise the educated man's account. Now, this man is also one who (in modern societies anyhow) reacts from time to time to social problems by crying 'there ought to be a law'. And I suspect if we were to cross-examine him about the general use of law to serve social goals, we might summarize his responses along these lines:

We have laws to serve social goals—communal functions. When officials set a goal and pass a law, the idea is to achieve, more or less directly, a specific end result (goal) by changing the behaviour of people. The law tells people what to do (provides guidance) and says what will happen if they fail (usually some kind of punishment). Thus, every effective law brings about social change. And it is officials who make the law effective by enforcing it.

The foregoing account, which I will call 'naïve instrumentalism', distorts reality and hides complexity. In particular, it incorporates misleading conceptions of legal goals, faulty theories of what 'a law' is, and inaccurate perceptions of how law serves goals. But the naïve instrumentalist is no man of straw. He is not only widely represented among the educated laity, but can be identified among jurists, too, though as jurist his position is more often implicit than explicit.[2] The

* Professor of Law, Cornell University.
[1] This essay is a shrunken version of a larger work in progress. The author wishes to thank the following persons for valuable discussion or comment: Peter Hacker, Geoffrey Marshall, Torstein Eckhoff, William Twining, Steven Lukes, A. M. Honoré, and David Lyons.
[2] Both Bentham and Austin espoused significant tenets of naïve instrumentalism.

nature of legal goals and the ways laws serve them are topics jurists have rarely considered frontally.[3] Here, it will only be possible for me to indicate the general character that work on these topics might take.

II. NAÏVE INSTRUMENTALISM AND LEGAL GOALS

Legal goals are the goals of those legal precepts adopted or accepted within a society. Such goals substantially determine preceptual content. Constitutions, statutes, court opinions, regulations, orders, custom, private contracts, wills and other voluntary arrangements comprise the precepts. By studying their content and the evidence surrounding their adoption or acceptance in a given society, it would be possible to compile an inventory (a very long one) of legal precepts and corresponding goals—the 'legal goals'—for that society. But would these goals all prove to be 'communal' or 'social' in nature, as the naïve instrumentalist might have us believe? Would they, for example, all take such forms as: 'preservation of democracy' (for, e.g., electoral laws), 'maintenance of community peace' (for, e.g., criminal laws), 'preservation of public health' (for, e.g., compulsory vaccination laws), etc.? That is, would they all be concerned with furthering mutual interests of all members of the society (whether or not so recognized as such)? Or if not this, would they all at least be dependent for their realization on joint co-operation by the mass of the populace? Or if neither of these, would they still at least be espoused by all members (or a majority) of society and be set by legal officials on behalf of all of us rather than by particular individuals, classes of individuals, or groups? The answers would vary from society to society.

In a libertarian, individualistic, and plural democracy, it is plain that most goals for legal precepts would not be communal or social in any of the foregoing senses. Most precepts would take the form of private arrangements between and among private individuals and entities. These arrangements include contracts, wills, corporate bodies, unions, families, churches, etc. The goals for the provisions of contracts, by-laws and official actions of corporate bodies and unions, terms of private associations, and so on are not concerned

---

For example, they both subscribed to relevant facets of the imperative theory of law. Both missed the primacy of private parties in the division of legal labour. Both neglected 'process values' and 'rule of law' values among legal goals. (I do not claim that a single jurist can be found who espoused *all* tenets of naïve instrumentalism.)

[3] For an exception, see R. Von Jhering, *Law as a Means to an End* (Macmillan, New York, 1924).

with furthering mutual interests of all the members of the society. Nor are such goals dependent for their realization on broad forms of joint co-operation by the mass of the populace. And it is evident that the particular goals of such arrangements are not espoused by all, or even a majority, of the society, nor are they set by officials purporting to act for us all. Yet the relevant goals are legal goals, for the corresponding arrangements have the force of law between or among the parties. Even in large democracies, private individuals, classes of individuals, and groups set far more goals for legal precepts in a given day than all of the officialdom combined in the course of a year.

Furthermore, even those goals actually set by officials in regard to statutes, regulations, administrative decisions and policies, and other officially created law will more often be faithfully represented as goals 'writ large' of specific individuals or classes of individuals or groups rather than as general goals espoused by all or even a majority of the society. That is, such goals, however officially formulated, are readily translated into generic goals of specific individuals, classes of individuals, or groups. For example, even such a seemingly 'social' goal of a collective bargaining statute as 'equality of employer-employee bargaining power' translates into something like: 'we employees want more say over our wages and working conditions, *qua* employees.' In addition, goals set by officials are not necessarily concerned with furthering mutual interests of all citizens, nor are they necessarily dependent for their realization on mass social co-operation.

Even in the clearest kind of case of what seems to be a communal or social goal, e.g. 'preservation of community peace', it is normally possible to reduce the goal (though not always without remainder) to a generic goal of specific individuals, classes of individuals or groups. Thus the foregoing goal, in part, reduces to 'facilitation of private economic activity free of wrongful interference', for such activity is not possible without criminal laws to keep criminals 'out of the way'.

Thus, at least in some societies, the assumed particular needs and wants of private individuals, classes of individuals, and groups are the primary sources of goals for laws, and therefore of the content of laws. Thus, private parties cannot be so readily conceived merely as subordinate subjects of a dominant sovereign, as in the simple 'top and bottom theory' Professor Hart has so ably criticized (on other grounds).[4]

[4] H. L. A. Hart, *The Concept of Law*, chs. 3, 4 (Clarendon Press, Oxford, 1961).

According to one version of instrumentalism, all legal goals consist of *specific end results* discretely realizable at some particular moment in time. Some goals are of this character. The goals of certain tax laws, for example, are to raise specified revenue as of given dates. Or the goals of laws designed to increase minority-group employment are sometimes stated in terms of quotas to be achieved within a given period. But many legal goals are not thus specific or precise. Many are deliberately formulated in general and imprecise language, e.g. 'to prevent unreasonable restraints of trade', or 'to secure that a fair price will be charged', or 'to guarantee a safe place of work'. Professor Hart has himself sought to explain why we sometimes opt for such generalized goal formulations (which can find their way into formulations of laws, too). Thus, owing to lack of foresight and consequent indeterminacy of aim, those who create laws may deem it wise to leave particularization of goal (and of law) to other officials situated at point of application when relevant facts are known.[5]

One familiar kind of 'specific end result' embodied in legal goals consists of particular *behavioural* change, e.g. fewer robberies, fewer rapes, and fewer homicides. But it is obvious that many other kinds of specific end results can be embodied in a legal goal, including: changes of attitudes, payments of money, modifications of statuses, provision of services, demarcation of boundaries, dissemination of ideas, increases in feelings of well-being, etc. Moreover, many legal goals are simply not reducible at all to specific end results of the foregoing nature. Thus, the goals for some laws are simply to set up a new legal institution (e.g. a fuel-conservation agency) or a new legal process (e.g. a special juvenile court procedure) or a new legal framework (e.g. collective bargaining), or the like. Of course, these institutions, processes, or frameworks may themselves be designed to bring about specific end results.

Many important kinds of legal goals are not realizable at some 'terminal' point in time. Consider, for example, two familiar goals of public-education laws: 'enhancement of literacy' and 'equality of opportunity'. And consider the 'preservation of community peace' and the 'promotion of public health'. All such goals are not short run and transient, but long run and continuous. To the extent they are realized, this takes the form not of specific end results achieved at some terminal point but general conditions or states of affairs secured

[5] Hart, op. cit., ch. 7.

or maintained (partly) through law over time. The goals of those laws that comprise the substantive core of any legal system (Professor Hart's 'minimum content') are [6] of this general character.

The naïve instrumentalist tends to think of legal goals as embodying policy directives for social change, e.g. 'reduction of air pollution', 'promotion of highway safety', 'increased employment', etc. But some legal goals are not affirmative public-policy 'directives'. Rather they are constraints. For example, in a humane and liberal society, the twin goals of humaneness and liberty will constrain the affirmative pursuit of many other goals. Thus, humaneness might be invoked to rule out castration of recidivist rapists, and liberty to rule out random police dragnets, thereby limiting the efficacy of certain policy-goal pursuits. A few constraining goals might be denominated 'high priced' for they rule out pursuit of numerous possible public policies over wide areas of human interaction. Liberty and humaneness are such goals. (Of course, what is generally a constraining goal in most contexts may in some be affirmatively directive in character.)

Nor do all legal goals incorporate substantive public policies for social change, as many instrumentalists would have it.[7] Justice, equity, and fairness can be and often are general legal goals within a society, too. When legal officials and others concerned to apply law and resolve legal issues implement these goals, they particularize and apply accepted moral-legal notions rather than implement substantive public policies for social change. Countless court decisions at common law and in equity illustrate as much. The distinction between such moral-legal notions on the one hand, and public policies for change on the other, is of central importance in jurisprudence, yet even Professor Hart has not always seemed totally cognizant of it. He often thinks of law as 'a means of social control';[8] and while it is that, it is also a means of 'doing justice and equity' between individuals, too.

Similarly, what might be called 'rule of law' values find their way into legal goals, too, e.g. legal predictability and reliability, non-arbitrariness, and equality before the law. And so do 'process values', e.g. participation, procedural rationality, process fairness, and humaneness.[9] Again, many judicial and other official decisions

---

[6] Hart, op. cit., pp. 189–95.

[7] For a modern version of such instrumentalism see V. Rosenblum, *Law as a Political Instrument* (Doubleday & Co., New York, 1955).

[8] See, e.g., Hart, op. cit., p. 151.

[9] On process values, see R. S. Summers, 'Evaluating and Improving Legal Processes

illustrate efforts to particularize and apply notions of this nature rather than to implement substantive public policies for social change.

And, of the totality of legal goals, more at any given time are concerned with preserving desirable features of the *status quo* than with changing it, at least in stable societies.

Finally, our instrumentalist thinks that means and goals are always separable and that it is therefore always appropriate to set goals first and then cast about for means. However true this may be of constructing houses or other artifacts, it is not always so in law. In law, when available means limit and in part define the goal, the means and the goal thus defined are to that extent inseparable. While this inseparability rarely comes about with respect to what I have called ultimate or highest-level goals, it can occur with lower-level goals. For example, because it is inherently difficult to prove in court that price fixing reduces competition in an industry, the law may provide that price fixing offends the anti-trust laws *per se* and not require proof of anti-competitive effects in the particular case. Here the lower-level goal of ruling out price fixing altogether is partly defined or shaped by the limited fact-finding machinery of the law ('the means') and it is thus not possible to divide means and goal ('lower-level') in any naïve fashion.

III. NAÏVE INSTRUMENTALISM AND THE NATURE OF LAWS

The naïve instrumentalist is also an imperativist and thus believes that all laws can be reduced to essentially one type—orders backed by threats. Professor Hart's attack on the imperative theory is a lasting contribution to jurisprudence. Among other things, he has shown that not all laws impose categorical duties—that the nature of laws is more varied and includes power-conferring laws. And nullity is the consequence of non-compliance with these, not liability to a sanction.[10]

But against the naïve instrumentalist, still more can be said, from a somewhat different angle. There are other important criteria for differentiating varieties of laws. The naïve instrumentalist thinks that all law is 'behavioural'—it sets forth 'dos and don'ts' telling people

---

—A Plea for "Process Values" ', 60 *Cornell Law Review* 1 (1974). It may help avoid confusion, if I remark on some of the relations between values and goals. In my scheme of things, a goal may be good or bad and this is to be judged by reference to the relevant values and disvalues. Also, I sometimes say a goal may 'incorporate' or 'embody' a value. (But I do not say a value may incorporate a goal.)

[10] Hart, op. cit., ch. 3.

what to do or not to do—it 'guides people in act-situations'. Professor Hart himself does not entirely escape the grip of this general conception, for he conceives his power-conferring rules as ones which, when the powers are exercised, operate to impose duties on people to act or not to act in specified ways, and does not explicitly provide for varieties that do not felicitously fit the behavioural guidance model.

It distorts reality to represent all laws as directly or indirectly marking out mandatory pathways. And it is not just that many laws authorize wide official (or private) choice or grant broad discretion. Again, Western law is concerned with particularizing and applying widely held moral notions of justice and equity to resolve disputes between individuals. (Not that the job is always done right.) This is so even in the contracts field in which, for example, two parties may have exercised power under Professor Hart's power-conferring rules to impose very specific behavioural duties on each other. Most contract disputes before courts come after any 'dos and don'ts' possibilities (for those parties anyhow) are entirely moot. Many judges then see their task to be primarily that of deciding (partly in light of prior law) a dispute *after the fact*, rather than that of providing future guidance for these or any parties. And in so deciding, these judges almost invariably take into account considerations of justice and equity as between the parties. Sometimes these considerations will be incorporated into what might be called a legal *rule*. Often they will be scattered through a line of prior authority in the form of stated *reasons* for decisions. Occasionally, they will appear in the form of *principles* or *maxims*, e.g. 'no woman should profit from her own wrong'. But they will not be reducible (directly or indirectly) to categorical or hypothetical behavioural injunctions, general or specific. In short, they are not the same as those forms of law that are to be 'complied' with.[11]

The behavioural-injunction model also fails to account for many other varieties of laws. For example, many laws invalidate, cancel, or excuse, rather than tell people what to do or not to do in the first place.[12] To cite a further example: many laws are addressed to classes of *beneficiaries*. In effect, they say: 'Here is *X*. Come and get it, or use it, as you wish'.[13] Laws that give or provide things and

[11] See also T. Eckhoff, 'Guiding Standards in Legal Reasoning', in D. Lloyd and R. W. Rideout, eds. *Current Legal Problems*, Vol. 29 (Stevens & Sons, London, 1976).
[12] I am indebted to Professor A. M. Honoré for discussion of this point.
[13] See further R. S. Summers and G. Howard, *Law, Its Nature, Functions and Limits*, ch. 4 (Prentice-Hall, Englewood Cliffs, N.J., 1972).

services to people must not be represented as species of behavioural or guiding laws. In sum, law's instrumentalities are highly varied.

Jurisprudence is replete with realizations that laws (especially laws that are behavioural injunctions) require 'implementive mechanisms or devices'. The naïve instrumentalist has but one type of such device or mechanism in his inventory: sanctions. Professor Hart has added nullity. But the reality is more varied and complex. Among other things, it includes educational effort, rewards and other incentives, symbolic deployment of legal forms, publicity (favourable or adverse), continuous supervision, public signs and signals, recognized statuses and entities, grants with strings attached, and on and on and on. Jurisprudence ('sociological'?) awaits an imaginative and systematic analysis of the wide-ranging varieties of implementive devices and mechanisms. It might turn out in the end that the relevant varieties could all be subsumed without distortion under the twin headings 'sanction' and 'nullity', but that is most unlikely.

The behavioural-guidance model of 'dos and don'ts' laws implicit in naïve instrumentalism is more appropriate to criminal laws than to any other type. Yet even with respect to these, the reality is far more complex, and here it is possible only to indicate in general ways how this is so. Imagine a person who wants a more or less *complete understanding* of the conditions under which she or he would incur penal liability pursuant to a simple criminal law. To provide this, it would be necessary to differentiate elements of the crime in terms of the conduct proscribed, the circumstances in which it is proscribed, any causal consequences part of the crime, and the mental element, if any, as well as any excuses, justifications, or other defences to liability, and the scope (territorial and otherwise) of the law. A really full account would also go into the nature of the penalty (and perhaps the mode of its imposition, along with such alternatives as suspended sentence and probation). Sometimes criminal law presupposes and thus calls for references to other branches of law, too. For example, to determine criminal liability for theft, it is frequently necessary to resort to the law of property.

Thus, the seeming simplicity even of 'dos and don'ts' laws is entirely deceptive and false. It is virtually impossible to capture these laws in a single sentence. This complexity is inescapable, given the range and variety of human activities, the conditions of human existence, and, above all, relevant legal goals. Goals largely determine content and are highly diverse: those figuring in scope provissions, those dictating the elements of the offence, those leading to recognition of defences, those concerned with penalties, etc.[14] Never is there any single and sole goal running through all these, and[15] when the same goal is relevant to more than one kind of issue, it will usually have different significance or weight. When goals unavoidably collide, provision must be made for this, too. Thus, self-defence, for example, is usually allowed to override competing goals.

The variety and internal complexity of laws other than criminal laws is frequently even greater, and some criminal laws are far more complex than here suggested.

IV. NAÏVE INSTRUMENTALISM AND HOW LAWS SERVE GOALS

In one crude version of naïve instrumentalism, it is thought to be typical that a single law serves a single goal. Both singularities falsify the reality. The efficacy of law is almost never attributable to a single law. A functioning legal 'unit' is not reducible to a single law. Legal goals cannot be served through single laws. Societies do not live by single laws alone. Also, more than one goal is always involved.

Those jurists who individuate legal 'units' solely in terms of single laws fail to take into account the relevant requirements of goal subservience in real life. At least in real life, the legal unit always takes the form of a *grouping* of various laws into a functional *technique*, or *programme*, or *process*, or *institution*, or *system*, etc. (or some combination of these). Elsewhere I have identified five common *techniques* of the law: the penal, the court remedial, the distributive, the regulatory, and the private arranging.[16] Each involves extensive combinations of socio-legal resources, including many varieties of individual laws. Within these techniques, legal processes, e.g. legislative and adjudicative, are constructed out of numerous individual laws. And frequently lawyers refer to 'systems' of laws, too, such as 'bankruptcy system', the 'juvenile-court system' and so forth. Again, each consists, in part, of articulated combinations of many different laws that operate together as functional units. Only through such units can legal goals be served. Even the isolated stop sign on a

---

[14] On the complexity of punishment goals, see the admirable essay by Professor Hart himself: 'Prolegomenon to the Principles of Punishment' in H. L. A. Hart, *Punishment and Responsibility*, ch. 1 (O.U.P., New York and Oxford, 1968).

[15] But for a different view, see L. Hall and S. Glueck, *Cases on the Criminal Law and Its Enforcement* (West Pub. Co., St. Paul, 3rd edn. 1958), p. 15.

[16] See R. S. Summers, 'The Technique Element in Law', 59 *California Law Review* 733 (1971).

lonely moor is part of an over-all technique which incorporates a variety of laws and other socio-legal resources into a functional whole.

Moreover, such legal units are never designed to serve but a single goal. Indeed, even a single law necessarily has more than one goal.[17] Legal goal structures are inherently complex in the following way: it is always possible to differentiate several levels of goals along an ascending means–end continuum in which the realization of lower-level goals (often explicitly formulated in the law) serves higher-level goals (often not so formulated). Thus, for any law we can identify one or more 'immediate'-level goals, one or more 'intermediate'-level goals, and one or more 'higher or ultimate'-level goals. Consider, for example, a law requiring private owners of handguns to register their ownership with the police. In terms of the foregoing analysis, we might distinguish at least the following different goals for this law: 'registration of all privately owned handguns' (immediate), 'deterrence and control of violence with firearms' (intermediate), 'general community peace' (ultimate). It should be evident that the means–end relations between these goals are not enough to convert them all into one and the same goal. At least, we can imagine ways of serving the intermediate goal that do not simultaneously also serve the immediate goal, and ways of serving the ultimate goal that do not simultaneously also serve the intermediate goal. And, while realization of the immediate goal serves the intermediate one, so would the realization of many other imaginable immediate-level goals. Of course, it is not possible to draw such distinctions between the goals of a single law in the abstract. They can only be drawn in relation to a specific law and relative to a scale or continuum appropriate to that law. Thus, one would begin with a law's 'immediate' goal and trace out how the pursuit of that lowest-level goal would in turn serve higher goals upward along the ascending means–end scale or continuum.

Moreover, at each of the three (there might be more) 'goal levels' so far identified, we will usually find more than one intended goal—indeed, this will be the case even for a single law. Consider, for example, the 'ultimate level' goals for the hypothetical firearm-registration law. Depending on the lawgiver's 'intent', these goals might consist of: community peace, facilitation of economic activity,

---

[17] See L. L. Fuller, *The Anatomy of Law* (Mentor, New York and Toronto, 1958), pp. 60-5, in which it is argued that laws *characteristically* serve more than one goal.

the intrinsic good of preserving life, enhancement of freedom, etc., each of which is distinct.

Furthermore, the lawgiver will always have at least one positive or affirmative goal, and will recognize that any law (almost any law) has its costs—economic costs, e.g. expense, time, and trouble, or other costs in the form of sacrifice of conflicting values.[18] Accordingly, the lawgiver will virtually always pursue the goal of minimizing such costs, too.

It is important to see, as well, that the plurality of legal goals in many legal systems includes goals other than those served by the standard outcomes of official law creating processes (statutes, regulations, etc.) and of official law-applying processes (judicial and administrative orders, court judgments, etc.). As already indicated, the legal goals of some societies include 'rule of law' goals such as predictability, consistency, freedom from arbitrariness, and equality before the law. In addition, the legal goals of some societies include what may be called 'process value' goals such as participation, procedural rationality, process fairness, and humaneness.[19] Neither of these two types of goals is served by the legal outcomes or 'output' of those processes as normally conceived, e.g. statutes passed through a legislative process or judgments rendered at the end of a court process. Rather, these two important kinds of goals are served (when they are served) by features of these processes themselves. For example, the right to a hearing is an important feature of court and administrative processes, and one goal that such a feature serves is that of securing 'say' for participants in the process. Such goal subservience occurs (when it does occur) not through process outcomes but *in the course of* the workings of those processes themselves.

The naïve instrumentalist tends to think that in so far as law, once made, serves goals it does so more or less exclusively through formal processes in which officials are the 'prime movers'. But this, too, falsifies reality in most modern legal systems in the West. It is true that in order for law to serve goals it must be applied to the facts of particular circumstances. But from this it does not follow that law is an instrument wielded solely by officials acting out roles within formal applicative processes.

Far more of the totality of law within advanced western societies is

---

[18] It may be noted that the nature and varieties of legal goal conflict is a fertile topic for jurisprudential investigation on which almost no work has been done.
[19] See, too, n. 9, pp. 123 f. above.

self-applied by private individuals and groups or organizations than administered by officials acting within formal processes. The main wielders of legal instrumentalities in western liberal democracies anyhow, are private parties, not officials, another elementary fact that profoundly embarrasses the simple 'top and bottom' theory of law in which officials on top ('sovereigns') dictate to subordinate citizens at the bottom ('subjects'). As noted earlier, Professor Hart has ably criticized this theory, though not on the grounds I stress here. Daily, private parties apply traffic laws to themselves, safety laws, laws entitling them to public benefits, property-boundary laws, laws on buying and selling, tax laws, penal laws, and on and on and on. Indeed, virtually the whole of that vast domain of privately created law (contracts, wills, trusts, corporate and other organizational norms, etc.) is very largely administered and applied in the first instance by private parties, groups, and organizations.

Even when *disputes* arise over the application or administration of law, it is far from universal that these are resolved through resort to official decision by formal processes. On the contrary, very nearly the opposite is true. Of the totality of disputes over the application and administration of law that arise annually within a modern legal order, it is safe to say that only a small percentage are formally processed through official decisional procedures that 'run their course'. Thus, a relatively small proportion of claimed torts and breaches of contract become the subject of court judgments. Only a relatively small proportion of alleged regulatory infractions become the subject of formal orders of regulatory bodies or courts. The same is true of disputed claims to public benefits such as welfare payments, accident compensation, and the like, and of disputes over tax liability. It is not even true that disputes over penal liability are typically resolved in criminal courts. When any legal dispute is not simply dropped or allowed to die away, and something is instead done about it, this is typically through informal processes of 'settlement'. Criminal cases are resolved through bargained or voluntary pleas. Tort and breach of contract disputes are 'settled out of court'. Alleged regulatory infractions are resolved through informal agreements. And so on. Moreover, in such cases, private parties will often be the 'prime movers' (with or without lawyer help), rather than officials (though officials will often play important roles). Indeed, in many vast fields of law, the initiative to put even the official applicative processes of the law in motion is more or less entirely left in the hands of private parties.

Nor must it be thought that the only way law can serve goals is by 'running its formal course' through prescribed legal processes presided over by officials. While some informal resolutions of disputes over law application doubtless serve relevant goals less fully than others, these informal processes typically serve goals to some degree. It is not even true that when a matter is dropped or allowed to die away entirely, no relevant goals can be served. It is familiar, for example, that in the face of indisputable evidence that an accused committed a crime, the prosecutor may *rightfully* and *properly* decide to drop the matter entirely. This implies (and it is usually true) that some relevant legal goals are served by such actions.

A natural corollary of naïve instrumentalism is that law always serves its goals by direct rather than indirect means. Long ago, in an admirable but neglected essay,[20] Bentham demonstrated that this is not so—indeed—that even with respect to such seemingly 'direct' modes of legal goal subservience as the penal law, a sophisticated legal order relies more on 'indirect' means (such as education) to serve the relevant goals.

Another corollary is that the implementive devices and mechanisms of law are not merely direct (which is in itself false), but inherently coercive—with punishment and the threat thereof paradigmatic. As I have already indicated, there are many other kinds of implementive mechanisms and devices.[21] Some of these are not punitively coercive and some not coercive at all.

CONCLUSION

Our instrumentalist is naïve about many other things, too, including the social effects properly attributable to law, and the unanticipated consequences of resort to legal means. But these must await another day. These concerns and most others I have taken up in this short essay (often only with brevity calling for further development) are rather more 'sociological' than 'analytical'. But this diminishes not at all the range of Professor Hart's inspiration. In almost single handedly reviving analytical jurisprudence he revitalized the subject in nearly all its branches. One simply cannot read *The Concept of Law* without being forced to reflect on questions of the kind I have introduced here.

[20] See *The Works of J. Bentham* (William Tait, Edinburgh, Bowring edn. 1843), Vol. i, pp. 533–80.
[21] See p. 126 above.

7

Positivism, Adjudication, and Democracy

G. MARSHALL*

RECENT criticism of 'law as a system of rules' and of legal positivism has made much use of arguments about the judicial process. Why should this be so? Is there any natural or obvious connection between belief in a positivist analysis of the nature of law and attachment to any particular theory about the nature of adjudication? Perhaps the anti-positivist might say that the limitations of the idea of law as a collection or system of positive rules are most likely to be exposed by an examination of rule-application at its limits, especially in difficult or contested instances. Just such an attack is conducted in 'Hard Cases',[1] where two opposed philosophies of adjudication are displayed. The dispute is personified in an implied debate between two philosophically inclined adjudicators—Hercules and Herbert. Hercules is pictured as being a judge in 'some representative American jurisdiction' (Connecticut, say)—a fact which may conceivably give him some special characteristics not shared by judges everywhere. He accepts that statutes have the power to create and extinguish legal rights and that judges should follow precedent, and he also accepts (civilly enough as it may seem) the rules of law operating in his jurisdiction. He is, moreover, 'a lawyer of superhuman skill, learning, patience and acumen'. Matched against him is Herbert. Herbert is not credited with these last-mentioned characteristics. He seems, by contrast with Hercules, a somewhat less muscular figure destined to have the juridical sand kicked in his face. Herbert is not altogether unfamiliar. He is a positivist and has appeared elsewhere.[2] His

---

* Fellow of The Queen's College, Oxford.
[1] Ronald Dworkin, 88 *Harvard Law Review* 1057 (1975).
[2] For example in 'Social Rules and Legal Theory', 81 *Yale Law Journal* 855 (1972), and 'Philosophy and the Critique of Law' in *Society, Revolution and Reform*, ed. Grimm and MacKay (1971).

probable beliefs are that law consists exclusively of rules; that in every legal system some identifiable standard or pedigree rule can be used to determine what is and what is not law; and that legal and moral standards can be clearly separated.

On this occasion, however, it is Herbert's theory about his role as adjudicator that is under inspection. This is held to be connected with his view about the nature of rules. Where rules are unclear or conflict, Herbert's reputed view is that the judge runs out of rules to apply, and brings his discretion to bear. Herbert J. has also imputed to him some extra-judicial views about democracy. He is said to believe that policy decisions should be made by elected persons and that the judiciary, being unelected, should be subordinate to the legislature. So pictured, his positivist philosophy of adjudication presents him with a dilemma. How can judicial decision-making, which in so many hard cases consists in mere discretion or judicial legislation, be reconciled with the democratic ideal? Only, he supposedly concludes, by ensuring that judges act both as deputies to the legislature and as deputy legislators. This has a number of related implications. When judges make new law they should, on the democratic theory imputed to Herbert, enact the law that the superior legislator would make if seized of the problem. In addition they should defer to legislative judgment in preference to their own; and they should make law in response to evidence and arguments of the same character as would move the legislature if it were deciding the issue.

Hercules, though we are not told his views about positivism generally, rejects this approach as being a 'positivist theory of adjudication'. There is, perhaps, some ambiguity in the phrase 'theory of adjudication'. The expression might perhaps refer to a theory about what is going on when judges apply rules (e.g. they 'legislate', don't 'legislate', 'legislate' interstitially, 'legislate' unconsciously, etc.). Alternatively it might be applied to the holding of certain kinds of beliefs about the attitude that judges *ought* to adopt towards the application of rules (e.g. a liberal, creative, 'legislative' role or a restrictive, literal, mechanical, or automatic role). Theorists might perhaps have a descriptive theory of the judicial role as being 'legislative' without having a normative theory to the effect that judges ought to legislate. One gathers, for example, from a reading of critics such as Bentham or Laski, that they thought judges could be said to legislate, though they were far from thinking it a good thing that judges should do so. Perhaps this misrepresents their position. Perhaps they thought that judges ought to legislate consciously and liberally rather than unconsciously and conservatively. At any rate, it would be possible to elaborate a number of possible permutations on descriptive and normative theories of adjudication (e.g. judges do legislate and should, do and shouldn't, don't and shouldn't, etc.). Traditionally 'positivist' used to go along with 'formal', 'mechanical', 'automatic', 'analytic', and so on, as a label attached to the belief that judges do not and should not legislate. But paradoxically Hercules' view of the positivist adjudicator is that legislating is just what he does and must do. It is this doctrine that gives Herbert J. and his positivist democratic friends their distressing problem. Hercules J., on the other hand, is undistressed. On his theory hard cases do not involve the judge in legislating, so he is not in competition with, or challenging the supremacy of, the legislature. He is not confined to a choice between the application of rules and the application of discretion since he is equipped with, or equipped to find, a stock of principles. He does not therefore direct himself to decide as, or in the way that,[3] the legislature would decide and he need not defer to its judgment or think too much about the actual views of voters or legislators. The solution of hard cases is a question requiring dialectical skill. Since this is not widely distributed among the electorate and their representatives the casual results of the ballot box are hardly likely to duplicate conclusions reached through the more sophisticated ratiocinative processes that Hercules J. can bring to bear. Hercules' conception of his role thus 'provides an alternative theory of adjudication that is more consistent with democratic ideals'—whether the unreflective voters grasp the fact, or (as seems quite possible) not. It rather looks, in fact, as if what Hercules is able to do is to avoid truckling to legislative judgment and to engage in an activist pursuit of principle without being exposed to the accusation that he is legislating. He can use his 'superhuman skill, learning, patience and acumen' to make progressive and enlightened legal advances without making new law (as the legislature makes law). If his decisions surprise the lawmakers or his fellow judges it is not

---

[3] Not that these are the same thing. To try to decide a case in the way that the legislature would have decided it if it had had the disputed point in contemplation may produce quite different results from trying to decide it (oneself) by the use of the same kinds of argument as the legislature would have used. Legislatures often reach absurd conclusions from the arguments they use and one might be able to guess quite accurately just what unwise or inequitable conclusions the legislature would be likely to have reached without its being the conclusion that anybody else would reach using the same kinds of evidence or argument.

because he is acting upon his mere personal view or discretionary preferences, but because he is contending for principles. In so doing he is probably setting out his conception of a commonly shared concept[4] of legal and moral rights.

What could Herbert J., if he were to summon up such reserves of skill, learning, patience, and acumen as he is capable of mustering, find to say against these Herculean claims? To begin with he will have to make some effort to clear his mind about the key distinctions on which they rest, namely those between principles and policies and between rights and goals. Both contrasts are matched with the differences between adjudication and legislation. Before grappling with them however Herbert might begin by querying some of Hercules' remarks about judicial independence and democracy. It is suggested that 'Philosophers and legal scholars have long debated the means by which decisions of an independent judiciary can be reconciled with democratic ideals'.[5] Why, he might wonder, should there have been any such debate and where has it taken place? Could it be that Hercules is confusing judicial independence and judicial 'originality' (or 'discretion' or 'legislation'), all of which are said to be at odds with the 'familiar story that adjudication must be subordinated to legislation', and popular theories that 'put judging in the shade of legislation'.[6] Herbert might well say that popular theory set out in this way seems to be further confusing subordination of the judge (in some respects, in some constitutional systems) with subordination of the judicial function. Even in systems where each and every judicial decision can be overturned by legislative action it is not usually supposed that the *function* of applying law is inferior or subordinate to the lawmaking function, rather than being a different, independent and co-ordinate function. Its inferiority is not in importance or dignity or constitutional standing. In none of these (or in remuneration) do judges walk in the shade of legislators. But how is the judicial role, subordinate or not, to be characterized? Hercules J. stands for the thesis that adjudication is to be understood as the resolution of unclear or 'hard' cases in terms of 'principle' and never in terms of policy. Herbert is said to operate differently. He applies rules and when these fail to reveal the answer he has nothing to fall back upon but naked policy or discretion. Conscious, however, of the fact that

---

[4] Dworkin, op. cit., p. 1107. Cf. on the concept/conception distinction Professor Dworkin's 'The Jurisprudence of Richard Nixon', *New York Review of Books*, 4 May 1972. Also John Rawls, *A Theory of Justice* (1971), pp. 5–7, 10.

[5] Ibid., p. 1057.   [6] Ibid., p. 1058.

he has not been elected to give effect to policy of his own invention, he tries to ensure that his discretionary decisions are informed by referred values derived from the goals of the community (or perhaps the legislature, or perhaps the majority of the legislature).

Arguments of policy are held to be distinguished from arguments of principle in the following way. Arguments of policy justify a political decision by showing that the decision advances or protects some collective goal of the community as a whole. Arguments of principle justify a political decision by showing that the decision respects or secures some individual or group right. Arguments about principles and rights are also characterized by 'articulate consistency' and promulgated in accordance with a doctrine of 'political responsibility'. There is thus a close association between principles and rights and between policies and goals.[7]

RIGHTS AND GOALS

The contrast pointed between goals and rights seems misplaced. Arguments of policy are said to relate to goals aimed at by the community as a whole, whereas a right is drawn in terms of principle and inheres in individuals or groups. Is the contrast here simply between what as a matter of fact promotes the ends that the community or) the majority group in it) happens to have and the ends, aims, and interests that individuals and minorities happen to have? Or is the term 'right' here used to indicate what individuals are entitled to have? If that is the contrast between rights and goals, then it obviously does not cut along the same lines as the distinction between individual or minority interests and community interests. Individuals and minorities may have goals, and communities or majorities may have rights. A goal is anything that is aimed at or perhaps anything that it would benefit an individual or a group or a community to aim at. But there is no reason why a goal might not be, or aim at, the protection of a right or the maximization of rights. So Herbert should not allow Hercules to assume that arguments about goals or policies cannot aim at the protection of rights or that arguments of principle cannot be given for the promotion of policies or goals.

POLICIES AND PRINCIPLES

There is, however, another way in which Hercules distinguishes

[7] 'Arguments of principle are arguments intended to establish an individual right; arguments of policy are arguments intended to establish a collective goal. Principles are propositions that describe rights; policies are propositions that describe goals' (Dworkin, op. cit., p. 1067).

arguments of principle and arguments of policy, which is quite different from their having to do with rights and goals. This is to do with the manner of their making. Principles are applied, it is suggested, in accordance with the doctrine of 'articulate consistency' which is demanded by the wider doctrine of 'political responsibility'. This doctrine is not to do with accountability or removability but refers to the requirement that decisions be made consistently and in accordance with some general theory. Policies and their related arguments, it is implied, do not demand articulate consistency. If a legislature awards a subsidy to one aircraft manufacturer in one month it is not (it is said) required to award a similar subsidy to another manufacturer the next month. A legislature is not required to behave consistently, to follow precedent or to derive its individual decisions from a general theory. Yet it does not quite seem on Hercules' theory that adjudication and legislation can be exactly equated with the presence and absence of the demand for articulate consistency since the doctrine is also said to apply to 'all political officials'. The demand for such consistency is, however, 'relatively weak' when policies are in play. This leaves it unclear whether legislation is also subject in some degree to the demands of articulate consistency or whether (as the subsidy example suggests) it is the very essence of legislative discretion to be totally free from the doctrine's requirements. (There are of course legislatures and legislatures. No constitution imposes a constitutional duty on a legislature to act consistently or to follow a doctrine of precedent; though some legislatures have an obligation at least to comply with the requirements of equality or equal protection.)[8] But it is necessary to be clear about what the legislative function generally or in essence is, if it is to be insisted that judges should not decide as legislators do, and if this is to be equated with applying principles rather than deploying policies.

DECIDING AS LEGISLATORS DO

The allegedly positivist theory that Hercules as adjudicator rejects is that he should act as a deputy legislator and as a deputy to the legislature. The meaning given by Hercules to the first expression is that a judge acting as a subordinate legislator would be using

---

[8] This is not perhaps the same thing as consistency since, as experience of the equal protection requirement in the United States shows, legislatures may not necessarily under the guise of respecting equality be required to treat all aspects of a question or to remedy all evils if they choose to remedy some. See, e.g., *Railway Express Agency* v. *New York* 336 U.S. 106 (1949).

arguments of policy of the kind used by legislators. The meaning given to the second expression is that by acting as deputy a judge would make the law that the legislature would enact if seized of the problem.

Would Herbert J. in fact propose either of these courses? The second contains an important ambiguity. Suppose we take a fairly normal problem of statutory construction involving a case in which the legislature has had no specific intention because in using a general term they had not considered the alternative ways in which it might be applied. Suppose for example they had used in a statute the word 'frequent' (as a verb) and the issue arises as to whether this can properly be applied to someone who is in a particular place for some extended period but not on a number of different occasions.[9] What then will it mean for Herbert to ask himself to decide as the legislature would have done? Is he to ask himself what the legislators would have thought about the application of the term 'frequent'? Or is he to ask himself what they would have done to meet the specific situation if they had been confronted with it? The answer to that may well be that they would have used a different term or made a different law. To answer this question would then not be to direct one's mind to what the law is but to what it would be if the legislature had been able to consider altering it. It does not seem likely that Herbert J. would want to do that. Nor that he would want to act as a deputy legislator in the sense of using arguments about community goals or policies of the kind that he might use if he were not a judge at all but a legislator.

JUDICIAL SUBORDINATION

A positivist/democratic objection of a different kind is also considered. If Hercules is to decide hard cases by appealing to principle— that is to his own understanding of rights—his decisions, it is argued, will reflect political convictions of a kind that reasonable men may disagree about. Will it not then be offensive to democratic feeling for him to rely merely on his own convictions. Hercules' answer is that there are two senses in which a man may rely upon his own opinion. One is that he simply appeals to his holding of an opinion as a reason for its soundness. The other is that he may rely upon his own belief in the sense of relying upon the truth or soundness of that belief. It seems doubtful, in fact, if any believers in judicial subordination have

---

[9] As in *Clarke* v. *The Queen* (1884) 14 Q.B.D. 92.

ever had the first sense in mind. What at least in constitutional contexts they may have proposed is that judicial reliance of the second kind should be subordinate in decision-making (especially about the validity of legislation) to what the judge perceives to be the convictions of legislators. Hercules' response to this view is to argue that such deference is not possible. Two arguments are given. First, if a judge were to defer to other people's standards it would then be his own opinion that the way to decide is to use other people's principles and standards, so that he would still in that sense at least be relying on his own opinion or standard. A second, perhaps more substantial argument is that deference is impossible since Hercules cannot readily discover what community morality is. The community's true morality is not just the sum or combination of the competing claims made in the community. It is what those claims really amount to and for that he must rely upon his own judgment. The alternative of deferring to what most members of the community *think* is required by their common morality is said to be impossible because the man in the street has not reflectively considered what it requires in particular cases. Hercules wavers here a little between the view that this fact is a reason for saying that the popular or majority view is undiscoverable and the assertion that the popular or majority view, even if discovered, need not be heeded. The decisive view in the end seems to be the second. The relevant questions he believes are sophisticated ones, requiring dialectical skill which, even if possessed by the voter, is not expressed systematically in his casual political preferences (i.e. in voting) and even if Hercules were satisfied that the ordinary man had expressed them systematically 'the question remains why Hercules should take the ordinary man's opinion . . . as decisive'.[10] Since an 'ordinary legal question' (i.e. a non-hard case) would not be settled by reference to popular opinion and since Hercules thinks that the parties to litigation have rights in hard cases as well as easy ones (since both have to be resolved by the application of principles) he will not submit to popular opinion in either case.

But is Hercules correct to suppose that either Herbert's positivism or his democratic inclinations will compel him to defer to popular opinion in hard cases or to deny that such cases involve arguments about rights? Perhaps Herbert's democratic leanings, if he has any, might at least prompt him to say that Hercules has not given much attention to whether his conclusions about the inscrutability and

[10] Dworkin, op. cit., p. 1108.

irrelevance of *community* opinion applies equally to the more reflectively considered opinions of *legislators*. In constitutional adjudication Herbert J. would not need to deny that rights are in issue to be able to assert that a balance between rights struck by a legislator ought to be set alongside a balance between rights struck by a judge. If he were not only a positivist but also a democrat and a believer in judicial restraint he would not need to base his argument for judicial subordination upon the ground that the judicial role involves legislative discretion. He could accept entirely Hercules' analysis of the judicial role in terms of the application of principle and still want to limit or moderate the judicial pursuit of principle (in the constitutional sphere at least) in deference to the opinions of the legislature.

Outside the constitutional field in which courts may be considering the validity of legislative enactments neither positivism nor democracy need lead Herbert J. to defer to legislative opinion. Nor do they compel him to embrace the view that disputed legal questions are of two classes—those that can be decided by the application of rules and those that require the application of 'legislative' discretion. Something like this view is attributed to 'the positivist theory of adjudication',[11] to 'classical jurisprudence'[12] and to popular, traditional, or familiar theories.[13] One form of the theory is that judges decide cases in two steps. They find the limit of what the 'explicit' law requires and they then use their discretion and legislate on issues 'which the law does not reach'.[14] This means that the positivist/democratic ideal according to which judges apply the law (and nothing but the law) that other institutions have made cannot apply 'outside' the law or beyond its reach or in novel cases. Novel cases are hard cases and they cannot be decided on this view even by stretching or reinterpreting existing rules; and so there is nothing left for it but legislation, albeit deferential and subordinate legislation.

Herbert J., whether as classicist, traditionalist, or populist, should feel no obligation to accept this description with its bifurcation of cases into soft and hard and its division of issues into the familiar and the novel. Every case, he might suggest, involves some novelty, some departure and some extension, stretching, or revision in the application of concepts or the weighting of analogies, or the balancing of cross-cutting principles or the application of precedent to new fact situations. No cases are totally novel, isolated, or disconnected from existing principles or rules. All adjudication involves asking: How

---

[11] Dworkin, op. cit., p. 1057.   [12] Ibid., p. 1103.   [13] Ibid., p. 1058.   [14] Ibid., p. 1103.

much is x like y? Can a plausibly be said to include b? Can p be reconciled with q? (Can derivative damage as well as directly caused economic damage be treated in similar ways?[15] Is electricity a form of property capable of being stolen?[16] Should the category of legally protected confidential relationships extend to those between Cabinet ministers?[17] Is disrupting a tennis tournament 'insulting behaviour'?[18] Hard cases are not entities that occupy a small untypical corner of the law. They fill a large part of the arena. Even the most hardened traditionalist would not propose that they are, or should be, typically resolved by asking only about social goals or the general welfare or community opinion, and criticism of inept decisions does not typically take the form of charging neglect of such interests.

The absence or avoidance of arguments about social policy is not of course inconsistent with its being the case that the outcome of a decision may in fact have the effect of furthering or promoting a particular social policy. Indeed over a very wide range of disputed issues this is bound to be the case. Most legislative measures have such policies written into them, though they occur at various levels of generality and may well appear in conjunction with other potentially conflicting policies. Whichever decision is reached in a contested case will frequently further some policy. Consumer-protection laws provide obvious instances. In a case involving the Supply of Goods (Implied Terms) Act 1973, for example, the Court of Appeal were split on the issue of whether a second-hand car sale had been a 'sale by description'.[19] Giving a wide interpretation to the phrase would certainly have the effect of promoting the interests of purchasers and consumers, whilst a narrow interpretation might further those of sellers. A decision to give a wide or liberal interpretation to the phrase might conceivably be motivated by a desire to protect the consumer and it does in fact protect the consumer. But it may be reached by other means and it may also be possible to reach the opposite conclusion that a 'sale by description' has not taken place without reaching it by applying the principle that the interest of the consumer ought not to be promoted. The implication of appeals to linguistic and analogical considerations is that there is never a clear point at

---

[15] *Spartan Steel and Alloy Ltd.* v. *Martin & Co. (Contractors) Inc.* [1972] 3 All E.R. 557.

[16] *Low* v. *Blease* [1975] Crim. L.R. 513.

[17] *Attorney-General* v. *Jonathan Cape Ltd.* [1976] 1 Q.B. 752.

[18] *Brutus* v. *Cozens* [1972] 2 All E.R. 1297.

[19] *McDonald* v. *Empire Garage (Blackburn) Ltd.* (*Times Law Report* 7 Oct. 1975).

which the rules simply run out and hard cases have to be resolved by the choice and direct invocation of some social purpose or policy; though it is often possible so to resolve them and some judges may seem to do it more than others.

POSITIVISM AND ADJUDICATION

If then Herbert J's positivism has any relevance to adjudication at all, it need have none that commits him to a belief in the classical or traditional fable about the resolution of hard cases by the methods of the quasi or deputy legislator. What he may, incidentally, be opposed to is the view that where statute or precedents are relatively clear and point in one direction they may properly be displaced by arguments drawn from considerations of equity, morality or justice. But dislike of that form of judicial boldness[20] and creativity has no relevance to cases in which the conclusion to be drawn from statute or precedent is admittedly unclear or ambiguous and where creativity (whether called legislative or not) is inevitable because words are general, because rules of statutory interpretation or common-law principles and precedents lead in different directions or because some analogy, distinction, or difference is contested. Most litigated cases are at least 'hardish' in this sense. There are no 'soft' cases if 'softness' implies an absence of any possibility of an alternative answer to a disputed point. The hard/soft contrast suggests misleadingly two categories into which cases might (perhaps roughly) be divided, as if on one side an answer is dictated by the law whilst on the other an answer is dictated by nothing in the law and can only be found outside it.

Conceivably Professor H. L. A. Hart in *The Concept of Law* unwittingly helped to confuse Herbert J. by suggesting too sharp a contrast between clear and unclear areas of rule-application. This may have had something to do with the fact that the relatively brief discussion of adjudication in *The Concept of Law* is devoted mainly to

[20] It is by picturing a positivist commitment to the notion of a *fixed body* of rules to which judges must have recourse that some have seen a connection and an emerging anti-positivist consensus in the judicial approach of Lord Denning and Professor Dworkin's attack on law as a system of rules. See Julius H. Grey, 'In re Vandervell The Jurisprudential Aspects', 21 *McGill Law Review* 160 (1975) (commenting on the decision in *Vandervell Trustees Ltd.* v. *White* [1970] 3 All E.R. 16). The suggestion is that on each theory the judge is being liberated from his imprisonment within fixed rules and free to deploy principles of a different kind.

It may be true that a number of the fundamental distinctions drawn in Professor Dworkin's writings favour a cluster of attitudes that might be dubbed 'anti-positivist liberationism' (e.g. the Rules/Principles distinction (Jurists' liberation); the Principles/Policies distinction (Judicial liberation); the Concepts/Conception distinction (Supreme Court liberation); and the Rights/Right Conduct distinction (citizens' liberation).

exposing the contrasting shortcomings of 'rule-formalism' and 'rule-scepticism'. By way of contrast with extreme scepticism emphasis is laid upon the existence of 'the plain cases' where there is general agreement about the application of a rule or the meaning of a term occurring in the statement of a rule. As against extreme formalism and 'mechanical jurisprudence' on the other hand, it is conceded that the open texture of rules and of language involves the development of law, by the judicial striking of a balance between circumstances of varying weight in cases where a *choice* between alternative applications is presented.[21] But it is argued that in resolving the indeterminacies that arise in and between rules the judge may 'add to a line of cases a new case *because of the resemblances which can reasonably be defended as both legally relevant and sufficiently close*'.[22] The criteria of relevance and closeness of resemblance, it is added, depend on *many complex factors running through the legal system.* Whatever they are, there is nothing in this description that implies the exhaustion of rules and a retreat to the kind of legislative discretion that is imputed to Herbert J. and that rests on the invocation of goals and policies.

Oddly, and happily, Hercules J., in rejecting decision in terms of goals and policies seems to be discarding what once was a central part of the anti-positivist case. In 'Social Rules and Legal Theory' Professor Dworkin, attacking the positivist 'rules model', argued that conflicts within the law could in the last resort only be resolved by invoking moral and political policies that took the argument outside the field of what positivists would be prepared to call law. Indeed it was the necessity of reference to such moral and political policies in adjudication that made it possible to urge that positivism must be false and that 'in countries like the United States and Britain . . . no ultimate distinction can be made between legal and moral standards'.[23]

If, as now appears, principle rather than policy is the basis of adjudication, even in hard cases there seems a basis for agreement between Hercules and Herbert. Positivists can find room for legal principles within the law as well as legal rules. They can also weigh and balance them in disputed cases without feeling vulnerable to the charge of allowing extra-legal elements to penetrate the sphere of positive law or befog the frontier between law and morality.

---

[21] *The Concept of Law*, p. 132 (italics added).
[22] Ibid., p. 124 (italics added).
[23] 81 *Yale Law Journal* 855 (1972).

Positivists may even properly insist that they have a choice between theories of adjudication. One who wished to admit that hard cases were resolved by the application of a strong sense of discretion having recourse to moral or extra-legal considerations might argue that if such recourse to moral principles or policies as an aid to resolving rule-conflicts were prescribed by positive law, there would be no penetration of law by morality that was inconsistent with a positivist analysis of a legal system.

The dialogue between Herbert and Hercules shows that positivists have other choices too. Just as they are not committed to any particular theory of adjudication, neither are they committed to other political or constitutional theories. They can urge either deference or activism in the relationship between legislators and judges and they can choose to support democracy or to cry it down. Between all these attitudes positivism properly so called should be neutral.

8

The House of Lords and the Rules of Precedent

RUPERT CROSS*

A statement read by the Lord Chancellor on 26 July 1966 announced that the House of Lords proposed to modify its existing practice of invariably following its past decisions and to 'depart from a previous decision when it appears right to do so'.[1] More recently two attempts by the Court of Appeal to modify its existing practice of following decisions of the House of Lords have been roundly condemned by the House. These developments are considered in this essay, the principal jurisprudential thesis of which is that the failure to recognize that judicial statements concerning the rules of precedent are neither *rationes decidendi*, nor *obiter dicta*, has caused spurious problems to be raised.

The three basic rules of precedent in English law are: (1) all courts must consider the relevant case-law; (2) lower courts must follow the decisions of courts above them in the hierarchy; and (3) appellate courts are generally bound by their own decisions. Rule (1) is historically the earliest and jurisprudentially the most important, but this essay is solely concerned with rules (2) and (3).

1. *Stare decisis* AND THE HIERARCHY OF COURTS

The two attempts of the Court of Appeal to escape from the fetters of a House of Lords' decision which it regarded as undesirable were made in *Broome* v. *Cassell & Co. Ltd.*[2] and *Miliangos* v. *George Frank (Textiles) Ltd.*[3] In the first of these cases the Court of Appeal held that it was not bound to apply the rules governing the assessment of exemplary damages laid down by the House of Lords in *Rookes* v.

---

* Vinerian Professor of English Law, All Souls' College, Oxford.
[1] [1966] 3 All E.R. 77.   [2] [1971] 2 Q.B. 354.   [3] [1975] Q.B. 487.

Barnard[4] because the decision on that point had been given *per incuriam*. In *Miliangos* v. *George Frank (Textiles) Ltd.* the Court of Appeal held that it was bound to follow its previous decision in *Schorsch Meier G.m.b.H.* v. *Hennin*[5] where a majority had held that the decision of the House of Lords in *Re United Railways of the Havana and Regla Warehouses Ltd.*[6] was not binding because the principle 'cessante ratione cessat ipsa lex' applied to the case. The decisions of the Court of Appeal in both the *Broome* and *Miliangos* cases were upheld by the House of Lords, but not before the appropriate reprimands had been uttered. The speeches in the *Miliangos* case have an added interest because two Law Lords made contradictory statements concerning the duty of the Court of Appeal to follow its own decisions, and the question whether they were *ratio* or *obiter* can fairly be raised with regard to a number of remarks in both the House of Lords and Court of Appeal.

1A. *Broome* v. *Cassell*

In a case which can only be described as a tragedy of errors Captain Broome, the commander of the ill-starred convoy PQ17, sailing to Russia in World War II, sued Irving as author and *Cassell & Co. Ltd.* as publishers of a libel contained in an account of the dispersal of the convoy with heavy losses. The attention of both author and publisher had been drawn to the libellous character of this account before publication. The trial judge directed the jury in accordance with the unanimous decision of the House of Lords in *Rookes* v. *Barnard* and the plaintiff was awarded £15,000 general damages together with £40,000 exemplary damages. Cassell & Co. and Irving appealed. The Court of Appeal held that the case came within the restricted rules governing exemplary damages laid down by Lord Devlin in *Rookes* v. *Barnard* because the tort was calculated to make a profit for the defendants in excess of the amount due to the plaintiff by way of compensation; but the Court's main holding was that *Rookes* v. *Barnard* was wrongly decided with the result that the exemplary damages should have been assessed in accordance with the punitive principles which had previously prevailed. The leading Court of Appeal judgment of Lord Denning M.R. contains the following remarks:

. . . [t]he common law of England on this subject was so well settled before 1964—and on such sound and secure foundations—that it was not open to the House of Lords to overrule it.

[4] [1964] A.C. 1129.   [5] [1975] Q.B. 416.   [6] [1961] A.C. 1007.

If ever there was a decision of the House of Lords given *per incuriam* this was it.

I think the difficulties represented by *Rookes* v. *Barnard* are so great that the judges should direct the juries in accordance with the law as it was understood before *Rookes* v. *Barnard*. Any attempt to follow *Rookes* v. *Barnard* is bound to lead to confusion.[7]

Cassell & Co. unsuccessfully appealed to the House of Lords, each member of which concurred in condemning the Court of Appeal's refusal to follow *Rookes* v. *Barnard*. To quote Lord Hailsham L.C.:

The fact is, and I hope it will never be necessary to say so again, that in the hierarchical system of courts that exists in this country, it is *necessary* for each lower tier, including the Court of Appeal, to accept loyally the decisions of the higher tiers. Where decisions manifestly conflict, the decision in *Young* v. *The Bristol Aeroplane Co. Ltd.*[8] offers guidance to each tier in matters affecting its own decisions. It does not entitle it to question considered decisions in the upper tiers with the same freedom.[9]

At the point in the above passage where it has been italicized, the word 'necessary' was not used solely in its imperative sense. No doubt the failure of a lower-tier court to follow a decision of a court in a higher tier is liable to excite unfavourable reactions such as those of the House of Lords in *Cassell & Co. Ltd.* v. *Broome*, but Lord Hailsham was also using the word 'necessary' in the sense of 'essential to the working of a judicial system like the English'. When a single decision can settle the law on a particular point, the court in the highest tier must have the last word and, when spoken, that last word must be followed by all lower-tier courts, however much they may believe it to have been mistaken. What the Court of Appeal was claiming in *Broome* v. *Cassell & Co. Ltd.* was a power to overrule decisions of the House of Lords which it considered to have been given *per incuriam*. To the great advantage of certainty in the law, that power is now clearly confined to decisions of the Court of Appeal itself and courts below it in the hierarchy.

1B. *Miliangos* v. *George Frank (Textiles) Ltd.*

In *Re United Railways of the Havana and Regla Warehouses Ltd.*[10] Lord Denning said '. . . [I]f there is one thing clear in our law, it is

[7] [1971] 2 Q.B. at pp. 380, 382, and 384 respectively.
[8] [1944] K.B. 718.
[9] *Cassell and Co. Ltd.* v. *Broome*, [1972] A.C. 1027 at p. 1054.
[10] [1961] A.C. 1007, at pp. 1068–9.

that the claim must be made in sterling and the judgment given in sterling.' This rule had represented English law for more than 300 years, and it was the basis of the decision of the House of Lords in the *Havana Railways* case in 1961, that for the purpose of English liquidation proceedings, a debt payable in American dollars had to be quantified in English currency as at the date when payment was due. In *Schorsch Meier G.m.b.H.* v. *Hennin*,[11] decided by the Court of Appeal in 1974, the balance of the price of goods sold and delivered was due to be paid to the plaintiffs in Deutsch marks in February 1972. The sterling equivalent was then £452 but, by the time the County Court summons was issued in July 1973, sterling had depreciated to such an extent that £452 was worth a thousand or so marks less than the amount claimed. Overruling the County Court Judge, the Court of Appeal held that, notwithstanding the earlier decision of the House of Lords, judgment should be entered for the amount of Deutsch marks claimed by the summons. Two reasons were given for this decision. The first was that it was required by article 106 of the Treaty of Rome. Although the court was unanimous on this point, its conclusion was treated with the utmost reserve by the House of Lords on the hearing of the appeal in *Miliangos* v. *George Frank (Textiles) Ltd.*[12] The second reason for the decision of the Court of Appeal in the *Schorsch Meier* case was that *Re United Railways of the Havana and Regla Warehouses Ltd.* ought not to be followed because things had changed since 1961 and the maxim 'cessante ratione cessat ipsa lex' applied. This reason was given by Lord Denning M.R. with the concurrence of Foster J.; Lawton L.J., the third member of the court, dissented. The respects in which things had changed since 1961 were said to be an alteration in the prescribed form of judgment and the decision of the House of Lords in *Beswick* v. *Beswick*[13] that specific performance may be granted of agreements to pay money. No great importance was attached to these matters by the House of Lords in the *Miliangos* case, but, whatever their significance may have been, it is clear that the Court of Appeal was claiming a far greater power to disregard decisions of the House of Lords than that claimed in *Broome* v. *Cassell & Co. Ltd.* The number of decisions to which the 'cessante ratione' maxim might, with at least plausible justification, be said to apply must be greater than those which can be said to have been given *per incuriam*, even after allowance has been made for the broad construction of that term which the Court of Appeal was

[11] [1975] Q.B. 416.   [12] [1975] 3 All E.R. 801.   [13] [1968] A.C. 58.

prepared to countenance in *Broome's* case. This new claim was destined to be as decisively rejected by the House of Lords as the previous one, but not on an appeal in the *Schorsch Meier* case, and not before some conundrums with regard to the duties of puisne judges and the Court of Appeal had been raised.

In *Miliangos* v. *George Frank* (*Textiles*) *Ltd.* the debt for which the plaintiff sued was due in Swiss francs, and the difference between the sterling value of the debt at the date when payment was due and at the date of the hearing by Bristow J. of what had become an un-defended action was some £18,000. Bristow J. found himself in a position of some embarrassment, being confronted with the choice of following the decision of the Court of Appeal in *Schorsch Meier G.m.b.H.* v. *Hennin* and following the decision of the House of Lords in the *Havana Railways* case. Emboldened by the conclusion that the decision of the Court of Appeal was given *per incuriam* because the case had only been argued on one side, he decided to follow the House of Lords and declined to give judgment for payment in Swiss francs. Bristow J. was of course only concerned with the second *ratio decidendi* of the Court of Appeal in the *Schorsch Meier* case for Switzerland is not a party to the Treaty of Rome, and it seems that the course which he adopted would probably not have been followed by at least one other puisne judge.[14]

The Court of Appeal allowed the plaintiff's appeal and gave judgment for the amount of Swiss francs claimed.[15] The antics of the biter bit are inevitably of interest in any context. Having failed to establish its claim to be under no obligation to follow decisions of the House of Lords given *per incuriam*, the Court of Appeal would have no truck with the claim of a puisne judge to act in the same way with regard to its decisions. The Court's unanimous opinion was that Bristow J. should have followed the *Schorsch Meier* decision. Points made in the leading judgment delivered by Lord Denning M.R. were that both of the *rationes decidendi* of the *Schorsch Meier* case were binding on courts of first instance and the Court of Appeal, the *Schorsch Meier* case was not decided *per incuriam* because it was only argued on one side, and a case is not decided *per incuriam* because all the relevant authorities were not cited.

The defendant appealed to the House of Lords where a majority of four to one was in favour of overruling the *Havana Railways* case

---

[14] *The Halcyon the Great*, [1975] 1 All E.R. 882. Brandon J.
[15] [1975] Q.B. 487.

with the result that the judgment of the Court of Appeal ordering the
defendant to pay the amount of Swiss francs due to the plaintiff at the
date when payment should have been made was upheld. The House
was, however, unanimously of opinion that the Court of Appeal
should have followed the *Havana Railways* case in *Schorsch Meier
G.m.b.H.* v. *Hennin*. All their Lordships agreed with Lord Wilberforce
when he said 'It has to be reaffirmed that the only judicial means by
which decisions of this House can be reviewed is by this House under
the declaration of 1966'.[16] The maxim 'cessante ratione cessat ipsa
lex' would be relevant to such a review, but it does not control the
rules of precedent in other respects.

As so often happens when an attack on established doctrine is
repulsed, the effect of the episodes of *Broome* v. *Cassell & Co. Ltd.*
and *Miliangos* v. *George Frank (Textiles) Ltd.* has been to render the
established rules rather more rigid than they were before the attacks
were made. To perceive this one only has to consider the concessions
to orthodoxy made by Lord Denning in his judgment in the *Miliangos*
case. In *Young* v. *The Bristol Aeroplane Co. Ltd.*[17] three exceptions to
the rule that the Court of Appeal is bound by its own decisions were
mentioned by Lord Greene. The first relates to conflicting decisions
of the Court of Appeal, a situation in which a choice obviously has
to be made; under the second, the Court of Appeal is bound not to
follow a decision of its own which, though not expressly overruled,
cannot, in its opinion, stand with a decision of the House of Lords;
the third exception relates to decisions of the Court of Appeal given
per incuriam. Neither *Broome* v. *Cassell & Co.* nor *Miliangos* v.
George Frank (Textiles) Ltd. has any bearing on the first exception,
but Lord Denning stressed the point that the second exception is
confined to cases in which a previous decision of the Court of Appeal
cannot stand with a *subsequent* decision of the House of Lords,
although there are instances in which this limitation does not appear
to have been recognized.[18] Lord Denning's conception of a case
decided *per incuriam* was clearly far narrower and more orthodox in
the *Miliangos* judgment than it was in his judgment in *Broome* v.
Cassell & Co. Finally he insisted that, where a case has two *rationes
decidendi*, both are binding although he took a different view on three
previous occasions.[19] These minor enhancements of the rigidity of the

---

[16] [1975] 3 All E.R. at p. 806.   [17] [1944] K.B. 718.
[18] *Fitzsimons* v. *The Ford Motor Co. Ltd.*, [1946] 1 All E.R. 429.
[19] *Betty's Cafes Ltd.* v. *Phillips Furnishing Stores Ltd.*, [1958] A.C. 20, at p. 53; *Browning* v. *The War Office*, [1963] 1 Q.B. 750; *Re Holmden's Settlement*, [1966] 2 All E.R. 661.

rules of precedent are to be welcomed in the interests of certainty, but the same cannot be said of the observations made in the House of Lords in *Miliangos* v. *George Frank* (*Textiles*) *Ltd.* about the way in which Bristow J. and the Court of Appeal should have acted with regard to *Schorsch Meier G.m.b.H.* v. *Hennin.*

1C. *The House of Lords and Decisions of the Court of Appeal*

Speeches in the House of Lords have previously stated that the Court of Appeal is bound to follow its own decisions,[20] but never with the inexorability of Lord Simon of Glaisdale; previous speeches have pointed to, and suggested solutions of, the difficulties of a court confronted with a conflict between a decision of the Court of Appeal and an earlier decision of the House of Lords,[21] but never with the dogmatic assurance with which Lord Cross of Chelsea contradicted Lord Simon of Glaisdale.

To begin with a remark of Lord Simon's which certainly runs counter to some previous judicial assumptions: 'It is clear law that the Court of Appeal is bound by a decision of your Lordships' House and (at least on its civil side) by a previous decision of the Court of Appeal itself. Any change in this respect would require legislation.'[22] There are several recent judicial statements to the effect that the Court of Appeal should remain bound by its past decisions, but in none of them is support for this view sought in anything said by the House of Lords, and, in *Gallie* v. *Lee*,[23] Salmon L.J. clearly contemplated the possibility of a practice statement on the lines of that of the House of Lords when he said:

Surely today judicial comity would be amply satisfied if we were to adopt the same principle in relation to our decisions as the House of Lords has recently laid down for itself by a pronouncement of the whole House. It may be that one day we shall make a similar pronouncement. But that day is not yet. It is, I think, only by a pronouncement of the whole court that we could effectively alter a practice which is too deeply rooted. In the meantime I find myself reluctantly obliged to accept the old authorities, however much I disagree with them.

But it seems that we will be denied the spectacle of a practice statement of the Court of Appeal made in the teeth of a considered statement of a Lord Ordinary of Appeal at least for some little time

---

[20] *Young* v. *The Bristol Aeroplane Co. Ltd.* [1946] A.C. 163, at p. 169 per Lord Simon.
[21] *Noble* v. *The Southern Railway*, [1940] A.C. 583, at p. 598 per Lord Wright (see below).
[22] [1975] 3 All E.R. at p. 815.   [23] [1969] 2 Ch. 17, at p. 49.

because past and present Lords Justice have indicated their opposition to the making of such a statement.[24]

The next remark of Lord Simon runs counter to an extremely tentative observation by Lord Wright. Lord Simon said:

It will be apparent that in my view the Court of Appeal in the instant case was correct in following its previous decision in *Schorsch Meier*. There were two concurrent *rationes decidendi* in *Schorsch Meier*, one, (art. 106 of the Treaty of Rome) that of all members of the court, the other ('cessante ratione') that of a majority. Both were subsequently binding on the Court of Appeal no less than on Bristow J.[25]

In support of his decision not to follow the Court of Appeal Bristow J. might have cited the following passage from Lord Wright's speech in *Noble* v. *The Southern Railway*.[26]

What a court should do when faced with a decision of the Court of Appeal manifestly inconsistent with the decisions of this House is a problem of some difficulty in the doctrine of precedent. I incline to think it should apply the law laid down by this House and refuse to follow the erroneous decision. But I cannot blame the Court of Appeal for leaving to this House to point out that the decision in *Clarke's* case[27] was at the time inconsistent with *M'Ferrin's* case . . .[28]

But there is a difference between the situation envisaged by Lord Wright and that which confronted Bristow J., for the Court of Appeal in *Schorsch Meier* deliberately departed from the earlier decision of the House of Lords. No doubt it was this fact which prompted the following remarks of Lord Cross of Chelsea in the *Miliangos* case:[29]

Moreover, although one cannot but feel sympathy for Stephenson and Geoffrey Lane L.JJ. in the embarrassing position in which they found themselves, I think that it was wrong for the Court of Appeal in this case to follow the *Schorsch Meier* decision. It is no doubt true that the decision was not given *per incuriam* but I do not think that Lord Greene, when he said in *Young* v. *The Bristol Aeroplane Co. Ltd.*[30] that the 'only' exceptions to the rule that the Court of Appeal is bound to follow previous decisions of its own were those which he set out, can fairly be blamed for not foreseeing that one of his successors might deal with a decision of the House of Lords in the way in which Lord Denning dealt with the *Havana* case. I propose therefore to consider this case as though the Court of Appeal had dismissed the appeal from Bristow J. and we were hearing an appeal to us by the respondents to depart from the *Havana* decision under the declaration of 1966.

---

[24] Russell L.J. in *Gallie* v. *Lee*, [1969] 2 Ch. at p. 41; Scarman L.J. in *Farrell* v. *Alexander*, [1976] 1 All E.R. at p. 147.   [25] [1975] 3 All E.R. at p. 823.
[26] [1940] A.C. 583, at p. 598.   [27] (1927), 20 B.W.C.C. 309.   [28] [1926] A.C. 377.
[29] [1975] 3 All E.R. at p. 837.   [30] [1944] K.B. 718.

The balance of practical convenience appears to be on the side of the course advocated by Lord Simon, but the merits of judicial statements in the House of Lords concerning the extent to which lower courts are bound by their own decisions are debatable, and the desirability of contradictory statements on the subject is highly questionable. There is something to be said for the discreet silence of Lords Wilberforce, Edmund Davies, and Fraser of Tullybelton in the *Miliangos* case.

1D. *Statements about precedent and the* ratio–obiter *distinction*

Diplock L.J., as he then was, must be included among those who thought that legislation was unnecessary to free the Court of Appeal from the rules by which it announced that it was bound in *Young* v. *The Bristol Aeroplane Co. Ltd.*, for, in *Boys* v. *Chaplin*[31] he said:

Indeed it is difficult to see how a pronouncement of the House of Lords which did not form part of the reasons for judgment in any appeal before it could have any binding effect upon any other court. In the Court of Appeal we are bound by decisions of the House of Lords, but, so far as concerns the binding effect of the Court of Appeal on its own decisions, our fetters too are self-imposed.

This suggests, wrongly it is submitted, that the distinction between *ratio decidendi* and *obiter dictum* applies to judicial statements about the rules of precedent. For the purposes of the ensuing discussion the *ratio decidendi* of a case may be taken to be any rule of law considered necessary by the judge who states it for the decision of the case before him. It is that part of the decision which has binding effect and the facts of the case play a large part in its identification. All other statements of law contained in a judgment are generally described as *obiter dicta*, but this practice may have to be reconsidered. Why should statements about the rules of precedent such as those which have previously been quoted be treated as either *ratio decidendi* or *obiter dictum* according to whether or not they were considered necessary for the decision of the case in which they were made?

To begin with statements by members of the House of Lords concerning the manner in which its decisions should be treated by lower courts: none of these could possibly have been considered

[31] [1968] 2 K.B. 1, at p. 35.

necessary for the decision of the cases in which the speeches were made, yet it would, to say the least, be odd to speak of them as *obiter dicta* which are not absolutely binding on lower courts. The mind boggles at the thought of a puisne judge or a member of the Court of Appeal declaring that he is not bound by decisions of the House of Lords given *per incuriam* or falling within the maxim 'cessante ratione cessat ipsa lex'.

What is the status of such remarks as those of Lord Denning in *Broome* v. *Cassell & Co.* or *Schorsch Meier G.m.b.H.* v. *Henin*, or, at the more ordinary level, any judge's statement that he is, or is not, bound to follow a decision of which he disapproves? Remarks of this sort are *necessary* for the decision of the case before the court. Professor Glanville Williams once said that one way of arriving at the conclusion that the rules of precedent cannot be based on precedent would be 'to say that every purported decision of a point on the doctrine of precedent must be *obiter*, because it is necessarily irrelevant to the issues of law and fact that have to be decided by the court'.[32] The suggestion seems only to be applicable to statements of higher courts about the way in which lower courts should behave. At the same time, although a judge's statement in case *A* to the effect that he is bound by case *B* and therefore follows it in spite of the fact that he would otherwise have decided case *A* in the opposite way is an essential step in the reasoning leading to the decision, there are weighty objections to treating such remarks as the *ratio decidendi* of case *A*. They are always in the same form, they are in no way dependent on the facts of the case, and they can never be solely determinative of the issue of law on which the parties are litigating. If this is true of specific statements such as 'I am bound by case *A*', it is *a fortiori* true of statements such as 'this court is bound to follow its past decisions', whether the court be the House of Lords or a court lower in the hierarchy.

In short, statements about the rules of precedent are statements about the way in which courts should act with regard to the *rationes decidendi* of other courts and they fall outside the *ratio–obiter* distinction. Three spurious problems, each connected with the House of Lords' practice statement of 1966, owe their existence to the failure to recognize this fact, and they ought not to be allowed to continue to trouble lawyers, academic or otherwise.

[32] 70 *Law Quarterly Review* 461 (1954).

2. SPURIOUS PROBLEMS AND THE PRACTICE STATEMENT OF 1966

2A. *Roy Stone's problem*

The late Mr. Roy Stone discussed logical problems which he considered to be raised by the Practice Statement with an admirable wealth of learning,[33] but they only achieve plausibility in relation to the context if it is assumed that the statement that a court is not bound by its own decisions is the same kind of statement as that which constitutes the *ratio decidendi* of a particular case. Put very briefly, Mr. Stone's main contentions were: (1) the Practice Statement is self-contradictory because, so long as it is operative, there is at least one decision of the House which cannot be departed from, namely, the decision mentioned in the statement not to be absolutely bound by its past decisions; (2) *London Tramways* v. *London County Council*,[34] the case in which the House decided that it was bound by its own decisions, was, subject to legislation, perpetually binding on the House of Lords.

The Practice Statement is said to involve the Cretan-liar paradox.[35] 'All Cretans are liars,' said Epimenides, himself a Cretan, meaning that everything said by a Cretan was always false. If this statement is true, it must be false, and logical difficulties arise which it would be imprudent for a mere lawyer to discuss. It would of course be quite unfair to Mr. Stone to point out that the verbal form of the Practice Statement does not give rise to the Cretan-liar paradox because the relevant sentence simply tells us that their Lordships propose 'to modify their present practice and, while treating former decisions of this House as normally binding, to depart from a previous decision when it appears right to do so.' But, even if the appropriate verbal adjustments are made, the Cretan-liar paradox can only be applicable to the Practice Statement if the word 'decision' is given the same meaning in both of the places where it occurs when it is said that 'our decision is not to be bound by any of our decisions.' When used for the second time it means *ratio decidendi*, a meaning which it cannot possibly bear in the context of the Practice Statement when used for the first time.

---

[33] 26 *Cambridge Law Journal* 35 (1968); 51 *Minnesota Law Review* 655 (1967).

[34] [1898] A.C. 375, not to be confused with *London Street Tramways* v. *London County Council*, [1894] A.C. 489. The 1898 case was given the same title in the Law Reports in error.

[35] See the discussion by J. C. Hicks, 29 *Cambridge Law Journal* 275 (1971).

The argument that, subject to legislation, the House of Lords had irretrievably bound itself to follow its own decisions when it announced that it was so bound in the *London Tramways* case only gains plausibility if it is assumed that the announcement was the *ratio decidendi* of the case. The statement 'we are bound by the *rationes decidendi* of all cases that have come, or ever will come, before us, including the *ratio decidendi* of this case' may be thought to confront a court proposing to modify its practice with logical difficulties; but no such difficulties arise once it is realized that the *ratio decidendi* of the *London Tramways* case was the same as the *ratio decidendi* of *Edinburgh Tramways* v. *Lord Provost of Edinburgh* and *London Street Tramways* v. *London County Council*,[36] two previous appeals to the House of Lords dealing with identically worded Tramway Acts. The view that the *ratio decidendi* of the *London Tramways* case was that the House of Lords is bound by its own decisions is superficially attractive because this was the only point on which argument was heard, but the order of the House was that the order of the Court of Appeal be affirmed, and the order of the Court of Appeal affirmed the order of the referee that a particular sum was due from the Council to the tramway company as representing the 'then' value of the companys' property taken over by the Council. This sum had been calculated in accordance with the principles laid down by the House of Lords in the two previous tramway decisions, and those principles might well have been applied again even if the House had held that it was not bound to follow its past decisions.

The propriety of referring to the proposition that the House of Lords is bound by its own decisions as the *ratio decidendi* of the *London Tramways* case becomes apparent if we ask whether that case would have been overruled if, in a subsequent case, the House had declared that it was no longer bound by its past decisions and had overruled one of them there and then. Clearly the *London Tramways* case would not have been overruled because all courts below the House of Lords would have been obliged to follow the earlier tramway decision on which the order of the House was based. *Rationes decidendi* are 'overruled', the rules of precedent are 'changed', 'modified', or 'departed from'. The Practice Statement is open to criticism because it speaks of the proposal to 'depart from a previous decision' when the proposal really is to overrule a previous decision. No doubt the point is too obvious to be likely to cause trouble, but

[36] [1894] A.C. 456 and 489 respectively.

failure to use the word 'overrule' could suggest to a court below the House of Lords that the decision 'departed from' was still there to be followed if the court were so minded, whereas it could only be resuscitated by the House of Lords. The author of the headnote of the *Miliangos* case in the Weekly Law Reports was not fooled for the note says that the *Havana Railways* case was 'overruled'.[37] Unfortunately the author of the headnote in the All England reports was more cautious for he says that the *Havana Railways* case was 'not followed'.[38]

2B. *Julius Stone's problem*

Professor Julius Stone argues that the Practice Statement was a non-statement because the House of Lords was acting neither in its legislative nor in its judicial capacity when it was made. 'If their Lordships were not acting in a curial capacity, then the rule enunciated could not have any *legal* force as part of the precedent system.'[39] After giving credit to Professor Glanville Williams for having foreshadowed something like the Practice Statement as long ago as 1957,[40] Professor Stone continues:

It still leaves unsolved the mystery of how any legal amendment of the rules of precedent (these being rules of law) can flow from the 1966 statement (this being itself only a mere extra-curial *ipse dixit* not arising from either judicial activity or delegated legislative power).[41]

The assumption seems to be that rules of precedent must be derived from legislation, *rationes decidendi*, or *obiter dicta*. This is to confuse statements of courts about their own practice with judicial statements about the rights and duties of litigants under the substantive law which must, in order to have any legal effect, be made in the course of a judgment. The question of the constitutional validity of the Practice Statement was mentioned but not pursued in the course of the argument in *Cassell & Co.* v. *Broome*,[42] but can there be any doubt that it owes its validity to the inherent power of any court to regulate its own practice. It is certainly going too far to describe a statement read by the Lord Chancellor at a sitting of the House of Lords before judgments were delivered and expressed to be on behalf of all the

[37] [1975] 3 W.L.R. 758.
[38] [1975] 3 All E.R. 801. Similar caution is shown in [1976] A.C. 443.
[39] 69 *Columbia Law Review* 1163 (1969).
[40] Salmond's *Jurisprudence*, 11th edn. (1957), pp. 187–8.
[41] 69 *Columbia Law Review* 1168 (1969).
[42] [1972] A.C. at p. 1038.

Lords Ordinary of Appeal as a 'mere extra-curial *ipse dixit*'. It could even be argued that the Practice Statement was on the verge of receiving parliamentary recognition while Professor Stone's article denigrating it was being written for there would not have been much point in including decisions of the House of Lords in the items justifying the leap-frogging procedure contemplated by part II of the Administration of Justice Act 1969 if there were no possibility of the House overruling such a decision.

2C. *Prospective overruling*

In two of the cases in which action on the Practice Statement was discussed in the House of Lords, Lord Simon of Glaisdale said that he would have been more ready to approve of such action if it were possible for the House to overrule the impugned case prospectively.[43] This is not the place for a discussion of the merits of prospective overruling, but it is right to point out that the irrelevant distinction between *ratio decidendi* and *obiter dictum* has been allowed to cloud thought on the subject. The point has been made that, if a court with power to overrule case *A*, were to say 'the *ratio decidendi* of case *A* will be applied to the instant case so that there will be judgment for the plaintiff, but, for the future, case *A* is overruled so that, on facts which cannot reasonably be distinguished from those of the instant case, judgment will have to be given for the defendant', everything said about case *A* would be *obiter dicta* because it was not necessary for the decision of the issue between the parties. One might have been pardoned for regarding the point as so uninteresting, and so remote from the issues raised by prospective overruling as not to be worth answering; but the point has been answered in a recent informative and helpful lecture and the answer is unconvincing:

Each part of the bifurcated decision springs from an actual controversy between the parties. The decision to liquidate the old rule springs from its unfitness to govern such cases. The decision to pay final respects to the doomed rule springs from such considerations as the justifiability of a party's reliance on an old rule, given that it may induce reliance by the very authority of its existence, if not by its fitness. It bears emphasis that each part of the decision is essential to a proper resolution of the case. Neither is dictum.[44]

[43] *Jones* v. *Secretary of State for Social Services*, [1972] A.C. 944, at p. 1026; *Miliangos* v. *George Frank (Textiles) Ltd.*, [1975] 3 All E.R. 801 at p. 832.

[44] 'Quo vadis—Prospective Overruling', a lecture delivered before the Holdsworth Club at Birmingham University in 1975, by Roger Traynor, at p. 13.

But this ignores the fact that the most difficult problem presented by a decision to overrule prospectively is that of the 'cut-off' date. In the example of case *A* given above, it can truly be said that, granted that prospective overruling was a recognized possibility, the issues between the plaintiff and defendant would have been: (1) Should the case be overruled? (2) If the answer to the first question is 'yes' should the *ratio decidendi* of case *A* none the less be applied to the instant case? There would have been no issue between the parties on the all-important third question of the date from which the overruling should be effective. Assume, for example, that the House of Lords had decided in *Miliangos* v. *George Frank (Textiles) Ltd.* to overrule the *Havana Railways* case prospectively, should that case have been treated as overruled for the purpose of all actions begun after the *Miliangos* decision, or only in relation to debts falling due thereafter, or only in relation to obligations contracted thereafter? These questions would have been of no interest to the parties, but it would be pointless for a court to have power to overrule prospectively if it could not deal with such matters. Let the *obiter–ratio* distinction be recognized for the red herring that it undoubtedly is in this context.

3. THE PRACTICE STATEMENT IN OPERATION

Whether prospective overruling becomes an accepted possibility in England is a question for the future. As to the past, it is already possible to say a few words about the effect of the Practice Statement during what is nearly the first decade of its existence, the period from the end of July 1966 to the end of January 1976. Only two decisions of the House of Lords have been overruled, *The Aello*,[45] in the *Johanna Oldendorff*,[46] and *Re United Railways of the Havana and Regla Warehouses Ltd.*[47] in *Miliangos* v. *George Frank (Textiles) Ltd.*[48] The *Aello* could have been distinguished but the majority of the House of Lords found it convenient to get rid altogether of the test laid down in that case for determining when a ship becomes an 'arrived ship'. There was no possibility of a reasonable distinction being drawn in the *Miliangos* case. Two overrulings in ten years is by no means insignificant, but it would be wrong to assess the effects of the Practice Statement solely by reference to cases overruled. The speeches in other cases, notably *British Railways Board* v. *Herrington*,[49] would have taken a very different form if the Statement had

---

[45] [1961] A.C. 135.   [46] [1974] A.C. 479.   [47] [1961] A.C. 1007.
[48] [1975] 3 All E.R. 801.   [49] [1972] A.C. 879.

not been in the background. In the *Herrington* case two of the law lords were for overruling *Robert Addie & Sons (Collieries) Ltd.* v. *Dumbreck*[50] and, even though the others did not go so far, it is difficult to escape the conclusion that, greatly to the detriment of the development of the law, we would have heard more about distinctions on the facts and the fiction of an implied licence to child trespassers if the *Herrington* case had come before the House of Lords in 1965. This point emerges clearly from the following passage from Lord Diplock's speech:

This House has since 1966 abandoned its former practice of adhering rigidly to the *ratio decidendi* of its previous decisions. There is no longer any need to discuss whether, to discard the fiction of a so-called 'licence' to enter granted by the occupier of land to the person who suffers personal injury on it, should be characterised as overruling *Addie's* case or as doing no more than explaining its reasoning in terms which are in harmony with the general development of legal concepts since 1929 as to the source of one man's duty to take steps for the safety of another.[51]

A few general points are emerging with regard to the criteria for the exercise of the House's new power. The mere fact that a past decision is considered wrong will not suffice, 'In the general interest of certainty in the law we must be sure that there is some very good reason before we act.' This remark was made by Lord Reid in *Knuller Publishing Promotions* v. *Director of Public Prosecutions*,[52] a case in which the majority declined to overrule *Shaw* v. *Director of Public Prosecutions*;[53] the *Knuller* case may also be cited for the proposition that decisions on broad questions of morals are unlikely to be overruled. The House will probably act on the Statement less readily in cases of statutory interpretation than in those involving points of common law,[54] and, perhaps, more readily when the decision to be overruled is a recent one.[55] The avoidance of over subtle distinctions,[56] and commercial convenience coupled with the avoidance of injustice in the instant case[57] are obviously relevant considerations. These points are no more than straws in the wind, but a jurisprudence of overruling may be developing and, for this reason alone, the Practice Statement cannot be regarded as the near nonevent which some writers appear to have thought that it was.

[50] [1929] A.C. 358.   [51] [1972] A.C. at p. 934.   [52] [1973] A.C. 435, at p. 455.
[53] [1962] A.C. 220.
[54] *Jones* v. *Secretary of State for Social Services*, [1972] A.C. 944.
[55] [1972] A.C. at p. 993 per Lord Dilhorne.
[56] The *Johanna Oldendorff*, above.
[57] *Miliangos* v. *George Frank (Textiles) Ltd.*, above.

9

Intention and *Mens Rea* in Murder

ANTHONY KENNY*

IN a characteristically energetic and wide-ranging paper of 1967[1] H. L. A. Hart discussed *inter alia* the role of intentionality in the definition of murder. It is commonly held that English law does not require that a killing, in order to amount to murder, should be something intended in the sense that the accused set out to achieve it, either as a means or an end. Here, as Hart pointed out, the law diverges from what is ordinarily meant by expressions like 'he intentionally killed those men'.

Some legal theorists, Bentham among them, have recorded this divergence by distinguishing (as '*oblique* intention'), mere foresight of consequences from '*direct* intention' where the consequences must have been contemplated by the accused not merely as a foreseen outcome but as an end which he set out to achieve, or as a means to an end, and constituted at least part of his reason for doing what he did. (pp. 120–1.)

Hart counted it a merit of the English law of homicide that—unlike the principle of 'double effect' favoured by Catholic moral theologians—it did not pay attention to the difference between direct and oblique intention, either being sufficient to constitute murder. Both the direct and oblique cases, he argued, share a feature which any system of assigning responsibility for conduct must treat as crucial. In each type of case the situation is that the accused

. . . had control over the alternative between the victims' dying or living, his choice tipped the balance; in both cases he had control over and may be considered to have chosen the outcome, since he consciously opted for the course leading to the victims' deaths. Whether he sought to achieve this as

* Fellow of Balliol College, Oxford.
[1] 'Intention and Punishment', *Oxford Review*, No. 4, February 1967; reprinted in *Punishment and Responsibility* (Oxford, 1968), pp. 113–35, to which references are given.

an end or a means to his end, or merely foresaw it as an unwelcome consequence of his intervention, is irrelevant at the stage of conviction where the question of control is crucial. (p. 122.)

Hart conceded, with some hesitation, that the distinction between direct and oblique intention might be relevant when determining the severity of punishment.

I have argued elsewhere[2] that even on a utilitarian theory of punishment there may be reason for distinguishing in the law of homicide between direct and oblique intention even at the stage of conviction. I will briefly return to the moral question later in the present paper. But the main question I wish to raise is not about the justification of the current law of homicide, but about its exact content. Assuming that Hart's paper gave an accurate account of the English law of homicide in 1967, does it remain exact as an account of the law today, after the 1974 decision of the House of Lords in *Hyam* v. *D.P.P.*?

In presenting the state of the law, Hart relied on the 1868 case *R.* v. *Desmond, Barrett and Others*. Barrett dynamited a prison wall in order to liberate two Fenians; the plot failed, but the explosion killed some persons living near by. It was clearly no part of Barrett's purpose, either as a means or an end, to kill or injure anyone, but he was convicted on the ground that he foresaw their death or serious injury. As the then Lord Chief Justice summed up, it is murder 'if a man did (an) act not with the purpose of taking life but with the knowledge or belief that life was likely to be sacrificed by it'. (pp. 119–20).

In *Hyam*'s case, Lord Hailsham of St. Marylebone, then Lord Chancellor, questioned whether any inference to the current state of the law could be drawn from *Desmond*. The words cited above, he pointed out, came after a passage in which the doctrine of constructive malice ('felony murder') had been expounded.

Like other 19th century cases, the direction given was at a time when no jury could have the prisoner's sworn testimony to consider, and when there was no adequate system of criminal appeal. Moreover, it is not really satisfactory to charge a jury on two parallel legal theories each leading to the same result and leave them with no means of saying which of the two their verdict is intended to follow. The jury itself may well have founded

---

[2] 'Intention and Purpose in Law', in R. S. Summers, *Essays in Legal Philosophy* (Oxford, 1968), pp. 146–63 esp. pp. 158–60. The arguments presented there were a modified version of those in an earlier paper (*Journal of Philosophy* 63 (1966)) searchingly criticized by Hart.

their verdict in *R.* v. *Desmond* entirely on the doctrine of constructive malice to which, at the time, the defence had, it would seem, no possible answer. [1974] 2 All E.R. 53.)

From several remarks in his speech it appeared that Lord Hailsham believed that since the abolition of constructive malice by the Homicide Act of 1957 a *direct* intention of some kind (to kill, say, or to cause grievous bodily harm) was necessary to constitute malice aforethought in murder. Thus he said 'I do not believe that know-ledge or any degree of foresight is enough' (p. 43). ' "Intention" is clearly to be distinguished alike from "desire" and from foresight of the probable consequence' (p. 52). 'I do not consider . . . that the fact that a state of affairs is correctly foreseen as a highly probable consequence of what is done is the same thing as the fact that the state of affairs is intended' (p. 52). Nor is it the case that foresight, if not identical with intent, is an alternative form of malice aforethought. 'I do not think that foresight as such of a high degree of probability is at all the same thing as intention, and, in my view, it is not foresight but intention which constitutes the mental element in murder' (p. 54). The innovation in Lord Hailsham's speech was the proposal that the list of intentions sufficient to constitute murder should include not only the intent to kill and the intent to cause grievous bodily harm, but also the intent to expose a potential victim to the serious risk of death or grievous bodily harm.

Lord Hailsham's speech, therefore, is of interest in the present context as setting out a view of intent in murder which is in direct opposition to that presented and defended by Professor Hart. But its interest is, of course, very much wider than an academic one. Because of the circumstances of its delivery in *Hyam*'s case it can be argued that it effected a significant change in law.

The verdict in *Hyam* was given by a majority of three to two. The other majority judges both accepted that oblique intention to kill or to cause grievous bodily harm was sufficient for malice aforethought in murder. Lord Dilhorne said:

Whether or not it be that the doing of the act with the knowledge that certain consequences are highly probable is to be treated as establishing the intent to bring about those consequences, I think it is clear that for at least 100 years such knowledge has been recognised as amounting to malice aforethought. [1974] 2 All E.R. 59.)

It was therefore not necessary to decide whether such knowledge amounted to intent; but Lord Dilhorne was inclined to think that it did. Lord Cross of Chelsea conceded that in a strict sense of intention foresight of consequences that are less than certain does not constitute intention. But foresight of death or grievous bodily harm was none the less sufficient for malice aforethought:

The first question to be answered is whether if an intention to kill—using intention in the strict sense of the word—is murder—as it plainly is—doing an unlawful act with knowledge that it may well cause death ought also to be murder. I have no doubt whatever that it ought to be. On this point I agree entirely with the view expressed by Cockburn C.J. in the passage in his summing up in *R.* v. *Desmond.* . . . I think that it is right that the doing of an act which one realises may well cause grievous bodily harm should also constitute malice aforethought whether or not one realises that one's act may endanger life. [1974] 2 All E.R. 71.)

In *Hyam* therefore we have a situation parallel to the unsatisfactory one to which Lord Hailsham drew attention in *Desmond*: the appeal was dismissed on the basis of three different parallel theories of intent and malice aforethought. But of the three theories the one which is crucial to study with a view to seeing the effect which the *ratio decidendi* of *Hyam* will have on the future history of the English law of homicide is that of Lord Hailsham. For, as I hope to show, it is that theory which draws the definition of murder in the narrowest manner: and though the actions of the appellant Hyam fell within the definition of murder on all three theories, it is not hard to think of cases which would be murder according to the accounts of Lords Dilhorne and Cross, but not according to Lord Hailsham's proposal.

Lord Hailsham did not in presenting his opinion make use of Bentham's distinction between direct and oblique intention, but at least in the first part of his speech it is obvious that it is direct intention that he has in mind. He distinguished between intention on the one hand and motive (in the sense of 'emotion prompting an act') and purpose (in the sense of 'ultimate end of a course of action') on the other (pp. 51–2). Direct intention, which is the intending something as a means *or* as an end, is likewise to be distinguished from motive and purpose in the senses in question. Lord Hailsham went on: 'Intention . . . embraces, in addition to the end, all the necessary consequences of an action including the means to the end and any consequences intended along with the end' (p. 52). This makes clear that intention for Hailsham, like direct intention for Bentham, includes means as well as ends. To clarify his position further Lord Hailsham quoted with approval the definition of 'intention' given by an earlier judge in a civil case:

An 'intention' to my mind connotes a state of affairs which the party 'intending'—I will call him X—does more than merely contemplate: it connotes a state of affairs which, on the contrary, he decides, so far as in him lies, to bring about and which, in point of possibility, he has a reasonable prospect of being able to bring about, by his own act of volition.

This definition, which clearly would exclude merely oblique intention, is said by Lord Hailsham to be a good definition for purposes of criminal law 'so long as it is held to include the means as well as the end and the inseparable consequences of the end as well as the means'. By 'inseparable consequences' he means those which follow with moral certainty from the achievement of the end. He cites an imaginary case from the Law Commission's disquisition on Imputed Intent: '. . . a man may desire to blow up an aircraft in flight in order to obtain insurance moneys. But if any passengers are killed he is guilty of murder, as their death will be a moral certainty if he carries out his intention' ([1974] 2 All E.R. 52).

Bentham, when he distinguished direct from oblique intention, did not consider the case of inseparable consequences. One might argue that these should count as merely obliquely intended, since foresight even with certainty, remains foresight, a cognitive and not a volitional state; or it might be argued that they should count as directly intended, since if a consequence is inseparable from an end it should count as part of the very same state of affairs as the desired outcome: in the case in point, blowing up the plane in flight just *is* killing the passengers, and a man should not be heard to say that he wanted the one but not the other. It is not necessary to inquire in which way Lord Hailsham would relate his terminology to Bentham's: what is clear is that if 'direct intention' is understood in this second way, then he can be said to be proposing that direct intent is necessary for murder.

There is little difficulty in applying the notion of direct intention, understood in this broad way, to the intention to kill or to cause grievous bodily harm. However, Lord Hailsham, while proposing a stricter requirement of directness of intent than his fellow judges, proposed also a broader interpretation of the content of the intent: namely, that not only the intent to kill, or the intent to cause grievous bodily harm, but also the intent to expose a potential victim to the serious risk of death or grievous bodily harm, should suffice for malice aforethought in murder. The question at once arises: is the intent to expose to risk that is here in question a direct intent, or does an oblique intent suffice? I do not find it altogether easy to answer this question in the light of Lord Hailsham's speech.

In the case of a defendant 'who knows that a proposed course of conduct exposes a third party to a serious risk of death or grievous bodily harm without actually intending those consequences, but nevertheless and without lawful excuse deliberately pursues that course of conduct regardless', Lord Hailsham says, 'there is not merely actual foresight of the probable consequences but actual intention to expose his victim to the risk.' It is hard to see how this is necessarily so, unless 'intention' as it occurs at the end of this quotation means 'oblique intention'. Quoting with approval Lord Reid's dictum 'a man who deliberately shuts his eyes to the truth will not be heard to say that he did not know it', Lord Hailsham asks, 'Cannot the same be said of the state of intention of a man who, with actual appreciation of the risks and without lawful excuse, wilfully decides to expose potential victims to the risk of death or really serious injury regardless of whether the consequences take place or not?' It is not at all clear what it would *be* to say the same about direct intention: when what we are considering is a volitional, not a cognitive state, what is the equivalent of shutting one's eyes? It is presumably pretending not to want what one in very truth does want. But a man who creates a risk of grievous bodily harm by an unlawful act may *genuinely* not want to create such a risk, in the sense that the creation of such a risk is neither an end of his, nor a means he chooses to an end, nor an inevitable consequence of such a means.[3] Of course, if Lord Hailsham in this passage is talking about *oblique* intention, then the relevance of the reference to shutting one's eyes to the truth becomes clear.

Lord Hailsham claims that his proposal does not bring back the doctrine of constructive malice, nor substitutes an objective for a subjective test of intent:

It simply proclaims the moral truth that if a man, in full knowledge of the danger involved, and without lawful excuse, deliberately does that which exposes a victim to the risk of the probable grievous bodily harm . . . or death, and the victim dies, the perpetrator of the crime is guilty of murder and not manslaughter to the same extent as if he had actually intended the consequence to follow, and irrespective of whether he wishes it. This is

[3] The appellant in *Smith* v. *D.P.P.* (1961) A.C. 290, for instance, if it is true that he 'merely swerved or zigzagged' his car 'to shake off the officer' who was trying to arrest him, and was horrified when he saw that he had caused the policeman to be run over.

because the two types of intention are morally indistinguishable, although factually and logically distinct . . . ([1974] 2 All E.R. 55.)

The principal difficulty is in seeing what are the two types of intention which are being claimed to be morally indistinguishable. Is it being claimed that there is no moral difference between the direct intention to do that which exposes a victim to the risk of grievous bodily harm or death and the direct intention to kill? Such a claim is surely extraordinary: any surgeon performing a difficult operation has a direct intention 'to do that which exposes a victim to the risk of grievous bodily harm or death'. (He does not, to be sure, have a direct intention, in the strictest sense, 'to expose a victim to the risk of grievious bodily harm'—it is not a means or end of his that the operation should be risky, and he will welcome any procedure which will diminish its riskiness—but the periphrasis 'to do that which exposes' was obviously chosen with care, and for good reason.) It would be even more preposterous to claim that there was nothing morally to choose between the *oblique* intention to do that which creates a risk and the *direct* intention to kill or cause serious harm. We are left with the possibility that Lord Hailsham's contrast is between two oblique intentions: the oblique intention to create the risk, and the oblique intention to kill or seriously harm. But that cannot be the correct interpretation of the passage, for it would render otiose the careful argumentation of the first part of the speech to the effect that foresight of death or grievous bodily harm does not suffice for malice aforethought.

It is only when he comes to apply his test to the case in hand that Lord Hailsham finally makes it clear beyond doubt that the intention to create the risk of grievous bodily harm, to suffice for malice aforethought, must be direct. The case was one in which the appellant Hyam, out of jealousy of another woman *B* who had supplanted her in the affections of her paramour, went to *B*'s house in the early hours of the morning, poured petrol through the letter box, stuffed newspaper through it and lit it, then went home leaving the house burning with the result that *B*'s two daughters were suffocated. Her defence was that she had set fire to the house only in order to frighten *B* into leaving the neighbourhood. Lord Hailsham said:

Once it is conceded that she was actually and subjectively aware of the danger to the sleeping occupants of the house in what she did . . . it must surely follow naturally that she did what she did with the intention of exposing them to the danger of death or really serious injury regardless of whether such consequences actually ensued or not. Obviously in theory, a further logical step is involved after actual foresight of the probability of danger is established. But in practice and in the context of this case the step is not one which, given the facts, can be seriously debated. ([1974] 2 All E.R. 56.)

If Lord Hailsham had been interested in the *oblique* intention to create a risk he could not have said that a further step was involved: for surely *no* step is involved in passing from 'I foresee that my actions make their death or serious injury probable' to 'I am aware that my actions are exposing them to a risk of death or serious injury.' The further step which Lord Hailsham mentions is the step between *seeing that* one is exposing to risk and *directly intending* to expose to risk. And surely he is right in saying that on the facts of this case there is no doubt that the intention as well as the foresight was present: as the appellant herself said, she wanted to frighten *B* into moving away from the neighbourhood; and the way she chose to frighten her was to put her and her family at serious risk.

But if we imagine the facts of the case slightly altered, an equally risky action might not have been an intentional placing at risk. Suppose that in order to vent her hatred of *B* Hyam had stolen all the love-letters and keepsakes exchanged between *B* and her own lover and had set them alight in *B*'s doorway with petrol; and suppose that the house had been burnt down as before and the children been killed. Here there would not necessarily have been any direct intention to set at risk. It is in a case such as this, it seems to me, that Lord Hailsham's *ratio decidendi* in *Hyam* would lead to an acquittal on a charge of murder, while the *ratio decidendi* of Lords Dilhorne and Cross of Chelsea would lead to a conviction (given that the accused realized it was highly probable that what she was doing would cause grievous bodily harm).

But we have not yet done justice to Lord Hailsham's full statement of his proposal. In answer to the question certified for appeal he put forward two propositions, of which the first runs:

Before an act can be murder it must be 'aimed at someone' as explained in *Director of Public Prosecutions* v. *Smith* (1961) A.C. 290, 327, and must in addition be an act committed with one of the following intentions, the test of which is always subjective to the actual defendant:
  (1) The intention to cause death
  (2) The intention to cause grievous bodily harm . . .
  (3) Where the defendant knows that there is a serious risk that death or grievous bodily harm will ensue from his acts, and commits those acts

deliberately and without lawful excuse, the intention to expose a potential victim to that risk as the result of those acts. . . .

Here, in addition to one of the various forms of intention we have hitherto discussed, there are two further elements required for malice aforethought: that the acts which result in death should be committed 'without lawful excuse' and that they should be 'aimed at someone'. From various passages in his speech it is clear that Lord Hailsham's final formulation takes the shape it does because he wishes to exclude from the definition of murder both the surgeon who performs a high risk operation and the motorist who kills on the road by dangerous driving, and because he wishes to include in the definition of murder the man who places a time bomb in an aeroplane to recover the insurance on its cargo when it blows up in flight.

Lord Hailsham devotes considerable thought to the question of the surgeon's intention, and he seems to give two quite different reasons why on his definition a surgeon would be free of malice aforethought. Early in his discussion he says:

The surgeon in a heart transplant operation may intend to save his patient's life, but he foresees as a high degree of probability that he will cause his death, which he neither intends nor desires, since he regards the operation not as a means to killing his patient, but as the best, and possibly the only, means of ensuring his survival. (p. 52.)

One can say equally that just as the surgeon does not intend to cause death, he does not intend—directly—to cause a risk to life. Hence he will not have any of the intentions which are required, on Hailsham's test, for *mens rea*. But later in his speech the Lord Chancellor said that the reason why the heart surgeon, exposing his patient to the risk, is not guilty is because he is 'not exposing his patient to the risk without lawful excuse or regardless of the consequences'. This move seems both unnecessary and dangerous. It is unnecessary because once it is recognized that the surgeon does not directly intend the risk to the patient's life, there is no need to ask whether he has an excuse or not. It is dangerous, because if it is admitted that there can be a lawful excuse for intentionally creating a risk of life, the question must be raised what such excuses are and how far they extend: and Lord Hailsham, in marked contrast with the erudition he displayed on the topic of intent, did not feel it necessary, or did not find himself able, to quote a single case on the topic.

On the other hand, if we omit the proviso 'without lawful excuse' then it seems that the rather obscure phrase from *Smith* 'an unlawful and voluntary act aimed at someone' will be neither sufficient to catch the aeroplane time-bomber nor necessary to acquit the motor manslaughterer. The motor manslaughterer will already not be a murderer on the grounds that he has no intent to cause death, serious harm, or the risk of either; the aeroplane time-bomber will not be clearly caught because it is not clear that the act of putting a bomb on a cargo plane is 'aimed at someone'. This rather improbable person creates a problem precisely because he has no direct intent to kill or hurt anyone and 'aim' is a word which connotes, if any word does, directness of intent.

In spite of these difficulties and uncertainties, it seems to me that in proposing that direct intent rather than oblique be the test for *mens rea* in murder, and in introducing the notion of the wilful creation of a risk, Lord Hailsham has thrown a great deal of light on a confused and obscure area of English law. I wish to end this paper by suggesting a way in which Lord Hailsham's insights could be reformulated with certain modifications in a way which avoids the unclarities we have detected. But before doing so, I must turn for a while to the other main topic discussed by the House of Lords in *Hyam*, the content, not the directness of the intent: namely, whether for murder there was necessary an intent to kill (or to bring about a risk of death) or whether an intention to cause grievous bodily harm (or to bring about a risk of grievous bodily harm) sufficed.

Prior to *Hyam*, it had commonly been accepted that *R. v. Vickers* (1957) had established that, after, no less than before, the Homicide Act of 1957, killing with the intention to do some grievous bodily harm was murder. (There remained some degree of uncertainty about the precise nature of 'grievous' harm, which we can for our purposes ignore.) In a learned and keenly argued speech in *Hyam* Lord Diplock argued that *Vickers*, and *Smith* subsequently, had been wrong in allowing the intent to do grievous bodily harm as an alternative; they should have accepted the submission that in order to be guilty of murder an offender, if he did not intend to kill, must have intended or foreseen as a likely consequence of his act, that human life would be endangered. The decisions in those cases, he argued, were based on a misreading of the history of the doctrine of constructive malice from Lord Ellenborough's Act of 1803 (which made it a felony to wound people with intent to do them grievous bodily harm) right up to the Homicide Act of 1957 (which abolished the doctrine of constructive malice which had made it murder to kill in furtherance of a felony). The House of Lords should now overrule *Vickers* and *Smith* and take the opportunity, which had been lost in those cases, to restrict the relevant intention on a charge of murder to an intention to kill or to cause a bodily injury known to be likely to endanger life.

Lord Kilbrandon agreed in this with Lord Diplock. The majority, however, refused to overturn *Vickers*. Lord Hailsham said:

If at this stage we were to overthrow the decision in *Vickers* a very high proportion of those now in prison for convictions of murder must necessarily have their convictions set aside and verdicts of manslaughter substituted. This consideration ought not perhaps logically to affect our decision, but I am personally relieved to find that I find myself in agreement with the decision in *Vickers*. ([1974]2 All E.R. 46.)

Apart from this consideration, which he very properly set aside, Lord Hailsham did not offer any argument in favour of the *Vickers* decision; and he admitted that 'technically this decision only rejected the ingenious argument of some academic lawyers that by enacting section 1 of the Homicide Act 1957, Parliament, despite the express words of the section, had inadvertently got rid of the doctrine of implied malice as well as constructive malice'. But of course if the intent to endanger life, and that alone, were allowed as an alternative to the intent to kill as *mens rea* for murder, then implied malice would remain a possibility.

Lord Dilhorne agreed with Lord Hailsham about the correctness of the decision in *Vickers*; but he drew attention to a paragraph in the 1953 report of the Royal Commission on Capital Punishment. 'We should therefore prefer to limit murder to cases where the act by which death is caused is intended to kill or to "endanger life" or is known to be likely to kill or endanger life' (p. 62). 'Our task', he went on, 'is to say what, in our opinion, the law is, not what it should be.' The intent to cause grievous bodily harm should therefore not be taken to be restricted to the intent to endanger life. 'To change the law to substitute "bodily injury known to the offender to be likely to cause death" for "grievous bodily harm" is a task that should, in my opinion, be left to Parliament if it thinks such a change expedient' (p. 62).

The third majority judge, Lord Cross of Chelsea, took an unusual course. He declared that he was unprepared to decide between the rival opinions of Lord Dilhorne and Lord Diplock about the correctness of *Vickers*. He went on: 'For my part, therefore, I shall content myself with saying that on the footing that *R. v. Vickers* was rightly decided the answer to the question put to us should be "Yes" and that this appeal should be dismissed' (p. 639). I do not know what the precedents are for such conditional rulings. But to the layman it appears that whatever *Hyam* may have decided, one thing it did not decide was that *Vickers* was correct, since two judges thought it was, two thought it was not, and one refused to say.[4]

Shortly after the decision in *Hyam* I wrote as follows:

> To the layman it seems a pity that the House of Lords did not combine the insights of both Lord Hailsham and Lord Diplock and define the *mens rea* for murder as being the direct intention to kill or to create a serious risk of death. If, as Lords Diplock and Kilbrandon believed, and as Lord Cross of Chelsea professed himself willing to believe, it was open to the court to reverse *Vickers* and *Smith*, then in restricting the content of murderous intent to killing and endangering life the House would have made the law of murder take the form which, in the opinion of all of them, and of all who have tried to codify the English law of homicide, it *ought* to take. And in restricting the nature of *mens rea* to direct intention instead of allowing it to embrace foresight they would have brought greater conceptual clarity into the law and brought legal terminology more closely to common parlance.[5]

Further reflection on the speeches of the judges in *Hyam* has made me think that it is possible to argue that the case has actually left the law in the state which I then described as a desirable position for which the opportunity has been lost. Because of the even division on the topic of *Vickers* it will be open for the House of Lords in future, and perhaps even for the Court of Appeal if not for a lower court, to rule against it. Because the *ratio decidendi* to which the Lord Chancellor appealed demanded that there should be direct and not oblique intention for malice aforethought, it will henceforth be open to an accused, who caused death by an act which he foresaw but did not intend to be likely to cause death, to plead that he lacked the necessary *mens rea* for a conviction of murder.

Whether or not this *is* the state of the law—and obviously that is in the end a question for the lawyer, not for the philosopher—I have no doubt it would be a good thing if it was. Murder would then be definable as doing an act which causes death with the intent either to

---

[4] I observe that the first question which follows the setting out of *Hyam* in the current edition of Smith and Hogan's *Criminal Law: Cases and Materials* (London, 1975) is 'What is the status of Vickers? Is it binding on (i) trial judges? (ii) the Court of Appeal?' (p. 355).

[5] *Will, Freedom and Power* (Oxford, 1976), p. 67.

kill or to create a serious risk of death: the intent in each case to be direct. The intent to kill should be taken to include the (direct) intent to bring about a state of affairs from which one knows death will certainly follow.

This definition will enable us to decide all the difficult cases in the way which—to me as to Lord Hailsham—intuitively seems correct. The surgeon in a risky operation will lack malice aforethought, if his patient dies, because he had no direct intent to kill or endanger him; there will be no need to invoke the sinister concept of 'lawful excuse'. The man who blows up the plane for the insurance money will be guilty of murder when the passengers are killed, because though he did not directly intend to kill or endanger life, he directly intended to bring about a state of affairs of which he knew death was the certain consequence.

The other cases which preoccupied their Lordships, namely terrorist bombings, would commonly not be difficult to bring under the definition proposed: the paradigm case of terrorist bombing is where the bombing is in order to spread terror precisely by creating widespread risk to life and limb. Where the creation of risk to life is not part of the plan, and therefore nor directly intended—as may be shown, for instance, by the placing of the bomb in a particular case, or by the nature of the precautions taken—then surely death which may result *should* not be taken as murder.

If this is the law, or if this were to become the law in England, that would be a significant change from the state which Hart, in the paper from which we began, regarded as a particularly fortunate one. I think that it would be a change for the better, not only because in cases of murder it would provide a simple and clear *ratio decidendi* which would accord with what Hart himself agrees to be the common man's notion of 'intention', but because it would be morally preferable to the state of the law as left by the Homicide Act, *Vickers*, and *Smith*. The Law Commission said in 1967 'In our view the essential element in murder should be willingness to kill, thereby evincing a total lack of respect for human life'. This seems to me correct. Unfortunately, the Law Commission's own definition of 'willingness to kill' was such as to make it tantamount to mere foresight of the likeliness of death: for it seems that if a man foresees death as a likely result of his actions, but does not therefore desist from his actions, he is willing for them to kill.[6] However, the Law Commission, like Lord Hailsham,

[6] See my 'Intention and Purpose in Law', p. 162.

was expressly anxious not to allow mere foresight to constitute the appropriate malice aforethought. The definition I have suggested enables us to capture the 'willingness to kill' which should be the essential element in murder in such a way that it does not collapse into mere foresight.

10

The Grounds of Responsibility

J. L. MACKIE*

'AN action is voluntary when what the agent does is controlled by his will; or, when what he wants straightforwardly determines what he does; or, when his desires issue in action.' It would be natural to give some such account as these, preserving the etymological connection between 'voluntary' and will, want, or desire, but also somehow indicating the double relation between the wanting and what is done, that the former both brings about the latter and is fulfilled by it. And we could sketch a related but more complicated account of intentional action. But Professor Hart (in the lectures and essays collected in *Punishment and Responsibility*) repeatedly criticizes accounts of this sort, on two main grounds. He does not believe that such an analysis can be coherently developed or applied in an illuminating way. But also, even in so far as it does point correctly to certain psychological elements, it focuses attention on the wrong things. What is important as a ground for liability to legal penalties is not that agents should ' "have in their minds" the elements of foresight or desire for muscular movement. These psychological elements are not *in themselves* crucial. . . . What is crucial is that those whom we punish should have had, when they acted, the normal capacities, physical and mental, for doing what the law requires . . . and a fair opportunity to exercise those capacities'. (*Punishment and Responsibility*, p. 152; all page references in the sequel are to this volume.) Capacity and opportunity, Professor Hart holds, are what matter, rather than foresight and the execution of desire as such. He thinks that mistakes about this have fostered bad arguments against responsibility for negligence and have delayed the recognition of other ways in which diminished capacities for self-control should limit responsibility. But I believe that what I have called the natural account can be defended against such objections.

* Fellow of University College, Oxford.

For the sake of clarity, let us introduce a distinction like that commonly drawn between a fact and a concrete event, and enshrine it rather arbitrarily in the words 'act' and 'action'. Acts, like facts and results, will be tied tightly to descriptions, though to gerundival phrases rather than to that-clauses: an act will always be the act of doing or bringing about such-and-such. An action will be the whole concrete performance, which will incorporate or involve as many acts as there are non-equivalent true descriptions of it. Then instead of saying, as we might have said without this distinction, that an action may be intended or intentional under one description but not under another which also applies to it, we can say simply that it is acts and results, not actions, that are intended or intentional, or that fail to be so, and that the same action can involve some acts that are intended and some that are not. We also need Bentham's distinction between what is directly intended, either as an end aimed at or as a means to such an end, and what is obliquely intended either as a second effect of a means or as a further consequence of an end, including as obliquely intended both results which the agent foresees with certainty and ones which he sees as likely to follow what he directly intends. *Mens rea* must relate, like intention, to specific acts or charges: the agent's *mens* can be *rea* with regard to a particular *actus reus*—which is an act, not an action—only if he intended that act either directly or obliquely.

In 'Acts of Will and Responsibility' Professor Hart examines the theory that besides the knowledge of circumstances and foresight of consequences required for *mens rea* there is another, more funda-mental, psychological, element required for responsibility, that the 'conduct' (including omissions) must be 'voluntary'; this is more fundamental in that it may still be required for offences of strict liability where *mens rea* or even inadvertent negligence is not. He agrees that there is in non-voluntary conduct some kind of defect, different from and more fundamental than lack of knowledge and foresight, but he finds obscure such phrases as 'acts of will', conduct 'not governed by the will', and the like, which have been used in attempts to describe it. There is, he notes, a theory which would give such phrases an exact meaning, which was expounded clearly, early in the nineteenth century, by Dr. Thomas Brown and, following him, by John Austin, remnants of which have come down into the legal textbooks. This theory is that a human action, strictly speaking, is 'merely a muscular contraction'—what are ordinarily called actions

are combinations of muscular movements and some of their consequences—and a voluntary action is a muscular contraction caused
by a pre-existing desire for that contraction. But, though simple and
clear, this account cannot, Professor Hart thinks, 'intelligibly or
correctly characterize . . . a minimum indispensable connexion
between mind and body present in all normal action and generally
required for responsibility' (p. 99). He criticizes it on two main
grounds, that it cannot account for the voluntariness and involun-
tariness of omissions, and that in ordinary positive actions desires for
muscular contractions do not occur. In its place he puts an account
which deals separately with positive interventions and omissions.
Involuntary movements are ones which 'were not appropriate, i.e.
required for any action (in the ordinary sense of action) which the
agent believed himself to be doing' (p. 105). An omission (for example
a failure to do some positive action demanded by the law) is involuntary if the agent either is unconscious and therefore unable to
perform any positive action or, though conscious, is unable to make
the particular movements required for the performance of the action
demanded by the law. In the Notes added later, Professor Hart
expresses dissatisfaction with this account of involuntary movements,
and suggests instead that the defective cases are 'those where the
bodily movements occurred though the agent had no reason for
moving his body in that way' (pp. 255–6). But this still seems wrong;
if a doctor is testing my knee-jerk reaction I may have a reason for
kicking up my leg—perhaps I want him to report that I am in sound
health—but the movement may still be involuntary. What would
make it voluntary is not my having a reason but my moving it for
that reason, and this leads us back towards the rejected theory of
movements caused by desires. The same is true of another phrase
Professor Hart uses, that involuntary movements are 'not subordinated to the agent's conscious plans of action' (p. 105).

Since it is difficult to formulate any stable alternative account, let
us look again at the Brown–Austin theory. This had two salient
features: the first, that it took something as both the object and the
causal product of the same desire; the second, that it identified this
something with a muscular contraction. Professor Hart's criticism is
fatal to this second feature, but it does not touch the first. (There is,
indeed, a well-known argument against the first feature, that a desire
is so logically connected with its object that they cannot also be
related as cause and effect. But this 'logical connection argument', it

is gradually being realized, is thoroughly fallacious. The fact that an adequate description of a desire will have to include a description of its object in no way prevents the desire and its object from being distinct occurrences, as a causal relation between them requires.) Let us see, then, if we can salvage this first feature while abandoning, as we must, the second—that is, find something other than a muscular contraction to play the double role of object and causal product of desire.

Suppose that I voluntarily shut a door. When I start to do this, I desire the result, the door's being shut, though perhaps only as a means to some further end. From long experience I know that I can shut the door and I know how to do so; hence when I desire the door's being shut and have no strong contrary motive I decide to shut the door; the movements that constitute my shutting of the door then take place and bring about that result. In such a straightforward case the desire leads causally to a pre-formed decision or intention to shut the door, this in turn leads causally to the appropriate muscular contractions and bodily movements, and these in turn to the door's being shut. I am normally aware of my bodily movements though not of the muscular contractions, but I do not normally desire or intend either of these. I do not need to. Long practice and habitually established skills enable me to bring about many results while thinking only about the result, not about any of the essential intermediate links in the causal chain.

This example suggests a general account: an action is voluntary if it incorporates some directly intended act, where a directly intended act is the bringing about of some result by a causal process which starts with a desire for that result and a decision to bring it about. The sense in which voluntariness is more fundamental than *mens rea* would then be that an action is voluntary if it incorporates *some* directly intended act, whereas there is *mens rea* only if the particular feature which is the *actus reus* is itself either directly or obliquely intended.

But this is not quite correct. First, the step of pre-formed decision or intention is not essential for voluntariness: an unopposed desire may lead directly to appropriate movements. I can just do something without deciding to do it. But, secondly, it is not necessary for voluntary action that any desired result should actually be realized. I want the door to be shut and in consequence begin the appropriate series of movements; but the door is jammed, so that I fail to shut it.

Though nothing that I desired has come about, those initial movements were voluntary. Though not themselves desired and not the object of any explicit decision, it is enough that they were such as would normally fulfil the desire that brought them about and that they came about because they were so associated with its fulfilment. They were what I had learnt to do in execution of such a desire, having been 'reinforced' in this respect by normal success. An action may be voluntary, then, even though nothing plays the double role of object and causal product of desire—the muscular contractions are not desired, and the result which is desired may not come about. It is enough that the action incorporates some movement which is (in the sense indicated) appropriate for the fulfilment of a desire that causally brings it about.

This resembles Professor Hart's formula that an action is involuntary if the movements that constitute it 'are appropriate to no action which [the agent] believes himself to be doing' (pp. 105–6). But there is the vital difference that in my account what the movements are to be appropriate to is the fulfilment of a desire that causes them, not just something that the agent believes he is doing, and the appropriateness can be explained by a more complex relation to that desire. Voluntariness is constituted by certain causal patterns in which desires play a leading role.

It is easy to check that this account gives the right answers in such cases of non-voluntary conduct as those listed by Professor Hart (pp. 95–6). It resembles what he calls a toned-down version of the Brown–Austin theory, which he admits to be 'broadly acceptable' but dismisses as 'not very informative' (p. 103). But I think that when it is spelled out a little more fully it gives just the information that we need to understand how voluntary positive actions differ from non-voluntary ones.

But it is still exposed to Professor Hart's other criticism, that it does not apply to omissions. Now an omission corresponds to what we have called an act rather than to an action, and even where the *actus reus* is an omission, it may be an aspect of a positive concrete action, and the latter can be voluntary in the way already explained. If I am driving a car in the normal way, while conscious, but go past a red light without noticing it, the *actus reus* is an omission, a mere negation, failing to stop, but all the time I have been doing something positive, maintaining a slight pressure on the accelerator, making small movements of the steering wheel, watching and responding to road conditions other than the unnoticed signal, and all this is (in the sense explained) appropriate to and a causal product of the desire that the car should proceed along the road. My failing to stop is merely a negative feature of a positive voluntary action. Of course, this does not make the omission itself voluntary. On the other hand if the omission is involved in a piece of positive behaviour which is itself non-voluntary, then *a fortiori* the omission will be non-voluntary.

Omissions, like positive acts, can be intended, either directly or obliquely, and will then be voluntary. But they can also be voluntary in a weaker, negative sense, that the failure to perform the omitted act was caused by the lack of any sufficiently strong desire. If the agent had had some sufficiently strong desire whose fulfilment would have involved the omitted act, or to whose fulfilment that act would have been appropriate, then it would have been performed in execution of that desire; so the omission can be causally ascribed to a lack of desire. Omissions which are involuntary in this sense will be so by Professor Hart's criteria too, since they will have to be causally ascribable to something other than either a desire or the lack of a desire, and this will be some lack of capacity or opportunity. But the converse may not hold. An omission could be voluntary in our sense but involuntary in Professor Hart's, since the lack of a desire that would have brought about the required action might itself be regarded, in some cases, as resulting from the lack of a capacity to form such a desire. Positive acts and actions can also be voluntary in this weaker sense: a habitual, semi-automatic, action may be causally ascribable not to any desire which it fulfils or to which it is appropriate, being a learned means to its fulfilment, but merely to the lack of any sufficiently strong desire. My aimless walking along the road is voluntary in that I would stop if I either wanted to stop or wanted to do something else.

The stronger and weaker senses of 'voluntary' are connected by the fact that in each case what is said to be voluntary is causally dependent upon what the agent wants: it is due to his wanting something or to his not wanting something strongly enough, and where it is due to his wanting something it is either a carrying out of what he wants or at least an appropriate step towards this.

This account of voluntariness, especially of the stronger, positive, sort, leads naturally to a further explanation of intending and intentionality. The central case is that of an act which is both directly intended and carried out. This is both the object and the causal product of a desire, but the intending combines with the desire the belief that the intending will lead straightforwardly to the fulfilment of the desire which it includes. There can be a bare intention to do something, where this combination of desire and belief occurs but the causal process stops short before it issues in any action. There can be intentions for the more distant future—I intend now to do something tomorrow—where the desire is for the future achievement and the belief is that this desire will persist until the specified time and will then lead to its own fulfilment. Attempts and doing something with some further intention also fit easily into this account.

The notion of something's being obliquely intended fits best into an admittedly ideal picture of a fully deliberate action. If an agent brings into consideration and weighs thoroughly everything he knows about the nature and circumstances and likely consequences of a proposed action, and performs the action as a result of this deliberation and in fulfilment of the decision in which it culminates, then he has intended a rather complex act which includes all the features of the action known to him. He has accepted its undesired or neutral components for the sake of the desired ones, knowing that he cannot have these without those. Aspects of the action which are not directly intended either as desired ends or as means may still be known parts of this complex intended act: it is in this that their being obliquely intended consists. But this is an ideal case, and as soon as we move from it to actions which are less deliberate, or impulsive, or result from passion, or rage, or terror, this description becomes less apt. An agent may have known that a certain further consequence would result from what he did, and yet through imperfect deliberation not have explicitly included it in the act which he literally intended. One can bring something about knowingly but not intentionally.

I think, then, that a coherent account of voluntariness and intentionality can be developed on fairly traditional lines and in a way that preserves the close connection between voluntariness and will, want, and desire. But does it lead, or allow, us to draw the boundaries of responsibility in the right places? Or is it easier to do this if we work, as Professor Hart recommends, with the notions of capacity and opportunity, asking 'Could he have done otherwise?' or 'Had he any real choice?'

One problem concerns duress and 'necessity'. Actions performed under duress or necessity—where acting otherwise would have led with practical certainty to the death of the agent himself, or of persons close to him, or to some similar disaster—are clearly voluntary in our stronger sense; but we may well feel inclined to excuse them on the ground that the agent had, in the circumstances, no real choice.

But though this is a colloquially natural way of speaking, it would be more accurate to say that he did have a choice but to spell out what that choice was—for example, between doing what some tyrant demanded and having his relatives safe, and defying the tyrant and having them tortured or killed. Though his being confined to just these alternatives was not voluntary, the agent's choosing one of these complex alternatives rather than the other was wholly voluntary and intentional. And to hold him responsible for his intentional act, adequately described, is appropriate and has no undesirable implications. Even if X is in itself morally wrong or dishonourable or illegal, it does not follow that X-rather-than-Y must be so.

Instead of taking duress or necessity as negating responsibility because it deprives the agent of any real choice, we should see each of these as helping to determine the precise act for which he is responsible, as adding justifying or mitigating circumstances to the description of what he intentionally did.

Another problem concerns the actions of the kleptomaniac, the compulsive drinker, the psychopath, and of one who executes a suggestion made under hypnosis. In some important sense each of these has no real choice, cannot do otherwise; yet his actions seem to be voluntary in terms of the proposed account, they carry some desires that he has into effect. But we may hope to identify some ground of responsibility that will make such people not responsible, or perhaps less than normally responsible, for these actions.

However, even if the question 'Could he have done otherwise?' gives the right answer in these cases, it gives it for the wrong reason. It is liable to mix up considerations relevant to the ordinary grounds of responsibility with the metaphysical problem of determinism and free will. If causal determinism holds, there is a sense in which no one could have done otherwise, and we need at least to do some work to distinguish the determinist's 'could not have done otherwise' from that which denies the ordinary grounds of responsibility. But, also, if we state the test in this way we may wonder why the compulsive drinker is not responsible for drinking whereas the compulsive mathematician presumably is to be given credit for his achievements, and likewise the compulsive reformer, the compulsive patriot, the compulsive scribbler, and the compulsive mountaineer.

An alternative explanation would qualify the voluntariness of certain actions by reference to one or both of two models, of which one impugns an agent's unity through time and the other his unity at any one time. First, what is a voluntary action of mine at a certain time may express motives which are very poorly representative of my relatively permanent character and personality; the self whose voluntary action it was may be less than normally continuous with my present self. 'I did it, but I wasn't myself at the time.' Secondly, we may follow Freud, or Plato, in comparing the mind of an individual with a society, and in distinguishing different groups of elements and different styles of interaction between them. There may be a central personality or ego within which desires and purposes interact by conscious deliberation that is an analogue of parliamentary debate, but other desires or impulses which arise in the same human being and which may causally determine and purposively control his movements, but which are outside this central personality and do not participate in this debate, but may either be 'censored' and suppressed or get their way by some less rational process. Thus a voluntary action of this human being may fail to be a voluntary action of his central personality.

Extreme variants of these two models work with the notion of an absolute self: my unity and identity are unequivocal, but completely alien spirits may fight with me for control of my limbs and sometimes take complete possession of my body. But the more plausible variants are built on the rejection of this metaphysical theory; they presuppose that such unity and identity as we have at the best of times depend upon connections and interactions and continuities which are themselves matters of degree. However, philosophical considerations could show only the possibility of these models. It must be an empirical question whether they are exemplified in particular cases or types of case. This will not be an easy question. No neat tests will directly decide the answer, and it is all too easy for someone to use one or other of these models as an excuse; but that does not prevent there being a real issue whether, or how far, they are exemplified. These models formulate questions which we should like psychologists to answer.

These models bring out, better than does the question 'Could he have done otherwise?', what is wrong about the actions of the kleptomaniac and the rest. The compulsive drinker at other times, and perhaps even when he is starting to drink, wishes that he did not get drunk, whereas the compulsive mathematician or mountaineer is on the whole happy with his addiction.

But the psychopath (or perhaps one kind of psychopath), the person who is quite lacking in sympathy and shows no capacity for moral feeling or moral reasoning, escapes both these accounts. His actions are, by our criteria, voluntary in relation to his whole permanent personality, whereas Professor Hart would say that they are not voluntary because he lacks the capacity for self-control. However, it is less confusing to say firmly that his actions are voluntary and his acts intentional, but that there may be other reasons for not holding him responsible, that voluntariness and intentionality are necessary but not sufficient conditions for legal responsibility. The reasons for not holding such a psychopath responsible are significantly different from those that cut other agents off from their unintended acts and non-voluntary actions. The psychopath is in some ways like a young child. Of him in particular it is plausible to say that he is not a moral agent; I shall try to show later how this bears upon legal responsibility.

Would our account lead us implausibly to rule out responsibility for negligence? Here we need some distinctions. If the agent foresees as likely certain harmful results of what he is about to do, but none the less deliberately goes ahead, and such results occur, then those results are themselves obliquely intended. If he is only vaguely and generally aware that harm of a certain sort could result from his carelessness, so that he knows that he is being negligent in that respect, it would be more accurate to say that his negligence itself is obliquely intended, but not its results. If we took it as a necessary condition of responsibility for a certain *actus reus* that that act should itself be intended, then this would exclude responsibility for the results of inadvertent negligence, though not for negligence itself. But if we took as our necessary condition for responsibility only voluntariness in the weaker sense, then there could be responsibility for the results of inadvertent negligence. Of these it may be true to say that if the agent had had a sufficiently strong desire that they should not come about he would have taken more care, and it is only where we can say this that it seems reasonable to impose responsibility for the results of negligence. (But I am not saying that voluntariness in the weaker sense, or even in the stronger, is in itself a sufficient condition of responsibility: as I have hinted with respect to psychopaths, there may be other grounds for excuse.)

Judgments about responsibility which are in themselves acceptable, and which indeed pretty well coincide with those which Professor Hart reaches by a different route, can be largely based on and at any rate reconciled with our version of the natural and traditional account of voluntariness and intentionality. But what of the charges that these psychological elements are not *in themselves* crucial, that what matters for liability for punishment is that those whom we punish should have had the normal capacities for doing what the law requires and opportunity to exercise them—in effect, that what matters is not so much what they did or how they did it, but what else they could have done? This charge is the more forceful since we have had to refer to a different principle to explain the non-responsibility of psychopaths, whereas this is already covered by Professor Hart's principles of capacity and opportunity.

Our view of what matters here will naturally depend upon our view of the aim and justification of legal penalties and of the point, in relation to these, of recognizing any excusing conditions. Bentham, having located this aim and justification in deterrence, tried to explain the excusing conditions by arguing that penalties which violated these restrictions would be ineffective in deterrence. But Professor Hart has shown that this argument is fallacious. Though one can be deterred only from voluntary acts (or omissions), one may be more effectively deterred by the annexing of penalties to all acts of a certain sort rather than just to the voluntary ones, since one might hope that one's own voluntary act might escape punishment by the false pretence that it was not voluntary. Alternatively, anyone who took retribution to be the aim and justification of legal penalties would naturally take the psychological elements to be what matters: it is only what an agent voluntarily does that can in itself deserve punishment. But Professor Hart also rejects this approach. He sees both legal penalties and the excusing conditions attached to them as parts of a compromise between the protection of society and the freedom of individuals, as elements in 'a method of social control which maximizes individual freedom within the coercive framework of law' (p. 23).

His argument is, I think, that penalties attached only to infringements of the law where the agent has the capacity and opportunity to comply with the law interfere less with individual freedom just because the agent can avoid them. This interpretation agrees with Professor Hart's use of the analogy between the mental conditions that excuse from criminal responsibility and those that invalidate wills, contracts, marriages, and the like (pp. 44–5). The function of these institutions of the private law is to carry individual preferences into effect, and the invalidating conditions tend to ensure that only genuine preferences, real choices, are thus made effective. Similarly, the excusing conditions maximize, within the coercive criminal law, 'the efficacy of the individual's informed and considered choice in determining the future and also his power to predict that future' (p. 46).

We must concede that individuals would be less free under a criminal law that did not recognize these excusing conditions, and also that there is some important analogy between these and the invalidating conditions in the civil law. But the analogy does not seem to hold in quite the suggested way. It is surely not that while the civil law tries to ensure that people enter into contracts, marriages, and the like only if they really want to, the criminal law tries to ensure that they go to jail only if they really want to. We must allow for the fact that whereas the aim of the civil law is to carry bequest-making choices, contract-making choices, and so on into effect, the aim of the criminal law is not to carry law-breaking choices into effect but to discourage them.

Let us, then, take this as the starting point of our explanation, noting that the criminal law is addressed primarily to rational agents who are presumed in general to have some tendency to respect the law. It seeks to regulate conduct in the first place by attaching an adverse legal characterization to certain types of voluntary and especially intentional acts and omissions, some but not all of which also have adverse moral characterizations. This legal characterization is the primary thing: it is intended to—and to a considerable extent does—control conduct independently of any sanction. Deterrence and penalties for non-compliance are secondary, reinforcing the motive of direct respect for the law. If we ask why, given that there is a social need for the regulation of conduct, we should have a device of this rather than of some other sort, the answer will be that it has many merits, but one of them is that it represents the compromise of which Professor Hart speaks between individual freedom and the protection of society. But this is an answer not to the more special question, why recognize excusing conditions, but to the very basic

question, why work with a law that is addressed primarily to rational
—and socially rational, not just egoistically rational—agents. Given
that this is the nature of the (criminal) law, and that penalties are
intended only to back up the immediate discouragement of adverse
legal characterization, it follows that penalties will be appropriate
only in so far as they are attached to the very items to which those
adverse characterizations are first assigned, that is, choices, or
voluntary and especially intentional acts and omissions. To be
punishable an act must first be legally wrong. Most of the excusing
conditions then follow immediately: they are signs of the absence of
intentional or at least voluntary acts to which adverse legal characterizations are typically applied. The true analogy between the
invalidating mental conditions in civil law and the excusing conditions
in criminal law is then this: they both negate the positive psychological
feature of action in fulfilment of desires which fairly represent the
agent as a coherent person, while it is contract-making (and the like)
with this feature to which the civil law seeks to give effect, and
harm-doing with this feature which the criminal law seeks to
discourage.

The psychopath who is 'not a moral agent' stands outside this
system of social control. Adverse legal characterizations do not make
sense to him, because he lacks moral responses with which they could
be linked. Punishing him may indeed help to deter others, but it
cannot have any of the normally intended effects on the psychopath
himself.

Of the psychopath, then, it is correct to say that he is not responsible
because he lacks the normal capacities for doing what the law requires.
But this is a very different reason from that which makes people
non-responsible for their non-voluntary actions and, in general, for
their unintended acts, and different even from the reasons for which
we may excuse the kleptomaniac and others whose actions, though
voluntary, are not voluntary actions of their relatively permanent
central personality. I think it is confusing to group all these different
excusing conditions under the heading of lack of capacity or opportunity, and to take as the decisive test such questions as 'Could he
have done otherwise?', 'Had he any real choice?', which misleadingly
suggest that if causal determinism—or even some approximation to
it—holds the essential requirement for legal responsibility is negated.

If we ask 'Why should we not punish unintended and even non-
voluntary harmful acts and omissions, or the voluntary and intended

acts of those who are not moral agents?', then Bentham's answer 'Because this would be ineffective as deterrence and would therefore be just useless further harm' is both false and irrelevant. A more relevant answer is retributivist in form, 'Because none of these acts is of the sort that can be legally wrong.' But we can go further and ask about the point of a system which works primarily by the legal characterization of voluntary and intentional acts of socially rational agents, and Professor Hart's stress on a compromise between individual freedom and the protection of society will be part of the answer to this basic question. But if it is here rather than as a direct answer to our previous question that Professor Hart's point is in place, the positive psychological elements of voluntariness and intentionality—an essentially traditional but slightly modified account of which I gave in the first part of this article—are crucial *in themselves*, not simply as signs of capacities and opportunites. The capacities summed up in the phrase 'moral agent' are indeed also crucial. But since these different factors are crucial in different ways, it is more illuminating to distinguish them than to run them together under a single heading; and our account will be less exposed to irrelevant intrusions if we ground responsibility on what a certain sort of agent did and how he did it then on the possibility of his having acted otherwise.

11

Rights in Legislation

D. N. MACCORMICK*

THERE must be many for whom the beginnings of wisdom in the understanding and analysis of legal systems and legal concepts have been found in the lectures and the writings of H. L. A. Hart. Being one of whom that is true, I take particular pleasure in joining in the tributes to him in this *Festschrift* by presenting an essay on the subject of 'Rights', upon which subject he has had so many illuminating things to say during his career.[1] While I shall here advance a thesis which is fundamentally at variance with Hart's own account of rights, I cannot claim to be doing more than applying techniques learned from Hart in criticizing and (I hope) transcending that account of his.

I

The first point to be made about legal rights must seem, when made, to be of breath-taking banality. The point is that legal rights are conferred by legal rules, or (if you will) by laws.[2] What could be more obvious? Obvious as it may be, the point is one which has not been given sufficient weight in much of what has been written by legal theorists. The point being made that legal rights are conferred by legal rules, it should at once lead any jurist of the school of Hart to ask the question: 'What are the general characteristics of those legal rules which confer rights upon individuals—as distinct from imposing duties, granting powers, or whatever?' (In *The Concept of Law*, for example, Hart quite rightly contends that to expound the meaning of

---

* Regius Professor of Public Law, University of Edinburgh.

[1] Hart's most interesting contributions on this subject in my opinion are: 'Definition and Theory in Jurisprudence', 70 *Law Quarterly Review* 37 (1954) at 47 f.; 'Bentham', *Proceedings of the British Academy* 48 (1962), 297; 'Are There Any Natural Rights', reprinted in *Political Philosophy*, ed. A. M. Quinton (Oxford, 1968); 'Bentham on Legal Rights' (herinafter cited as 'B.L.R.') in *Oxford Essays in Jurisprudence*, 2nd series, ed. A. W. B. Simpson (Oxford, 1973).

[2] Cf. J. Raz, *The Concept of a Legal System* (Oxford, 1970), pp. 175–83.

terms such as 'duty' and 'obligation' one must first show that any particular obligation or duty arises in virtue of some legal rule, and one must then complete one's exposition by elucidating the general characteristics of those rules which impose duties or obligations.)[3]

That question which ought to be asked has not been asked and answered with clarity, partly indeed because of a false trail laid by the master himself in 'Definition and Theory in Jurisprudence', in which he based a famous account of the meaning and use of the term 'right' upon the supposition that the term was standardly used in sentences such as '*x* has a legal right to . . .' which, as he put it, express 'conclusions of law'. The meaning of the phrase was thus best elucidated by explaining the conditions in which the statement '*x* has a legal right' can be appropriately used as expressing a *true* conclusion of law. Such conditions are presupposed by, though not expressed in, the statement itself.[4]

All that depended upon a view which Hart used to state in his (unpublished) lectures on 'Legal Rights and Duties', delivered in Oxford in the early 1960s, the view that 'right' is a term used in discourse *about* the law, used for making statements *about* individual's positions as seen in terms of the law, rather than a term used *in* the law itself. 'Right' in this view is a term or concept used by the jurist or the commentator upon the law, used discursively, but not used dispositively in the law. The derivation from that view of the theory that 'expressing conclusions of law' is the *standard* use of the term is obvious enough.

At a quite simple empirical level, these assumptions underlying the early Hartian analysis can be falsified completely. The term 'right' and its congeners is in fact used regularly and frequently in dispositive legal utterances and documents. Consider for example section 2(1) of the Succession (Scotland) Act 1964:

Subject to the following provisions of this Part of this Act—
(a) where an intestate is survived by children, they shall have right to the whole of the intestate estate.
(b) . . .

Of that Act, indeed, the first eight sections alone, comprising Part I of the Act, use the word 'right' twenty-four times, a tally which would be greatly swollen were one to incur the labour of counting its appearances throughout the whole Act. And if it were desired to

---

[3] H. L. A. Hart, *The Concept of Law* (Oxford, 1961), esp. at pp. 82–6.
[4] 'Definition and Theory in Jurisprudence', pp. 49 f.

demonstrate that this is by no means an entirely Caledonian eccentricity of the Scottish draftsman, one might cite a plethora of examples from the English property legislation of 1925, such as section 96(1) of the Law of Property Act 1925 which indeed piles entitlement *expressis verbis* on top of no less explicit 'right'.

A mortgagor, so long as his right to redeem subsists, shall be entitled from time to time, at reasonable times, on his request, and at his own cost, and on payment of the mortgagee's costs and expenses in this behalf, to inspect and make copies or abstracts of or extracts from the documents of title relating to the mortgaged property in the custody or power of the mortgagee . . .

There is no need for further multiplication of examples such as these; they show conclusively that the language of 'rights' and of being 'entitled' is as well adapted to stating general premisses of law (and indeed to establishing them by legislation) as it is to expressing particular conclusions of law. In fact to establish the conclusion that *A* (a Scotsman) has the right to a certain 'intestate estate' or that *B* (an Englishman) is entitled to make copies of certain documents of title held by a Building Society as mortgagee, one would have to refer to the rules of law in s.2(1) of the Succession (Scotland) Act and s.96(1) of the Law of Property Act. If the 'investitive facts' as set out in these and related provisions are satisfied in *A*'s or in *B*'s case, then each has indeed the right in question. But the premisses from which the conclusions as to individual rights follow are rules which expressly purport to confer the postulated right on persons in general whenever the relevant investitive facts are realized. An inquiry into the nature of rights must therefore be an inquiry into the nature and character of the legal rules which concern the conferment of legal rights.

One characteristic which it would be a mistake to postulate as a necessary distinguishing feature of rules which confer rights would be that of expressly using the term 'right'. Consider section 46(ii) of the Administration of Estates Act 1925, which is in the following terms:

The residuary estate of an intestate shall be distributed in the manner or be held on the trusts mentioned in this section, namely:
. . . .
(ii) If the intestate leaves issue but no husband or wife, the residuary estate of the intestate shall be held on the statutory trusts for the issue of the intestate.

The effect of that provision is very broadly similar to the effect of section 2(1)(a) of the Succession (Scotland) Act quoted above. But in this case the statute confers a right without saying so *expressis verbis*. While it is wrong to suppose that legislative provisions never speak of 'rights', it would be equally wrong to suppose that they always do whenever rights are being conferred.

II

Legal theorists have traditionally divided into two camps on the issue of the proper explanation of rights.[5] One line of thought, which may be called the 'will theory', asserts that an individual's having a right of some kind depends upon the legal (or, *mutatis mutandis*, moral) recognition of his will, his choice, as being preeminent over that of others in relation to a given subject matter and within a given relationship. The 'interest theory', by contrast, contends that what is essential to the constitution of a right is the legal (or moral) protection or promotion of one person's interests as against some other person or the world at large, by the imposition on the latter of duties, disabilities, or liabilities in respect of the party favoured. It is against the background of this clash of theories that we must pursue the question announced as to the general characteristics of those rules which confer legal rights. Are these to be conceived primarily in terms of giving a special status to the choice of one individual over others in relation to a given subject matter, or primarily in terms of the protection of the interests of individuals against possible forms of intrusion (or the advancement in other ways of individuals' interests)?

The answer which I shall offer to that question will be that the 'interest theory' is the more acceptable, though not to be accepted without modification. The essential feature of rules which confer rights is that they have as a specific aim the protection or advancement of individual interests or goods. The reasons for holding that view, and the necessary refinements of the view itself, can best be set out by showing the defects of the rival view, and so I shall proceed to expound, and criticize, what seems to me the strongest version of the

[5] For a review of opposed theories see, e.g., G. W. Paton, *A Text-Book of Jurisprudence*, 4th edn. (Oxford, 1972, ed. G. W. Paton and D. P. Derham), at pp. 285–90. Cf. also W. J. Kamba, 'Legal Theory and Hohfeld's Analysis of a Legal Right', [1974] *Juridical Review* 249–62.

In 'B.L.R.' Hart expounds Bentham's theory as an instance of 'interest theory' or (*per* Hart) 'benefit theory'; and he asserts the preferability of his own version of 'will theory' or, as he prefers to call it, 'choice theory'.

'will theory', that advanced by Professor Hart[6] (appropriately enough to the present occasion).

(i) One class of rights is the class of rights which have correlative duties. Duties exist when there exist legal or social rules of a particular kind, in virtue of which individuals in certain circumstances are required to act or abstain from acting in certain ways. For any individual whose circumstances are an instance of those specified in the rule, it is true to say that he has a duty to act or abstain from acting as specified.

Of those rules which impose duties, some provide that the performance of the duty-act is to be conditional upon some other person's choice, either in the sense that it is to be performed only if and when he so requests, or in the sense that the other person can waive the requirement, and, if he does, the act (or abstention) need not be performed. When *A*'s duty is in either sense made conditional upon *B*'s choice, *B* may properly be said to have a right against *A*, a right that *A* act or abstain in the manner laid down in the rule. So also, when it is the case that in the event of *A*'s breach of duty *B* has the power to take appropriate remedial action at law, at least if *B* has a discretion as to the use or non-use of that power.

Thus, for this class of right (sometimes called 'claim rights'[7] or 'rights of recipience'[8]) the 'will theory' asserts that what is constitutive of rights is the way in which the law confers on certain individuals or classes of individuals power to waive or enforce the duties of other individuals, or other classes of individuals.

(ii) There are other classes of rights, for example liberty rights and power rights, in case of which the right-holder is, so to say, the active rather than the passive subject of the law. In so far as the law imposes no duty on me not to do so, I have a right to speak my mind (and you have no right that I should hold my tongue)—and that is a 'liberty right', a right constituted by freedom from legal duty to act or abstain in some specified way. What is more, it is sometimes the case that my acting in a certain way is not merely not impeded by the law, but is indeed recognized by law as achieving a certain change in the legal position of myself, or others, or both; for example, when an utterance of mine (intended as such) is recognized as a declaration of

[6] Variously in the works cited in n.1 above.

[7] Cf. W. N. Hohfeld, *Fundamental Legal Conceptions* (New Haven, 1919; 3rd reprint, 1964); for variants of nomenclature, see W. J. Kamba, op. cit.

[8] The term favoured by D. D. Raphael, in *Problems of Political Philosophy* (London, 1970), pp. 68–71.

trust in favour of some other person over certain property. Such is a case of 'power right'.

In both these cases, yet more obviously than in the case of 'claim right' it is the law's recognition of the freedom or the legal efficacity of the choices of individuals which is central to the notion of 'a right'.

(iii) A further class of 'right', the so-called 'immunity right' presents on the face of it more difficulty for the will theory. This is the right which corresponds to lack of power in others. It may be the case not only that I have a (liberty) right to enter my place of work and to do my job, and a (claim) right to be paid for it, but also that I have a right not to be dismissed save on certain specified grounds proven by certain stipulated processes, and that because my employer cannot *validly* dismiss me from my job, because he has a disability to sack me. And so by way of general characterization of immunity rights we may say that whenever A's legal position is in certain respects protected from change by any act of B, in the sense that B lacks power to change it, A has an immunity (as against B) from having his legal position changed in that respect.

Professor Hart admits to a certain difficulty in accommodating 'immunity rights' within his over-all theory.[9] But he suggests that the characteristic manifestation of immunity rights within the law is their manifestation in constitutionally entrenched 'Bills of Rights' which protect various claims and freedoms against derogation or abrogation even by acts of legislation. He therefore regards these as being beyond the ordinary interests of the lawyer and belonging more to the province of the political or moral theorist. While some theory of rights other than that given by will theorists might be necessary to account for such entrenched immunities, the fact (it is alleged) remains that the specific terminology of 'rights' is of peculiar utility to lawyers only when restricted to those instances of 'small-scale sovereignty' which the will theory takes to be constitutive of the notion of 'a right'—and to be the unifying thread among various types of right.

(iv) Subject to that qualification, it is asserted that what gives the concept 'right' its particular function and utility in legal language is that it draws attention to those relationships in which rules of law confer on one individual special recognition of his will or choice as

---

[9] See 'B.L.R.', pp. 198–200.

predominating over that of others in the relationship. Such are the outlines of the theory which in the succeeding sections of the present essay I intend to refute.

III

There is something, on the face of it, odd about Hart's concession that immunities cannot be properly taken into account within the four corners of the 'will theory' as propounded by himself. For it is often the case that A's immunity is waivable by A's choice. If A owns a car, B cannot divest him of ownership by any unilateral act (if B is another private citizen); in other words, A's rights over the car are in this respect protected by (or do they simply include?) an immunity against B. But, of course, A's immunity from being divested of ownership in favour of B is not absolute, but conditional on his own choice to transfer or not transfer the property—otherwise sale, exchange, and gift would be impossible.

That being so, it follows that there is a class of immunities which could comfortably be brought within the Hartian version of the will theory, namely, the whole class of those immunities in relation to which the immunity-holder has a power of waiver. Looked at from the other party's point of view, from the point of view of the party B who is under a disability to alter A's legal position in some respect, such a disability may be absolute (B cannot enslave A, even if A should consent to be enslaved); or it may be conditional upon A's will; A has a right not to be assaulted by B, and B can't take that away from A, unless A agrees—for example, in a boxing match.

In the light of those facts, the reasonable extrapolation to make from Hart's thesis in relation to claims, liberties, and powers would be along the lines of including within the genus 'rights' only those immunities which lie within the immunity-holder's own power, those which he can waive or assert at will. Such would be 'immunity rights' (a species of the genus 'rights'); unwaivable immunities would belong outside of the genus 'rights'.

But surely the moment we make that extrapolation we hit upon the fundamental implausibility of the 'will theory'. It seems to me unproblematic to say that I have (legally and morally) a right not to be deprived of my personal freedom and a right not to be deprived of my property. The two rights seem to me to be on all fours with each other, at any rate when we are concerned with the propriety of using the noun 'right' in the statement of such propositions of law (or of morals); in my view, which I believe to be widely held, the former right is of greater importance than the latter—I would rather, if it came to the bit, be propertyless than be a slave. The laws of the U.K. certainly place a higher value on the right of freedom than on the right of property in a certain highly important respect: the former is regarded as absolute in the sense that no person can enslave any other, not even a person willing to be enslaved; whereas the latter is conditional upon the property-holder's will—no person can deprive another of his property *without his consent*.

Let us take note of the point. *A*'s right to personal freedom involves *B* in having (a) a duty not to reduce *A* to a servile condition, e.g. by clapping him in irons; and (b) a disability to impose upon *A* the status of a slave; and (c) a disability to change the relation (a) and (b) *even with A's consent*. *A* does not himself have power to waive his immunities in these respects—he too is under disability here, though it may well be said that the disability is to his own advantage in preventing him ever from bartering away his freedom, whatever the temptation. That, indeed, is one of the grounds upon which untutored common sense would found the assertion that the right to personal freedom is yet more securely protected in our law than any right of property.

But there's the rub, there, for the 'will theory', the paradox. For it appears that this legal dispensation, be it ever so advantageous from the point of view of securing liberty, is so forceful as to thrust liberty beyond the realm of 'right' altogether. If there be no power to waive or assert the immunity, the claim, or whatever, upon some matter, upon that matter there is, *by definition*, no right either. In the matter of non-enslavement no person in any contemporary western legal system can *de jure* waive his immunity; the same is true of other interests characteristically protected by Bills of Rights (whence, perhaps, Hart's embarrassment over these in connection with the notion of 'immunity'). Are we really to conclude that here the terminology of 'rights' is inapposite? Really to conclude that the language of the practical lawyer does such violence to common understanding as to extrude such protections of human interests, when arguably at their most efficacious, from the category which it is interesting or useful to describe as 'rights'? The paradox would seem to me altogether too violent; the ascription of concerns to the practical lawyer, unconvincingly ethnocentric.

Admittedly, we are to some extent in the realms of stipulative

definition when we enter into contention over the essential characteristics of the concept 'right'. Yet we are entitled to ask somebody
who stipulates that there shall be held to be 'rights' only where there
are choices, whether that stipulation does not go wholly against
common understanding, and whether there is any profit derived
from it.

What seems to me strangest is the way in which the will theory
seems to cut off the use of 'rights'-language at a predetermined
point on the scale of protection which the law may confer upon
people's interests. To take a somewhat trivial case: the law relating to
assault prohibits any person from offering or inflicting physical
interference or harm on another. *A* has a duty not to interfere with *B*.
So far as concerns the 'will theory', *B* has a 'right not to be harmed'
only if and in so far as he, *B*, can in some way regulate *A*'s duty not to
interfere with him. That seems all very well: in relation to minor
interference, or manly sports, or bona-fide surgical operations, *B* can
waive *A*'s duty. So, for the 'will theory', *B* has a right not to be trivially assaulted, or assaulted in the course of manly sports, or assaulted by
a surgeon conducting an operation. Yet in relation to serious assaults,
or 'unmanly' pastimes (e.g. flagellation by or of a prostitute),[10] or
operations by unqualified persons, no valid consent can be given
which releases the assaulting party from the duty of non-interference.[11]
It is rather bewildering to suppose that none of us has a right not to
be thus grievously assaulted, simply because for various reasons of
policy the law denies us the power to consent to these graver interferences with our physical security.

Students of Dicey's *Law and Opinion* will recall his ill-disguised
disapproval of those collectivist measures which were introduced in
the later nineteenth century in order to protect various elements in
the poorer sections of the population.[12] The technique which he
deplored was as follows: first, the legislature conferred protection on
people which they could have conferred on themselves by contract,
e.g. in matters of safety at work; secondly, the legislators, discovering
that too many of the protected class exercised the power 'voluntarily'
to contract out of the protection, removed the matter from the option

[10] See *R*. v. *Donovan* [1934] 2 K.B. 498 for discussion of this instance, and of consent
generally.
[11] G. H. Gordon, *Criminal Law* (Edinburgh, 1967), pp. 773–6; J. C. Smith and B.
Hogan, *Criminal Law*, 3rd edn. (London, 1973), pp. 287–90.
[12] A. V. Dicey, *Law and Opinion in England during the Nineteenth Century*, 2nd edn.
(London, 1924), pp. 260–9.

of the protected party altogether by depriving of legal effect such waivers of the statutory protection. Perhaps such legislation was as disgracefully paternalistic as Dicey so evidently thought it (though it cannot be said that this century has seen any reversal of its increase, far from it) but can it really be said that the second stage of protection is a stage at which a 'right' disappears? At stage one, the employer is obliged to take certain steps to protect his employee's safety, unless his employee 'contracts out'—here, for the 'will theory' is a classic case of 'right'. At stage two, the employer's duty is made unconditional upon the employee's will, and that with a view to protecting better the interests of employees individually and as a class—and now, for the will theory, the 'right' has gone. How odd that, as the protection is strengthened, the right disappears![13]

There is no point in multiplying such examples, of which there is certainly an abundance; the ones here given reinforce the particular case of the legal and moral protections of children which I have discussed in my recent paper on 'Children's Rights'.[14] If I may immodestly quote, and adopt from, that argument, I should like to repeat what I said in relation to what I conceive to be a child's (legal and moral) right to care and nurture:

We are put . . . to our election. Either we abstain from ascribing to children a right to care and nurture [on the ground that no one has discretion to waive the responsible adult's duty of care and nurture] or we abandon the will theory. For my part I have no inhibitions about abandoning the latter. It causes me no conceptual shock or mental cramp to say that children have that right. What is more, I will aver that it is *because* children have that right that it is good that legal provision should be made in the first instance to encourage and assist parents to fulfil their duty of care and nurture, and secondarily to provide for its performance by alternative foster parents when natural parents are disqualified by death, incapacity, or wilful and persistent neglect. *Ubi ius, ibi remedium.* So far from its being the case that the remedial provision is constitutive of the right, the fact is rather that recognition of the right justifies the imposition of the remedial provision.

We are all accustomed to talking and thinking about some rights

---

[13] But note that in 'B.L.R.' at p. 192 Hart shows that the 'fullest measure of control' by one person over another's duty need not be present in every case of a right; there are several distinguishable elements in that 'fullest measure' of which powers of waiver or enforcement are only one (remedial powers and powers of waiver of remedial rights being others). But it must be at least embarrassing to him if measures conceived of as strengthening rights standardly involve derogation from the fullest forms of control.

[14] A paper read to the conference of the Association of Legal and Social Philosophy in Cambridge, April 1975, to be published in 1976 *Archiv für Rechts und sozial Philosophie.*

as 'inalienable'. But if the will theory is correct, the more they are inalienable, the less they are rights. So far at least as concerns claim rights and immunities, I find the paradoxes with which the will theory is faced so great that, rather than swallow them, I am driven to seek an alternative. As a first step towards doing so, I should like to probe some of the grounds which have been suggested as foundations for the will theory with a view to showing that they are not as sound as they sound. In doing so I shall resume consideration of the statutory provisions referred to in my opening section.

IV

The principal advocates of benefit or 'interest' theories of rights correlative to obligations have shown themselves sensitive to the criticism that, if to say that an individual has such a right means no more than that he is the intended beneficiary of a duty, then 'a right' in this sense may be an unnecessary, and perhaps confusing, term in the description of the law; since all that can be said in a terminology of such rights can be and indeed is, best said in the indispensable terminology of duty.[15]

In that statement we find one of the principal grounds of Hart's case in favour of this theory, and against any version of interest theory. By introducing 'the idea . . . of one individual being given by the law exclusive control, more or less extensive, over another person's duty so that in the area of conduct covered by that duty the individual who has the right is a small-scale sovereign to whom the duty is owed', Hart claims to have shown us an idea by reference to which the 'terminology of . . . rights' can be used without redundancy to say things which cannot be said in the 'indispensable terminology of duty' by itself.[16]

This argument of Hart's perhaps has a certain force as against Bentham's account of rights—even in the brilliantly polished version of it expounded by Hart in his essay thereon. To rest an account of claim rights *solely* on the notion that they exist whenever a legal duty is imposed by a law intended to benefit assignable individuals (in which case all the beneficiaries of the law have rights as against all the duty bearers) is to treat rights as being simply the 'reflex' of logically prior duties. Accordingly, for any statement about rights there could always be substituted a statement about duties which would be at a more fundamental level analytically and which yet would say just the same as the 'rights statement'.

---

[15] 'B.L.R.', p. 190.   [16] Ibid.

It is however no part of my intention here to advance a theory according to which even 'claim rights' are conceived as being merely the reflex of duties,[17] as though the latter must always be understood as being in every way prior to rights. Here I return to the importance of my introductory point, that legal rights are conferred by laws, and that scrutiny of those laws which confer rights must therefore be profitable, not to say essential, for understanding rights. In relation to the point in hand, let me refer again to section 2(1) of the Succession (Scotland) Act 1964: '(a) Where an intestate is survived by children, they shall have right to the whole of the intestate estate.'

It is worth taking a few moments (and repeating a point which I have made elsewhere)[18] in explaining the context and effects of that provision. Under it, whenever a person domiciled in Scotland dies intestate leaving children, there automatically vests in those children a right to the whole of that part of his estate statutorily entitled 'the intestate estate' (i.e. the residue after certain statutorily established prior claims have been satisfied). At the moment at which the right vests, it is not a 'real right' involving ownership of the estate or any particular assets included in it. Rather, each child's right is a right to receive in due course an equal share in the assets remaining in the executor's hands after satisfaction of prior claims. So it seems that we have a normal right–duty relationship, which could as well have been stated in the 'indispensable terminology of duty' as in the terminology which commended itself to the draftsman.

The problem, however, is that whereas the right vests at the moment of the intestate's death, there is not at that moment an executor to bear a correlative duty. Vesting of the right is temporally prior to the vesting in any other individual of the correlative duty, which can occur only when an executor has in due course been judicially confirmed or appointed. The executor dative has then the duty to wind up the estate and to transfer appropriate shares in the intestate estate to those having right thereto. What is more, when the question of confirmation of an executor dative is raised before the relevant court, a person who has beneficial rights in the estate is normally *on that ground* to be preferred to other parties, at least if the

---

[17] To this extent disagreeing with Geoffrey Marshall 'Rights, Options, and Entitlements' (in Simpson, ed., op. cit., pp. 228–41) with which otherwise I substantially agree. Cf. A. M. Honoré, 'Rights of Exclusion and Immunities against Divesting', 34 *Tulane Law Review* 453 (1959–60).

[18] Op. cit. For a general account of the matters sketched here, see M. C. Meston, *The Succession (Scotland) Act 1964*, 2nd edn. (Edinburgh, 1970).

estate appears to be solvent. So one of the intestate's children may, *because of this right conferred on him by the Act*, have a resultant preferential right to be confirmed as executor. His confirmation as such will in turn result in his incurring the duties of executor, including the duty of distributing the intestate estate to those (including himself) who have right thereto under section 2(1)(*a*) of the 1964 Act.

In this case, therefore, it is not only the case that the vesting of a given right is temporally prior to the vesting of the correlative duty, but it is also the case that the vesting of the right in a given individual is a ground for confirming him in that office to which is attached the duty correlative to the like rights of his brothers and sisters; so that in this context right is logically prior to duty as well. Here then we have a concrete instance of a 'right of recipience' which correlates with 'duty' indeed, but in a much more interesting way than as being a mere 'reflex' of a duty which the legislator might have as readily imposed in simpler and more straightforward terms. An 'interest theory' of rights which can take account of such subtleties as this may well avoid the reproach of redundancy, as well as escaping the paradoxes in which (as the last section showed) the will theory is inevitably drawn.

In drafting a law to deal with intestate succession, a legislator might indeed be very likely to regard the crucial and primary question, as being who is to take the benefit of the estate left by the intestate, and to treat as secondary the means (appointment of executors or administrators, and imposition of appropriate duties upon them) of securing that the benefit in view should actually reach the hands of the intended beneficiary. It is the end which makes sense of the means, not vice versa. This is as obvious in relation to section 46 of the (English) Administration of Estates Act 1925, which likewise confers rights of succession on intestacy though without saying so expressly, as in relation to Section 2 of the Succession (Scotland) Act 1964.

In such a case, given that the legal system recognizes and establishes a system of private property, there is necessarily a vacant 'estate' whenever somebody dies possessed of property. The system must make *some* provision as to the destination of that estate. Whoever gets it, to him will be owed all the duties which are owed to property owners, and to him will ensue also the various liberties, powers, and immunities which accrue to property owners, but *that* person gets all that only because—only if—the law has already vested in him the right of ownership of the property in question. And the step before that is the conferment on some generically identified type of person(s) of the right to have ownership of some part of or share of the property comprising the estate invested in him. What is essentially at stake is, who is to get the more or less substantial advantage of inheriting what share of what part of the estate. It is a quite secondary question to settle by what precise means (imposition of duties and disabilities on *whom*?) that advantage shall be secured to him.

It seems obviously—even trivially—true that at least one function, and that a prominent one, of such laws as those concerning succession, is that they are concerned with the conferment and securing of advantages to individuals; or, rather, to members of given classes severally.[19] To explain the idea of 'members of given classes severally': section 2(1)(*a*) of the Succession (Scotland) Act protects and promotes the interests of a certain class, the class of children of a parent who has died intestate but possessed of some property. But the protection is not of the interests of the class indiscriminately, taking them all together as a group—as, perhaps, aircraft-noise-control legislation indiscriminately protects everybody living or working or doing anything else in the near vicinity of airports. The protection, in the succession case, is rather of each and every individual who is within that class each in respect of some separate share of an identified estate.

It is not necessarily the case that each individual acquiring a right under the law should experience it as a benefit, an advantage, an advancement or protection of his interests. Perhaps there are some people who have been more harmed than benefited by an inheritance. Perhaps in some cases property inherited—e.g. slum properties subject to statutory tenancies at controlled rents—are literally more trouble than they are worth, and, besides, something of an embarrassment to their proprietor. None of that is in any way inconsistent with the proposition that the function of the law is to confer what is considered to be normally an advantage on a certain class by granting to each of its members a certain legal right.

The case of the mortgagor's entitlement (under s.96(1) of the Law of Property Act 1925) to inspect and make copies of title-deeds, also quoted as an example in the introductory section of the present paper,

---

[19] For Hart's account of an essentially similar view of Bentham's see 'B.L.R.', pp. 186–8. For another similar account, see John Austin on 'absolute' and 'relative' duties in the seventeenth chapter of *Lectures in Jurisprudence* (London, 1862).

further indicates the way in which a legislator's concern with protecting what are conceived to be legitimate interests of the members of a given class of individuals leads naturally to the framing of legislation in terms of the rights or entitlements of the given class rather than in terms of the correlative obligations of the mortgagee. In just this sense, what is essential to a clear and comprehensible law relating to mortgages is that the relevant legislation should make clear the respective advantages, protections, and powers accruing to each of the parties to any mortgage. Judicial enforcement of the legislation may then proceed by elucidation and enforcement of duties etc. as necessarily consequential upon conferment of the relevant rights.

By contrast with this branch of the law, the criminal law is no doubt primarily concerned with duties,[20] with laying down in clear and precise terms the prohibitions infraction of which may expose the citizen to prosecution and punishment. This of course follows from a respect for the right of individuals to freedom from interference by the state save for breach of clear rules of the criminal law. Thus, in so far as it is an important function of the criminal law to protect important individual rights—to freedom, to physical and mental security, and so on—it is nevertheless not surprising that the law is not expressly framed in terms of rights, but rather in terms of duties, or through the imposition of duties by the denomination of offences. Even at that, however, there is a large part of the criminal law which deals with crimes against property, and which therefore necessarily presupposes the existence of that elaborate and interlocking set of laws which define and regulate the institution of property and the many and various rights in relation thereto which the law confers. Rights of, and rights in relation to, property—e.g. a mortgagor's right to redeem, a child's right of intestate succession—are on the face of it much too complex to be dissoluble into a set of bare reflexes of correlative duties. But that is not an objection to the thesis that right-conferring laws are best understood in terms of a standard intention to confer some form of benefit or advantage or protection of interests upon the members of a class severally rather than collectively. There may indeed be simple cases in which some general duty—e.g. a duty not to assault—is imposed upon everyone at large with a view to protecting the physical security of each and every person in society, and where the 'right not to be assaulted' is simply the correlative of the duty not to assault; no doubt in such simple

20 Cf. 'B.L.R.', pp. 191–5.

cases the 'terminology of rights' does not enable us to say very much more than can be said in the terminology of duty. But it may be well adapted even in this simple case to expressing a reason why people aggrieved by breaches of certain duties *should* be empowered to take various measures and actions at law to secure remedies therefor, and why they *should* be permitted, at least when there are no strong countervailing reasons of policy, to waive other people's duties in this respect. If I'm allowed to be the best judge of my own good, and if such laws (being right-conferring) are aimed at securing what's good for me, why should I not be allowed to have a say over their operation when only my own protection is at stake?

What is more, there are other, more complex, cases in which the legislative decision to confer certain benefits on individuals who satisfy certain generic qualifications ('institutive' or 'investitive' facts) is logically prior to the vesting or the enforcement of a correlative duty. Taken as a whole, there is no reason to suppose that an 'interest theory' so defines 'rights' as to make the term redundant.

In another context, I have expressed as follows the conclusion which follows from arguments such as the foregoing:[21]

To ascribe to all members of a class C a right to treatment T is to presuppose that T is, in all normal circumstances, a good for every member of C, and that T is a good of such importance that it would be wrong to deny it to or withhold it from any member of C. That as for moral rights; as for legal rights, I should say this: when a right to T is conferred by law on all members of C, the law is envisaged as advancing the interests of each and every member of C, and the law has the effect of making it legally wrongful to withhold T from any member of C.

That is certainly not a perfect or watertight formulation, nor am I sure that I can at present make it so. But it does bring out the three features which must be included in any characterization of rules which confer rights.

First, they concern 'goods' (or 'advantages', or 'benefit', or 'interests', or however we may express the point). Whatever *x* may be, the idea of anyone's having a right to *x* would be absurd unless it were presupposed that *x* is normally a good for human beings, at any rate for those people who qualify as having the 'right' in question. That does not mean that in every case the *x* which is subject matter of a right need be beneficial to a particular potential right-holder, or be thought so by him. Some *hereditates* may be *damnosae*, but our

[21] Op. cit.

general view of the law of succession as conceding '*rights*' of succession is founded on the firm supposition that most are not.

Secondly, they concern the enjoyment of goods by individuals separately, not simply as members of a collectivity enjoying a diffuse common benefit in which all participate in indistinguishable and unassignable shares. But since necessarily the qualifications and conditions which must be satisfied for the application of such a rule of law in favour of any given individual have to be expressible and expressed in generic terms, it is therefore correct to say that such rules of law must be concerned with classes of individuals, but the benefit secured is secured to each and every individual severally upon satisfaction of the 'institutive' or 'investitive' conditions.

Thirdly, benefits are secured to individuals in that the law provides normative protection for individuals in their enjoyment of them. No doubt it is too narrow to envisage such protection purely in terms of its being 'legally wrongful to withhold T from any member of C'. 'Normative protection' may be understood as involving any or all of the various modes identified by Hohfeld and others. Thus an individual *A* may in the relevant sense be 'protected' in his enjoyment of *x* if

(a) some or all other people are under a duty not to interfere with him in relation to *x* or his enjoyment of *x*,

or (b) he is himself not under any duty to abstain from enjoyment of, or avoid or desist from *x* (being therefore protected from any complaint as to alleged wrongful use, enjoyment, etc. of *x*),

or (c) some or all other individuals lack legal power to change the legal situation to the prejudice of *A*'s advantage in respect of *x* (the case of disability/immunity),

or (d) *A* himself is in some respect enabled by law to bring about changes in legal relations concerning *x* in pursuit of whatever he conceives to be his advantage.

Not every right entails protection at all these levels or in all these modes simultaneously, though more than one may be and all sometimes are (this being contrary to the Hohfeldian picture of rights as atomic relations between paired individuals). Consider section 5(1) of the Trade Union and Labour Relations Act 1974: '. . . [E]very worker shall have the right not to be—(a) excluded from membership (b) expelled from membership, of a trade union . . . by way of arbitrary or unreasonable discrimination.' That confers protection of at least the first three kinds; it being presumed that membership of a union is beneficial to any worker in normal circumstances (a) people at large are put under a duty not to injure any worker by getting him excluded or expelled from a trade union, (b) every worker is in law free to apply for membership of a union of his choice, and (c) any act of purported expulsion of a worker from his union lacks legal effect if it is judged to be 'by way of arbitrary or unreasonable discrimination'. Consequentially, of course, A has various legal remedies which he may pursue for alleged infractions of the primary right conferred by the Act.

Thus using the terminology (in my view indispensable) of 'rights' the legislature can in short and simple words achieve complex legal protections for the several members of a given class. What is more, it can do so in a way which draws attention to the end in view, the protection of those people in relation to a supposedly advantageous condition of things. This serves better than would any alternative formulation the function of conveying to the population in general and to the judiciary in particular the intended aim and object of the measure.

The example most recently used can be used to show why we should not accept the Hohfeldian view of 'rights' as being reducible without residue to atomic relationships (belonging to one or other of his four types) between pairs of identified individuals; or even to sets of such relations. During the whole period when the 1974 Act was in force, any individual who was a worker had the right conferred by Section 5(1) of the Act. For any worker at any moment of time his having that right would have entailed a large set of Hohfeld-type atomic relationships with other individuals in a position to affect his membership (actual or projected) of some union. But although such individual atomic relationships are derivable from the existence of the right conferred by the Act, the converse is not true. The legislature can establish that vast myriad of atomic relationships by establishing the right to non-exclusion and non-expulsion. It could not establish the latter by establishing the former. (Of course, the legislature could establish a whole set of such 'atomic' relationships, but no particular set would be equivalent to the right actually established, which, depending on the circumstances which emerge, results in a variable set of claims, powers, etc.).

Rights, in short, may be more or less simple or complex and might be ranged on a scale of relative complexity. The more complex they are, the more it is necessary, at least for practical understanding, to envisage them as 'institutional' concepts, as I have elsewhere analysed that term.[22] For any given right, e.g. a right of real security, it is (at least for practical comprehension) necessary to distinguish 'institutive' (*per* Bentham, 'investitive') provisions which establish the conditions upon which the right in question vests in qualified individuals; 'consequential' provisions establishing the various normative protections enjoyed by 'right-holders' as such; and 'terminative' or 'divestitive' provisions establishing the conditions in which the 'right' is 'lost' or 'transferred'. In the case of complex provisions of this kind, the concept of 'right' is for practical purposes indispensable. Even if it were theoretically the case that the whole set of rules comprising a developed legal system could be restated purely in terms of the imposition of duties and the conferment of powers, which I doubt, it would be of no advantage for the practical comprehension of the law were anyone to do so. (The difficulties can be gleaned from a scrutiny of Bentham's heroic attempt to show, by way of prolegomenon to a codification project, how it might in principle be done.)

Even in the case of very simple legal provisions expressed in the duty-imposing mode, the interpretation of such rules as also conferring rights is not wholly without point. First of all, if it be supposed that the law was made with a view to protecting the good of individuals severally, so that every qualified individual has a correlative right to the duty (a Hohfeldian 'claim right'), that would supply at least a prima facie reason for supposing that individuals adversely affected by anybody's breach of the duty imposed ought to be entitled to seek a private law remedy, 'Ubi ius, ibi remedium'; to interpret a law as right-conferring is to give a justifying reason why there should be a remedy at private law for its breach. Secondly, and by a similar line of argument, it would appear that when such a law is conceived as conferring individual rights, individuals ought normally to have the power of waiving the duty in particular cases affecting only themselves.

If it be accepted that the identifying feature of right-conferring laws is to secure certain goods to individuals, and if it be accepted (as liberals accept it) that people should have free choice as to the pursuit or not of their own good, that constitutes a reason why, when the law confers rights on people, they *ought* to have the kind of choice which the will theory conceives to be analytically entailed by

[22] D. N. MacCormick, 'Law as Institutional Fact', 90 *Law Quarterly Review* 102 (1974).

the term 'right'. But surely it is better to conceive of such 'powers of waiver', like remedial powers, not as being essential to the definition of, but as being consequential on the recognition or conferment of, rights. Paternalistic legislation which seeks to protect people's rights by preventing them from waiving them may be objectionable, but that is for argument. Surely it cannot be the case that, by definition, it destroys as 'rights' the rights which it seeks better to protect? Freedom of choice is a good, but it is not necessarily the only good.

The more one considers the matter, and the more one looks at rights in legislation, the more implausible become the contentions of the 'will theory' as to the definition and elucidation of rights. Rights must be understood in terms of the type of 'interest theory' advanced in this essay. From that it may be seen that there are powerful reasons why people should be free to exercise or not exercise their rights. But these reasons are points of moral and political substance, not analytic truths about rights. What is more, the experience of the past century suggests that in contexts of economic inequality the value of freedom of choice (in its guise as freedom of contract) may justifiably be overridden by other values, at least sometimes. That gives a further reason for not erecting the liberal principle about freedom of choice into an analytic truth following from the definition of 'right'. To follow Hart's example by seeking to elucidate the character not of 'rights' directly, but of the laws that confer them, is to find grounds for rejecting his own theory of rights.

ENDNOTE: *Ius quaesitum tertio*

Of the arguments adduced by Hart against the 'benefit theory', the only one not dealt with here is that which concerns contracts in favour of third parties.[23] If A and B make a contract which has a provision for the benefit of C, it follows that there is a duty under the contract, which is intended to be for the benefit of C. Therefore, if the benefit theory is true, C has a right under the contract, but in some (indeed most) legal systems the existence of third-party rights under contract is not recognized, so the benefit theory cannot be true.

Observe that the argument proves too much, for with an obvious modification it applies to the will theory too. If A and B make a contract containing a provision in favour of C, to be carried out by

[23] 'B.L.R.', pp. 195-6.

B if *C* requests, but not if *C* does not request, is there a right in favour of *C*? Not under English law, even though that duty of *B*'s has been set up so that its performance is at *C*'s option.

The point in both cases is that under English law (unlike Scots law in either case) *A* and *B* retain the power to alter the provisions of their contract without *C*'s consent. Since the term in *C*'s favour remains precarious until performed, it is not called a 'right'. What is crucial is the presence or absence of immunity. That embarrasses the will theory, but not the interest theory here propounded.

12

Promises and Obligations

J. RAZ*

SOME authors consider that the distinction between 'ought to ϕ' and 'has an obligation (or duty) to ϕ' is important and should not be obscured. Others regard it as a matter of style or emphasis of no practical significance however interesting the historical origins of the distinction may be. I side with the latter in viewing the distinction as of philosophical significance only if it reflects a practical difference, i.e. only if the way to justify a statement of an obligation is different from the way to justify 'ought' statements, or, if the entailments of statements of obligations are different from those of 'ought' statements.

On many occasions 'obligation' and 'duty' (and I will make no attempt to draw a systematic distinction between them) are used in ways which from the point of view of practical philosophy do not differ from uses of 'ought', except in emphasis. There are many people whose practical principles allow for no distinction of significance between 'ought' and 'duty'. It is too late to rebuke them for misusing language. We should note, however, that language incorporates features which reflect a different view by which duties have a special role in practical reasoning. My purpose is to probe a little the features of 'duty' which point to a conception assigning it a special role, and to take a few steps towards identifying the kind of practical principles presupposed by this conception ('the narrow concept of duty' as I shall refer to it). I am assuming that statements of the type: 'x ought to ϕ' are logically equivalent to statements of the type 'There is a reason for x to ϕ'.[1] This implies among other things that 'ought' means 'prima-facie-ought'. I shall further assume that if x has a duty to ϕ then he ought to ϕ (there is a reason for him to ϕ). The question

---

* Fellow of Balliol College, Oxford.

[1] On the background to this assumption as well as to the general line of reasoning pursued here see my *Practical Reason and Norms* (Hutchinson, London, 1975), ch. 1.

of the special role of duties in practical reasoning is, then, how do statements of duty differ from 'ought' statements.

I shall approach the question by concentrating on the special case of promises. The discussion of promising will lead to and illustrate the examination of the concept of obligation.

1. 'ONE OUGHT TO KEEP ONE'S PROMISES'

My purpose is neither to defend nor to criticize any particular view of the grounds for keeping promises but to explain the normative institution of a promise. To do this is not to explain the meaning of any word, though it may help to account for the meaning of certain words. We can promise without using the word 'promise' or any of its synonyms or part-synonyms as by saying 'You can rely on me', 'I will . . .', etc. We also use 'I promise' without promising—e.g. to threaten ('I promise I'll get you'). Some promises are mere resolutions (e.g. 'I promised myself a holiday abroad this summer'). Others are emphatic statements (e.g. 'I didn't do it, I promise'). Such promises are not instances of the normative institution with which we are concerned. We shall confine ourselves to promises which are a kind of voluntary obligations or thought to be so.

In the next two sections I shall examine and contrast *the intention* and *the obligation* conceptions of a promise. According to the first, promises are expressions of firm intentions to act. According to the second, promises are expressions of intentions to undertake obligations. Principles of roughly the following form correspond to these conceptions:

PI: Whoever communicates, in circumstances of kind *C*, a firm intention to perform an action, being aware that the addressee may rely on him, ought to perform it and his addressee has a right that he shall do so (unless released from this requirement by the addressee).

PO: Whoever communicates, in circumstances of kind *C*, an intention to undertake by the very act of communication an obligation to perform an action and invest the addressee with a right to its performance ought to perform that action and his addressee has a right that he shall do so (unless the addressee releases him from this requirement).

The circumstances alluded to in both principles concern marginal conditions: Was the promise induced by duress? Is it a promise to perform an intrinsically immoral act? etc.

Before we engage in an examination of these contrasting conceptions it may be well to clear three subsidiary issues which affect both conceptions equally. It has been claimed that promising principles unlike other rules such as those prohibiting killing or rape or assault do not regulate ordinary actions. They concern actions which *cannot* be explained except by reference to rules. If principles of either of the kinds just described are promising principles then this claim is mistaken. Promising principles are ordinary rules regulating ordinary actions just like 'Don't kill'; 'Don't imitate such people and don't listen to their advice'; 'Every day perform one good action—the first that anybody mentions to you that day'; etc. It is clear also that a society may endorse and practice a promising principle without having the word 'promise' or its equivalents. But what about the word 'promise' itself? Is it to be explained in a way according to which the statement that one ought to keep one's promises is analytic or not? Philosophers seem unanimous that the statement is analytic. But the linguistic evidence is ambiguous.

There is no doubt that explanation of action taken or intended in terms such as 'But I promised I'll do it' do sound complete. To add 'therefore it was my duty to do it' is, we feel, to unpack what is already contained in the first statement, not to add to it. To say 'I promised to ϕ but I have no reason to ϕ' is paradoxical. It can be explained, e.g. by adding 'since the promisee released me from my promise'. But all such explanations presuppose rather than deny that promises ought to be kept.

On the other hand we have only to turn our attention to other contexts in which 'a promise' is used and the evidence becomes more blurred. If 'promises ought to be kept' is analytic then disputes about the scope of the promising principles are disputes about the meaning of the word 'a promise'. This is sometimes reflected in usage. A person who believes that a promise made in private to a dying man provides no reason for action may say that death-bed promises are not promises. But he is more likely to say that death-bed promises are not binding. Similarly some who hold such views say that promises to perform intrinsically immoral acts or that promises extracted under duress are not promises. But people who have these views are more likely to express them by saying that such communications are promises but they are not binding promises—meaning thereby that one has no reason at all to keep them.

So the evidence gives some support both to the view that an action is a promise only if it creates for the agent a reason to perform another action in virtue of a binding promising principle and to the view that it is an action of a kind often thought to bind the agent according to some (not necessarily valid)[2] promising principle. The second view is defensible only if coupled with the assumption that there exists a conversational convention that unless otherwise indicated explicitly or by context he who uses the word 'promise' (a) accepts some promising principle, and (b) his interest in the case under discussion is as a case falling under a principle which he accepts. On this view, by saying 'You promised' or asking 'Did you promise?' one does not assert any promising principle or anything which entails the existence of such a principle. But one is expressing oneself in a way which implies endorsement of such a principle and belief that the present case falls under it, or interest whether it does.

Some words are value-laden. That generosity is good is analytic. We can argue which acts are generous, but not whether generous acts are as such good. Other words much used in practical contexts designate an area generally thought by some people or others to be good (or bad etc.) but which is not necessarily good (or bad etc.) nor necessarily held by the speaker to be such. 'Privacy' or 'Democracy' are perhaps such examples. 'A promise' is used in a way which makes its classification with one kind or the other very difficult. I tend to feel that the second view fits all the facts better than the first.

Assuming the second view, one can turn to examine two popular views about promising.

It has often been maintained that it is a necessary condition of promising that the promisee will benefit from the performance of the promise or wants the promised act to be performed, or that at the time of promising the promisor believes so.[3] This may be true as a matter of practical principle (though I do not believe so) but is certainly wrong as a piece of conceptual analysis. Counter-examples abound. Imagine a man who solicits a promise, hoping and believing that it will be broken, in order to prove to a certain lady how unreliable the promisor is. Imagine further that the promisor is aware of this and makes his promise intending to disappoint the promisee by keeping it. Imagine a youth who promises his father never to smoke despite his father's protestations at the time that he sees nothing

---

[2] i.e. justified, well-founded, or binding principle.

[3] Cf. e.g., J. Searle, *Speech Acts* (Cambridge U.P., Cambridge, 1969), ch. 3; J. Schneewind, 'A Note on Promising', *Philosophical Studies* 17 (1966), 33–5.

wrong in smoking. The son insists that *he* believes smoking is undesirable and therefore, he makes the promise in order to strengthen his resolve, even though he is aware that his father would prefer him to smoke. The father reluctantly accepts the promise as a favour to his son. We may think that the boy is not bound, or at least not bound to his father. But assume that he holds himself to be bound and regards his father as having a right to insist on the promise being kept. Would we have to accuse him of a conceptual confusion before we can ascribe to him a belief that he promised?

One might be tempted to counter such examples by modifying the benefit condition. But this is a mistake. The appeal of the benefit condition is vicarious and derives entirely from the fact that promises are commitments undertaken through being communicated to an addressee who acquires a right to demand the performance of the promise and the right to release the promisor from his obligation. It is this power to release which accounts for the attractiveness of the benefit condition. The promisee can be expected to release the promisor from a promise if its execution is against his interest, but he need not do so.

Another common belief is that promises can exist only if there is a social practice to that effect.[4] It is admittedly difficult to conceive of a human society in which some form of promising is not practised. But it is imaginable. Could not promises be made in it and wouldn't they be binding? Of course it will be impossible to promise by saying 'I promise . . .' or by any other conventional means. We are imagining a society in which there are no conventional ways of promising. But these conventional means, useful as they are in helping to clarify people's intentions, are not essential.[5] If in our imagined society a man communicates to another his intention to undertake by the very act of communication, an obligation to perform an action and confer a corresponding right on his interlocutor, I cannot see how we can avoid regarding his act as a promise. Some may believe in promising principles by which promises are binding only in a society in which

---

[4] This is endorsed by almost all the writers on promising. For example, H. L. A. Hart, 'Legal and Moral Obligation', in A. I. Melden, ed. *Essays in Moral Philosophy* (University of Washington Press, Seattle, 1958); J. Searle, op. cit.

[5] Some hold principles by which he who unwittingly performs an action conventionally used to promise has promised unless he has made clear to the addressee that he does not intend the act as a promise. More commonly it is held that in such cases a person acting in good faith is bound by his 'promise' only if his interlocutor was misled to believe that he promised and changed his position so that he will suffer if the so-called promise is not kept. Here we rely on a principle of estoppel, not of promising.

such principles are practised. But if our promisor has a different view neither he nor others can be accused of a conceptual confusion for describing his action as a promise.

2. THE INTENTION CONCEPTION AND ITS LIMITATIONS

Several authors have defended the view that to promise to ϕ is to communicate a firm intention to ϕ when knowing that the addressee may rely on the information, or variants of it.[6] Several considerations seem to support this view. The most common way of promising is also the standard way of expressing intentions, namely by means of 'I will ϕ' type of sentence. It is true that it is less common to promise by saying 'I intend to ϕ'. But, then, to express an intention in this way rather than by the 'I will ϕ' formula, when knowing that the addressee may rely on one's ϕ-ing is often to indicate that one's intention is less than firm and could not be safely relied upon. Similarly, 'I intend to ϕ, and that's a promise' is an indication that the intention is firm and presupposes that the speaker is aware that his addressee may rely on it. 'I intend to ϕ but I don't promise' indicates that the intention is less than firm and cannot be safely relied upon.

It seems reasonably clear that when promising to ϕ in normal circumstances, one is expressing a firm intention to ϕ. This is the case regardless of the language used when promising and is true also of promises made by the use of 'I promise to ϕ' kind of sentence. But are there any further assertions, presuppositions, implications or any other elements which are necessary for promising, at least in normal circumstances?

One way to approach this question is through the considerations on which promising principles are based. These justify one or more promising principles by relating them to some general human concerns. Thereby they also indicate what a promise has to be like to be binding. If these considerations justify only a principle of the (PI) variety then promises are communications of firm intentions when aware that these may be relied upon by the addressee. Most of the common philosophical defenses and explanations of promising principles justify (PI) or its cognates but not (PO) nor any other strong kind of principle. This is particularly true of utilitarian

---

[6] See especially P. S. Ardal, 'And That's a Promise', *Philosophical Quarterly* 18 (1968), 225–37; but also, e.g., J. Narveson, 'Promising, Expecting and Utility', *Canadian Journal of Philosophy* 1 (1971), 207–33; P. Singer, 'Is Act-Utilitarianism Self-Defeating?', *Philosophical Review* 81 (1972), 94–104.

justifications but not only of them.[7] In general, reasons of two kinds are most commonly advanced in justifying the requirement that promises ought to be kept: *Firstly*, the promisee may rely on the promise and be inconvenienced, harmed or disadvantaged if it is not kept. *Secondly*, a person who does not normally keep his promises cannot be expected to keep them in the future. Similarly a society in which people do not normally keep their promises is one in which people cannot be expected to keep their promises. Thus such a person and such a society lose the advantages of greater possibilities of social co-operation and exchange which presuppose the improved predictability secured by a practice (personal and social) of keeping one's promises.

It is clear that whatever reasons for action these considerations establish apply to all expressions of intentions which may be relied upon by anybody. We may harm people who count on us acting in accord with our expressed intentions and we benefit from having a reputation of reliability as people who do not change their minds too often and who do not mistake fleeting inclinations for firm intentions. Considerations of the kinds described support principles of the (PI) variety. We shall see below that they are insufficient to justify any principle of the (PO) variety. Given these facts one can either endorse the intention conception[8] or show that despite common theories it is insufficient to account for common beliefs about the obligation to keep promises.

It is easy to find features of our common conception of promising which do not readily fit the intention conception.[9] There is the direct challenge of the case of A who, knowing that B will decide his plans in the light of his estimate of A's likely action, tells him that he firmly intends to ϕ but that he refuses to promise to do so. Is he conceptually confused? More persuasive is the fact that the intention conception fails to distinguish adequately between promises and other pheno-

[7] F. G. McNeilly's 'Promises Demoralized', *Philosophical Review* 81 (1972), 63–81, is an interesting instance. His plan is to elucidate the reasons for having a promising principle. These in fact point to the intention conception, though McNeilly does not draw that conclusion himself.

[8] Some would maintain that I left out some necessary elements the addition of which strengthen the intention conception without converting it into the obligation conception. In particular an intention to induce or encourage reliance and actual reliance are added. See, for a very forceful defence of such a view, D. N. MacCormick, 'Voluntary Obligation and Normative Powers', *Aristotelian Society*, Suppl. Vol. 46 (1972). I have tried to refute such views in my reply to MacCormick's paper in the same volume.

[9] For a powerful criticism of the intention conception which influenced my own comments below see G. J. Warnock, *The Object of Morality* (Methuen, London, 1971), pp. 94 ff.

mena. This is a result of the fact that the considerations on which (PI) principles rest apply to many non-promising cases. The resulting difficulty is not that a promise-based reason can be equal in weight to a differently based reason. This is a harmless truism. The difficulty is that on this account both promises and other circumstances are reasons for action of precisely identical quality differing only in the style of their description—a difference which does not reflect any difference of practical importance. This fact is disturbing, for our linguistic and cultural intuitions indicate the existence of practical— and not merely stylistic—differences between promises and mere expressions of intention and other phenomena which the considerations we examined identify with promises in their practical character.

I'll give two examples to illustrate the point: (1) A communicates to B his firm intention to ϕ. At the time he does not know that this is of practical significance to B. But later circumstances change and it becomes obvious to A that B may well rely on his knowledge concerning A's intentions. (2) A promises C to ϕ. B is present at the time and A is aware that B may rely on A's ϕ-ing in making his own plans. According to the common conception, in neither case does A promise B to ϕ. Similarly, following the (PI) conception, it is easy to define promises in a way which excludes these cases. But the considerations on which (PI) principles are based apply with equal force to both cases. In both, A is aware that B may rely on his expressed intention. In both, if A does not ϕ he may reduce his general reliability, and more indirectly, the reliability of people generally in such cases. In some situations promises will be weightier reasons than expressions of intentions of the kinds I described. In other circumstances the reverse will be the case. But basically promises and such non-promises rest on the same basis. There is no difference of principle between them or in the practical reasoning on which the requirements to keep to them are based.

The common view that promises differ in important practical respects from other reasons for action is usually reflected in three features: They are said to be based on *rules*, to impose *obligations* which are of a special kind, namely *voluntary*. The intention conception of promises cannot do justice to any of these features. The reasons for keeping promises on which the intention conception is based are, in essence, that keeping the promise will have, other things being equal, the best consequences. The (PI) principle functions merely as a statement to this effect. It has no independent force. A

(PI) principle is not itself a reason for action. It is merely a statement that such a reason exists. But rules are characteristically reasons for action in themselves, as we shall see below.

Our intuition that promises differ in important practical respects from 'mere' expressions of intention like those in my examples is reflected also in the common belief that promises, unlike many other expressions of intentions, give rise to obligations. The intention conception need not deny this, but according to it this difference is of no practical significance. It is reduced to a minor stylistic difference. The intention account of promises minimizes, even trivializes, the difference between obligations and other reasons for action.

Finally, the intention conception does less than justice to our intuitions concerning promises as the paradigmatic case of voluntary obligations. To be sure, according to the (PI) conception, the obligations which promising imposes result from intentional action, but so does the duty of a highwayman to compensate his victim. Neither of them acts with the intention of creating an obligation.

3. THE OBLIGATION CONCEPTION

I shall try to show that all the features commonly associated with promising for which the intention conception has no use play an essential role in the main alternative conception based on (PO) type principles. This is most easily shown with respect to the third feature mentioned above, the character of promises as *voluntary* obligations. Promises are voluntary obligations not because promising is an intentional action, but because it is the communication of an intention to undertake an obligation, or at any rate to create for oneself a reason for action. It may be objected that promising is the undertaking of an obligation, not the communication of an intention to do so. But this objection is met once it is realized that the intention communicated is a reflexive one: To promise is, on this conception, to communicate an intention to undertake by the very act of communication an obligation to perform a certain action.

The fact that by promising one communicates an intention to undertake an obligation does not 'produce' an obligation by any form of magic which then can be 'intuited'. Indeed some such communications do not create any obligation, e.g. when the promise is induced by threats to life. If others do impose obligations that can only be because of the validity of some (PO) principle to the effect that if one communicates an intention to undertake, by that communication, an obligation to ϕ, then one has an obligation to ϕ, provided some further conditions are met. It is the fact that there is such a valid (PO) principle which is the reason to keep those promises which fall under it. It is this fact together with the fact that one promised to ϕ that is a reason for ϕ-ing.

Thus according to the obligation conception, both the promising rule and the promise can be said to be reasons for performing the promised act. Each is a partial reason, and together they are a complete reason. The fact that the promising principle is itself a reason for action, that the statement of that principle is an essential premiss in the practical inference yielding the conclusion that one ought to do as one promised, is the key to the dependence of promises on rules. The dependence is not in the explanation of what a promise is, but in the way the requirement to keep promises is justified. I am referring to the two-level view of its justification. First one justifies the rule, then—on its basis—those instances which fall under it. The rule is the reason for acting in certain ways in particular circumstances. There are reasons for believing that the rule is valid. But these are different reasons.[10]

The fact that the obligation conception of promises invokes rules in this special way also helps to explain the reason why according to it promises impose obligations. The obligation conception of promises can be related to a narrow conception of obligation according to which an action is obligatory if its performance is required by a categorical rule, i.e. a rule not dependent for its validity on the goals and desires of the agent.

4. PROMISES AND RULES

In the last section I stated the basic elements of the obligation conception. Throughout the rest of the article I will elucidate and defend these statements.

We often invoke rules as reasons for action,[11] both in explaining action (he did it because he believes in a rule that . . .) and in practical deliberation ('What should I do ? On the one hand it is a rule that . . .'). We tend to overlook the fact that viewing rules as reasons is not easy

[10] They should not be confused with reasons for enacting the rule, advocating its acceptance, etc. These are ordinary reasons for different actions and they do not presuppose the two-level analysis.

[11] Strictly speaking only facts are reasons. It is the fact that it is a valid rule that one ought to φ which is a reason for φ-ing. I shall, for reasons of convenience, refer to rules as reasons.

to reconcile with some other features of our practical thinking. The reasons for a rule are those justifying its validity. They are reasons for belief. If the rule is that one ought to ϕ then the reasons justifying the rule are reasons for believing that one ought to ϕ. But in general these are also the reasons for ϕ-ing. Thus we said above that the reasons for (PI) principles are the reasons for keeping those promises to which they apply. (PI) principles themselves are not such reasons. They are merely statements that there are reasons for keeping those promises. In this respect (PO) principles are radically different. They are themselves reasons for action.

The motives for assigning (PO) principles such a status are clear. Most commonly these days they stem from a desire to avoid some of the consequences of extreme utilitarianism. Yet there is something seemingly paradoxical about such arguments. They are often advanced by people who accept a utilitarian value theory, and agree with the utilitarians on what are the ultimate reasons for action.[12] They are concerned with certain cases in which though on the balance of reasons (including considerations of reliability and the risk of harming the promisee by misleading him) one ought to break the promise, nevertheless, in their view, the promise should be kept. They invoke rules as a justification for the need to act against the balance of reasons in some of the cases to which the rule applies.

It will be objected that I am misrepresenting the arguments of those supporters of the two-level justification whose position I am trying to portray. Surely they claim that act-utilitarians made a mistake. In working out what ought to be done on the balance of reasons the act-utilitarians overlooked the existence and independent weight of rules, like the promising rule. But the two-level justification cannot be analysed in such a way. The act-utilitarians, to be sure, did not regard the rule as a reason with an independent force. But they did take account of the considerations on which the rule is supposed to rest, namely considerations of reliability and harm to promisees. If the reasons for the rule are also reasons for action conforming to the rule then surely the weight of the rule as a reason for action is the same as that of the reasons for the rule considered as reasons for action conforming with the rule. The two-level justification procedure, on this interpretation, merely substitutes the rule for the considerations

---

[12] Both J. Rawls's 'Two Concepts of Rules' *Philosophical Review* 64 (1955), 3–32, and D. H. Hodgson's *Consequences of Utilitarianism* (Clarendon Press, Oxford, 1967) are examples of this approach.

on which it is based, which are relegated to a higher level. Thus it redescribes the practical reasoning involved but makes no difference to its outcome. Since two-level justifications were developed to show how to reach conclusions which can't be justified on the basis of rival theories, the above interpretation must be rejected.

The problem for a two-level analysis which we have noted applies generally to all conceptions of rules which regard them as fulfilling a significant role in practical reasoning, as being more than a statement that there are some reasons. They have to explain why the rule that one ought to ϕ affects practical reasoning in a way different from the reasons for the rule when interpreted as reasons for ϕ-ing.

One way to solve the problem is to regard rules as ultimate, to deny that they rest on any other reasons which justify their validity. Rules, however, seem to belong to the middle and lower levels of practical reason. They do not share the heights which values, principles, and ideals share. Rules are on the whole more mundane, pragmatic, creatures. At the very least it cannot be denied that many rules (like many principles, values, and ideals) have the more humble position of depending for validity on more ultimate considerations. The problem is how to reconcile the derivative status of rules with their relatively independent role in practical reasoning; how to combine their dependence on justifying considerations with their power as reasons for action in their own right.

The nature of the problem points to the terms of its solution. The reasons for the rule that one ought to ϕ cannot be just reasons for ϕ-ing. If so, then justifying such a rule is not merely a matter of pointing to reasons for ϕ-ing. What else can it be? The answer was already pointed out in the beginning of this section. To justify a rule is, among other things, to justify not acting, on occasions, on the balance of reasons. It is to justify assigning a peremptory status to the rule. Obviously if the reasons for the rule are more than mere reasons for ϕ-ing, then the rule itself is more than merely a reason to ϕ. The point is that whatever else the rule is, it is something which bears on the question 'Ought one to ϕ?' This is the nub of the problem: How can a rule bear on whether one ought to ϕ without being a reason for or against ϕ-ing?

Here is my proposal: The fact that it is a valid rule that one ought to ϕ is both a reason for ϕ-ing and a reason for not acting for certain reasons for not ϕ-ing. In so far as the rule is a reason for ϕ-ing it merely relays the force of the reasons for ϕ-ing on which it is based.

But a rule is also an exclusionary reason—namely a reason for not acting on certain conflicting reasons, and this explains its independent force as a reason. I have explained and defended this analysis of rules elsewhere.[13] The following example may illustrate the way in which the fact that rules are also exclusionary reasons explains the possibility of two-level justification. Imagine a revolutionary group taking a vow to disregard the government and its laws. They do not deny the authority of the government as the only effective civil authority. But despite their recognition of reasons for obeying the law they make their anti-social contract regarding it as justified as part of a revolutionary plan. Their vow is not for them a reason to do the opposite of what the law requires. It is not a reason to break every contract, trespass on all land, steal every property, violate every copyright, etc. It is simply a reason not to perform any action for the reason that the law requires it. One of the revolutionaries considers whether to steal his neighbour's money for revolutionary purposes. He weighs the reasons for so doing (facilitating some revolutionary activities) and against so acting (1) the harm to his neighbour, (2) the law, and (3) the risk to himself if caught. On balance he ought not to steal the money but of the reasons against so doing he should exclude the law because of his vow. It may be that if one excludes the law, the remaining reasons against the theft are overridden by the reason for it. If this is so the vow leads to the conclusion that in this case he ought to act against the balance of reasons. It is important to see that the exclusionary reason itself does not 'belong' to the balance of reasons. It is neither a reason for stealing nor against it. If the non-excluded reasons against stealing override those for it then he ought not to steal and the vow, unlike the reasons for the theft, would not be overridden. It will be conformed with provided he does not refrain from stealing because of the law.

We could stipulate a distinction between 'On the balance of reasons, one ought to ϕ' and 'All things considered, one ought to ϕ'. The second kind of judgment reflects the ultimate verdict of practical reason based on all the considerations which bear on the question. The first is a partial judgment being based on the reasons for and against ϕ-ing only. Our anti-social contract example shows how the vow affects the reasoning without being either a reason for or against stealing. Since rules are both reasons for the act they require and for disregarding some reasons against it, they can affect the all-things-

[13] *Practical Reason and Norms*, chs. 2 and 3.

considered judgment without changing the balance of reasons. This explains their special position in practical reasoning without denying their prima-facie character (they need not exclude all conflicting reasons and may be overridden). The analysis also explains how despite the fact that a reason for believing that one ought to ϕ is a reason for ϕ-ing, a rule requiring ϕ-ing affects the all-things-considered judgment that one ought (or not) to ϕ on a given occasion in a different way from the reasons for ϕ-ing on which it is based: It is also an exclusionary reason for disregarding certain reasons for not ϕ-ing. Finally it is the fact that rules are reasons for the action they require, defended so to speak, by reasons to exclude conflicting reasons which explains their relative independence despite their derivative status. Indeed we may say that their independence depends on their derivative status. Most commonly they represent a partial conclusion concerning what ought to be done in certain situations bringing together various, sometimes conflicting, considerations. These conclusions crystallize in the form of a rule with prima facie, but exclusionary force.

5. OBLIGATION

The preceding discussion of promises and rules clears the way to an account of the special or narrow concept of obligation: An action is obligatory if it is required by a categorical rule, i.e. a mandatory rule which applies to its subjects not merely because adherence to it facilitates achievement of their goals.

This account is meant to overcome four difficulties in the elucidation of the narrow concept of duty. *Firstly*, how to explain the peremptory force of duties. The temptation is to assign to them absolute or at least great weight. But this is contradicted not only by the belief in conflict of duties which shows that they are merely prima facie reasons, but also by the belief in many duties of little consequence—like the obligation to keep promises of a trivial nature, or some obligations of porters. The difficulty is solved if duties are imposed by mandatory rules. They are exclusionary reasons and thus have a special peremptory force, and yet the rules may have but little exclusionary force. Their special role is explained without entailing great importance or weight.

Secondly, there is the problem of why duties are felt to be particularly *binding* and the agent *bound* by them. This is explained by the combination of both features of the proposed account. Since obligatory acts are required by mandatory rules with exclusionary force, they are acts which the agent must sometimes perform even if they should not be performed on the balance of reasons. The agent is faced, in such situations, with two assessments of what ought to be done. On one level he ought, on the balance of reasons, to perform an act. On another and superior level he ought to do the opposite. This conflict of the results of two levels of hierarchically related evaluations creates the sense of being bound against (one-half) of one's own self. Not all mandatory rules, though, impose obligations. Many of them apply only to persons who pursue certain goals and are binding on them because they help promote these goals. Thus, aspiring opera singers must, in pursuit of their own goals, observe certain rules requiring practice of their voices, etc. Persons who want to be healthy must obey certain rules concerning their diet and physical fitness. Not all such rules are mandatory rules. But some are and they are not rules of obligation because they depend on the agents' own goals. Obligations derive from consideration of values independent of the person's own goals and that is another reason why he is thought of as bound by them despite himself.

Some rules depend on the agent's goals in more subtle ways. Rules of games apply only to persons who play the game, i.e. who pursue (or pretend to pursue) the goal of winning that game. Rules of thumb apply to people who because of ignorance, lack of time, emotional bias or similar reasons cannot trust their own judgment at the time for action. They are designed to remedy deficiencies which every rational person wants to remedy and thus are not rules of obligation. Naturally, rules of thumb are designed to produce greater efficiency in promoting some further good. They may serve a purpose which may be of value independently of the agent's goals. But in themselves they are meant to remedy deficiencies which are recognized as such by every rational person. Rules of etiquette are not regarded as imposing obligations by people who justify their adherence to them as a means to facilitate human relations. But they may be regarded as duty-imposing by people who regard them as binding on themselves for other reasons.

Voluntary obligations are the one exception to the rule that rules facilitating realization of the agent's goals do not impose obligations. An agent can incur an obligation by behaving in a way which normally communicates an intention to undertake by that very act an obligation.

I shall say little on *the third* main problem in any explanation of 'obligation', namely how to present a unified account of both moral and non-moral obligations. It is a problem which raises the general question of the nature of morality. Two points which avoid this large question can be briefly made: (1) Nothing in my account of either promises or obligations suggests that they are exclusively moral notions. If the obligation to keep a certain promise is moral this is because of the content and circumstances of that particular promise, and is not entailed merely by its being a binding promise. (2) Often when we make a qualified statement of obligation like 'one has a legal duty to . . .', one is making a suspended judgment, presenting the situation from a certain point of view, without either subscribing to or rejecting it. (Such sentences are also used to make full-blooded statements of obligation.) These statements from a point of view should not be confused with statements that certain people hold certain views. They are not about their point of view. They are statements from their point of view, representing things as they seem to those who hold the point of view but indicating that it is not thereby endorsed.

The *fourth* difficulty is of explaining 'obligation' by its formal features, as a concept with a special role in practical reasoning and at the same time accounting for our intuitions that the notion is particularly apt in certain areas such as undertakings and positions of special responsibility. My explication of the notion of duty is in terms of its formal character (imposed by mandatory rules) and the kind of reasons on which it is based (not subservient to the agent's own goals). Which acts are held to be obligatory depends on the substantive practical principles one adopts. Yet my account makes clear why the narrow notion of duty is commonly associated with roles and positions of special responsibility. The interests of all people should be equally respected. Yet many who believe so also believe that parents should attach greater importance to the interests of their own children, that statesmen owe a special duty to their own people and should prefer (up to a point) their interests to those of other nations, etc. There are many ways to reconcile such apparently paradoxical views. It all depends on the precise nature of the principles involved. Some could be easily explained on act-utilitarian grounds. But some hold stronger principles, wishing to combine an underlying universalistic value theory with a strong notion of the obligations involved in assuming roles or in any other position of special responsibility.

Some such commonly held principles are best explained on the basis of the proposed explanation of obligation, combining as it does two levels of evaluation: The general balance of reasons and the impact of exclusionary reasons requiring a special bias on the part of those who have certain special responsibilities.

These remarks do little more than suggest lines of inquiry which cannot be pursued here. Their explanation requires a full scale examination of the bases of the special duties of office-holders and other cases of special responsibility. Instead I shall turn in the last section to a brief and tentative consideration of the basis of promising principles and the way they fit in the general account of obligation proposed above.

6. ON JUSTIFYING PROMISING PRINCIPLES

There is no denying that the considerations of reliability and risk to the promisee on which the intention conception rests are sufficient to show that a firm expression of an intention to ϕ is, if the addressee is likely to rely on it, a reason for ϕ-ing. The intention conception does not fail because it cannot show that we have reasons to do as we promised. Since normally a communication of an intention to undertake an obligation expresses an intention to keep it these considerations do point to reasons for keeping most promises. The failure of the intention conception stems from the failure of these considerations to establish (PI) principles as categorical rules. They cannot show that every promisor whose act falls under a (PI) principle has not merely a reason to do as he promised, but also a reason for disregarding conflicting reasons which is based on categorical considerations.

Many authors have shown that these considerations justify a variety of rules of thumb (several of which are mandatory rules) designed to save time and effort or avoid error or bias by requiring the agent who made a (PI) promise to disregard conflicting considerations in circumstances which may lead to error, bias, etc. But these are not categorical rules and do not impose obligations, nor do they apply to all promises which fall under (PI) principles. They are merely auxiliary rules and cannot even show that any plausible (PI) principle (namely one covering all binding promises) is a valid mandatory rule.

To be sure if (PI) principles are valid mandatory rules then the requirement to keep (PI) promises is stronger than if they are not. The reasons for keeping them lose nothing of their force and to them are added reasons excluding action for certain conflicting reasons. It follows that if a person accepts and follows the view that (PI) principles are mandatory rules, he is less likely to break his promises than if he rejects this view. We could, therefore, say that such a person is the more reliable because of his belief that (PI) principles are mandatory rules. Does not that show that they are valid mandatory rules? I don't think it does. The increased reliability is excessive. The needs of reliability were admitted as reasons for keeping (PI) principles anyway. Allowing them extra force as exclusionary reasons as well would be to tip the balance unduly in favour of this consideration at the expense of conflicting considerations and would not be justified. Moreover, considerations of reliability cannot justify exclusion of reasons. By their nature they are reasons to be added to the balance of reasons rather than to justify possible deviation from the balance (contrast them with the anti-social contract).

No doubt this is all too brief a dismissal of an argument which was not adequately explored. But let us turn, finally, to (PO) principles. It may be thought that if considerations of reliability and risk to the promisee cannot establish (PI) principles as mandatory rules *a fortiori* they cannot establish the validity of (PO) principles. But one may try to use such considerations in a more discriminating way. It can, e.g., be argued that reliability is best served and the best consequences are achieved if there are two kinds of reason-creating expressions of intention to ϕ—one corresponding to (PI) principles, the other to (PO) principles—so that a person can bind himself more or less strictly. I am doubtful of the success of such arguments or any arguments which attempt to base (PO) principles on these considerations. For one thing it seems that (PI) principles can do full justice to the requirements of reliability and risk to the promisee. They also allow great flexibility (by explicit stipulation or implicit understanding) concerning the circumstances under which the promisor will hold himself bound by the promise. Secondly, such arguments seem to assume that promises are generally more weighty or more binding than other expressions of intentions. My account of (PO) principles does not assume this. The weight of the reasons to keep a promise and the scope of its exclusionary force depend on its content and on the circumstances.

(PO) principles present promises as creating a relation between the promisor and promisee—which is taken out of the general competition of conflicting reasons. It creates a special bond, binding the promisor to be, in the matter of the promise, partial to the promisee. It obliges the promisor to regard the claim of the promisee as not just one of the many claims that every person has for his respect and help but as having peremptory force. Hence (PO) principles can only be justified if the creation of such special relationships between people is held to be valuable. Thus the justification of (PO) principles, like that of (PI) principles, explains not only why one ought to keep promises one made, but also why it is good to make promises. Both inevitably create possibilities of abuse, of promises which should not have been made, but which, once made, should be observed.

It is not my purpose to argue that the special relationships the desirability of which would validate (PO) principles are indeed desirable. Nor will I try to explain the nature of such relationships. Instead, I shall conclude with two brief remarks about the importance of promises to practical philosophy.

First, the dependence of (PO) principles on the intrinsic desirability of forms of life in which people create or acknowledge special bonds between them and certain other individuals explains how the analysis of (PO) promises can serve as the model for the analysis of all kinds of obligations, for all depend for their validity on the value of special bonds and many of them are, like promises, constituent elements of special human relations (husband–wife, parent–child, leader–led, etc.). Secondly, the analysis of (PO) promises indicates that to acknowledge the validity of voluntary obligations (when 'obligation' is taken in the narrow sense) is to accept a rather unfashionable view of practical reason. It is a view according to which what a man ought to do depends not only on the ways things happen to turn out in the world (drought in another country; war, poverty, and social strife in one's own, the fact that more people enjoy soccer than classical music, etc.). What one ought to do depends in part on oneself, and this not only because the behaviour, needs, tastes, and desires of the agent count just as much as those of any other person, but because the agent has the power intentionally to shape the form of his moral world, to obligate himself to follow certain goals, or to create bonds and alliances with certain people and not others. It seems to me that many have become so preoccupied with the way considerations of human welfare affect what one ought to do that they become blind to the existence of this other dimension to our practical life.

13

Approval and Disapproval

PHILIPPA R. FOOT*

WHEN anthropologists or sociologists look at contemporary moral philosophy they must be struck by a fact about it which is indeed remarkable: that morality is not treated as essentially a social phenomenon. Where they themselves would think of morals first of all in connection with moral teaching, and with the regulation of behaviour in and by society, philosophers commonly take a different starting-point. What the philosopher does is to ask himself what it is to make a moral judgment, or take up a moral attitude, and he tries to give the analysis in terms of elements such as feeling, action, and thought, which are found in a single individual. Controversy persists between emotivists, prescriptivists, and those who have been labelled 'neo-naturalists' as to just which elements are needed and how they must be combined; all are agreed, however, in looking to the individual for their location. We are first to find out how it must be with him if he is to think something right or wrong, or to have an attitude such as that of moral approval; then we may go on, if we choose, to talk of shared moral beliefs and of the mechanism by which morality is taught. The essentials are found in the individual; social practices come in at a later stage in the story.

In a way it is strange that so few people question the methodological assumption just described, since we are well aware that many concepts cannot be analysed without the mention of social facts. For example it is a commonplace that writing a cheque, or going bankrupt, is impossible without the existence of particular social institutions such as banks and debts; no one would think that he could say what it is to write a cheque without giving an account of the social practices which give these marks on these bits of paper their significance. Examples may easily be multiplied. One recognizes at once, for

* Senior Research Fellow of Somerville College, Oxford; Professor in Residence, University of California, Los Angeles.

instance, that voting is something that a man can do only in the right social setting. Other people come in to the matter not just as being voted for, but also as the creators or perpetuators of the arrangements which make voting possible. Voting requires conventions about what counts as voting, and voting on a certain side; and a special piece of social stage-setting is needed for each election in so far as lists of candidates must be drawn up, or the possible choices established in some other way.

We are, therefore, well aware that the analysis of certain concepts cannot proceed without the description of social institutions and conventions. Why is it thought that we can ignore such things in analysing the fundamental concepts of ethics? One answer is that it is the attitude, not the act, of approval that we speak about in our moral philosophy, and that it is easier to believe that acts may require an appropriate social setting than that attitudes may do so. Another answer is that we have in mind the analysis of emotions such as fear, and that for these concepts the individualistic assumption seems to be justified. Whatever precisely is to be said about fear, however such elements as feelings, desires, actions, and thoughts are involved in *being afraid*, it does not seem necessary to look beyond the individual in order to understand the concept. Other people come in as the possible objects of fear, and conventions are needed for its verbal expression; but there seems to be no reason why a single individual should not feel fear whatever the social setting in which he finds himself. In this instance it is, therefore, right to start with the individual, going on, if one chooses, to shared fears and fears that can be attributed to social groups. No fact about society is implied by the attribution of fear to an individual as facts about society are implied by saying that he voted or signed a cheque. There are, therefore, mental concepts for which the individualist assumption is correct. The question is whether it is also right for the case of approval and disapproval. Are approving and disapproving more like voting in this respect, or more like feeling afraid?

The thesis to be put forward in this paper is that it is no more possible for a single individual, without a special social setting, to approve or disapprove than it is for him to vote. This will be argued for non-moral approval and disapproval; moral attitudes will be considered briefly later on.

It is evident that there is one case of approval which is more like voting than feeling fear so far as the relation to a specific social setting is concerned; this is the case of approval by an inspector passing e.g. plans for buildings in a city. The distinguishing mark of this kind of approval (apart from the fact that it is opposed to rejection rather than disapproval) is that the approving is something done, whether by a performative use of 'I approve' or by some other recognized device; if told that the inspector has approved the plans we can ask 'When did he do so?', asking not for the period during which he had the attitude (which perhaps he never did) but rather for the time at which the act of approval was performed. For such an act of approval a special social setting is obviously required. In the first place anyone who approves plans must be appointed to do so; the appointment may be formal or informal, but it must exist. Someone not designated as competent in the matter cannot be said to approve the plans; if he imagines himself to be doing so he must also imagine himself to occupy the relevant position. Moreover to each inspecting position belong not only conditions of appointment but also the standards which are to be used by the inspector. He is required to see if certain standards are met, and this is one of the things that makes his act one of approving rather than merely giving permission. In some cases he will be given the tests that he must apply; in others he will rather judge, in his own way, how far particular ends are served, as a school inspector may license a school on the basis of his judgment, however arrived at, that the pupils are well educated and cared for.

It is clear that we cannot describe this kind of approving without mentioning the social practices which create and maintain the position of inspector. There is, it seems, no need to prove the thesis of this paper so far as the acts of approval are concerned; the debatable proposition concerns the attitudes not the acts. It does not, however, seem right to argue from the features of one to the features of the other. No doubt it is not an accident that we use the same word 'approval' in both cases; but who can say just where the similarities lie?

We must, then, start afresh and ask whether the attitudes of approval and disapproval can exist only in a determinate social setting? Why is it commonly supposed that nothing of the kind is required? The main reason is, I think, that approving and disapproving are thought to be rather like wanting and not wanting. The chief element in their composition is supposed to be a readiness to work towards or away from some result, or perhaps from some *kind* of result. When one approves of the thing one is thought to favour it, which means working towards it, and the ill-defined term of art 'pro-attitude' is used to slide between wanting and approving.

I shall first try to show that such things as promoting and wanting are quite different from approving, and that wanting and promoting may exist without the possibility of approving; the same going for the opposites. For this I shall use a number of examples, all of approval and disapproval on non-moral grounds. Let us consider, for instance, parents who approve or disapprove of the marriage of one of their children; it is common for parents to do so, and we understand very well what this means. We notice, however, that a stranger cannot approve or disapprove of the marriage as the parents can, and we must ask why this is so. Why is it that I can approve of my own daughter's marriage, or disapprove of it, but not of the marriage of some girl who is not a relative, or even a friend? (Perhaps I have read of her in the local paper, or heard of her from a gossiping neighbour.) No doubt it will be objected that approval and disapproval of a marriage is not in fact confined to parents or even relatives and friends. For surely many white men in South Africa disapprove of the marriage of any white man's daughter to any black man, and surely there are grounds on which even reasonable people might disapprove of the marriage of some girl with whom they had no special connection, for instance because it was a case of child marriage, or a marriage that was forced upon the girl. This is true, but it should be noticed that these examples all come within the sphere of public manners and morals. The fact that anyone can approve or disapprove on such grounds is something we shall discuss later on. It is enough for the present argument, which confines itself to other areas, that there are grounds on which a parent can disapprove and a stranger cannot. Parents may disapprove of their daughter's marriage because the man is too old for her, or not rich enough, or not well enough connected; they may disapprove because they think that the marriage will not work out well, or because the family's honour or pride is at stake. Now the very same opinions may be held by someone unconnected with the family. Why is it that this other person cannot disapprove? One might think that it is because the stranger will not care about the girl's fortunes, or the fortunes of the family. But this may not be true. One may very well care about what happens to a stranger, either through a kindly disposition, or because there is some other factor at work. Then one will hope that the marriage will not take place and be sorry if it does; but it will still be wrong to say that one approves or disapproves. Nor is it a matter of having or not having actual power. Perhaps the parents are not able to influence what happens, and perhaps the stranger has this power; he decides to prevent the marriage, and by some means or other, perhaps by an anonymous letter to one of the parties, he is able to do so.

Nor does this appear to be an isolated case, which might be thought to depend on some ancient ritual aspect of parental approval. One can find other examples with the greatest ease. Suppose, for instance, that an elderly couple are thinking of retiring to some seaside resort, and the evidence is against the success of the venture. A relative or close friend who knows how things are likely to turn out may therefore disapprove of the idea. But what about a stranger? Or what about one who though a neighbour is not a friend? He too is of the opinion that if they go they will regret it, and being of a kindly disposition he cares, and may actually care more than the friends and relations, about whether they are unhappy or not. Moreover, he may, by chance, be in a better position than the others to make a difference to what the old people do. Perhaps there is only one bungalow in the seaside town, and he can buy it himself; or perhaps he can send an anonymous letter that will frighten them off. Even with the caring, and the power, we still cannot say of him that he disapproves of their idea unless, surreptitiously, we introduce some new role for him, such as that of the family doctor or the social worker in charge of elderly persons' welfare. If, not having such a position, he went and offered them *advice* he would merely be impertinent or officious; if, however, he said that he disapproved he would be saying something that could not, in the circumstances, be true.

Exactly the same point, about some people being able to approve or disapprove where others cannot, is illustrated by examples in which some but not others are involved in a particular enterprise, like giving a dinner party, or robbing a bank, or where some but not others belong to a particular institution like a college, or support an organization such as a sporting club. If my team captain chooses a certain player I may approve or disapprove of his choice; if your team captain chooses a player I may be glad or sorry, but barring a special circumstance such as bribery or blackmail I cannot approve or disapprove.[1]

---

[1] Someone who resolutely denies what is said here might be asked if he really thinks that an American might disapprove of the British Government's bill giving a measure of Home Rule to Scotland.

It seems, therefore, that there is this first difference between approval and disapproval and, e.g., wanting and liking. What anyone can want or like is not restricted, logically speaking, by facts about his relationship to other people, as for instance that he is the parent or friend of one, and engaged in a joint enterprise with another. Such facts can, however, create possibilities of approving and disapproving that would otherwise not exist.

Another contrast lies in the fact that approval and disapproval are logically connected with specific opinions as wanting and liking are not. It would be, at most, a requirement of rationality that one wanted or liked things for a reason, whereas attitudes of approval and disapproval are impossible without grounds. One could not say that one disapproved of the marriage, the retirement plans, the nomination of a player, or the choice of guests, but that one had no reason for doing so. And only some considerations will count as grounds for approval or disapproval in each case. A parent cannot disapprove of the marriage of one of his children on the grounds that a neighbour, with no particular standing in the matter, will be annoyed by it, or that his, the parent's income will be somewhat reduced. If he disapproves he must hold an opinion about the way the marriage will work out for his son or daughter, or about the way the family fortunes will be affected by it. Similarly, the relatives or friends of the elderly couple can disapprove of their projected move on the ground that they will be unhappy, but not because a neighbour will be put out by the sale of their house. With special assumptions these, too, could be grounds of disapproval of a moral kind, but for the moment we are putting morality aside. In the case of the joint enterprise the grounds of approval and disapproval are similarly limited but now the restriction is that they must have to do with the success or failure of the enterprise or with other shared ends of the participants. If we are giving a joint dinner party I may disapprove of your choice of guests or food or wine if I maintain that these are unfavourable to the success of the party, or, e.g., that they will ruin us financially. I may, however, have some reason of my own for disliking and working against some idea of yours for the dinner party which is nevertheless not a ground of disapproval. Perhaps some friend of mine in another town will be annoyed by the fact that we did not take his advice about where to eat, and I do not want to offend him. It does not follow that I can disapprove of what you have in mind.

Incidentally, examples such as these help one to get away from the idea that the grounds of disapproval must be lofty, or at least respectable. If two men are engaged together in some murderous project one may disapprove of the other's choice of assassins because the man chosen is not ruthless enough for the job.

The immediately preceeding paragraphs have shown that approval and disapproval are possible attitudes only in one who has an opinion from a determinate range. The opinion itself is not, however, enough any more than the right position or relationship would be. Everyone has opinions about what is and is not a good idea in the matter of marrying, house-buying, the choosing of players, the running of dinner parties, and a thousand other matters of everyday life. And each could be a ground of approval or disapproval given the right context. We do not, however, say that everyone has thousands of approvals and disapprovals, one to each of his everyday maxims. This alone should give pause to anyone who wants to insist that he does *disapprove of* retirement to the seaside, of putting a long and a short man in a team together, of inviting to a dinner party guests who see each other every day, or whatever it may be that he thinks not a good idea.

Having seen something of the part played by opinion in making approval and disapproval possible, we may now add another to our list of the special positions which may enable someone to approve or disapprove. So far we have said nothing about the position of experts, but this is obviously one which can allow one to approve and disapprove where others cannot. I am thinking, naturally, of expertise in some practical field such as the curing of illnesses or mending of motor cars. The doctor can approve and disapprove of treatments as the layman cannot, and the mechanic is in a similar position *vis à vis* the design of an engine or the mending of a car. Anyone can, of course, disapprove of a particular form of medical treatment if moral or other social issues are involved: for instance of the treatment of a patient against his will. And anyone can disapprove of the practice of dishonest mechanics who 'mend' a car in such a way that it is temporarily in running order but liable to break down at any moment. But as before we are leaving such considerations aside. What a person without medical expertise cannot do is to disapprove of a form of treatment on purely medical grounds, any more than one who knows little or nothing about car engines can approve or disapprove of something done to mend a car on the grounds that the mechanic can. And the point is not that he cannot have the opinion which they have;

even if he happens to have it that is not enough to allow him to approve or disapprove.

It may be objected that one sometimes says to someone not in fact expert on motors 'Do you approve of my new car?' or to one not versed in fashion or dress designing 'Do you approve of my outfit?' But when we notice the point of doing so the examples turn out to be ones which support the 'special position' thesis. 'Do you approve?' is, in such circumstances, a complimentary and friendly thing to say, and the reason it is so is the pretence that the conditions for approval are fulfilled. We are treating the person as if he were an expert, or alternatively as a close friend to whose scrutiny purchases would naturally be brought.

It seems, then, that the position of an expert is one of those giving the standing necessary for approving or disapproving in non-moral matters. If a doctor thinks a form of treatment a bad form of treatment he can be said to disapprove of it. *His* disapproval is general, and can be applied to any case without the need for a special relationship. The position of an expert is like that of close friend or relation, or partner in a joint enterprise, in that it is enabling with regard to approval and disapproval. It is unlike the other positions in giving standing for approvals and disapprovals of a general kind. To illustrate the difference we may use an example in which expertise but also public policy is involved. An economist may, for instance, disapprove of certain kinds of taxes both in general and in any particular case. I, on the other hand, can disapprove of a measure of taxation only in my country. Nor is it hard to see why I should be able to do so if we notice that public policy in my community is like policy in a joint enterprise in which I am taking part.

Let us now ask how all this is related to the thesis that approval and disapproval is dependent on a specific social setting? Has this been proved, at least for the range of approvals and disapprovals to which we have so far confined our attention? In fact the thesis has not yet been argued even for this set of cases. We have indeed seen that the possibility of approval and disapproval may depend on what could, I suppose, be called a social fact, as that *A* and *B* are engaged together in a joint enterprise. But this was not the kind of thing that I had in mind in suggesting the thesis. I was thinking of social practices that might underly this and all other forms of approval and disapproval.

To broach this topic let us consider again what it is to approve or disapprove, still thinking of the non-moral cases, but mostly because they seem to present less difficulty than the others. So far we have said something about the occasions for possible approval or disapproval, but nothing of its consequences. It is as if we had said who is appointed inspector, and what standards he must use in his inspection, but nothing about the fact that, by and large, it is only the plans that he approves that are put into effect. It is obvious that in the case of the inspector and his acts of approval it doesn't just happen that approval has these consequences. Without the agreement that gives his words or other actions these consequences, acts of approval would not exist. What I want to consider is whether something of the same kind may not be true for the attitudes of approval and disapproval? Obviously the same consequences are not in question for the attitudes and the act. The inspector disallows plans which he refuses to approve, and no one would suggest that this kind of command is the general rule where the attitude is concerned. What is the general rule is rather some kind of influence. Even this may be too strong a word; we should rather say that those able to approve or disapprove are as a general rule taken account of or listened to. And we must notice that 'as a general rule' is not put in for caution's sake, but rather to imply that there may well be instances of the attitude which do not have any such feature, either because it is both unexpressed and unnoticed, or for some other reason. Parents, we said, can approve or disapprove of their offspring's marriage; it does not follow that some parents are not totally disregarded in decisions of this kind. Going back to inspectors and acts of approval we see that there is nothing nonsensical about the idea of an individual inspector so personally feeble or badly situated that none of his acts of approval made any difference to what was done. Nevertheless it is impossible to describe the concept of an inspector, or an act of approval, without talking about the practice of building the buildings he approves rather than those he turns down.

Nobody will deny that when other people approve or disapprove of what we are thinking of doing, or have done, we do take account of it. The question is whether it is a contingent fact that we do so, or whether it is not. On one view of the matter we could have had approval and disapproval—the attitudes—without any presumption that this would make any difference to what happened, rather as we could in theory have wanting which no one took any account of. On the other view, which is the one for which I am arguing, the attitudes of approval and disapproval would not be what they are without the existence of tacit agreement on the question of who listens to whom and about what. On this view where we have approval or disapproval we necessarily have such agreements, though it may not be necessary that we have just the agreements that we do. Thus it may not be a necessary fact about approval and disapproval that, e.g., relations are able to approve where others are not. It could be that different classes of persons were able to approve and disapprove, or even that anyone could approve or disapprove of anyone in respect of anything. But a society in which the latter were so would necessarily have very different social practices from ours. For if it is true that where there is approval and disapproval there must be the understanding that as a general rule other people's views are taken account of there would have to be a lot more taking account of other people's views in that society than there is in ours.

That approval and disapproval can, logically speaking, exist only against a background of agreement about the part that other people's views shall be given in decision making, seems to me to be correct. It seems that it is anomolous to join a supposition about approval and disapproval with statements such as 'no one is expected to take any notice of that'. And if this is not obvious it is because the presumption that account will be taken is only a presumption, and may be destroyed in an individual case. What may destroy it is for instance the fact that some individual forfeits our respect by his habitually foolish opinions.

It will not be surprising if many find this thesis unacceptable on account of a picture that they have of what an attitude is. An attitude, they say, is something mental, and who can rule out in advance the possibility of any mental occurence or state in any social setting? Suppose that in the 'wrong' social setting, where there was no understanding that others were to be listened to, some individual just did have the attitude of approval or disapproval? (The 'wrong' social setting is either that in which there is no presumption that anyone will listen to anyone about anything, or else one which does not accord the right standing to someone placed as he is placed.) The idea is that whatever the social background this might be *how it was with him*. The proper reply for one who agrees with my thesis is that the hypothesis is impossible: that that couldn't be how it was with him. If they say that approving and disapproving are states of mind, and states of mind may logically exist in an individual whatever social setting he is in, one would reply that on that definition of 'state of mind' (which does not particularly recommend itself) what is at issue is whether approving or disapproving of something is a state of mind.

More powerful, perhaps, is the thought that approving is being *for* something, and disapproving *against* it. Surely it cannot be argued that these attitudes too require a tacitly recognized position? Curiously enough this is just what can be argued. If we go back, once more, to our old examples, we find that the stranger can no more be against the elderly couple's move to the seaside than he can disapprove of their going. If a relative or close friend says that he is against their going we understand him. To say to them 'I am against your going' may be ineffective, ill judged, or impertinent, but we understand the attribution of the attitude as conceptually in order. He is against their going. But what could it mean to say that the stranger was against their going, or to say it even of the neighbour who does not want new tenants next door? Either could want the old people to stay, but wanting-that-not is not the same as being against.[2] They could hope that the old people would not go, and could work against the project, but without some addition to the story we could not describe them as being against it. If the stranger, or the neighbour not a friend, went up to them and said 'I'm against your going', this would not be merely impertinent, like offering them advice; it would be presumptuous because presuming a relationship which did not in fact exist. Nor is the rule simply a social rule against expressing an attitude impertinently: 'he is against it' is just as bad as 'I'm against it', said to the people concerned. If this is not obvious it is because what is said at a distance, and not to their faces, leaves more room for fantasies of a special relationship.

What, then, is the relation between approving and disapproving on the one hand and on the other being for and against? It seems that approving and disapproving are special cases of being for and against, and that the two are practically indistinguishable in cases like the one described above. There are, however, examples of being for or against something which are not also instances of approval or disapproval. Let us consider the following example. A group of people are

---

[2] The only case I know of where to say one is for or against is the same as to say that one wants something, is in the locution 'I'm for so and so', meaning that one wants him to win. In this example, which was given me by Gilbert Harman, one is simply, perhaps in imagination, taking sides, and for that no special position or social setting is required.

deciding how to spend the evening together. Should they go to a cinema? Should they go into town? If they go to a cinema, which one should it be? Some are in favour of one thing, some of another. And this need not be a matter of approval or disapproval; they may simply be for or against.

The characteristic of this class of examples is that we do not always have shared ends, as with the joint enterprise, but ends that may conflict. And here each man may, though he need not, favour a course of action on the ground that it suits himself. Each has in theory a voice in the decision even if in practice some particularly ineffective or unpopular individual may be ignored. What we now want to ask, as in our question about approval and disapproval, is whether the tacit agreement about how such questions are to be settled is necessary if the attitudes of being for or against different courses of action are to exist? It seems to me clear that it is so. That the agreement is necessary for one use of the expressions 'I'm in favour of X' or 'I'm against X' is obvious. For these expressions sometimes function rather like a device for registering a vote, and it seems clear that if you are going to register a vote you must have it, and that if you have it the relevance of what you say to the decision cannot be denied. Of course even formal votes can be miscounted, falsified, wasted, etc. Nevertheless where the words 'I'm in favour of X' are used in this way there must be some presumption that what the speaker wants is to be taken into account. Now it may be said that this is all very well when we are considering the use of the expression 'I'm in favour of X' as if it were the casting of a vote. Perhaps it is a different matter when an attitude is involved. This seems a strange position because it drives a large wedge between two things apparently so closely connected. One would have thought that the expression of the attitude required rather more in the way of conditions than the 'voting' use. But on the present hypothesis a social background would be presupposed by the latter but not by the former.

If being for or against, in favour of or opposed to, are atitudes that do require a particular social background, then even where approval and disapproval are not themselves in question we have social conditions which are required for the attitudes. It is not, however, to be suggested that the agreement behind each is the same. When one approves or disapproves of something it seems to be one's opinions which are to be taken into account, and hence it is right to speak of being listened to. In the cases of being for or against just discussed the understanding is rather that one's wishes are to be taken into account.

The thesis that being for and against are attitudes which, like approval and disapproval, presuppose a determinate social background is strengthened by consideration of the following example. There is a prison camp in which the prisoners have no say whatsoever in the running of the place. The camp commandant takes decisions to suit himself or his superiors, and the prisoners' wishes are considered irrelevant. Now it is easy to suppose that some ruling, as e.g. about the work they are to do, affects the prisoners adversely. They do not like the new rule; perhaps they even hate it. Nevertheless in the circumstances imagined we cannot say that they are opposed to it or against it. This might seem to be because there is no way in which they can work against it, but actually this might not be so. They might, for instance, scheme to kill the commandant in the hope that his successor would change the rule, and might actually have more effect on things than the members of some group, in a different setting, whose wishes were supposed to be taken into account. Nevertheless, since the position of being against something is one that only society can create, it is the former, not the prisoners, to whom it is available.[3]

Turning back to approval and disapproval we may at last raise the question of approving or disapproving of something on moral grounds. Does this, too, presuppose particular social practices? My intuition is strongly that it does, and that the practices and expectations necessary for moral approval and disapproval share at least some of the features of those which other kinds of approval and disapproval require. It is not, of course, that customs about who is to be listened to here establish classes of persons able to approve or disapprove where others cannot. In matters of morality we do not need experts, and such things as relationships are irrelevant to moral approval and disapproval. If anyone can approve or disapprove on moral grounds, then everyone can do so, or any sane person over a certain age. What is understood is that anyone is to listen to anyone when considerations are brought forward which are moral considerations.

There is, therefore, no difficulty in the idea that although no exclusive position is needed for moral approval or disapproval determinate social practices are nevertheless presupposed, and one

[3] This way of putting it was suggested by Jerrold Katz, who has given me much help in the writing of this paper.

might ask at this point why it is supposed that the possibility of moral approval and disapproval must be independent of social facts? It is not, after all, that *all* moral concepts must have such independence. Obviously, promising and owing are things that require a particular social background, and it has been argued by H. L. A. Hart that obligations are in the same boat so far as this is concerned.[4] Without the institutions that give these concepts application a man could not truly think that he had promised this, was owed that, or had a certain obligation. And if he, on his own, dreamed up the ideas, he would have to dream up the social practices as well.

One cannot say that just because moral approval and disapproval are *moral* we can see, ahead of any investigation, that they cannot require a determinate social setting. But does anything, apart from the analogy with the inspector's act of approval and (if the preceeding arguments have been right) with non-moral attitudes of approval and disapproval, suggest this link between social practices and moral attitudes? The crucial experiment is to suppose a world in which the practices are different in the relevant respects, and then to see what would be possible for an individual in a world such as that.

What is it, then, that we have, which may make moral approval and disapproval possible? What we have, which we might not have had, and perhaps will not always have, is a certain assumption about the determination of conduct within a certain area. It is our custom, and for all I know the custom of every society in the world, to take matters such as killing, stealing, and lying as the concern of the community. Everyone has a voice in the matter of whether or not these things are to be done; actions within this range are up for scrutiny, and by and large men take account of what others say about such matters. The actions are 'passed' or 'not passed', and moreover people are accepted or not accepted on the ground that they do or do not do them. This is, of course, so familiar to us that it is hard even to see it as a particular social setting which might be necessary for moral approval and disapproval. Perhaps this will be easier if we try to think the familiar setting away. Suppose, for instance, that no one took much notice of what anyone else did, except when it affected him, or him and his family. Cows and horses behave like this. Suppose that human beings did so as well? Or suppose that people were interested in each others' actions but only aesthetically. They liked to

---

[4] 'Legal and Moral Obligation' in *Essays in Moral Philosophy*, ed. A. I. Melden (University of Washington Press, Seattle and London, 1958).

watch rescues and not murders, or murders and not rescues, but this
had no effect on the number of murders or rescues that were performed. In such settings people would not have a 'say' in what other
people did as they do in a society such as ours. No one would be
taught not to murder or ostracised for stealing; these things would be
treated as the affair of the agent and his victim.

Now let us place in this world an individual of universal benevolence, hating the suffering that these people inflict on each other.
And suppose that he sets out to try to prevent murders and to get
other people to hate them too, and to refrain from such acts. Can we
now say that his attitude to murder is one of moral disapproval? It
seems to me that we cannot; and that the reason is that we cannot
think of him, situated as he is, as refusing to 'pass' acts of murder. In
this situation, where by hypothesis there is no social regulation of
behaviour, and no one cares what anyone else thinks of what he does,
no one has any authority to speak against murder. Then does a man
who disapproves of something on moral grounds necessarily speak
with the authority of society? In one way, of course, he need not do
so, or else it would be impossible for anyone to come out against
established moral opinions. But it matters here what our moral
theory allows. If we think that there are no limits, logically speaking,
to the considerations that may be argued by a moral dissenter, that is
a would-be moral reformer, then his moral opinions need relate to no
standards or goals accepted by others who have a morality. If,
however, this seems on other grounds implausible, we shall think that
even the most radical moral reformer must, if he is to keep within
morality, refer to more or less determinate standards or ends. He and
others must have common ground, and it is this that allows him to
speak with authority even when he is criticizing those among whom
he lives.

What, however, are we to say about those who altogether reject
morality? Surely we think it possible to disapprove of their actions,
although they do not agree to take any account of what we say? This
is true, and it is an important fact about the phenomenon we call
'morality' that we are ready to bring pressure to bear against those
who reject it. But this no more shows that moral attitudes do not
depend on agreement within human society than the possibility of
asserting other kinds of authority against those who do not accept it
shows that authority requires no agreement. The position of the one
man described in the last paragraph is not at all like our position,

given that we are able to bring the pressure and authority of society against those who reject the ends of morality. Nor do we get a position like his if we think of discovering some tribe whose members behave in the way we described earlier, having no morality and not, initially at least, caring whether we accept or reject them. For it matters that if we do find such a tribe we will confront them with the confidence that we have the world with us—the world that pays at least lip service to morality. Perhaps we would coerce them; perhaps, whatever might be their cruelties, we would not. In neither case would it be nonsense to speak of disapproving of what they did. 'But might we not be in the position of this tribe?' What are we supposing here? That we have discovered thousands of inhabited planets or stars, whose inhabitants have no morality and, though they have commerce with us, take not the slightest notice of how their actions seem to us? To say 'We could still disapprove of them' seems to me to carry no conviction if we really get our minds round such an idea. 'But we wouldn't', it may be said, '*accept* them'. In this situation neither accepting nor rejecting makes any sense at all.

Finally, I want to consider whether what was said earlier about the need for reasons for attitudes of approval and disapproval could be true also in the moral case. Must there not be some basic moral approvals and disapprovals for which no reasons are given?[5] To see how we should answer this question it will be useful to go back to our earlier examples of non-moral approval and disapproval. We were talking, for instance, of friends and relations who disapproved of an elderly couple's plan of retiring to the seaside, and of partners in joint enterprises who disapproved of choices of dinner guests. In one case the reason for the disapproval was the thought that the couple would be unhappy; in the other cases what was in question was the success of the joint enterprise, or some other shared end, these being the standards dictated by the particular context. And we see that indeed we cannot suppose the question 'Why do you disapprove?' applied to the objects specified in the standard. It is not that we could not understand questions such as 'Why do you disapprove when your partner makes a choice disastrous to the enterprise in which you are both engaged?' or 'Why do you disapprove when there is a plan afoot that will probably turn out badly for one of your friends or relatives?' But we would have to understand these questions differently from

---

[5] This problem was put to me by Bernard Gert, and I am grateful to him for making me think about it in this context.

'Why do you disapprove of their moving to the seaside?' or 'Why do you disapprove of the choice of so and so?' Perhaps what is being asked is why we go in for this kind of disapproving, which is not something that everyone does. But to *this* question we could answer that we didn't know and perhaps had no reason at all. Similarly, in the case of moral approval and disapproval, the question 'Why do you disapprove?' requires an answer so long as the standard itself has not been reached. Here even those who have not decided on prescriptivist or emotivist grounds that there could not be such a standard will agree that it is much harder to say where it is reached. Perhaps there is more than one 'good' to which moral standards relate, as for instance both the common good and the liberty of the individual. But given that these are standards one does not need a reason for applying them. The question 'Why do you disapprove of pointless cruelty?' is not to be treated like 'Why do you disapprove of breaking promises?' One can ask whether, and if so why, someone goes in for the approvals and disapprovals we call moral, but if there is no answer to the question 'Why?' no doubt is thrown on the attitude itself.

In conclusion, I should like to go back to the main thesis of this paper and ask about the implications of the idea that moral approval and disapproval can exist only in a setting in which morality is taught and heeded. Does it imply that outside this setting all moral judgment would be impossible? The answer to this question must depend on the connection we see between moral judgment and approval and disapproval. If there are any expressions—'right' and 'wrong' for instance—that serve only to express these attitudes, these would obviously not be in the language. But it is not clear that the whole of our moral language has an essential connection with the expression of attitudes, even if any part does so. When, for instance, we speak of good men and bad men, or good actions and bad actions, we are using a form of expression ('good *A*') which is, in general, linked to standard interests rather than speakers' attitudes. There seems to be no reason why an individual who observes that there is a certain interest in a given class of persons or things should not have the materials for the invention of a new expression of this form—as he might have been the first to put 'good' together with 'friend' or 'neighbour' or 'singer' or 'speaker'—and similarly he might introduce 'good man' or 'good action' even into a setting in which the attitudes of moral approval and disapproval were not possible. Whether he would then be said to have introduced 'moral judgment' is another matter, and one not easily decided given that the expression 'moral judgment' is for the most part a term of art. What is clear is that the expression of approval and disapproval is part of the complex phenomenon we call 'morality', and that if approval and disapproval are essentially social in the sense explained here, then the morality we are trying to analyse is so too.

14

Scepticism, Self-Refutation, and the Good of Truth

J. M. FINNIS*

I

By inviting and inciting us to reflect on the implications of our own dispositions to act, *The Concept of Law* restored the theoretical vigour of jurisprudence and its openness to all the other philosophy and sciences of human affairs. Throughout that book, we are asked to reflect on what we would say when . . . But having been coaxed beyond the observation and correlation of external events and behavioural responses, we are asked not merely to relate such patterns of activity with patterns of language use, but also, and more fruitfully, to relate both external activity and use of language with the attitudes, dispositions, desires, interests, acceptances, presuppositions, and, indeed, the reasons, which we either have, or could understand having, in relation to such ways of acting and speaking. Patterns of behaviour and patterns of linguistic activity alike *display* patterns of reason(ing) and will(ingness); jurisprudence advances by going behind the display.

The present essay is a reflection on the implications of our willingness to further our understanding, to raise questions, to seek clarifications, and to make efforts to sharpen our perception. I do not take it for granted that the reader's desire is to further his understanding of law, coercion, or morality as social phenomena (though I digress, in section III, to tilt at a bad argument that has had some social success among lawyers). I assume no more than that the reader has sometime come across an assertion (or has himself entertained an idea) which he wished to dispute because it seemed disputable, to challenge because it seemed challengeable, to disagree with because it seemed to him foolish to agree.

* Fellow of University College, Oxford.

My own reason for undertaking this reflection is my wish to dispute Hart's view that *knowledge* is more disputable and more debatable as an aspect of the good for man than *survival*.[1] By examining what is implied in any profound disagreement I wish to dispute Hart's assertion that 'men may profoundly disagree'[2] with the classical view that 'the specific human end or good is in part . . . a condition of biological maturity and developed physical powers, but . . . also includes . . . a development and excellence of mind manifested in thought and character.'[3]

I do not wish to raise any objection about the course of argument on the relevant pages of *The Concept of Law* (pp. 186–8), pages which after all may be controlled by their author's desire to persuade hard-bitten lawyers and tough-minded social scientists to join him in seeing how far the *phenomena* of law and morality can be explained by reference to *at least* one, rather *minimal*, aim: survival. Nor do I wish merely to equivocate on a phrase such as 'men may profoundly disagree', which after all may have signified no more than that men violently or frequently disagree, or often act as if they disagreed. Nor do I wish to speculate on the historical causes for the present situation of any philosophy or science of human affairs, in which the fact that values 'may be' (in some sense of 'may') 'and have been challenged' is explicitly or implicitly treated as methodologically controlling. Nor do I wish to explain the ways in which that methodological decision controls the arguments and conclusions not only of a Hobbes (who first publicly rejected concern for any *summum bonum*)[4] but also of such apparently disparate enterprises as Hart's *The Concept of Law*, Rawls's *A Theory of Justice*, and Nozick's *Anarchy, State and Utopia*, and seriously obscures the purport of Fuller's *The Morality of Law*.

Rather, my concern is to contribute to a more exact understanding of a practical principle which Plato, Aristotle, and Aquinas regarded —rightly—as self-evident. What most sharply differentiates the classical from the modern philosophy of human affairs is that the one asserts while the other denies that truth (and knowledge of it) is as self-evidently and intrinsically good for man as life is. Not that I wish

---

[1] H. L. A. Hart, *The Concept of Law* (Clarendon Press, Oxford, 1961), p. 187.
[2] Ibid.
[3] Ibid., p. 186.
[4] Hobbes, *The Elements of Law*, ed. F. Tönnies (Cambridge U.P., Cambridge, 1928), I, 7, § 6; 9, § 21; 14, § 6; 17, § 14; II, 9, § 3; 10, § 8; *Leviathan*, ch. XI, ed. A. D. Lindsay (Dutton, New York, 1950), p. 49; ch. XLVI (pp. 366, 372).

to defend any of the classical expositions of this principle and its self-evidence. Certainly I regard Aristotle's (apparent) view that truth is *more* self-evidently and fundamentally good than life[5] as more nearly correct than the modern view that knowledge is *less* self-evidently and fundamentally good than survival. But both views are wrong: self-evidently, both life and truth are intrinsically, underivatively, fundamentally good, and there is no priority, ranking, or hierarchy of the fundamental forms of human good.

I consider (but cannot on this occasion argue) that life and truth are not the only fundamental aspects of human good. There are also such basic forms of good as may be summarily labelled play, aesthetic experience, friendship, practical reasonableness (including freedom and authenticity), and what may be with particular crudity labelled religion. In the usual senses of that modern and opaque word 'moral', not all of these are moral goods. They can best be described as the basic (underived) principles of practical reason. From them are derived (by an operation of practical reason which cannot be expounded here) conclusions which we would call moral principles, rules, obligations, counsels . . .

Aristotle had an explicit and definite account of the self-evidence and indemonstrability of fundamental principles,[6] but seems never to have applied it in working out an account of first principles of practical reason. As it happened, it was Thomas Aquinas who repaired the omission.[7] But his account of these principles, notwithstanding its clarity, has much more often than not been thoroughly misunderstood, by theologians in a hurry to claim for concrete moral rules the status of self-evidence, and by philosophers content to take it for granted that practical reason is just theoretical or speculative reason (misunderstood by them, moreover, as a kind of passive looking) supplemented by acts of will.[8] The present essay is a contribution to an investigation of the self-evidence and indemonstrability of fundamental practical principles. It relates to one particular practical principle, and it

---

[5] See *Eudemian Ethics* vii: 1244^{b}23 ff.; cf. *Nicomachean Ethics* ix. 9: 1170^{a}26–b14. I leave aside the ambiguities in the notion of survival; they are underlined by Stephen Clark, *Aristotle's Man: Speculations upon Aristotelian Anthropology* (Clarendon Press, Oxford, 1975), pp. 19, 22, 172.

[6] See *Posterior Analytics B*, 18: 99^b 16 ff.

[7] See *Summa Theologiae*, I–II, q. 94, a. 2; q. 10, a. 1; II–III, q. 47, a. 6.

[8] For sound interpretation see Germain G. Grisez, 'The First Principle of Practical Reason: A Commentary on the *Summa Theologiae*, 1–2, Question 94, Article 2' *Natural Law Forum* 10 (1965), also (slightly revised) in A. Kenny, ed. *Aquinas: A Collection of Critical Essays* (Macmillan, London, 1969).

demonstrates that the principle can be defended against sceptical objections. But that demonstration is not to be understood as an attempt to demonstrate the principle itself.

The principle that truth (and knowledge of it) is a good objectively worthy of human pursuit cannot be demonstrated. But it stands in need of no demonstration and itself is presupposed, as we shall see, in all demonstrations whatsoever. It is self-evident. That does not mean that it is understood and accepted, even implicitly, by everyone. If it were understood and accepted by everyone, that fact would be neither ground for inferring the principle nor compelling evidence for its objectivity. Correspondingly, the fact that it is not universally accepted is neither a ground for denying it nor compelling evidence against its objectivity. Still, it is self-evident to anyone who has the experience and intelligence that are necessary to understand the terms in which it is formulated (though I am not implying that only those who formulate it act on it). To know that other men have valued knowledge for its own sake is relevant as a source of vicarious experience, as a relevation or reminder of opportunities open to one. Taking it for granted that the reader has some knowledge of the opportunities for human knowing, the present essay eschews any attempt to evoke an understanding of those opportunities or their worth, and restricts itself to the negative role of refuting a form of sceptical doubt.

II

I shall use the terms 'retorsive argument' and 'argument from retorsion',[9] synonymously, to signify any argument which refutes a statement by showing that that statement[10] is self-refuting. That is a

---

[9] For want of any accepted English term I adopt this term from a continental usage. G. Isaye, 'La justification critique par rétorsion', *Revue philosophique de Louvain* 52 (1954), 205, introduces the topic as follows: 'Nous appelons "rétorsion" le procédé de discussion que saint Thomas nomme *redarguitio elenchica*. Il est essentiel à cette démarche d'être une *réponse*. Certaines objections sont ainsi faites que l'objectant, par le fait même de son objection, *in actu exercito*, concède la thèse qu'il voulait nier ou mettre en doute. Porter l'attention de l'objectant sur la concession qu'il vient de faire implicitement, c'est retourner l'objection en ma faveur, c'est rétorquer, c'est faire une rétorsion.' (Rétorquer: to retort, or to turn back.)

[10] Throughout I adopt the following standard terminology (there are other standard usages, some of which are used by some of the authors cited): 'sentence' signifies a form of words, a grammatical entity, without reference to a particular utterance; 'statement' signifies an event in which a declarative or assertive sentence is uttered, an act of stating something, a kind of performance; 'proposition' signifies what is expressed by a sentence, e.g. what is stated by a statement.

broad and rough characterization of the term, and will be refined by differentiating the types of self-refutation.

A first type of self-refutation is instanced by *propositions* which refute themselves either because they are directly self-contradictory or because they logically entail their contradictory.[11] Examples of this first type of self-refutation are such propositions as: 'I know that I know nothing'; 'It can be proved that nothing can be proved'; 'All propositions are false'. Slightly more subtle examples are: 'It is not the case that something is possible'; 'All propositions are true'. In the latter instances there is required some translation or logical manipulation and analysis before the self-refutation of the proposition is evident.[12] None the less, the retorsive argument which makes the required translation or analysis should be clearly distinguished from all *ad hominem*[13] arguments which seek to show that one and the same speaker is here asserting that *p* and elsewhere asserting that not-*p*. There is self-refutation of this first type only when one and the same proposition either is of the form 'both *p* and not-*p*', or is of the form '*p*' and logically entails 'not-*p*'.

A second type of self-refutation is instanced by statements whose occurrence happens to refute their content. I shall call this 'pragmatic self-refutation'.[14] An example of pragmatic self-refutation is afforded by someone singing 'I am not singing'. It might seem that pragmatic self-refutation is just a sort of trivial lie, of no philosophical interest. But the significance of pragmatic self-refutation is that it introduces us to the notion of performative inconsistency,[15] that is, inconsistency between what is asserted by a statement and facts that are given in and by the *making* of the statement.

The third type of self-refutation is instanced by propositions which cannot be coherently asserted, because they are inevitably falsified by

[11] See J. L. Mackie, 'Self-Refutation—A Formal Analysis' *Philosophical Quarterly* 14 (1964), 195–6. I am following Mackie's taxonomy of types of self-refutation.

[12] For 'It is not the case that something is possible', see Mackie, op. cit., p. 195; for 'All propositions are true' see Aristotle, *Metaphysics*, Γ 8:1012^{b}13; K 6.

[13] The term '*ad hominem* argument' is used very variously. A retorsive argument can be called '*ad hominem*', but only in a sense very different from arguments that point to inconsistency between different parts of a speaker's discourse, and *a fortiori* from arguments that undermine a speaker's assertions by demonstrating *his* unreliability, insincerity, etc.

[14] I follow Mackie's terminology, which has a more precise sense than the same phrase in, e.g. John Passmore, *Philosophical Reasoning* (Duckworth, London, 1961), ch. 4.

[15] For a useful review, see Joseph M. Boyle, Jr., 'Self-referential Inconsistency, inevitable Falsity and Metaphysical Argumentation', *Metaphilosophy* 25 (1972), and works there cited.

any assertion of them. The proposition 'I am not singing' is not such a proposition, since it can be asserted (say) in writing. Similarly, the propositions 'Descartes cannot speak English' and 'Descartes does not exist' are not inevitably false, even though the first is pragmatically self-refuting when uttered by Descartes in English and, in that sense, cannot be coherently asserted by Descartes in English, while the second is pragmatically self-refuting when uttered by Descartes in any language or other mode of expression. But the proposition 'I do not exist' is inevitably falsified by *any* assertion of it: the sentence 'I do not exist', if uttered in a statement, inevitably states a false proposition. Equally incapable of being coherently asserted is the proposition 'No one can put words (or other symbols) together to form a sentence'. I shall call all propositions such as the last mentioned 'operationally self-refuting'.[16]

Operationally self-refuting propositions cannot be coherently asserted. But they are not, themselves, logically incoherent. Nor are they meaningless or empty, or *semantically* paradoxical. Examples of semantic emptiness or paradox are: 'This sentence is false', or the norm 'This norm may be repealed by a two-thirds majority' where 'this sentence' or 'this norm' in each case is not a colloquial reference to some other sentence or norm, but, rather is self-referential and fails to establish any definite reference.[17] Operationally self-refuting propositions have a quite definite reference and hence can be (and inevitably are) false. Any such proposition is false because it is inconsistent with the facts that are given in and by any assertion of it. It itself is not self-refuting, but trying to assert it *is*.

A point similar to that made in the preceding sentences is made in more formally logical terms by J. L. Mackie. He prefers to say that any operationally self-refuting proposition either contradicts the proposition 'someone asserts that *p*' or else contradicts some proposition entailed by 'someone asserts that *p*'.[18] That is why the assertion of an operationally self-refuting proposition is said to be incoherent: one cannot coherently assert a self-contradiction; one who asserts a proposition *p* is implicitly committed to asserting, not merely whatever is entailed by *p*, but also any proposition entailed by

[16] Following Mackie, op. cit., p. 197.

[17] See H. L. A. Hart, 'Self-Referring Laws', in *Festskrift tillägnad Karl Olivecrona* (P. A. Norstedt & Sons, Stockholm, 1964), pp. 315–16; Alf Ross, 'On Self-Reference and a Puzzle in Constitutional Law', *Mind* 73 (1969), 7–17; J. L. Mackie, *Truth, Probability, and Paradox* (Clarendon Press, Oxford, 1973), pp. 242–7, 285–90.

[18] Mackie, 'Self-Refutation—A Formal Analysis', op. cit., pp. 196, 198.

'someone asserts that p'; but where p is operationally self-refuting p contradicts one or more of those entailed propositions.

Hence the work to be done by a retorsive argument exploiting operational self-refutation consists in drawing out the 'implicit commitments' of the interlocutor, i.e. the propositions entailed[19] by 'someone is asserting that . . .', i.e. by the facts given in and by the interlocutor's statement. This is the most interesting and fruitful type of retorsive argument. Henceforward, references to self-refutation are (unless otherwise indicated) to operational self-refutation.

It is important to observe that, even where it is cast into logical form (as by J. L. Mackie, and as in section V of this essay), a retorsive argument from operational self-refutation achieves its effect by appealing to facts, which, of course, are not deduced by some logical operation but have to be recognized by the interlocutors in the ordinary 'empirical' ways. For 'p' does not entail 'someone asserts that p'. Hence the peculiar force of a retorsive argument comes from the unavoidable *proximity* of the relevant facts. The self-refuting interlocutor is overlooking these facts, but is himself creating or instantiating them by and in his act of asserting (disputing). And here we may further observe that the interlocutor whom I refute retorsively may be either a person other than myself or, equally well, a voice of my own intelligence, a moment in that inner debate through which I pursue knowledge by raising questions, and supposing and rejecting or accepting hypotheses. So the self-refuting proposition may be expressed as an assertion, or as an argumentative hypothesis, or simply as an open question. One who asserts that p is implicitly committed to whatever is entailed by 'someone asserts that p'. One who considers p or asks whether p is not yet implicitly committed to asserting anything; but since he is considering whether or not he should assert p, he is implicitly committed to considering what would be entailed by 'someone asserts that p'. Moreover, most if not all that is entailed by 'someone asserts that p' is equally entailed by 'someone considers that p may be the case'.

What is entailed by 'someone asserts that p' very largely depends, of course, on what is meant by 'assert'. As Mackie's use of the notion of implicit commitment suggests, an assertion will be operationally self-refuting only if it is located in a universe of rational discourse and is (or is treated as) an authentic contribution to be assessed and

---

[19] I follow Mackie's notion of entailment. One could also speak of implication: see C. K. Grant, 'Pragmatic Implication', *Philosophy* 33 (1958), 303.

judged at least primarily in terms of its correctness or rational justification and not (or not primarily) in terms of its utility as a conversation-filler, joke, ruse . . . nor for its euphony as a collection of vocables . . . As we shall see in section V of this essay, a retorsive argument when fully developed is in large part an analysis of the relevant sort of assertion, namely, that sort of assertion which would be *considerable* as a contribution to or solvent of some profound (but rational) disagreement about what is the case.

III

This section digresses, to illustrate a use of retorsive argument to expose self-refutation in a popular contention which, though legal, is not itself simply normative in form.

The contention may first be considered as it was expounded in Lord Birkenhead's defence of legislative 'sovereignty', i.e. legislative freedom from the restraints of legal rules defining areas of legislative incapacity:

Some communities, and notably Great Britain, have not in framing constitutions felt it necessary, or thought it useful to shackle the complete independence of their successors. They have shrunk from the assumption that a degree of wisdom and foresight has been conceded to their generation which will be, or may be, wanting to their successors, in spite of the fact that those successors will possess more experience of the circumstances and necessities amid which their lives are lived.[20]

The polemical irony of the passage is a device for *expressing* (under the guise of reporting) *a claim to a degree of wisdom and foresight*, and for rhetorically asserting that claim against anybody who might doubt or deny that those who live at a given time will be as wise and far-seeing as the people of any other time and hence will know what it is best to do at and for their own time. But this claim of Lord Birkenhead's (unless it is a mere prediction that wisdom simply *will* not fail amongst certain peoples, a prediction always liable to be overturned by events) is significantly comparable with the implicitly but absolutely self-refuting claim that all claims are true. For it is certainly possible that amongst Lord Birkenhead's successors (call them S1) there might be some (perhaps the ruling class or party)

---

[20] *McCawley* v. *R.* [1920] A.C. 691 at 703. This passage from the judgment of the Privy Council was much quoted in the great debate in the Indian Supreme Court about whether any parts of the Indian Constitution were immune from amendment: *Kesavananda* v. *State of Kerala*, All India Reporter 1973 Supreme Court 1461 at 1592, 1835.

holding and acting on the view that *their* successors (S2) were likely (for specifiable reasons, perhaps) to be unwise (perhaps generally, or perhaps just in relation to some specific question such as the question of the likely wisdom or unwisdom of their successors (S3)!). Is Lord Birkenhead committing himself to the contention that all his successors are going to be wise, even when they assert that some (or all) of their successors are going (or likely) to be unwise? If he is, he refutes himself, operationally as well as absolutely. For his contention (i) logically entails that his successors (S1) would be correct in thinking his contention incorrect and unwise, but (ii) implicitly commits him (by operational entailment) to the view that his contention is correct and wise.

What I am touching on here is, of course, what has often been called the paradox in the orthodox English view of Parliamentary sovereignty. In Hart's conveniently precise rendering of it, that view stipulates that Parliament enjoys 'a *continuing* omnipotence in all matters not affecting the legislative competence of successive parliaments'.[21] Thus it rejects the alternative view 'that Parliament should *not* be incapable of limiting irrevocably the legislative competence of its successors'.[22] How would the orthodox view or doctrine be expressed or embodied in legal rules? For convenience (and without reference to Hart's distinction between primary and secondary rules), I describe as 'second-order rules' rules about the enactment of rules, and as 'first-order rules' rules about matters other than the enactment of rules. The second-order rule embodying the orthodox view of Parliamentary sovereignty stipulates that the enactment of first-order rules is not restricted by reference to any subject matter, and that the enactment of second-order rules *is* restricted by reference to subject matter, namely, by the requirement that no second-order rule may (validly) be enacted which would contradict or limit the operation of the second-order rule embodying the orthodox view itself. Now this second-order rule is not itself self-contradictory or self-refuting. But any attempt to employ Lord Birkenhead's argument to support this rule (or the doctrine embodied by this rule) will fall into self-refutation. For those who attempt to defend the orthodox rule and doctrine by reference to *any* general principle (e.g. Lord Birkenhead's principle about the temporal distribution of wisdom) are thereby implicitly committed to maintaining

[21] Hart, *The Concept of Law*, p. 146. (Hart is reporting, not supporting.)
[22] Ibid., p. 145.

that they possess (in their principle) precisely 'a degree of wisdom and foresight' and that this wisdom 'will be, or may be, wanting to their successors . . .' viz. to any successors who might wish to set aside the principle and the doctrine founded on it and (on the basis of 'the circumstances and necessities' amid which *their* lives will be lived) enact a second-order rule contradicting or limiting the operation of the second-order rule embodying the orthodox doctrine itself.

So my reason for making the present digression has been simply to point out that the oddity of the orthodox view lies deeper than the commonly identified verbal antinomies or semantic paradoxes about 'omnipotence', 'unrestricted' sovereignty, etc. Rather, the 'paradox' is the oddity—indeed, absurdity—of at time t_1 asserting (and acting on) the principle (A) that *all* decisions falling to be made at t_2, $t_3 \ldots t_n$ will be made more satisfactorily at t_2, $t_3 \ldots t_n$ than at t_1, while at t_1 also asserting (and acting on) the principle (B) that any decision at t_2 to restrict the range of decisions able to be made at $t_3 \ldots t_n$ would be a decision less satisfactory than the decision at t_1 to act upon principle A.

I am not claiming that the orthodox doctrine of Parliamentary Sovereignty inevitably involves the assertion of principle A as well as principle B. The doctrine might be defended as being, not a claim of principle, but simply a judgment, made at t_1 and contingently repeated at $t_2 \ldots$, that *now* is not the time (i.e. there is no good reason *now*) to restrict the competence of successor Parliaments. But this would be a very weak version of the doctrine, for it allows that in principle any moment might be a good time to adopt (or to authorize the adoption of) some restrictions on the competence of successor Parliaments.[23] And when anyone suggests that some such restrictions be adopted now, at t_1, the defender of the established doctrine is likely to fall back on some version of principle A, for example, Lord Birkenhead's.

IV

Retorsive arguments have been exploited against sceptics not only by

[23] The doctrine might also be defended by drawing a sharp distinction between those who decide and act upon the doctrine (viz. the English establishment, officials or, if you prefer, 'the people') and the body whose powers of enactment the doctrine concerns (viz. the Parliament). But then the 'paradox' reappears in the form, not of inconsistent (or at best arbitrary) attributions of wisdom and unwisdom as between a decision-maker and his successors, but of inconsistent (or at best arbitrary) attributions of wisdom and unwisdom as between one decision-maker (e.g. 'the people') and another (Parliament).

Plato[24] and Aristotle,[25] the Stoics[26] and Augustine,[27] by Aquinas[28] (to a much lesser extent), and perhaps by Descartes,[29] but also by latter-day philosophers as diverse as Lonergan[30] and Wittgenstein.[31] Can a retorsive argument be used against one who denies, not the objectivity of truth, identity, proof, meaning, or existence, but the objectivity of every value, every form of *good*?

There seem, in fact, to have been rather few attempts to develop retorsive argument in this direction. Augustine conjoined with his well-known 'Si fallor, sum' the further claim that one is secure from the arguments of the Academic sceptics, not only in respect of 'we are' and 'we know that we are', but also in respect of 'we love to be and to know that we are'—which, being translated out of Augustine's terminology of 'love', is to say: we are secure in affirming that our life is of value, and our knowledge of it likewise.[32] But he makes no attempt to work out any explicit argument for this.

Augustine had been profoundly affected by reading the now lost *Hortensius* of Cicero.[33] This work seems to have contained an argument in favour of philosophizing, along the lines that one who says that philosophizing is not worthwhile is himself philosophizing (since to argue about what is and is not worth doing is precisely to philosophize).[34] Now the *Hortensius* is assumed to have been based on Aristotle's also lost work, the *Protrepticus*, and certainly Aristotle's

---

[24] *Theaetetus* 171.

[25] *Metaphysics* Γ 4:1005^{b}35 ff.; Κ 4. See Pierre Aubenque, *Le Problème de l'être chez Aristote*, 2nd edn. (Presses Universitaires de France, Paris, 1966), pp. 124–6; Joseph Boyle Jr., op. cit., p. 27.

[26] See the arguments assembled by Sextus Empiricus, *Pyrrhonean Hypotyposes* II. 185–6; *Adversus Mathematicos* VIII. 463.

[27] *De Civitate Dei* XI. 26; *De Libero Arbitrio* II. 3; *De Trinitate* X. 10, 16; XV. 12, 23; *Enchiridion* 20; *De Vera Religione* 39, 73; *Contra Academicos, passim*. Some of these texts are analysed by Gareth B. Matthews, 'Si Fallor, Sum', in R. A. Markus (ed.), *Augustine: A Collection of Critical Essays* (Doubleday, New York, 1972), p. 151; he interprets them as (in our present terminology) retorsive.

[28] *De Veritate*, q.10, a.8 ad 2; a.12 ad 7; *Summa contra Gentes* II. 33.

[29] See J. L. Mackie, 'Self-Refutation—a Formal Analysis', op. cit., pp. 197–8, refining J. A. Passmore, op. cit., pp. 60–4; Jaakko Hintikka, '*Cogito, ergo sum*: Inference or Performance?' *Philosophical Review* 72 (1962), 3. Against this interpretation, see A. Kenny, *Descartes: A Study of His Philosophy* (Random House, New York, 1968), pp. 42–8.

[30] B. J. F. Lonergan, *Insight: A Study of Human Understanding* (Longmans, London, 1957), ch. XI.

[31] Wittgenstein, *On Certainty* (Basil Blackwell, Oxford, 1969), paras. 363, 459, 460; cf. also paras. 506, 507, 514, and contrast para. 519.

[32] *De Civitate Dei* XI. 6.

[33] *Confessions* III. iv. 7; VIII. vii. 18; P. R. L. Brown, *Augustine of Hippo* (Faber, London, 1967), pp. 40, 107.

[34] Lactantius, *Institutiones Divinae* III. 16 (Cicero, *Hortensius*, frag. 12 Müller; also in W. D. Ross, ed. *Aristotelis: Fragmenta Selecta* (Clarendon Press, Oxford, 1955), p. 28).

commentators between the second and sixth centuries A.D. constructed and, in many instances, attributed to the *Protrepticus* an argument of the form: (1) 'If we ought to philosophize, then we ought to philosophize; and (2) if we say we ought not to philosophize then we ought to philosophize [in order to make out this assertion]; in any case, therefore, (3) we ought to philosophize'.[35] But a comparison of the various forms of this argument in the ancient sources reveals its obscurity. In particular, step (2) badly needs clarification, and, for want of clarification, is liable to be (and is) read in a non-normative sense. W. M. Kneale adopted this interpretation of step (2) when he said 'the most we can properly assert is "If *anyone says* there should be no philosophizing, then there must inevitably be some philosophizing, namely that which he has just begun" . . .'[36] This reading deprives the argument of interest for anyone who, like us, is looking for retorsive support for a practical (i.e. normative or at least evaluative) principle. For the following argument is quite obviously fallacious: (1) One who says philosophizing is worthwhile philosophizes; (2) one who says that philosophizing is not worthwhile philosophizes; therefore (3) philosophizing is worthwhile.

In recent times philosophers of such widely differing traditions as C. I. Lewis[37] and Gaston Isaye[38] have sketched retorsive arguments against scepticism about practical or normative or moral principles. But their presentations suffer from failure to distinguish between the different types of broadly retorsive argument, and from a too rapid assimilation of practical with moral principles. Hence there remains room for the present enquiry.

V

The retorsive argument which I wish to expound can be given the following rather extended formulation (among others):

For all *p*

(1) If I assert that *p* I am implicitly committed to 'I assert that *p*'.

[35] See the fragments from David and Elias in David Ross, ed. *The Works of Aristotle*, vol. xii, *Select Fragments* (Clarendon Press, Oxford, 1952), p. 28. W. M. Kneale, 'Aristotle and the *Consequentia Mirabilis*', *Journal of Hellenic Studies* 77 (1957), 62, and W. and M. Kneale, *The Development of Logic* (Clarendon Press, Oxford, 1962), p. 97, accept that Aristotle is the author of this argument, but this view is vigorously rejected by A.-H. Chroust, *Aristotle: Protrepticus: A Reconstruction* (U. Notre Dame P., Indiana, 1964), pp. 48–9.

[36] Kneale, *Journal of Hellenic Studies* 77 (1957), 63.

[37] C. I. Lewis, *Values and Imperatives*, ed. John Lange (Stanford U.P., California, 1969), esp. pp. 64–74, 79–81, 123–5; cf. Carl Wellman, review, *Philosophical Review* 80 (1971), 398–9.

[38] G. Isaye, op. cit., pp. 229–30, n.9.

(2) If I assert that p I am implicitly committed to anything entailed by 'I assert that p'.

(3) 'I assert that p' entails 'I believe that p [is true].'

    (4) 'I assert that p' entails 'I believe that p is worth asserting'.

    (5) 'I assert that p' entails 'I believe that p is worth asserting *qua* true'.

(6) 'I assert that p' entails 'I believe that truth is [a good] worth [pursuing or] knowing'.[39]

Therefore from (1)

(7) If I assert 'It is not the case that truth is [a good] worth [pursuing or] knowing' I am implicitly committed to 'I assert that it is not the case that truth is [a good] worth [pursuing or] knowing'.

And from (3) and (7)

(8) If I assert 'It is not the case that truth is [a good] worth [pursuing or] knowing' I am implicitly committed to 'I believe that it is not the case that truth is [a good] worth [pursuing or] knowing'.

But from (2) and (6)

(9) If I assert 'It is not the case that truth is [a good] worth [pursuing or] knowing' I am implicitly committed to 'I believe that truth is [a good] worth [pursuing or] knowing'.

So, from (8) and (9)

(10) If I assert 'It is not the case that truth is [a good] worth [pursuing or] knowing' I am implicitly committed *both* to 'I believe that truth is a good worth pursuing or knowing' *and* to 'I believe that it is not the case that truth is a good worth pursuing or knowing'.

Thus, if I assert that truth is not a good, I am implicitly committed to formally contradictory beliefs.

The argument (as I shall henceforth call it) indicates that I could never coherently deny that truth is a good. But if p seems to be the case (whether as self-evident or as warranted by evidence or reasons) *and* could never coherently be denied, p can reasonably be affirmed to be objectively the case.[40] Indeed, the argument can and should be

---

[39] The bracketed terms indicate alternative formulations (of which there are indeed many more: there need be and are no canonical formulations of first principles of reason).

[40] This is sometimes denied: e.g. Norman Malcolm, 'The Conceivability of Mechanism', *Philosophical Review* 77 (1968), 71: 'The inconceivability of mechanism, in

read as if the term 'objectively' preceded each instance of the terms 'good' and 'worth'. (I return to this matter of objectivity later in the argumentation.)

Steps (1) to (6) of the argument elaborate the sense and force of 'assertion', as that term is employed here. So I explain them in turn.

Steps (1) and (2) may be taken together. As I remarked at the end of section II of this essay, to assert that p is not merely to utter 'p' (which might be by way of an elocution lesson, microphone testing, quotation, recitation, word-game or guessing-game . . .). One's utterance does not amount to asserting that p unless it implicitly commits one to denying that not-p, and to affirming whatever is entailed by p, and to denying whatever else would entail not-p. To say this is not only to draw attention to an obvious feature of the word 'assertion' and its cognates in ordinary philosophical usage; it also is to express one of the elementary conditions of rational thought and discourse: that it be coherent. Now 'X asserts that p' is, of course, *not* entailed by p. So step (1) is a substantive step. It states that if someone says that p, he is not to be counted as asserting that p unless he has at least the (rather minimal degree of) self-consciousness sufficient to recognize that it is also true that he is asserting that p is true. Without that degree of self-consciousness, connected rational thought is impossible and argumentative discourse not worth bothering about. This point does not need labouring. Step (2) is entailed by step (1), given the definitional relation (stated earlier in this paragraph) between asserting that p and implicit commitment to whatever is entailed by p. For 'I assert that p' is an instance of 'p'.

Step (3) states the generally accepted results of the intensive philosophical analysis (initiated by G. E. Moore) of assertions of the form 'p, but I don't believe that p'.[41] The reason why the present retorsive argument is not cast in the third person is that step (3) cannot be transposed directly into the third person. For 'X asserts that p' does not entail 'X believes that p', since X may be lying. (In discussing step (1) we have already excluded the possibility that X is

the two respects we have elucidated, does not establish that mechanism is false.' But there seem to be no good reasons for this denial: see Joseph M. Boyle, Jr., Germain Grisez, and Olaf Tollefsen, 'Determinism, Freedom and Self-Referential Arguments', *Review of Metaphysics* 26 (1972), 34–5.

[41] See G. E. Moore, 'Russell's Theory of Descriptions' in P. A. Schilpp (ed.), *The Philosophy of Bertrand Russell* (Library of Living Philosophers, New York, 1944), pp. 203–4; M. MacDonald, ed. *Philosophy and Analysis* (Basil Blackwell, Oxford, 1954), ch. IV; C. K. Grant, 'Pragmatic Implication', *Philosophy* 33 (1958), 312–22; J. L. Mackie 'Self-Refutation—A Formal Analysis', op. cit., p. 196.

merely reciting, joking, etc.). Of course, this possibility that x is insincere could be accommodated in a somewhat expanded (third-person) version of steps (3) and (8), yielding the conclusion that if x asserts that truth is not a good, he is either implicitly committed to contradictory beliefs (as in (10)) or is a liar. Such an expanded version would, I think, be equally serviceable as a retorsive argument.[42]

Steps (4) and (5) are indented because they are introduced into the argument only in order to prepare for step (6); together these three steps carry the whole argument out of the ordinary run of retorsive exposés of operational self-refutation, by stating an *evaluative* implication of assertion. Step (4) itself is, however, hardly controversial as it stands, prior to any analysis of the term 'worth'. For if 'I assert that p but I don't believe p' is an absurd, pointless and (in *some* senses of 'self-contradictory') self-contradictory remark (unless it is to be taken in some non-straightforward sense), so equally is 'I assert that p but I don't believe that p is worth asserting'. Remember: 'asserting' is here not restricted to external utterances, but includes also, and even primarily, the internal operations of judgment, affirmation, assent, and the like.

Step (5) advances the analysis of the evaluative implications of assertion. It states that my thinking or saying that p does not count as an assertion of p unless I am thinking or saying that p (rather than either (i) not thinking or saying that p, or (ii) thinking or saying that not-p) because p (so it seems to me) is true, i.e. is correct, is-the-case.[43] For 'p [is true] but [in asserting this] I don't care whether p is true or

---

[42] The possibility of lies, deceptions, and insincerities calls for more detailed attention than I can give it here. Ramchandra Gandhi, *Presuppositions of Human Communication* (Oxford U.P., Delhi, 1974), argues 'that no account of assertion which was not also an account of *insincere* assertion could be regarded as satisfactory' (p. 15). But then, his book, unlike this essay, 'is very largely an attempt to understand the action of "telling" somebody something' (p. 141), and treats the role of a thinker as 'parasitic upon the roles of speaker and audience' (p. 140, n.1). But his analysis has its value in indicating (as against H. P. Grice, and by way of subtle attention to the possibilities of deceit) that for a speaker (*S*) to assert to an audience (*A*) that p, is for *S* to perform communicatively an act which *both* (i) implies, prima facie, that *S* wants *A* to believe that p (or that *S* believes that p), but *also* (ii) does *not* imply, prima facie, that *S* is trying to get *A* to believe that p (since, if this second requirement is not met, *S*'s action carries a prima-facie implication of deceitfulness). As Gandhi argues, to understand assertion (in his wide sense) is to understand how these two apparently contradictory requirements are not really contradictory (pp. 141-2; 15-24).

[43] Commenting on perhaps the earliest known instance of retorsive argument (Plato, *Theaetetus* 170 a-171 c), J. H. McDowell remarks 'If all that Protagoras can say to us is "(P) is true *for me*; it may not be true *for you*", we are justified in wondering why we should find what he says interesting. It seemed to be interesting originally because he seemed to be asserting the truth *simpliciter*, not just the truth for himself, of (P)': McDowell, ed. *Plato: Theaetetus* (Clarendon Press, Oxford, 1973), p. 171.

not' is absurd, pointless and (in a sense) self-contradictory (except in some special sense or context). If the reader has misgivings about this last point, he will at least grant that '*p*, but I don't care whether *p* is true or not' robs the speaker's assertion that *p* of any title to be regarded as a 'profound disagreement' with any assertion that not-*p*; it disqualifies the speaker from participation in any serious discussion of the question whether *p* or not-*p*.

Step (6) is the crucial step. Its meaning is quite ordinary and straightforward, and is standardly expressed when one exclaims 'good!' on successfully concluding an investigation. But because philosophical debate about these matters has a history that is not straightforward it is necessary to bracket out misunderstandings, as follows:

 (i) 'truth is worth knowing' is to be understood as meaning that truth is a good to be pursued, and is good to attain in one's judgments; and ignorance and error are to be avoided.

 (ii) 'truth is worth knowing' is not to be understood either as having a moral sense or implication or as incompatible with a moral sense, force or implication. Similarly, in (1), 'truth is a good' is not to be understood as a moral proposition; and 'truth is to be pursued' is not to be understood as stating a moral obligation, requirement, prescription, or recommendation.

(iii) 'truth is worth knowing' is not to be understood as stating that knowledge is the only thing worth pursuing or having, i.e. is the only good; nor is it to be understood as stating that knowledge is to be pursued under all circumstances, or at all times.

(iv) 'truth is worth knowing' is not to be understood as claiming that knowledge is the supreme good, or that knowledge is to be pursued at all costs.

 (v) 'truth is worth knowing' is not to be understood as claiming that every true proposition is equally worth knowing or that every subject matter is equally worth investigating.

(vi) 'truth is worth knowing' is to be understood as affirming that truth is an *intrinsic* good, in that

    (a) the correct answer to the question 'Is it the case that *p*, or is it the case that not-*p*?' is sought at least partly for its correctness as an answer, and not exclusively under some such description as 'whatever will satisfy my audience, whether or not they care for correctness or can distinguish correctness from error' or 'whatever answer first gives me satisfaction' or 'whatever position contributes to my survival'; and

(b) p is considered worth asserting *qua* true, and is not merely the object of an *urge* to assert p for some reason other than that p is the case; the process of gathering data, raising hypotheses and testing them, and judging that there is sufficient evidence or argument to warrant affirming p, will be a rational process only if the man who is going through it remains open to the possibility that what in the end should be asserted is, not p, but not-p; furthermore, he must be willing to consider the truth or otherwise of any propositions $q, r, s \ldots$ that bear on correctness of p or not-p, and in turn on the truth of $q, r, \ldots$

What has been said in (vi) (b) indicates a sense in which truth is a *general* form of good: truth is, so to speak, participated in by *all* correct propositions, judgments and assertions, but is not exhaustively realized in (nor to be identified with) any of them.[44] But what is said in (vi) (b) also indicates why and in what sense the whole argument holds for all p, notwithstanding that we have countless casual beliefs (and thus make countless casual assertions) which we (casually) believe to be true but about whose truth we don't really care (except, perhaps, for some instrumental reason; consider, e.g., the coffee-drinker's belief that coffee is cheap in the supermarket today). What determines whether p is or is not seriously asserted is not the content of p, but the dispositions and interests of particular persons. Provided we remember what was said in (v) above, we can say that there are no 'fields' in which truth in judgment is not a good. To say that truth is a good is to say that for any p it is better to believe (assert) p where p is true than to believe (assert) p where p is false, and than to disbelieve (deny) p where p is true.

With these clarifications of its meaning, step (6) is, I believe, self-evidently true. The clarified meaning of step (6) has been fixed by reflecting on the conditions under which *assertions* are worth making, worth testing, worth evaluating as true or false (rather than as popular or satisfying), worth profoundly disagreeing with . . . This reflection makes it quite clear that truth is a good, that ignorance and error are to be avoided, that to attain to the truth is *pro tanto* to be well off while to remain in ignorance and error is *pro tanto* to be

---

[44] It is tempting to add to the analysis of 'assertion' completed in step (6) one further element, viz.: I assert p only if I consider truth (and knowledge of it) to be good not just for me but for any person (subject to the provisos in (iii) and (iv) above). For otherwise my asserting p would not be a real participation in truth-seeking discourse or debate with others. But it is probably clearer to handle this requirement in the way I have proposed handling the requirement of sincerity in relation to step (3), viz. as a distinct element in a third-person version of steps (6) and (9).

badly off, and that to lose one's desire for truth would be a bad thing. But at the same time, the reflection makes it clear that in seriously asserting that truth is a good (in the clarified sense), one is neither merely reporting nor merely expressing a desire one happens to have; nor is one making a moral claim; nor is one reporting or relying on a universal or even a common belief of others. Still, the self-evidence of the proposition that truth is a good is no more queer or suspect than the self-evidence of, say, steps (1) or (3), or than the self-evidence of logical operations such as those which generate, say, step (8) from steps (3) and (7).

Once the meaning and force of step (6) are established by reflection on one's performance as a questioner and knower, there remains only the question whether the belief expressed in steps (6) and (9) (viz. 'truth is [a good] worth [pursuing and] knowing') is a genuine contradictory of the sceptical belief expressed within steps (7) and (10) (viz. 'it is not the case that truth is a good worth pursuing or knowing'). For someone might exploit a distinction between 'factual' and 'evaluative' utterances to argue that the former belief is 'evaluative' while the latter (sceptical) belief is 'factual', so that the contradiction appearing in step (10) in only apparent.[45]

But in evaluating both the retorsive argument as a whole and the counter-argument just mentioned, it is important to bear in mind that the relevant question is not how to apply the problematic philosophical labels 'factual' and 'evaluative'. It is whether the belief expressed within step (6) is genuinely contradicted by the sceptical denial within step (7). I have explained the meaning and force of the belief within step (6). So, if someone argues that there is no genuine contradiction, he must show that the denial in step (7) has some other meaning. If he says that what is denied in step (7) is that truth is *objectively* a good, I reply that, in my understanding, what is asserted in step (6) means that truth is objectively a good, as I understand 'objectively'. A judgment or belief is objective if it is correct; a proposition is objective if one is warranted in asserting it, whether

[45] A more extreme version of this move would be the claim that 'believe' is a term confined to factual assertions (so that the expressions of 'belief' in steps (4), (5), and (6) are ill-formed, and, where 'I assert that *p*' is evaluative, step (3) does not hold). But this claim involves a drastic stipulative restriction of ordinary usage, a restriction which could be justified only as a device for signalling the importance of the distinction which, in the less extreme version of the move, is alleged between evaluative and factual utterances. The same is true of a further version of the move, in which it might be claimed that the retorsive argument is ill-formed and unsound because 'assert' is confined to factual as opposed to evaluative assertions.

because sufficient evidence is in, or because there are compelling grounds, or because (to one who has the experience and intelligence to understand the terms in which the proposition is expressed) it is obvious or self-evident that in asserting it one asserts what is the case.

Now the belief or judgment or assertion, in step (6), about the good of truth, can be described as 'evaluative' (or in classical terminology 'practical') while the sceptic's denial in step (7) may be intended to be 'factual' (or in classical terminology 'speculative'). I am quite content (as were Aristotle and Aquinas) to stress the difference between 'factual' and 'evaluative' judgments, and to affirm that the latter are not derived by inference from the former and are *sui generis*. But I see no reason to admit that evaluative judgments cannot state, in their own way, what they seem to state, viz. what is objectively the case (about the good of human beings, their opportunities, and their actions).[46] The *differences* between 'factual' judgments, such as 'this book is blue' or 'iron melts at 1535°C', and 'evaluative' judgments, such as 'truth is a good', do not warrant the conclusion that only the former class of judgments can be objective—any more than that conclusion would be warranted by the different but equally considerable differences between the aforementioned type of factual judgments and 'philosophical' ('second-order factual'?) judgments, such as the judgment expressed in the present sentence (or its contradictory).

Suppose someone objects that this all goes to show that I am assuming, in relating step (6) to step (7), that it is possible to have a coherent belief which is at once evaluative and factual (in the sense, now, of 'factual' corresponding to 'it is the case that', 'it is true that' and 'objective'), and that this assumption is both gratuitous and a *petitio principii* against the sceptic. I make two replies. First: my interpretation of step (6) is not gratuitous, but sets out a sober and straightforward analysis of what is involved in the rational activity of asserting that p; if this analysis turns out to be inconsistent with a philosophical thesis about the non-'factual' character of evaluative judgments, that is reason for denying or restricting the thesis (which characteristically was worked out in relation to moral exhortations and resolutions, and never adequately tested in relation to pre-moral 'evaluative' judgments such as that expressed within step (6)). Second:

---

[46] The logic of ascribing truth and objectivity to (some) value judgments has been well worked out by Georges Kalinowski, *Le Problème de la verité en morale et en droit* (Paris, 1967), ch. IV.

my interpretation of step (6) as both evaluative and objective does not beg the question; the meaning of the proposition which the present retorsive argument defends is established not by the sceptic but by ourselves when we assert (as self-evident) what the sceptic *then* denies, viz. that (it is the case that) truth is a good worth pursuing. By showing only that that assertion straddles his distinction between the evaluative and the factual, the sceptic does not succeed in raising an objection.

Suppose, finally, the sceptic (a) grants that the belief expressed within step (6) not only expresses an evaluation which (*qua* evaluative) he does not contest but also, in *my* sense, is objective and states what is the case, but (b) says that his denial within step (7) is restricted to *his* sense of 'objective', 'factual', 'what is the case', etc. Then his denial can safely be ignored. For what he is denying now is not what was classically asserted about the good of truth. Indeed, his denial is now itself thoroughly obscure. What *does* he mean by 'objective', 'factual', 'what is the case', etc.? Usually, his meaning is indicated by the arguments he uses to defend his sceptical objections, viz. arguments from the diversity of moral beliefs, and from the impossibility of inferring evaluative from non-evaluative propositions. But those arguments simply do not apply to the belief expressed within step (6), as I have explained that belief.

Anyone, sceptic or not, who reflects on the whole argument and accompanying argumentation in this section might reasonably ask whether the retorsive argument set out in ten steps adds anything to what is asserted, without much argument, in step (6) and in the explanation of step (6). Well, any retorsive argument has its efficacy by testing the sceptic's objection against the facts (including implicit commitments to recognition and pursuit of values) that are provided in and by the sceptic's own performance as an objector. If the sceptic will not assent to the retorsive analysis of his own performance, he must be challenged to produce a more satisfactory analysis of his own performance as an objector (and, now, as an analyst of objections, too). The analysis will be satisfactory only if it shows that his objection is worth bothering about. And it will show this only if it departs from at least the most basic and radical sceptical tenets. The utility of retorsive argument is that it demonstrates that the sceptic is *bound* to produce this more satisfactory analysis (here, as an alternative to step (6)) if he is not to be involved in formal self-contradiction.

VI

Though one can toy with the notion that truth (and knowledge) is not a good worth pursuing, the retorsive argument should persuade the sceptic to cut short idle doubting. For the argument shows the irrationality of supposing that the doubt could ever mature into a correct affirmation that truth (and knowledge) is not an intrinsic good. The sceptic can always maintain coherence by *asserting* nothing (and so the ancient sceptics commended the *epoche* or suspension of judgment).[47] But the price of this is that he does not maintain a *position*, i.e. any part in rational discourse or in a 'profound disagreement'. Coherence is not the only requirement of rationality (animals never fall into self-contradiction). Is there, then, any reason to make the effort which is required to maintain a complete suspension of judgment, a complete abstinence from affirmation and denial? (Mere idleness will hardly suffice!) Is not the sceptic's reason for this effort his strong (though misdirected) grasp of the value of truth (as we explained it in relation to step (6))? Is not his effort his tribute to the stringent and authoritative demands of a form of good which he sees corrupted by the conventionality, hastiness, prejudice, muddle, wishful thinking, and partisanship of dogmatists (including dogmatists who offer to defend the objective value of truth)?

And so, if someone were to claim that truth has its value, not for its own sake, but only instrumentally, as a means of survival, we should make a threefold reply. First, it is true that truth has instrumental as well as intrinsic value. Secondly, it is true (as martyrs who value truth for its own sake have always been aware) that there are occasions when treating or regarding truth as merely instrumentally good has survival value. But, thirdly, it would be incoherent (but also mistaken) to make the claim, or even tacitly to assume its validity, as part of one's commitment and contribution to scientific objectivity or philosophical reasonableness.

[47] Sextus Empiricus, *Pyrrhonean Hypotyposes* I, 8. But of course Sextus Empiricus goes on, and on, making judgments . . .

15

Justice Between Generations

B. BARRY*

Suppose that, as a result of using up all the world's resources, human life did come to an end. So what? What is so desirable about an indefinite continuation of the human species, religious convictions apart?[1]

MY object in this paper is to ask what if anything those alive at any given time owe their descendants, whether in the form of positive efforts (e.g. investment in capital goods) or in the form of forbearance from possible actions (e.g. those causing irreversible damage to the natural environment).[2] We scan the 'classics' in vain for guidance on this question, and, I think, for understandable reasons. Among human beings, unlike (say) mayflies, generations do not succeed one another in the sense that one is off the scene before the next comes into existence. 'Generations' are an abstraction from a continuous process of population replacement. Prudent provision for the welfare of all those currently alive therefore entails some considerable regard for the future. The way we get into problems that cannot be handled in this way is that there may be 'sleepers' (actions taken at one time that have much more significant effects in the long run than in the short run) or actions that are on balance beneficial in the short run and harmful in the long run (or vice versa).

More precisely the problem arises (as a problem requiring decision) not when actions actually have long-run effects that are different in scale or direction from their short-run effects but when they are

* Professor of Politics, University of British Columbia.
[1] Wilfred Beckerman, 'The Myth of "Finite" Resources', *Business and Society Review* 12 (Winter 1974–5), 22.
[2] I am indebted for exceptionally detailed and helpful comments on an earlier and longer draft to G. C. Archibald, David Donaldson, John Gray, and Derek Parfit. Parts of the paper have been presented to the Colloquium on Decision Theory in London, Ontario, the Carlyle Club, and faculty seminars at the University of British Columbia and the University of Washington, and I am grateful for suggestions and criticisms made in discussion.

believed to do so. The increased salience of the problem for us comes about not just because we are more likely to have the opportunity, thanks to technology, of doing things with long-run consequences not mediated by similar short-run consequences but also because there is more chance of our knowing about it. A useful new technology that we have no reason to believe has adverse long-term effects does not present any problem of decision-making for us, even if in fact, unknown to us, it has the most deleterious long-run consequences. Conversely, new knowledge may suggest that things we have been doing for some time have harmful long-term effects. Even if people have been doing something with adverse long-term effects for hundreds or thousands of years, so that we are currently experiencing the ill effects in the form of, say, higher disease rates or lower crop yields than we should otherwise be enjoying, it may still require some break-through in scientific understanding to show that the current situation has been brought about by certain human practices.

In recent years, we have all been made aware by the 'ecological' movement how delicately balanced are the processes that support life on the earth's surface and how easily some disequilibrium may ramify through a variety of processes with cumulative effects. The stage is set for some potentially very awkward decisions by this increased awareness that apparently insignificant impacts on the environment may, by the time they have fully worked themselves through, have serious consequences for human life. We may, any day, be confronted with convincing evidence for believing that something on which we rely heavily—the internal-combustion engine, say—is doing irreversible damage to the ecosystem, even if the effects of our current actions will not build up to a catastrophic deterioration for many years (perhaps centuries) to come.

If we ask what makes our relations with our successors in hundreds of years time so different from our relations with our contemporaries as to challenge the ordinary moral notions that we use in everyday affairs, there are two candidates that come to mind, one concerned with power and one with knowledge. I shall consider these in turn.

A truistic but fundamental difference between our relations with our successors and our relations with our contemporaries, then, is the absolute difference in power. The present inhabitants of Britain may believe that, although they have some discretion in the amount of aid they give to the people of Bangladesh, they have little to hope or fear from the present inhabitants of Bangladesh in return. But they cannot be sure that later geopolitical events may not change this in their own lifetime. We can be quite certain, however, that people alive in several centuries time will not be able to do anything that will make us better off or worse off now, although we can to some degree make them better off or worse off.

Admittedly, our successors have absolute control of something in the future that we may care about now: our reputations. It is up to them to decide what they think of us—or indeed whether they think about us at all. And presumably what, or whether, they think of us is going to be in some way affected by the way that we act towards them. I must confess, however, to doubting that this does much to level up the asymmetry of power between us and our successors, for two reasons. First, although they control a resource which may matter to us, we have no way of negotiating an agreement with them to the effect that they will treat our reputations in a certain way if we behave now in a certain way. We therefore have to guess how they will react to the way we behave, and in the nature of the case such guesses are bound to be inexact. Second, and more important, although individuals are undoubtedly moved by thoughts of post-humous fame for their artistic achievements or political records, it does not seem plausible to suppose that the same motivation would lead a mass electorate to support, say, measures of energy conserva-tion. Altogether, therefore, I do not think that the fact of later generations determining our reputations deserves to be given much weight as an offset to the otherwise completely unilateral power that we have over our successors.

How important is this asymmetry of power between us and our successors—the fact that we can help or hurt them but they can't help or hurt us? It is tempting to say at once that this cannot possibly in itself make any moral difference. Yet it is perhaps surprising to realize that a variety of commonly held views about the basis of morality seem to entail that the absence of reciprocal power relations elimi-nates the possibility of our having moral obligations (or at any rate obligations of justice) to our successors.

There is a tradition of thought running from Hobbes and Hume to Hart and Warnock according to which the point of morality is that it offers (in Hobbes's terms) 'convenient articles of peace': human beings are sufficiently equal in their capacity to hurt one another, and in their dependence on one another's co-operation to live well, that it is mutually advantageous to all of them to support an institution designed to give people artificial motives for respecting the interests of others.

It seems plain that such a view cannot generate the conclusion that we have moral obligations to those who will not be alive until long after we are dead. Thus, G. J. Warnock, in *The Object of Morality* (Methuen, London, 1967), offers two reasons for saying that moral principles should have universal application rather than being confined to particular groups. 'First, everyone presumably will be a non-member of some group, and cannot in general have any absolute guarantee that he will encounter no members of groups that are not his own; thus if principles are group-bound, he remains, so to speak, at risk. . . . Second . . . if conduct is to be seen as regulated only *within* groups, we still have the possibility of unrestricted hostility and conflict *between* groups . . .' (p. 150). Obviously, neither of these reasons carries weight in relation to our successors, since we do precisely have an absolute guarantee that we shall never encounter them and cannot conceivably suffer from their hostility to us. It should be added in fairness to Warnock that he himself suggests that morality requires us to take account of the interests of future generations and also of animals. But my point is that I do not see how this squares with his premises.

It is, indeed, possible to get some distance by invoking the fact with which I began this paper, that the notion of 'successive generations' is an artificial one since there is a continuous process of replacement in human populations. Once we have universalized our moral principles to apply to everyone alive now, there are because of this continuity severe practical problems in drawing a neat cut-off point in the future. In the absence of a definite cut-off point, it may seem natural to say that our moral principles hold without temporal limit. But could what is in effect no stronger force than inertia be sufficient to lead us to make big sacrifices for remote generations if these seemed to be called for by atemporal morality? Surely if morality is at basis no more than mutual self-defence, we would (whether or not we made it explicit) agree to ignore the interests of those coming hundred of years after us.

There is an alternative line of argument about the basis of moral obligations, also involving reciprocity, from which the denial of obligations to future generations follows directly. This view is seldom put forward systematically though it crops up often enough in conversation. This is the idea that by living in a society one gets caught up in a network of interdependencies and from these somehow arise obligations. A recent statement of this view may be found in Burton Zwiebach, *Civility and Disobedience* (Cambridge University Press, London, 1975), who says that 'the basis of our obligation is the common life' (p. 75). The same idea—that obligations to others arise from actual relations with them—underlies Michael Walzer's *Obligations* (Harvard University Press, Cambridge, Mass., 1970). Obviously, this more parochial view, which makes obligations depend on actual rather than potential reciprocal relationships, rules out any obligations to subsequent generations, since there is no reciprocity with them.

As T. D. Weldon recognized when he put forward a similar view in the last chapter of *States and Morals* (John Murray, London, 1946), it is very close to basing obligations on sentiments. This further move is made in one of the very few papers addressed explicitly to the present topic (M. P. Golding, 'Obligations to Future Generations', *Monist* 56 (1972), 85–99) and permits some consideration to be given to future generations—but in a way that I personally find more morally offensive than a blunt disregard of all future interests. According to Golding, obligations rest on a sense of 'moral community'. Whether or not we have any obligations to future generations depends on whether we expect them to live in ways that would lead us to regard them as part of our 'moral community'. If we think they will develop in ways we disapprove of, we have no obligations to them. This view is obviously a diachronic version of the common American view that famine need only be relieved in countries with the right attitude to capitalism.

A third view which appears to leave little room for obligations to future generations is the kind of Lockean philosophy recently revived by Robert Nozick in *Anarchy, State, and Utopia* (Basic Books, New York, 1974). Indeed, it is scarcely accidental that the uniquely short-sighted destruction of trees, animals and soil in the U.S.A. should have been perpetrated by believers in a natural right to property. According to Nozick, any attempt to use the state to redistribute resources among contemporaries in order to bring about some 'end state' is illegitimate, so presumably by the same token any deliberate collective action aimed at distributing resources over time would fall under the same ban. Provided an individual has come by a good justly, he may justly dispose of it any way he likes—by giving it away or bequeathing it, trading it for something else, consuming it, or destroying it. No question of justice arises in all this so long as he does not injure the rights to property and security from physical harm of anyone else. Since we have a right to dispose of our property as we wish, subsequent generations could not charge us with injustice if we were to consume whatever we could in our own lifetimes and direct that what was left should be destroyed at our deaths. (Having one's property destroyed at death has been popular at various times and places and could presumably become so again.) It would clearly be, on Nozick's view, unjust for the survivors to fail to carry out such directions.

Once again, we can see that the problem is the lack of bargaining power in the hands of later generations. Those without bargaining power may appeal to the generous sentiments of others but they cannot make legitimate moral demands, as Nozick's examples of the men on their desert islands vividly illustrates. He asks us to imagine a number of men washed up on desert islands with the possibility of sending goods to each other and transmitting messages by radio transmitter but no means of travelling themselves. Sternly resisting the temptation to comment further on the outlook of a man for whom the paradigm of human relations is a number of adult males on desert islands, let us ask what moral obligations they have to each other. Nozick's answer is simple: none. Even if one has the good fortune to have landed on an island flowing with milk and honey while his neighbour is gradually starving on a barren waste, there is no obligation on one to supply the other's needs. Where could such an obligation possibly come from? To get a parallel with the relations between generations all we have to do is imagine that the islands are situated along an ocean current. Goods can be dispatched in one direction only, down the current. Even if those further down the line could call for help (as later generations in fact cannot) they could make no moral claims on those higher up.

I have so far concentrated on one potentially relevant fact about our relations with our successors: the asymmetry of power. The second one, which is invariably mentioned in this context, is the fact that we have less and less knowledge about the future the more remote the time ahead we are thinking about. Whether or not this is (like the asymmetry of power relations) an absolutely necessary truth derivable from the very concept of the future is a question any attempt to answer which would involve opening the can of worms labelled 'Determinism'. I shall therefore simply accept the basic assertion as true—since it is surely true for us now, anyway—and ask what its implications are.

The answer seems to be fairly clear. As far as I can see, no theory that survives the first consideration and still holds that we have some sort of obligation to take account of the interests of remote future generations would have its conclusions upset by our unavoidable ignorance about the future. Of course, it may be held that we have *no* knowledge of the way in which our present actions will affect the interests of those who come after us in more than k years' time— either because we don't know what effects our actions will have on the state of the universe then or because we can have no idea what their interests will be. In that case, it obviously follows that our accepting an obligation to concern ourselves with their interests does not entail our behaving any differently from the way we would behave if we did not accept such an obligation. We can decide what to do without having to bother about any effects it may have beyond k years' time. But the obligation still remains latent in the sense that, if at some future date we do come to believe that we have relevant information about the effects of our actions on people living in more than k years' time, we should take account of it in determining our actions. The obligation would have been activated.

Ignorance of the future may be invoked to deny that obligations to remote descendants have any practical implications so that we can ignore them with a good conscience in deciding what to do. Thus John Passmore, in his book on *Man's Responsibility for Nature* (Duckworth, London, 1974), canvasses among other possibilities the rigorous atemporal utilitarianism put forward by Sidgwick, according to which 'the time at which a man exists cannot affect the value of his happiness from a universal point of view' (*Methods of Ethics* (Macmillan, London, 1962), p. 414). But he says that, because of the existence of uncertainty, even Sidgwick's approach would lead us to the conclusion that 'our obligations are to *immediate* posterity, we ought to try to improve the world so that we shall be able to hand it over to our immediate successors in a better condition, and that is all' (p. 91, italics in original).

I think this all too convenient conclusion ought to be treated with great mistrust. Of course, we don't know what the precise tastes of our remote descendants will be, but they are unlikely to include a desire for skin cancer, soil erosion, or the inundation of all low-lying areas as a result of the melting of the ice-caps. And, other things being equal, the interests of future generations cannot be harmed by our leaving them more choices rather than fewer.

Even more dubious, it seems to me, is the habit (especially common among economists for some reason) of drawing blank cheques on the future to cover our own deficiencies. The shortages, pollution, over-population, etc., that we leave behind will be no problem for our successors because, it is said, they will invent ways of dealing with them. This Micawberish attitude of expecting something to turn up would be rightly considered imprudent in an individual and I do not see how it is any less so when extended to our successors.

My own view is that, especially in the context of universalistic utilitarianism, the appeal to ignorance normally functions as a smoke-screen, to conceal the fact that we are simply not willing to act in the kind of saintly way that a serious application of the doctrine must entail. Professor Passmore writes (claiming to paraphrase Rawls) that 'the utilitarian principle of impartiality, taken literally, demands too much of us; we cannot reasonably be expected to share our resources with the whole of posterity' (p. 86). He is, I think, more to the point here than when introducing ignorance as a 'fudge factor' to make the answer come out where in any case he feels it should be.

I entirely share the reluctance I have attributed to others to accept the full rigours of universal utilitarianism. Of course, reluctance to accept a theory about our obligations is hardly enough to disqualify it. Presumably the whole idea of talking about obligations is to put to us a motive for doing things that we would (at least sometimes) not be inclined to do otherwise. But the demands of universal utili-tarianism—that I should always act in such a way as to maximize the sum of happiness over the future course of human (or maybe sentient) history—are so extreme that I cannot bring myself to believe that there is any such obligation.

At the same time, I find it impossible to believe that it can be right to disregard totally the interests of even remotely future generations, to the extent that we have some idea of the way in which our current actions will affect those interests. If I am correct in saying that it is an implication of the three theories of morality that I briefly considered earlier that there are no obligations to distant future generations, they too have to be rejected.

But if we dump mutual self-protection, entitlement, and com-munity (with which we may roughly identify the holy trinity of political theory, first identified by T. H. Green and still faithfully worshipped by P.P.E.—Hobbes, Locke, and Rousseau) what are we left with? Unless we are prepared to fall back on an appeal to intuitions (and it may come to that), the only general approach remaining is as far as I can see some sort of ideal contractarian construction: what is required by justice is that we should be prepared to do what we would demand of others if we didn't know the details of our or their situation.

The name of Rawls naturally, and rightly, springs to mind here. But it should be recognized that the ideal contractarian formula is open-ended and does not have to be identified with Rawls's use of it. Nevertheless, Rawls's *A Theory of Justice* (Oxford University Press, London, 1972) is the obvious place to start and I shall therefore now set out and criticize Rawls's contribution to the problem of justice between generations. The first point to notice is that Rawls discusses the problem only in the context of the 'just savings rate' and this imposes two limitations on the generality of his conclusions. The obvious one is that if we concentrate on the question how much we are obliged to make our successors better off, we miss the whole question whether there may not be an obligation to avoid harm that is stronger than any obligation to make better off. This is after all a common view about relations among contemporaries.

The second, and ultimately perhaps more serious, limitation is that investment has a characteristic that enables discussion of it to dodge the most awkward difficulties. The only way in which we can leave people in *n* years (where *n* is a large number) more productive capital than they would otherwise have had is to create the additional capital now and hope that the intervening generations will pass it on, or more precisely to create it now and hope our immediate descendants and their successors will each pass on a larger total to *their* successors than they would have done had we left them less ourselves. If they do, then members of remote future generations will indeed be better off than they would otherwise have been thanks to our efforts. But there is no way in which we can be confident that our efforts will have any net effect because everything depends on the behaviour of the intervening generations, whom we have no way of binding.

Although it does not strictly follow from all this, it is easy to reach the conclusion if we concentrate on the 'just savings rate' that the problem of relations between generations can be reduced to the question of the relations between one generation and its immediate successors. There is no way of making remoter generations better off

by making savings now that does not involve making nearer generations better off and, conversely, if we make our immediate successors
better off by making savings now we at any rate make it possible for
them to make *their* successors better off than they would otherwise
have been.

Obviously, it might still be held that if we take account of remoter
generations this should lay on us a greater obligation to build up
capital now than would arise if we knew that our immediate successors
would be the last generation ever. But since we have no way of
ensuring that our immediate successors will not go on a binge and run
down the capital we leave them this must surely weaken the case for
our having to make extra efforts to save merely so as to make it
possible for our immediate successors to pass on more than they
would otherwise have done.

When, by contrast, we look at the bads rather than the goods that
we have the opportunity of passing on to our successors, we can see
that the same convenient assumption (which is a sort of diachronic
equivalent of 'chain connection' in Rawls's theory) is not generally
applicable. True, resource depletion has something of the same
characteristic. The only way in which we can leave more to our
remote successors is to leave more to our immediate successors; and
if we make extra efforts to conserve resources so as to give our
immediate successors more scope to pass on resources in their turn,
we take the risk that they will simply blue the lot anyway.

But this is not necessarily the case with other bads that we might
pass on. There could in principle be some ecological sleeper-effect
that we set off now with no ill effects for some hundreds of years and
then catastrophic effects. And there are in any case real examples
(such as the use of fluorocarbon sprays) of things that we do now that
may well have continuous and irreversible ill effects during the rest
of the period during which there is life on the planet and that can
either not be counteracted at all or only counteracted at great cost or
inconvenience.

Of course, our successors may make things even worse for remotely
future generations, adding further ecological damage to that done by
us. And if we refrain from causing some kind of ecological damage,
there can be no guarantee that our successors will not cause it themselves. But this does not suffice to destroy the distinction between
investment, which has the property that our successors can choose
whether to pass on the benefits we leave them, and ecological damage,

which has its own adverse effects on remote future generations
whether or not our successors add to it. It is, I think, because of the
reduction of the problem that follows from taking investment as the
paradigm of relations between generations that Rawls is satisfied
with a solution that would otherwise be manifestly inadequate.

He postulates throughout *A Theory of Justice* (without, I think,
ever adequately explaining why) that the people in the 'original
position' (whose choices from behind the 'veil of ignorance' are to
constitute principles of justice) know that they are all contemporaries,
although they do not know to which generation they belong. The
obvious problem that this raises is a sort of n-generation prisoner's
dilemma. Generation k, who happen to be behind the veil of ignorance, may be willing to save on condition that their predecessors have
saved. But there is no way in which they can take a conditional
decision of this kind because there is no way of reaching a binding
agreement (or indeed any agreement) with their predecessors. All *they*
can do is to decide themselves whether to save or not. As Rawls says,
setting out the problem: 'Either previous generations have saved or
they have not; there is nothing the parties [in the original position]
can do to affect it' (p. 292). How can we escape this difficulty?

It might appear that the obvious way out of the difficulty is to drop
the postulate that the people in the 'original position' are contemporaries, and this is I believe the path that Rawls should have
taken to be true to his own theory. But he does not take it. Instead,
the tack that he takes is, he says, to 'make a motivational assumption'.
The 'goodwill' of the parties in the original position 'stretches over
at least two generations'. We may, though we need not, 'think of the
parties as heads of families, and therefore as having a desire to
further the welfare of their nearest descendants'. He concludes as
follows:

What is essential is that each person in the original position should care
about the well-being of some of those in the next generation, it being
presumed that their concern is for different individuals in each case.
Moreover for anyone in the next generation, there is someone who cares
for him in the present generation. Thus the interests of all are looked after
and, given the 'veil of ignorance', the whole strand is tied together. (All
quotes from pp. 128-9.)

One slightly technical objection that must be made to this is that
the conditions stated by Rawls as necessary for the interests of all to
be looked after are unnecessarily strong. Given the veil of ignorance,

it is not necessary for each party to *know* that there is someone in the next generation he cares about. He will have a motive to support principles giving weight to the welfare of the next generation provided he knows that he will probably care about somebody in the next generation. Similarly, there is no need for everybody in the next generation to have someone who cares for him in this one so long as the uncared-for cannot be identified as a category and thus made the object of discriminatory principle-choosing from behind the veil of ignorance. And as far as I can see they are pretty safe from that risk.

This, however, is just a skirmish. There are two powerful objections to the use Rawls makes of his 'motivational assumption'. The first, which I have already foreshadowed, is that even if it does everything Rawls wants it to do, that is still not enough. The really nasty problems (to some extent actual but even more potential) involve obligations to remote descendants rather then immediate descendants and on these Rawls has nothing to say. It has been suggested that we might boost the extension of concern into the future derivable from sentiment (which is what Rawls's derivation amounts to) by pointing to the fact that if we care about our grandchildren and they care about their grandchildren we should care about our grandchildren's grandchildren, and so on *ad infinitum*. But those who base themselves on sentiment must follow where it leads, and if primary concern is as short-winded as Rawls suggests, it is scarcely plausible that secondary concern will alter the picture much. Certainly, by a few centuries' time it would be asymptotically approaching zero.

The second objection, which seems to me decisive, is that the derivation of obligations to future generations from the 'motivational assumption' is a pretty thin performance. The only justification offered for the 'motivational assumption' is that it enables Rawls to derive obligations to future generations. But surely this is a little too easy, like a conjurer putting a rabbit in a hat, taking it out again and expecting a round of applause. What it comes to is that we impute to the people in the original position a desire for the welfare of their descendants, on the basis of this we 'deduce' that they will choose principles requiring some action in pursuit of that welfare, and on the basis of the general theory that what would be chosen in the original position constitutes principles of justice we say that the principle governing savings that they would choose is the 'just savings principle'. But if it is acceptable to introduce desires for the welfare of immediate descendants into the original position simply in order to get them out again as obligations, what grounds can there be for refusing to put into the original position a desire for the welfare of at least some contemporaries?

For the whole idea—and the intellectual fascination—of 'justice as fairness' is that it takes self-interested men, and, by the alchemy of the 'original position', forces them to choose principles of universal scope. In relation to subsequent generations, the postulate of self-interest is relaxed to allow concern for successors, but this naturally limited sympathy is not forced by the logic of the 'original position' to be extended any further than it extends naturally. Our limited sympathies towards our successors are fed into the sausage-machine of 'justice as fairness' and returned to us duly certified as obligations. We come seeking moral guidance and simply get our existing prejudices underwritten—hardly what one would expect from a rationalist philosopher.

The alternative route out of Rawls's difficulties is to pursue the logic of his own analysis more rigorously. This entails scrapping the part of the construction specifying that all the people in the 'original position' are contemporaries and know that they are. We should now have to imagine that there is a meeting to decide on intergenerational relationships at which all generations are represented. Clearly, the 'veil of ignorance' would be required to conceal from them which generation each of them belonged to. Otherwise, an earlier generation would always have the whip-hand over a later one in the negotiations.

There are, obviously, formidable difficulties involved in the very notion of a meeting of all generations. But those difficulties are equally inherent in the bare notion of an individual choosing criteria for relations between generations either without knowing to which he belongs (Rawlsian individual choice) or on the basis that whatever criteria he chooses will apply to all generations (Kantian individual choice). It might therefore be offered as a point in favour of the 'general meeting' construction that it brings out the difficulties graphically.

If the whole notion of collecting representatives from all generations is difficult there is a special problem introduced by the fact that actions taken at one time may affect the number of subsequent generations by making the tenure of human life on the planet longer or shorter than it would otherwise have been. (In the extreme case, the actions of one generation may be such as to make it the last.) If every generation that *might* exist is represented at the meeting, everybody knows that the criteria chosen may turn out to make his or her generation non-existent.

This is an awkward problem and it is understandable that David Richards, who differs from Rawls in saying that 'the class of members of the original position includes, in a hypothetical sense, *all* persons, who have lived, live now, or will live' should seek to rule it out. In suggesting that the rational contractors would adopt a principle limiting population so as to make those who do live as well off as possible (I omit the details) he adds that 'the egoistic desire to exist of the contractors does not influence their consideration of this problem, for *ex hypothesi* the contractors know they exist in some point of time, and are thus only concerned to ensure that their existence be as satisfying as possible' (David A. J. Richards, *A Theory of Reasons for Action* (Clarendon Press, Oxford, 1971), pp. 81 and 134, italics in original).

It seems to me, however, that there are two objections to this way of disposing of the problem. First, although we may in the end want to say that people who don't get born don't count, this should surely be the conclusion rather than the premise, built in by virtue of the construction. And, more fundamentally, isn't there something incoherent in combining the idea that people in the original position are choosing among policies which will produce different total numbers of people with the idea that they know at the outset that they are all the people who ever have existed or ever will exist? It is surely a curious sort of choice if the results of it are already instantiated in the composition of the group of people doing the choosing!

We do therefore presumably have to ask whether the interests of potential people in being born should be taken into account or whether each possible decision-rule should be evaluated simply by estimating how those who would actually be born under it would fare, and ignoring those who might have been born under some other decision-rule.

I confess that this is an area in which the light is, for me, fitful. I am clear that the first alternative (extended Pareto optimality) is to be rejected. The criterion for a Paretian improvement is that as between two situations some people should be better off in the second and nobody worse off. As Ian Little pointed out in *A Critique of Welfare Economics*, the applicability of this criterion depends on there being the identical people in both situations. It seems to me plainly illegitimate to assimilate the case of someone who is alive at one point in time and not born at an earlier time and who does not regret having been born to the case of someone who is alive at two points in time and prefers the second to the first. It is essential to 'clear the mind of cant' and in particular to avoid the kind of Chestertonian whimsy that involves imagining that unborn people are hanging about somewhere, with all the usual human attributes of consciousness and desire, waiting to be born. It is a serious drawback of the idea of a convention of all possible generations (or all possible people) that it makes it almost impossible to escape from such a way of thinking. Not to be born after you have already attended a meeting of representatives takes on too much of the aspect of dying extremely prematurely. Admittedly, David Hume remarked on his death-bed that there is no more to being dead than to not having been born, but there is the crucial difference between them that one can have a conscious prospect of being dead but not one of not being born.

However, if we can somehow exclude this artefact of the construction, I do not see how coming into existence can itself be regarded a good from the point of view of the potential person, since potential people do not have points of view. And yet I must admit to feeling uneasy with the alternative conclusion that we should take into account only the conscious states of those who get born.

I find no difficulty in accepting this with regard to the numbers of people alive at any one time. In asking whether the world will be better off in the year 2000 with seven billion inhabitants than it is with four billion now, I do not feel any temptation to say that the extra numbers are themselves, other things being equal, an improvement—even if most of the enlarged population do not regret having been born. But in asking whether it would matter for human beings (or life on earth in general) to come to an end in 500 years' time rather than 500,000, I do not find irrelevant the fact that in the first case many generations that might have come into existence will not have the opportunity of doing so.

It may, of course, be argued that good reasons can be given in terms of the interests of actual human beings for not choosing to do something that brings about a substantial risk of ending human life in 500 years' time. The people in the original position would not care to risk the distress at the prospect or the suffering entailed in the process. But human life will presumably come to an end eventually anyway and in a congress at which all potential generations are represented, the risk of being the last generation that actually exists is the same whether that occurs early or late, and the risk of being non-existent (we are saying) is not to count. In any case, I feel fairly sure that my conviction that it would be monstrous to take risks with the existence of future generations in order to secure advantages or avoid hardships for those who will live during the shortened time-span left does not rest on such calculations.

The Hobbesian, Lockean, and Rousseauan theories give only the most tenuous and contingent security to the interests of future generations. It now appears that no theory confining its attention to the states of actual human beings will do. If we say that those who do not get born do not count in the choice of an 'ideal contract', the relatively early end of the human race may be preferred to a longer history at a somewhat lower level. The solution chosen would not be exactly equivalent to average utilitarianism (maximizing the average happiness of those who actually live) if we accept Rawls's arguments that people choosing in the 'original position' would be more concerned to avoid very bad outcomes than to obtain very good ones. But we can certainly say that 'average utilitarianism' where only those who get born count in the denominator runs into the same problem as an 'ideal contract' where only those who get born have a vote. The highest average for those who live may entail not merely a relatively small population at any given time (which seems to me a quite unexceptionable conclusion) but a relatively short time-span for the human race, as those who are alive splurge all the earth's resources with an attitude of 'après nous le deluge'.

The 'total utility' view (that the sum total of happiness should be maximized) in effect enfranchises potential people. (It does not however follow that an 'ideal contract' chosen by all potential people—if we can make sense of that notion—would be for maximizing total happiness. If they were, in Rawlsian fashion, much more concerned to avoid very bad outcomes than to obtain very good ones, it would seem prudent to vote for not bringing the human race into existence. All this would require would be that there should be *some* people of whom Sophocles' 'highest of all is not to be born' would apply.) However, the unpalatibility of this form of utilitarianism, which I have already remarked upon, seems to me greatly increased when we realize that it would call upon us to make sacrifices merely so that there could be more people, so long as each extra person adds any positive amount to the notional sum total of happiness. It may also be noted that, although the total utility doctrine is biased towards actualizing a lot of potential people, it is not biased towards spreading them over a long time-span. It is consistent with total utilitarianism that we should have a massive population for another two centuries and then nothing. Perhaps it is unlikely that this is the way to maximize total happiness, but the point is that at least as far as I am concerned the continuation of human life into the future is something to be sought (or at least not sabotaged) even if it does not make for the maximum total happiness.

Certainly, if I try to analyse the source of my own strong conviction that we should be wrong to take risks with the continuation of human life, I find that it does not lie in any sense of injury to the interests of people who will not get born but rather in a sense of its cosmic impertinence—that we should be grossly abusing our position by taking it upon ourselves to put a term on human life and its possibilities. I must confess to feeling great intellectual discomfort in moving outside a framework in which ethical principles are related to human interests, but if I am right then these are the terms in which we have to start thinking.[3] In contrast to Passmore, I conclude that those who say we need a 'new ethic' are in fact right. It need not entail the kind of half-baked ideas that Passmore criticizes, but should surely as a minimum include the notion that those alive at any time are custodians rather than owners of the planet, and ought to pass it on in at least no worse shape than they found it in.

[3] Although I was not aware of Derek Parfit's work on population at the time I drafted this paper, I was later encouraged to discover that he had arrived at a substantially similar conclusion to mine. For a much more sophisticated treatment of the problems arising in talking about potential people and their interests, see his forthcoming articles on 'Overpopulation' in *Philosophy and Public Affairs*.

16

Harm and Self-Interest

J. FEINBERG*

THE study of *kakapoeics*, or the general theory and classification of harms, should be a central enterprise of legal philosophy. Most writers agree, after all, that the prevention of harms is a legitimate aim of both the criminal law and the coercive parts of the civil law, though of course there is much disagreement over whether it is the *sole* proper concern of coercive law, over *whose* harms are properly considered, and over which types of harm have priority in cases of conflict. There are also conceptual riddles concerning the scope of the term 'harm', three of which provide the excuse for this essay, namely, whether there can be such things as purely *moral harms* (harm to character), *vicarious harms* (as I shall call them), and *posthumous harms*. My discussion of these questions will assume without argument the orthodox jurisprudential analysis of harm as invaded interest, not because I think that account is self-evidently correct or luminously perspicuous, but rather because I wish to explore its implications for the borderline cases of harm, the better to test its adequacy, and to determine the respects in which the concept of self-interest still needs clarification.

The theory of the nature of harms assumed here can be sketched quickly. A person is harmed when someone invades (blocks or thwarts) one of his interests.[1] A person has an interest in Y when he has a *stake* in Y, that is, when he stands to gain or lose depending on the condition or outcome of Y.[2] A person's interest in the singular

---

* Professor of Philosophy, The Rockefeller University.

[1] Interests can be blocked or defeated by events in impersonal nature or by plain bad luck. But they can only be 'invaded' by human beings, either oneself, acting negligently or perversely, or by others, singly or in groups and organizations. It is only when an interest is invaded by self or others that its possessor is harmed in the usual legal sense, though obviously an earthquake or a plague can cause enormous harm in the ordinary sense.

[2] Strictly speaking, this definition is circular since a person would probably have to know what it is to have an interest in something before he could know what it is to

(his personal interest or self-interest) consists in the harmonious advancement of all his interests in the plural. We speak not only of the things a person 'has an interest in' but also of the various things that are 'in his interest', that is, the things that promote his interests as a group. 'Welfare interests' are interests in the indispensable means to one's ulterior goals, whatever the latter may be. These include health, financial sufficiency, and the like. 'Ulterior interests' are based on stable, long-range objectives, achievements of goals valued at least partly as ends in themselves—for example producing a book, raising a family, building a dream house, advancing a cause. Characteristically human well-being consists in the advancing of such interests.

Welfare and ulterior interests bear somewhat different relations to wants or desires. Anything we believe we have a stake in, whether it be mere minimal health or ultimate achievement, we will desire to some degree, in so far at least as we are rational. But we have some welfare interests in conditions that are good for us even if we should not want them (for example, health), whereas in respect to our more ultimate goals, we have a stake in them because we desire their achievement, not the other way round. In these instances, if our wants were to change, our interests would too. It is not true, however, that wants, even strong wants, are *sufficient* to create interests. Few non-betting football fans, for example, have ulterior interests in their favourite team's victory, though many may have very intense desires for that outcome. As a psychological generalization, it is probably true that few persons can 'invest' enough in a wanted outcome to create a stake in it unless promoting that outcome becomes a personal goal or objective. Surely, no mere 'desire of the moment', like a desire to go to the cinema,[3] can generate an ulterior interest, but only a relatively deep-rooted and stable want whose fulfilment can be both reasonably hoped for (mere idle wishes won't do) and influenced by one's own efforts.[4]

'gain or lose' as well as vice versa. But even a circular definition can have some practical utility in providing an equivalent expression for the *definiendum* that is more easily manipulated to good purpose, or which is more suggestive, or productive of insight. The word 'stake', e.g. brings out with intuitive vividness the connection between interests and risks. The word 'stake' has its primary or literal use to refer to 'the amount risked by a party to a wager, or match, or gambler, a thing whose existence, or safety, or ownership depends on some issue'.

[3] Cf. Brian Barry, *Political Argument* (Routledge & Kegan Paul, London, 1965), p. 183.

[4] There is, I suppose, a respect in which anyone who has a strong desire for anything

1. *Moral harm.* Is interest, then, a wholly 'want-regarding' concept, or does the analysis sketched in the preceding paragraphs leave out something important? The label 'want-regarding' comes from Brian Barry[5] who contrasted it with what he called 'ideal-regarding' concepts and principles. A concept is want-regarding if it can be analysed entirely in terms of the 'wants which people happen to have', whereas it is ideal-regarding if reference must also be made to what would be ideal, or best for people, their wants notwithstanding, or to the wants they ought to have whether they have them in fact or not. The ideal-regarding theory of interest holds that it is in a person's interest ultimately not only to have his wants and goals fulfilled, but also (and often this is held to be more important) to have his tastes elevated, his sensibilities refined, his judgment sharpened, his integrity strengthened: in short to become a better person. On this view, a person can be harmed not only in his health, his purse, his worldly ambition, and the like, but also in his character. One's ultimate good is not only to *have* the things one wants, but (perhaps more importantly) to *be* an excellent person, whatever one may want. We not only degrade and corrupt a man by making him a worse man than he would otherwise be; on this view, we inflict serious *harm* on him, even though all his other interests flourish. Socrates and the Stoics even went so far as to hold that this 'moral harm' is the *only* genuine harm. Epictetus was so impressed with the harm that consists simply in having a poor character that he thought it redundant to punish a morally depraved person for his crimes. Such a person is punished enough, he thought, just by being the sort of person he is.

To a certain extent, the conflict between the two accounts of interest is entirely academic. That is because most forms of excellence, most of the time, tend to promote want-based interests. If there is an antecedent desire for excellence, as there often is, then the achievement of excellence is want-fulfilling, and even in the absence of such a

---

at all stands to 'gain' or 'lose' depending on whether it is satisfied. The pleasant state of mind we call satisfaction is itself a kind of reward or form of 'gain' (although it does not come automatically when we get what we desire) and intense disappointment is a kind of 'loss'. But one cannot do without the inverted commas. There is a distinction, crucial for our present purposes, between being disappointed *because* one has suffered a personal loss, and the 'loss' that consists entirely in disappointment, and between the 'gain' that consists entirely in satisfaction at some outcome, and the satisfaction that occurs *because* there has been some personal gain. The 'losses' and 'gains' in inverted commas have no direct connection with interests or with harms. We are commonly enough disappointed, dissatisfied, even frustrated without suffering harm.

[5] Barry, op. cit., pp. 38 ff.

desire, personal excellence is likely to contribute to the joint satisfaction of other wants. But contrary to Plato and many other ancient
sages, there is no necessity that excellence and happiness always
coincide, no impossiblity that morally inferior persons can be happy,
and excellent persons miserable. There is still room for controversy
then over what is truly good for persons in the latter two cases. In
particular, philosophers have disagreed over whether it is *in the
interest* of the contented moral defective to become a better person.
This disagreement can persist even when it is agreed on all sides that
it is desirable that the defective's character improve. Desirable, yes;
a good thing, to be sure; but in *his* interest? That is another thing.

The source of the appeal of the ideal-regarding theory, I think, is
evident: Few of us would wish to exchange places with people we
regard as morally flawed, no matter how content they seem to be. It
is easy to understand and sympathize with Epictetus' attitude toward
the morally depraved criminal. We would not want to be *him* even if
he escaped punishment, indeed even if he profited richly from his
crime and suffered no remorse for it. Neither would we wish to be
contented and vulgar, contented and dull, contented and stupid. We
would in fact be prepared to sacrifice a good deal of our (other)
want-fulfilments to avoid becoming flawed in these ways. But that is
surely because we already have *desires* for excellences of character
construed in accordance with our own standards. It is because we
have such wants that we think it in our *interest* to be excellent, or at
least not defective. Without those antecedent wants, it would not be
in our interest to be excellent at all, except of course indirectly through
the happy effects (not always to be relied upon) of excellent character
on popularity and material success. By the same token, it is not in the
interest of the contented moral defective to have *our* idea of virtue,
which he doesn't share, imposed on him, unless, of course, we speak
of thrift, prudence, diligence, etc., all of which could improve his
chances of fulfilling his *other* ulterior wants. But if he is clever enough
to make a 'good thing' in material terms out of dishonesty and
unscrupulousness, even while he is cold-hearted, mean, vulgar,
greedy, and vain, then it can hardly be in his interest to become warm,
sensitive, cultivated, and generous; much less witty, perceptive,
tactful, disinterested, and wise. We would not trade places with him
to be sure, for it would not be in *our* interests to do so in so far as we
have a stake, through the investment of our wants, in excellent
character. We think, and rightly so in most cases, that we could only

lose by becoming worse persons, and that the change itself would constitute a loss, whatever further losses or gains it caused to our other interests.

Partisans of the ideal-regarding theory often rest their case on the example of child raising. Surely, it is said, we do not educate our children simply to become good want-fulfillers; rather we wish them to have the right wants in the first place, and to acquire the traits of character from which right wants emerge. Thus Stanley Benn claims that we are promoting the interests of the child when, at a time before he has achieved a good character, we commence with 'educating him to be a person of a certain sort'.

His desires are beside the point [Benn writes], for it is often a question of whether he is to be encouraged to have desires of some approved sort instead of undesirable ones. It might be in the child's interests to deny him satisfaction of some of his desires to save him from becoming the sort of person who habitually desires the wrong thing.[6]

Benn's example supports an important point, but not the one he claims to be making. The point of moral education at the time it is undertaken is not simply to serve the child's interests either as they are or as they might one day become; not simply to promote his gain, profit, or advantage, his happiness or well-being. The aim is rather to lead the child, through creating new wants in him, to seek his happiness *by* pursuing personal excellence: to give him a *stake* in having a good character. The parent who values good character will want to give the child his own interest in it, so that the child's pursuit of his own interests will necessarily involve seeking and preserving virtues of character. The effect of making goodness one of a person's ulterior interests is to make the achievement of happiness impossible without attention to it. So, far from showing that a good character is in a person's interest even if it does not promote want-satisfaction, Benn's example shows instead that good character can be something that is directly in a person's interest only when the person has a want-based interest in *it*.

One of the advantages of the want-regarding theory is that it enables us all the more forcibly to praise personal excellence. Good character would be a good thing to have even if it didn't advance a person's self-interest. Self-interest, after all, isn't everything. It is no aid to clarity to insist that everything that is good *in* a person must be

[6] S. I. Benn, ' "Interests" in Politics', *Proceedings of the Aristotelian Society* 60 (1960), 130–1.

good *for* the person. Nor does it help to say that the evil in a person must be harmful to him. The contented moral defective is an ineligible model for emulation even though his faults cause no harm to himself. He is both evil and well off, and his evil character does not detract from his well-offness. Epictetus's 'pity' for him then is ill-placed. Vice is its own punishment, just as virtue is its own reward, only to the person who has a stake in being good.

It is not merely useful but morally important to preserve in this way the distinction between being good and being well off, for it saves us from speaking as if, and perhaps really believing, that well-offness is the sole good. It is important to be a good person and not merely a happy or fulfilled one. That is why we train children to seek their happiness in part through seeking their goodness. In that way we ensure that they will not be completely happy unless they are good.

Morally corrupting a person, that is, causing him to be a worse person than he would otherwise be, can *harm* him, therefore, only if he has an antecedent interest in being good. (It may in fact harm no one to corrupt him if he is corrupted in a way that does not make him dangerous to others.) The moral corruption or neglect of an unformed child, then, is no direct harm to him, provided that he has the resources to pursue his own interests effectively anyway, but it can be a very real harm to his parents if *they* have a powerful stake in the child's moral development.

2. *Other-regarding wants and vicarious harms.* There are two ways in which one person can have an interest in the well-being of another. In the one case, A may be dependent upon the help of B for the advancement of his own (A's) interests, so that if B's fortunes should decline, B would be less likely to help A. What promotes B's interest, in this case, indirectly promotes that of his dependent A as well. It is therefore in A's interest that B's interest be advanced. In the extreme version of this case, where A is *wholly* dependent on B's help, and so long as B's personal interest flourishes the help is sure to continue, B's good is, in effect, one of A's welfare interests, the advancement of which (like his own health) promotes the whole economy of his ulterior interests and is absolutely essential to his well-being, whatever his ulterior interests happen to be.

In the second kind of case, C has 'invested' a desire so strong, durable, and stable in D's well-being, that he comes to have a personal stake in it himself. It becomes, therefore, one of his ulterior interests or 'focal aims'.[7] This should be contrasted with the more common phenomenon of spontaneous sympathy, pity, or compassion which can be directed at total strangers. It may make A very unhappy to see B (a stranger) suffer, and A may do what he can to help B, from genuinely disinterested, compassionate motives. But the harm that has been done B, say, by a hit-and-run motorist who knocked him down, is not *also* harm done A. The interests of A have not been invaded by the harm done B; he has only suffered some vicarious unhappiness on B's behalf which will leave his own personal interests largely unaffected. In the case of genuinely other-regarding interest that I have in mind, C has an abiding interest of his own in D's well-being which is not merely an episodic 'passing desire'. Further, he desires D's good not simply as a means to the promotion of the other ulterior aims that are components of his own good, but quite sincerely as an end in itself. Such cases are, of course, rare, but no rarer than disinterested love. Indeed, there is one sense of 'love' (that which the New Testament writers called *agape*) which is well defined by the presence of purely other-regarding interest. Ralph Barton Perry once defined 'love' in this sense as an interest in the advancement of someone else's interests.[8] When C has a loving interest in D's personal interest, then anything that harms D directly *ipso facto* harms C indirectly. Can anyone doubt that one harms a loving parent by maiming his child (or as in the previous example, by corrupting his child) or that one harms a loving husband or wife by causing a disappointment that plunges his or her spouse into despair?

The separation of the two kinds of cases distinguished in the preceding paragraphs is somewhat artificial. The distinction is clearly enough conceived, but in real life psychological elements rarely separate so neatly. Most of the things we desire for their own sakes we *also* desire as means to other things. Harm to a child may itself be harm to its loving parent in that it directly violates the parent's 'purely' other-regarding interest, but it may also be instrumentally damaging to various self-regarding interests of the parent, in that it creates a drain on his funds, a burden on his time and energy, and a strain on his emotional stability. Similarly, when one spouse sinks into despair, this not only harms the other person's wholly other-regarding interest in the ailing mate's well-being; it also

---

[7] This phrase is C. L. Stevenson's. See his account in *Ethics and Language* (Yale U.P., New Haven, 1944), p. 203.

[8] Ralph Barton Perry, *General Theory of Value* (Longmans, Green, & Co., New York, 1926), p. 672. His exact words: '. . . a favourable interest in the satisfaction of the interest of a second person'.

deprives him or her of the myriad services and pleasures that a cheerful partner would contribute.

Loving interests are so commonly intertwined with, and reinforced by, instrumental, essentially self-regarding interests, that many observers are led to discount the former, or even deny altogether their existence in given cases. Others have embraced the apparently cynical view that there are no purely other-regarding interests at all, that human nature being what it is, no one 'really cares' about the well-being of other persons, except in so far as it affects his own self-regarding interests. All interests in the well-being of others, on this view, are of the first type distinguished above. This extreme form of psychological egoism rules out not only disinterested love, but episodic sympathy and compassion as well. Egoism of this sort can never be persuasive to those who are deeply impressed by the genuine purity of their own love for others, so its advocates must posit a good deal of self-deception in their opponents. Since the purity of people's motives is not readily subject to careful scrutiny, the egoistic theory, as a matter of empirical psychology, is not easily refuted, though the stronger philosophical arguments *for* the view are invariably muddled.

Some types of apparently other-regarding interests are so familiar, however, that the burden of explaining them away should be placed on the egoist. One common example is the case of pooled interest, where, either through design or accident, separate persons are so related that they share a common lot. Such common interests, 'all for one and one for all', are found wherever parties are led (or forced) by circumstances to act in concert and share the risk of common failure or the fruits of an indivisible success.[9] Whatever the ultimate truth of the matter, common sense reports that persons with pooled or interdependent interests are sometimes drawn even closer by bonds of sentiment directed toward common objects or reciprocal affection (of an *apparently* disinterested kind) between the parties. And when this happens, as it sometimes seems to in marriages and family groups, each has a genuine stake of a not merely instrumental kind in the well-being of the others, a stable ulterior goal, or focal aim, that the others flourish, partly as an end in itself, partly as a means to a great diversity of other ends.

Despite the familiarity of these observations, some very able philosophers have chosen to exclude purely other-regarding wants

---

[9] See my 'Collective Responsibility' in *Doing and Deserving* (Princeton U.P., Princeton, N.J., 1970), pp. 233–41.

altogether from their otherwise want-regarding analyses of interest. The writers in question do not necessarily deny that there are purely other-regarding wants. Professor Barry, for example, admits that some of us, some of the time, genuinely want other persons as well as ourselves to enjoy increased opportunities to satisfy ulterior wants. Indeed, he concedes that some persons, some of the time, even voluntarily suffer a diminution of their opportunities for want-satisfaction in order to increase the opportunities of other persons to satisfy *their* wants. But the latter cases, Barry insists, are best described as cases where our *principles* are allowed to override out interests.[10] Barry is right about the cases he seems to be considering, where persons voluntarily sacrifice their own interests for others out of a sense of justice, or for ideal-regarding reasons, or for charity. But he doesn't even consider cases of the kind discussed above where help to others is not thought to be a *sacrifice* at all, but a direct promotion of one's own other-regarding interest in the advancement of the interests of another party.

I think the theoretical motives of writers who exclude other-regarding wants from their analyses of self-interest are clear enough, and worthy of respect. They are simply taking the easiest way out of a kind of linguistic muddle. They are afraid that inclusion of purely other-regarding aims as eligible constituents of a person's own self-interest would commit them to saying various odd-sounding things. They fear that we would have to say when Jones gives his last cent to promote the cause of his favourite political party, or to finance his child's education, or to secure the very best doctor for his sick wife, that he is advancing his own interest *merely* (treacherous word, 'merely'). Hence, we must think of his act as 'selfish', since it was done in his own self-interest, after all. The less paradoxical alternative, they think, is to deny that the act is in the actor's own interest at all, and to say instead that Jones was acting from conscience, or out of principle, or for charity, and against his own interest. After all, how could his act be at once disinterested and self-interested, unselfish yet self-advancing?

There is, however, a more satisfactory, if less direct, way out of the muddle. That is simply to consider very carefully what it means to call an act 'unselfish' and 'disinterested', and to come by this route to appreciate how unselfish and disinterested conduct, without affecting any of the actor's interests other than those he has in the well-being

[10] Barry, op. cit., p. 77

of others, can nevertheless be in his own personal interest. A person who has such a stake in the happiness of other people that his own well-being depends on the advancement of their interests is not the proper model of a selfish person. A selfish person is one who pays insufficient attention to the interests of other people, and thus comes to pursue his own self-regarding interests at the expense of, or in disregard of, the interests of others. That is quite another thing than pursuing one's own interest in *promoting* the interests of others. The loving parent or spouse and the public-spirited zealot can make no distinction between their own interests and that of their children, or spouse, or party. Far from indicating their selfishness, that identity of interests shows how unselfish they probably are. They might yet be blamably selfish, however, if they pursue those of their own interests which include the interests of *some* other people (for example, a daughter and a son) at the expense of the interests of still *other* people (for example, their neighbours' children). It is in fact an advantage of our analysis (as opposed to Barry's) that it enables us to explain why conduct of the latter kind is selfish. On Barry's analysis, neither want—that for the well-being of my children nor that for the well-being of my neighbours' children—is one of my own interests. Hence, when I promote the interests of some of these parties at the expense of those of the others, I am acting neither for nor against my own interests. I can be acting oddly or wrongly in that case, but not specifically selfishly. That judgment, however, seems plainly false. It surely *is* selfish wrongly to benefit one's own loved ones at the expense of others.

The best way, it seems to me, to conceive of the relation between self-interested, selfish, unselfish, and disinterested acts is that indicated in a chart with two genera, one of which is further sub-divided (see diagram 1 on p.295).

The generic distinction in the chart is that on the top line between self-interested acts and acts that are not self-interested, particularly those that concerned Barry, namely, conscientious or charitable acts that are not predominantly in the actor's interest. Self-interested acts are then divided into self-regarding and other-regarding species. Depending on our purposes, of course, we would classify the acts in this motley category in various alternative ways, but it is especially useful for our present purposes to divide them into these mutually exclusive and jointly exhaustive categories. The self-regarding class is then further divided into directly and indirectly self-regarding subclasses. For an example of directly self-regarding activity (A1a) consider an unmarried home-owner's labour at improving his property so that he can take more enjoyment and pride in it, impress those in a

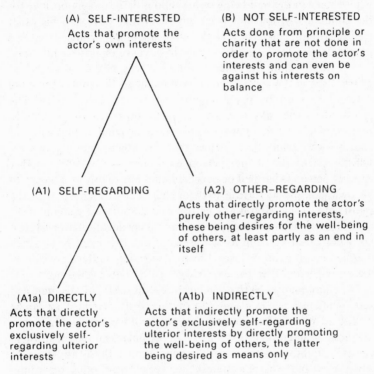

(A) SELF-INTERESTED

Acts that promote the actor's own interests

(B) NOT SELF-INTERESTED

Acts done from principle or charity that are not done in order to promote the actor's interests and can even be against his interests on balance

(A1) SELF-REGARDING

(A2) OTHER–REGARDING

Acts that directly promote the actor's purely other-regarding interests, these being desires for the well-being of others, at least partly as an end in itself

(A1a) DIRECTLY

Acts that directly promote the actor's exclusively self-regarding ulterior interests

(A1b) INDIRECTLY

Acts that indirectly promote the actor's exclusively self-regarding ulterior interests by directly promoting the well-being of others, the latter being desired as means only

position to help, and disproportionately increase its resale value in a rising market. Such a person is promoting his own purely self-regarding ulterior interests in material possession, career advancement, and capital accumulation. An example of indirectly self-regarding activity (A1b) is found in the story of the gambler, A, who bets B \$50,000 that C will recover from a serious illness. Thus C's health is in A's interest, and A has a stake (in a literal sense) in C's recovery. To protect that stake he works hard to promote C's recovery, providing at his own expense, the best medical and nursing care that he can find. He thus promotes the well-being of another as ardently as a lover or a saint would, though the other's well-being, his immediate goal, is desired only as a means to the advancement of his own self-regarding interest.

In contrast, acts in the genuinely other-regarding species of the self-interested genus (A2) aim at the promotion of another's good at least partly as an end in itself. An example would be that of a parent whose stake in the well-being of his child is derived from his love for the child simply, and not from any incidental service to his other (self-regarding) interests that the child might contribute. If such a parent depletes his own life savings to advance or protect his child, his act would fall in the other-regarding species of the self-interested genus. This is the species which is thought to be empty, for quite different reasons, by psychological egoists and Brian Barry. The egoists deny that any acts are genuinely other-regarding (that is, motivated by a desire to promote or retard the good of another as an end in itself), while Barry denies that any other-regarding acts are self-interested. But if any person ever does 'really care' whether another person is harmed or benefited, and not simply as a means to his own gain but at least in part for the other's own sake, then the egoists are wrong. And if any person ever does have a genuine stake in the happiness of another person—an independent ulterior interest not wholly derived from its service to other ulterior interests—such that he himself gains or loses directly depending on the condition of the other person, then the view suggested by Barry is wrong.

The chart enables us to distinguish several senses of 'disinterested action' and also two kinds of selfish action. A disinterested act can be defined in a first approximation, as one not done simply to advance the actor's interests.[11] One class of disinterested actions, then, consists of those in the chart's second genus: those not done to advance *any* of the actor's interests, self-regarding or other-regarding. These are actions done from conscience, or out of a sense of justice, or from charity, or from a spontaneous benevolent impulse, often with the conscious expectation that they will be against the actor's own interest. A second kind of disinterested action is one which meets a stricter test; it is neither done to promote the actor's own interest or to favour the interests of any second parties unfairly at the expense of third parties when the actor's own interests simply aren't involved one way or the other. Thus, a judge's decision is disinterested when it is unbiased and impartial. These related senses of the word 'disinterested' are well established in usage. A third sense

---

[11] Cf. *Webster's New International Dictionary*, 2nd edn. (1954): 'not influenced by regard to personal advantage . . .' and *The Oxford English Dictionary*: 'not influenced by self-interest . . .'

(one which is suggested by our chart) is not so clearly established and may in fact be somewhat extended beyond what is recognized in ordinary usage. I am not sure. Still, it stands for an important category that deserves to be distinguished from the others, whatever name it bears. I refer to actions in the other-regarding species of the self-interested genus (A2), acts done out of the perfectly genuine desire to help another whose well-being is actually a constituent of the actor's own good. When a person promotes the well-being of a loved one in a self-sacrificing or otherwise 'selfless' way, it may be misleading to call his act disinterested since he does have a personal stake, even a predominant ulterior interest, in the outcome. But it can be equally misleading to deny that his act is disinterested since apart from the well-being of the loved one that is his goal, there may be no 'personal advantage' in his action, and no trace of self-interest in his motivation. In an extreme case, he might even sacrifice all his other interests for the good of another person or cause in which he has 'invested' everything. The least misleading thing to say about such conduct is that it is not disinterested in one very familiar sense of the term, but that it is disinterested in another, less familiar, sense. In any event, extreme psychological egoists are likely to deny that there are disinterested acts of either kind, and sometimes put that view by saying that all voluntary actions are 'selfish'.

Now a selfish act, whatever else it may be, is one that is morally defective. A person acts selfishly when he pursues his own interests (or the satisfaction of transitory desires and appetites) *wrongly* at the expense of others. Sometimes, of course, there is nothing blamable in the pursuit of self-interest at the expense of others, as for example, in legitimately or unavoidably competitive contexts. An act is selfish only when its pursuit of self-interest is somehow in excess of what is right or reasonable in the situation.

The more familiar kind of selfish act is a defective specimen of those in the self-regarding species of self-interested actions (A1a and b). The father who refuses to spend money on his children for anything beyond their minimal needs, and uses his surplus instead to buy fine clothes and wines for himself is selfish in this way. But as we have seen, defective specimens of acts in the other-regarding species of the self-interested genus (A2) can also be selfish, as when a parent with a genuinely independent stake in his own children's advancement (an 'other-regarding interest') pursues that interest wrongly at the expense of his neighbour's children. We would be reluctant, I think, to call the latter actions 'disinterested' in *any* sense, since it would be intolerably odd to think of an act as both disinterested and selfish. Hence I am forced to qualify the account given above of the self-interested acts that can also be, in an 'unfamiliar sense', disinterested, as follows: an act is disinterested in that third sense provided that (i) it is done in order to advance the good of another party, but (ii) not merely as a means to the advancement of the actor's own self-regarding interests, *and* (iii) it is not done to promote the actor's other-regarding interest in the well-being of one party wrongly at the expense of still another party. (This third condition amends the definition, in effect, by requiring that a disinterested act not be a selfish act of the second kind.)

Selfish actions, then, can be defined as those which pursue the actor's self-interest *wrongly* at the expense of, or in disregard of, other people, and the two main types of selfish actions are those which are appropriately defective instances of category A1 on the chart, and those which are appropriately defective instances of A2. (Morally defective instances of B, as we shall see, are not called 'selfish'.) It is best, I think, to define 'selfish' and 'unselfish' as logical contraries rather than contradictories, in recognition of a large and motley class of actions that are neither selfish nor unselfish. An unselfish act then can be defined as one which pursues the interests of others (or the fulfilment of their transitory wants or appetites) *rightly* at the expense of, or in praiseworthy disregard of, the actor's own interests (or wants and appetites).[12] Voluntary actions in the middle group that qualify neither as selfish nor as unselfish include those which pursue the actor's own self-regarding wants or interests (A1) in a non-defective way (not wrong or blamable, not deficient in concern for others) as well as those whose motivation does not include concern for self-interest one way or the other, as in the case of the judge in a controversy between two persons who are strangers to him.

There are blamably defective specimens of acts even in the non-self-interested genus (B on the chart), but these characteristically bear names other than 'selfish'. Acting entirely out of principle, for example, a person might be rigid, cruel, or intolerant. A person might, in another case, act honestly in accord with a dictate of his

---

[12] Two kinds of unselfish actions then can be distinguished in terms of the categories in the chart: those in category B and those actions in category A2 that are not done wrongly at the expense of, or in blamable disregard of, the interests (or passing wants) of third parties.

own mistaken or confused conscience. Another person might act unjustly or imprudently out of spontaneous compassion. All of these morally defective acts can be against the actor's interest and known to be such, yet deliberately chosen anyway. They may be blameable, but they are not selfish.

According to our provisional definition of 'harm', a violation of an interest in any of the categories in the chart is a harm to its possessor. Any action, omission, or rule that interferes with a person's self-interested action, thus thwarting his interest, causes him harm. But does it follow from the definition that interferences with voluntary acts in the non-self-interested genus (B) are *not* harms? That would seem at first sight to be the case. Since acting out of conscience or benevolence is not acting to advance one's own interest, interference with such action does not violate one's interest, and therefore is not, by definition, a harm to one. Moreover, such interference, when it prevents a person from acting contrary to his own interest, actually *serves* his interest, and would seem therefore to be beneficial to him. Any interference, however, with a voluntary action, even with a non-self-interested one, is an invasion of a person's interest in *liberty*, and is thus harmful to him to that extent. If that seems too trivial a harm in the case at hand to be the basis of a powerful claim to non-interference, the liberal will have to retreat from the harm principle and seek a stronger defensive position, perhaps in the principle that infringements of an actor's *autonomy* are seriously wrongful even when they do him, at most, only trivial harm.

3. *Death and posthumous harms.* If a murderer is asked whether he has harmed his victim, he might well reply: 'Harmed him? Hell no; I killed him outright!' The victim's mourners too might feel that it is something of an understatement to describe the death of their loved one as a harm (to him). The death of the victim, it would seem, is not merely a 'harmed condition' he is put in; it is no 'condition' of him at all, but rather his total extinction. Consider the purest possible hypothetical case of the infliction of death, where all extraneous and distracting harms have been excluded from the example. A man in the prime of his life, with many on-going projects and enterprises, but with no dependents or friends close enough to mourn him, is shot by an unseen assailant in the back of the head. Without ever being aware even that he was in danger, much less that he has been fatally wounded, he dies instantly. Right up to the very instant he was shot, he was unharmed; then at that very moment, perhaps one second

after the killer squeezed the trigger, he was dead. At the very most, he was in a 'harmed condition' for the one half-second, or so, before he died. As for death itself, one might agree with the ancient Epicureans: 'Where he was, death was not, and where death was, he was not'.

Yet for all of that, it seems clear that the murderer did violate his victim's interest in remaining alive. One second before the trigger was pulled, it was true of the victim (as it is now true of both the author and reader of these words) that continued life was something *in his interest*. Indeed, there is nothing a normal person (in reasonable health and tolerable circumstances) dreads more than his own death, and that dread in the vast majority of cases, is as rational as it is unavoidable, for unless we continue alive, we have no chance whatever of achieving the goals that are the ground of our ultimate interests. Some of these goals perhaps might be achieved for us by others after our deaths, publicly oriented and other-regarding goals in particular. But most of our interests require not simply that some result be brought about, but rather that it be brought about *by* us, or if not by us, then *for* us. My interest in producing an excellent book, or a beautiful art object, is not fully satisfied by another person's creation of such objects. My interest was not simply that such objects exist, but that *I* bring them into existence. Similarly my aim to build a dream house, or to achieve leisure in security, is not satisfied when such a house or such leisure comes into existence, but only when I am present to enjoy and use it. Our interest in avoiding death is a supreme welfare interest, an indispensable condition for the advancement of most, if not all, of the ulterior interests that constitute our good. There is something bare minimal about it on the one hand, yet something supremely important on the other. Apart from the interests it serves, it has no value in itself; yet unless it is protected, hardly any of a person's ulterior interests will be advanced. To extinguish a person's life is, at one stroke, to defeat almost all of his self-regarding interests: to ensure that his on-going projects and enterprises, his long-range goals, and his most earnest hopes for his own achievement and personal enjoyment, must all be dashed.

There is a case then both for saying that death is not a harm and that it *is* a violation of an antecedent interest in staying alive. That makes death a very hard case indeed for the analysis of harm as invaded interest. There may be no way out of this for the writer who has strong theoretical incentives for saving the invaded interest theory other than to stipulate an admittedly extended sense of 'harm' broad enough to include death as a harm.[13] This would be a minor and quite excusable departure from the conventions of ordinary language for the sake of theoretical economy; still, it would make things tidier all around if we could *show* that, ordinary language to the contrary—and not as a matter of mere arbitrary stipulation—death *is* a harm.[14] It would be unreasonable to expect that this conclusion could be demonstrated, and indeed, there are various common sense considerations other than the oddness of its sound to the ear that militate against it. But there is also a way of conceiving death (even without the assumption of survival or immortality) that mitigates its paradox and lends it some plausibility. That is all that can be claimed, at best, for the view that death can be a harm to the one who dies.

To be sure, death is not always and necessarily a harm to the one who dies. To the person in hopeless, painful illness, who has already 'withdrawn his investments' in all ulterior interests, there may be nothing to lose, and cessation of agony or boredom to be 'gained', in which case death is a blessing. For the retired nonogenarian, death may not exactly be ardently desired, but still it will be a non-tragedy. Those who mourn his death will not think of themselves as mourning *for him*, but rather for his dependants and loved ones, if any, or simply in virtue of the capacity of any *memento mori* to evoke sadness. In contrast, when a young vigorous person dies, we think of *him* as chief among those who suffered loss.

One way of saving the 'invaded interest' theory of harm, at minimal cost to common sense, is to think of all harm as done to interests themselves, and interpret talk of harm done to men and women as convenient elliptical references to, and identification of, the interest that was thwarted or set back. Thus, when Cain harms Abel by punching him in the nose, it is Abel's interest in the physical integrity of his nose that is the immediate object of the harm, and

---

[13] For the writer who is interested in formulating a more precise and defensible version of Mill's 'harm principle' there is another alternative. He can simply amend his statement of that principle so that it restricts interferences with liberty to those necessary to prevent *harm or death* (implying that they are not the same thing). The cost of this amendment, however, would be the abandonment of the analysis of harm as 'any invasion of interest', for there *is* an interest in avoiding death, yet the amendment implies that death is not a harm.

[14] Thomas Nagel has argued ingeniously but inconclusively that death is an 'evil' or a 'misfortune' to the one who dies. This is not quite the same perhaps as saying that a person is *harmed* when he is killed, but it is close. See his article 'Death' in its expanded form in *Moral Problems*, edited by James Rachels (Harper & Row, New York, 1971), pp. 361-70.

Abel himself is harmed in the derivative sense of being the owner of a harmed interest. This is perhaps a step beyond (but only a small step beyond) saying what is obviously true: that it is only in virtue of having interests that people can be harmed, and that the only way to harm any person is to invade his interests. If Abel had no interest of the usual welfare kind in the integrity and normal functioning of his body, then Cain could not have harmed him by punching him in the nose, but at most only hurt, annoyed, or disappointed him. The next step is to point out that most of a person's self-regarding interests, at least, are thwarted permanently, and thus harmed, by his death. Although *he* no longer exists, we can refer to his earlier goals (as a matter of identification) as *his* interests, and *they* were the interests directly harmed by his death.

What then does it mean to say that an *interest* has been harmed? Our answer to this question will depend on which of two conceptions of interest enhancement and impairment we adopt. As we have seen, interests are 'stakes' that are derived from and linked to wants, in the case of ulterior interests to more ulterior goals or focal aims. Now we can apply to these wants W. D. Ross's distinction between want-fulfilment and want-satisfaction.[15] The *fulfilment* of a want is simply the coming into existence of that which is desired. The *satisfaction* of a want is the pleasant experience of contentment or gratification that normally occurs in the mind of the desirer when he believes that his desire has been fulfilled. When the object of a want does not come into existence, we can say that the want has been *unfulfilled* or *thwarted*; the experience in the mind of the desirer when he believes that his desire has been thwarted is called *frustration* or *disappointment*. Notoriously, fulfilment of desire can fail to give satisfaction. There is no more melancholy state than the disillusionment that comes from getting what we wanted and finding it disappointing. Such disillusionment can usually be explained as the consequence of a rash or ill-considered desire and unrealistic expectations. On other occasions, the original desire will bear up under retrospective scrutiny, and yet its fulfilment gives no pleasure. Indeed, the occurrences of subjective satisfaction is a highly contingent and unreliable phenomenon. Sometimes when our goals are achieved, we don't experience much joy, but only fatigue and sadness, or an affective blankness. Some persons, perhaps, are disposed by temperament normally to receive their achievements in this unthrilled fashion. Still, even in these cases,

[15] W. D. Ross, *Foundations of Ethics* (Clarendon Press, Oxford, 1939), p. 300.

re-examination of the goal whose fulfilment failed to satisfy may disclose no hidden defects, no reasons for regret, in a word, no disillusionment. Not only can one have fulfilment without satisfaction; one can also have satisfaction of a want in the absence of its actual fulfilment, provided only that one is led to believe, falsely, that one's want has been fulfilled. Similarly, pleasant states of mind resembling 'satisfaction' can be induced by drugs, hypnosis, and other forms of manipulation that have no relation whatever to prior wants.

Similarly, one's wants can be thwarted without causing frustration, or disappointment, and one can be quite discontented even when one's wants have in fact been fulfilled. These negative cases are perfectly parallel with the positive ones. Non-fulfilment of a want yields no disappointment when the want was ill advised in the first place. In such a case, the want can happily be renounced after rational reassessment. Disillusionment, however, is often not involved. A perfectly genuine and well-considered goal may be thwarted without causing mental pain when the desirer has a placid temperament or a stoic philosophy. And discontent does not presuppose thwarting of desire any more than satisfaction presupposes fulfilment. One can have feelings of frustration and disappointment caused by false beliefs that one's wants have been thwarted, or by drugs and other manipulative techniques.

For these reasons, harm to an interest is better defined in terms of the objective blocking of goals and thwarting of desires than in subjective terms; and the enhancement or benefiting of an interest is likewise best defined in terms of the objective fulfilment of well-considered wants than in terms of subjective states of pleasure. Most persons will agree, I think, that the important thing is to get what they want, even if that causes no joy.[16] The pleasure that normally attends want-fulfilment is a welcome dividend, but the object of our efforts is to fulfil our wants in the external world, not to bring about states

---

[16] This judgment is probably too confident if understood to extend to cases where what is wanted is expected to cause actual *disappointment*. Derek Parfit has reminded me of the distinction between cases where fulfilment *can't possibly* produce satisfaction because the person will never be in a position to know that his want has been fulfilled, and cases where fulfilment can produce satisfaction but in fact won't. In the former case, all would agree that the important thing is that what we want to happen will happen (our desire will be fulfilled). But in the latter case, if people know or confidently expect that fulfilment will not only 'not cause joy' but will actually produce disappointment, it is not so clear, as Parfit points out, that the important thing is 'to get what one wants'. There is some question, however, whether the existence of the want could even survive such conditions.

of our own minds. Indeed, if this were not the case, there would be no way to account for the pleasure of satisfaction when it does come; we are satisfied only because we think that our desires are fulfilled. If the object of our desires were valuable to us only as a means to our pleasant inner states, those inner glows could never come.

The object of a focal aim that is the basis of an interest, then, like the object of any want, is not simply satisfaction or contentment, and the defeat of an interest is not to be identified with disappointment or frustration. Hence, death can be a thwarting of the interests of the person who dies, and must be the total defeat of most of his self-regarding interests, even though, as a dead man, he can feel no pain.

This account helps explain, I think, why we grieve for a young, vigorous 'victim of death' himself, and not *only* for those who loved him and depended on him. We grieve for him in virtue of his unfulfilled interests. We think of him as one who has invested all his energies and hopes in the world, and then has lost everything. We think of his life as a whole as not as good a thing as it might have been had he lived on. In some special circumstances, death not only does its harm in this wholly 'negative' way, preventing the flowering of the interests in which a person's lifetime good consists, it also does direct and 'positive' harm to a person by undoing or setting back important interests that were already prospering. Death, in these cases, leads to the harming of surviving interests that might otherwise have been prevented.[17]

Because the objects of a person's interests are usually wanted or aimed-at events that occur outside of his immediate experience and at some future time, the area of a person's good or harm is necessarily wider than his subjective experience and longer than his biological life. The moment of death is the terminating boundary of one's biological life, but it is itself an important event within the life of one's future-oriented interests. When death thwarts an interest, the interest is harmed, and the harm can be ascribed to the man who is no more, just as his debts can be charged to his estate.

The interests that die with a person are those that can no longer be helped or harmed by posthumous events. These include most of his self-regarding interests, those based, for example, on desires for personal achievement and personal enjoyment, and those based on 'self-confined' wants that a person could have 'if he were the only

---

[17] The most vivid example I know in literature of a 'positively harmful' death is that foreseen by Pip at the hands of the villainous Orlick in Dickens's *Great Expectations*.

person that had ever existed',[18] for example, the desire to be a self of a certain kind, or the desire for self-respect. Other self-regarding wants, in contrast, seem more like other-regarding and publicly oriented wants, in that they can be fulfilled or thwarted after the death of the person whose wants they are. I refer to some of a person's desires to stand in certain relations to other people where 'the concern is primarily with the self . . . and with others only as objects or as other terms in a relation to me'.[19] These desires can be called 'self-centred', and include as a class such wants as the desire to assert or display oneself before others, to be the object of the affection or esteem of others, and so on. In particular, the desire to maintain a good reputation, like the desire that some social or political cause triumph, or the desire that one's loved ones flourish, can be the basis of interests that survive their owner's death, in a manner of speaking, and can be promoted or harmed by events subsequent to that death. Fulfilment and thwarting of interest, after all, may still be possible, even when it is too late for satisfaction or disappointment.

The above account might still contain elements of paradox, but it can be defended against one objection that is sure to be made. How can a man be harmed, it might be asked, by what he can't know? Dead men are permanently unconscious; hence they cannot be aware of events as they occur; hence (it will be said) they can have no stake one way or the other, in such events. That this argument employs a false premiss can be shown by a consideration of various interests of *living* persons that can be violated without them ever becoming aware of it. Most of these are 'possessary interests' whose rationality can be doubted, for example, a landowner's interest in the *exclusive* possession and enjoyment of his land—an interest that can be invaded by an otherwise harmless trespasser who takes one unobserved step inside the entrance gates; or the legally recognized 'interest in domestic relations' which is invaded when one's spouse engages in secret adulterous activity with a lover. The latter is an interest in being the exclusive object of one's spouse's love, and has been criticized by some as implying property in another's affections. But there is no criticizing on such grounds the interest every person has in his own reputation, which is perhaps the best example for our present purposes. If someone spreads a libellous description of me,

[18] C. D. Broad, 'Egoism as a Theory of Human Motives' in *Ethics and the History of Philosophy* (Routledge and Kegan Paul, London, 1952), p. 220.
[19] Op. cit., p. 221.

without my knowledge, among hundreds of persons in a remote part
of the country, so that I am, still without my knowledge, an object of
general scorn and mockery in that group, I have been injured in
virtue of the harm done my interest in a good reputation, even though
I *never* learn what has happened. That is because I have an interest,
so I believe, in having a good reputation *as such*, in addition to my
interest in avoiding hurt feelings, embarrassment, and economic
injury. And *that* interest can be seriously harmed without my ever
learning of it.

How is the situation changed in any relevant way by the death of
the person defamed? If knowledge is not a necessary condition of
harm before one's death why should it be necessary afterward?
Suppose that after my death, an enemy cleverly forges documents to
'prove' very convincingly that I was a philanderer, an adulterer, and a
plagiarist, and communicates this 'information' to the general public
that includes my widow, children, and former colleagues and friends.
Can there be any doubt that I have been harmed by such libels? The
'self-centred' interest I had at my death in the continued high regard
of my fellows, in this example, was not thwarted by my death itself,
but by events that occurred afterward. Similarly, my other-regarding
interest in the well-being of my children could be defeated or harmed
after my death by other parties overturning my will, or by thieves and
swindlers who cheat my heirs of their inheritance. None of these
events will embarrass or distress me, since dead men can have no
feelings; but all of them can harm my interests by forcing non-
fulfilment of goals in which I had placed a great stake.

This liability, to which we are all subject, to drastic changes in our
fortune both before and after death was well understood by the
Greeks. Aristotle devotes a chapter of his *Nicomachean Ethics* to a
saying already ancient in his time, and attributed by some to Solon,
that we can 'call no man fortunate before his death'.[20] On one
interpretation, this dark saying means that 'only when he is dead is it
safe to call a man . . . beyond the arrows of outrageous fortune'. On the
day before he dies, his interests can be totally smashed and his life thus
ruined. But as Aristotle shrewdly observes (attributing the point to
the general popular wisdom), some of a person's interests are not
made safe even by his death, and we cannot call him fortunate with
perfect confidence until several more decades have passed; 'For a
dead man is popularly believed to be capable of experiencing both

[20] Aristotle, *Nicomachean Ethics*, I. 10.

good and ill fortune—honour and dishonour, and prosperity and the loss of it among his children and descendants generally—in exactly the same way as if he were alive but unaware or unobservant of what was happening'.[21]

Three hypothetical cases can illustrate the 'popular belief' mentioned by Aristotle, and the case for posthumous harm must rest with them.

Case A. A man devotes thirty years of his life to the furtherance of certain ideals and ambitions in the form of one vast undertaking. He founds an institution dedicated to these ends and works single-mindedly for its advancement, both for the sake of the social good he believes it to promote, and for the sake of his own glory. One month before he dies, the 'empire of his hopes' collapses utterly as the establishment into which he has poured his life's energies crumbles into ruin, and he is personally disgraced. He never learns the unhappy truth, however, as his friends, eager to save him from disappointment, conceal or misrepresent the facts. He dies contented.

Case B. The facts are the same as in Case A, except that the institution in which the man had so great an interest remains healthy, growing and flourishing, until the man's death. But it begins to founder a month later, and within a year, it collapses utterly, while at the same time, the man and his life's work are totally discredited.

Case C. The facts are the same as in Case B, except for an additional surmise about the cause of the decline and collapse of the man's fortune after his death. In the present case, a group of malevolent conspirators, having made solemn promises to the man before his death, deliberately violate them after he has died. From motives of vengeance, malice, and envy, they spread damaging lies about the man and his institution, reveal secret plans, and otherwise betray his trust in order to bring about the ruin of his interests.

It would not be very controversial to say that the man in Case A had suffered grievous harm to his interests although he never learned the bad news. Those very same interests are harmed in Case B to exactly the same extent, and again the man does not learn the bad news, in this case because he is dead, and dead men hear no news at all. There seems no relevant difference between Case A and Case B

---

[21] Ibid., first paragraph. Aristotle's primary concern in this chapter, however, was not to show that a person's interests can be affected after his death, but rather that well-being, whether before or after death, cannot be destroyed by the caprice of events, but at worst, only somewhat tarnished. The point about interests surviving death he simply assumed as beyond need of argument.

except that in Case B there might seem to be no subject of the harm, the man being dead. But if we consider that the true subjects of harms are interests, and that interests are harmed by thwarting or non-fulfilment rather than by subjective disappointment, we can think of posthumous harms as having subjects after all. But if that point is not convincing, the argument must depend on its reinforcement by Case C. In that example, the man is not *merely* harmed (if he is harmed at all); rather he is exploited, betrayed, and wronged. When a promise is broken, someone is wronged, and who if not the promisee? When a confidence is revealed, someone is betrayed, and who, if not the person whose confidence it was? When a reputation is falsely blackened, someone is defamed, and who, if not the person lied about? If there is no 'problem of the subject' when we speak of wronging the dead, why should there be, when we speak of harming them, especially when the harm is an essential ingredient of the wrong?

To summarize then: Death can thwart a person's ulterior, self-regarding interests in personal achievement and enjoyment, by totally defeating the welfare interest that is necessary for fulfilment of the goals and focal aims that are their bases. It is for this reason alone that death is a harm to the one who dies suddenly, in the prime of life, never knowing what hit him, and unmourned by loved ones or dependents. We grieve for such a person (as opposed to grieving for our own loss) because of his unfulfilled interests. Events after death can thwart or promote those interests of a person which may have 'survived' his death. These include his publicly oriented and other-regarding interests, and also his 'self-centred' interests in being thought of in certain ways by others. Posthumous harm occurs when the deceased's interest is thwarted at a time subsequent to his death. The awareness of the subject is no more necessary than it is for harm to occur to certain of his interests at or before death.

Bibliography of H. L. A. Hart*

1. 'The Ascription of Responsibility and Rights', *Proceedings of the Aristotelian Society* 49 (1948-9), 171-94.
2. 'Is There Knowledge by Acquaintance?', *Proceedings of the Aristotelian Society*, Supplementary Volume 23 (1949), 69-90.
3. Book review of Jerome Frank's *Law and the Modern Mind* in *Mind* 60 (1951), 268-70.
4. 'A Logician's Fairy Tale', *Philosophical Review* 60 (1951), 198-212.
5. 'Signs and Words' (on J. Holloway, *Language and Intelligence*), *Philosophical Quarterly* 2 (1952), 59-62.
6. *Definition and Theory in Jurisprudence*: an inaugural lecture delivered before the University of Oxford on 30 May 1953, Clarendon Press, Oxford, 1953. 28 pp.
7. 'Philosophy of Law and Jurisprudence in Britain (1945-52)', 2 *American Journal of Comparative Law* 355-64 (1953).
8. 'Justice', *Philosophy* 28 (1953), 348-52 (on G. del Vecchio, *Justice*).
9. Introduction to *John Austin, The Province of Jurisprudence Determined etc.*, Weidenfeld & Nicholson, London, 1954, pp. vii-xxi.
10. 'Are there any Natural Rights?', *Philosophical Review* 64 (1955), 175-91.
11. 'Theory and Definition in Jurisprudence', *Proceedings of the Aristotelian Society*, Supplementary Volume 29 (1955), 239-64.
12. Book review of Axel Hägerström's *Inquiries into the Nature of Law and Morals* in *Philosophy* 30 (1955), 369-73.
13. 'Blackstone's Use of the Law of Nature', *Butterworths South African Law Review* (1956), 169-74.
14. Book review of Hans Kelsen's *Communist Theory of Law* in 69 *Harvard Law Review* 772 ff. (1956).
15. 'Murder and the Principles of Punishment: England and the United States', 52 *Northwestern University Law Review* 433 ff. (1957).
16. 'Analytic Jurisprudence in Mid-twentieth Century; a reply to Professor Bodenheimer', 105 *University of Pennsylvania Law Review* 953-75 (1957).
17. 'Legal and Moral Obligation', *Essays in Moral Philosophy*, ed. A. I. Melden, University of Washington Press, Seattle, 1958, pp. 82-107.
18. 'Legal Responsibility and Excuses', *Determinism and Freedom*;

---

* Excluding translations and reprints of Hart's work, as well as further minor items.

Proceedings of the First Annual New York University Institute of Philosophy, ed. S. Hook, New York, 1958.

19. 'Positivism and the Separation of Law and Morals', 71 *Harvard Law Review* 593–629 (1958).

20. with S. Hampshire: 'Decision, Intention and Certainty', *Mind* 67 (1958), 1–12.

21. 'Dias and Hughes on Jurisprudence', *Journal of the Society of Public Teachers of Law* N. s. 4 (1958), 143–9.

22. 'Immorality and Treason', *Listener* (30 July 1959), pp. 162 ff.

23. 'Scandinavian Realism', 17 *Cambridge Law Journal* 233–40 (1959) (on Alf Ross's *On Law and Justice*).

24. with A. M. Honoré: *Causation in the Law*, Clarendon Press, Oxford 1959. xxxii, 454 pp.

25. 'Prolegomenon to the Principles of Punishment', *Proceedings of the Aristotelian Society* 60 (1959–60), 1–26.

26. *The Concept of Law*, Clarendon Press, Oxford, 1961. x, 263 pp.

27. 'Negligence, *Mens Rea* and Criminal Responsibility', *Oxford Essays in Jurisprudence*, ed. A. Guest, Clarendon Press, Oxford, 1961, pp. 29–49.

28. 'The Use and Abuse of the Criminal Law', *Oxford Lawyer* 4 No. 1 (1961), 7–12.

29. Book review of Dennis Lloyd's *Introduction to Jurisprudence*; *with selected texts* in 77 *Law Quarterly Review* 123 ff. (1961).

30. 'Acts of Will and Responsibility', *The Jubilee Lectures of the Faculty, Sheffield University Faculty of Law*, ed. O. R. Marshall, London, 1961.

31. 'Bentham' (Lecture on a Mastermind), *Proceedings of the British Academy* 48 (1962), 297–320.

32. *Punishment and the Elimination of Responsibility* (Hobhouse Memorial Trust Lecture, 16 May 1961), Athlone Press, London, 1962. 32 pp.

33. Book review of Richard A. Wasserström's *The Judicial Decision* in 14 *Stanford Law Review* 919–26 (1962).

34. 'Acts of Will and Legal Responsibility', *Freedom of the Will*, ed. D. F. Pears, Macmillan, London, 1963, pp. 38–47.

35. Introduction to C. H. Perelman: *The Idea of Justice and the Problem of Argument*; tr. J. Petrie, Routledge & Kegan Paul, London, 1963, pp. vii–xi.

36. Book review of Oliver Wendell Holmes: *The Common Law* in *The New York Review of Books* 1 (1963–4), 15–16 (No. 4, 17 October 1963).

37. 'Kelsen Visited', 10 *UCLA Law Review* 709–28 (1963).

38. *Law, Liberty, and Morality* (The Harry Camp Lectures), Oxford University Press, London, 1963. viii, 88 pp.

39. 'Self Referring Laws', *Festkrift tillägnad Professor, Juris Doktor Karl Olivecrona vid hans Avgäng frän professorsämbetet den 30 Juni 1964 av kolleger, larjungär och vänner.* Kungl. Bocktryckeriet P. A. Norstedt & Söner, Stockholm, 1964, pp. 307–16.

40. *The Morality of the Criminal Law*, two lectures (Lionel Cohen Lectures, 1964), Magnes Press, Hebrew University, Jerusalem; Oxford Univers-

ity Press, London, 1965. 54 pp. (a. Changing Conceptions of Responsibility; b. The Enforcement of Morality).

41. Book review of Lon L. Fuller's *The Morality of Law* in 78 *Harvard Law Review* 1281–96 (1965).

42. 'Il Concetto di obbligo', trad. di G. Gavazzi, *Rivista di Filosofia* 57 (1966), 125–40.

43. 'Beccaria and Bentham', *Atti del convegno internazionale su Cesare Beccaria*, Accademia delle Scienze di Torino, Memorials of the Academy Series 4a no. 9, Turin, 1966.

44. 'Bentham on Sovereignty', *The Irish Jurist* N. s. 2 (1967), 327–35.

45. 'Intention and Punishment', *Oxford Review* 4 (1967), 5–22.

46. 'Varieties of Responsibility', 83 *Law Quarterly Review* 346–64 (1967).

47. 'Legal Positivism', *Encyclopedia of Philosophy*, ed. P. Edwards, Vol. 4, Macmillan and Free Press, New York, 1967, pp. 418–20.

48. 'Problems of Philosophy of Law', *Encyclopedia of Philosophy*, ed. P. Edwards, Vol. 6, Macmillan and Free Press, New York, 1967, pp. 264–76.

49. 'Social Solidarity and the Enforcement of Morality', 35 *University of Chicago Law Review* 1–13 (1967–8).

50. *Punishment and Responsibility, Essays in the Philosophy of Law*, Clarendon Press, Oxford, 1968. x, 271 pp. (including items no. 15, 18, 25, 27, 30, 32, 36, 40a, 45, and 46 of this bibliography).

51. 'Kelsen's Doctrine of the Unity of Law', *Ethics and Social Justice*, ed. M. K. Munitz and H. E. Kiefer, pp. 171–99. Vol. 4 of Contemporary Philosophic Thought: The International Philosophy Year Conferences at Brockport; State University of New York Press, Albany, 1968–70.

52. 'Duty', *International Encyclopedia of Social Sciences*, ed. David L. Sills, Vol. 4, pp. 320–3, Macmillan and Free Press, New York, 1968.

53. with J. H. Burns, Introduction, critical notes, and index to Jeremy Bentham: *An Introduction to the Principles of Morals and Legislation*, ed. J. H. Burns and H. L. A. Hart, Athlone Press, London, 1970 (Collected Works of Jeremy Bentham).

54. Introduction, critical notes and index to Jeremy Bentham: *Of Laws in General*, ed. H. L. A. Hart, Athlone Press, London, 1970 (Collected Works of Jeremy Bentham).

55. 'Jhering's Heaven of Concepts and Modern Analytic Jurisprudence', Jhering's Erbe; *Göttinger Symposium zur 150 Wiederkehr des Geburtstags von Rudolph von Jhering*, pp. 68–78; hrsg. von F. Wieaker und Chr. Wollschläger, Vandenhoeck & Ruprecht, Göttingen, 1970.

56. 'Bentham's "Of Laws in General" ', 2 *Rechtstheorie* 55–66 (1971).

57. 'Bentham on Legal Powers', 81 *Yale Law Journal* 799–822 (1972).

58. 'Abortion Law Reform; the English Experience', 8 *Melbourne University Law Review* 388–411 (1972).

59. 'Bentham on Legal Rights', *Oxford Essays in Jurisprudence* (2nd series), ed. A. W. B. Simpson, pp. 171–201, Clarendon Press, Oxford, 1973.

60. 'Bentham and the Demystification of the Law', 36 *Modern Law Review* 2–17 (1973).
61. 'Rawls on Liberty and Its Priority', 40 *University of Chicago Law Review* 534–55 (1973).
62. '1776–1976: Law in the Perspective of Philosophy', 51 *New York University Law Review* (1976).
63. 'Bentham and the United States of America', *1776: The Revolutlon in Social Thought*, ed. R. H. Coase, forthcoming.